MW00331146

CALLED TO BE SAINTS

Benjamin T. Peters

CALLED TO BE SAINTS
JOHN HUGO, THE CATHOLIC WORKER,
AND A THEOLOGY OF RADICAL CHRISTIANITY

APPENDIX
Dorothy Day's Retreat Notebooks

MARQUETTE
UNIVERSITY

PRESS

MARQUETTE STUDIES IN THEOLOGY
NO. 85
ANDREW TALLON, SERIES EDITOR

LIBRARY OF CONGRESS CATALOGING-IN-PUBLICATION DATA

Names: Peters, Benjamin T. (Benjamin Tyler), 1973- author.
Title: Called to be saints : John Hugo, the Catholic Worker, and a theology
of radical Christianity / Benjamin T. Peters.
Description: first [edition]. | Milwaukee, Wisconsin : Marquette University
Press, 2016. | Series: Marquette studies in theology ; No. 85 | Includes
bibliographical references and index.
Identifiers: LCCN 2016000683| ISBN 9781626007086 (hardcover : alk.
paper) | ISBN 162600708X (hardcover : alk. paper)
Subjects: LCSH: Hugo, John, 1911-1985. | Catholic Worker Movement.
Classification: LCC BX4705.H7947 P48 2016 | DDC 282.092—dc23
LC record available at http://lccn.loc.gov/2016000683

**Appendix by permission of the Department of Special Collections and
University Archives, Marquette University Libraries**

Cover art, *Foot Washing of a Reluctant Fisherman*, original drawing by Brian
Kavanagh, for the Lent 2009 cover of the *Hartford Catholic Worker
Newsletter*, courtesy of the Department of Special Collections and
University Archives, Marquette University Libraries.

*Marquette University Press wishes to thank the University of Saint
Joseph, School of Humanities and Social Sciences, West Hartford,
Connecticut, for generous support toward the printing of this book.*

*Marquette University Press also wishes to thank the Rev. Tad Burch, SJ,
Book Fund for generous support of the production of this book.*

Association of American
University Presses

MARQUETTE UNIVERSITY PRESS
MILWAUKEE

The Association of Jesuit University Presses

TABLE OF CONTENTS

Preface & Acknowledgments 7

Introduction 11

I. Father Hugo from Pittsburgh 15

II. "The Retreat" 53

III. Ignatian Radicalism 93

IV. Kindred Spirits 141

V. The "Retreat Controversy": 1945-1948 171

VI. Why Hugo Still Matters 207

Conclusion 241

Bibliography 245

Appendix: Dorothy Day's Retreat Notebooks 259

Index 583

I could write a great deal about that retreat, and all it brought to us, the new vistas which it opened out before us. But I will simply say that it gave us spiritual direction... The retreat gave us hope and courage, as retreats were supposed to do, and we will be everlastingly grateful for it, grateful to Father Lacouture, who made the retreat possible for us. We feel that we have been participants of a great spiritual movement which is still going on, though it is perhaps now in shadow. The seed has fallen into the ground and died. But we know that it will bear fruit.

☞ Dorothy Day[1]

---

1   Day, "On Retreat," *The Catholic Worker*, (December 1951).

PREFACE AND
ACKNOWLEDGMENTS

In his address to Congress in September 2015, Pope Francis surprised many when he included Dorothy Day and Thomas Merton along with Abraham Lincoln and Martin Luther King, Jr, as examples of four "great Americans" he wished to extol. While perhaps better known than Merton, adding Day to the pantheon of great figures in American history was certainly significant and rather startling. If nothing else, the Pope gave credence to Michael Harrington's claim from the 1950s—made to William F. Buckley, no less—that when the history of 1950s American Catholicism is written, "Francis Cardinal Spellman will be a footnote and Dorothy Day will be a chapter."[1]

For much of her life, Day and the Catholic Worker were regarded as being on the margins of the U.S. Catholic Church—in Harrington's words "a small band of nuts. Catholic purtians. Totally marginal radicals"—especially when compared with the Cardinal Archbishop of New York. But since her death in 1980, there has been a steadily growing recognition of the importance of Dorothy Day along with a steadily growing body of scholarship on her. All of which has only been bolstered by the move to have Day canonized, a cause which itself has been championed by Spellman's successors in New York.

Unfortunately, absent from all this study and promotion of Day and her causes has been much attention on the retreat that exerted such a profound effect in the 1940s, bringing about what Day called her "second conversion." Outside of a few short studies, little has been written on this important theological resource for Day.[2] There seem to be many reasons why the retreat has been overlooked or even ignored,

1   Harrington recounted this story in Rosalie Riegle, *Dorothy Day: Portraits of Those Who Knew Her* (Maryknoll, NY: Orbis Books, 2003), 58.

2   See, "The Significance of the Retreat Movement" in Brigid O'Shea Merriman, OSF, *Searching for Christ: The Spirituality of Dorothy Day*, (Notre Dame, IN: University of Notre Dame Press, 1994), 131-169; and "The Hidden Life of Father John Hugo: An Introduction" in *Weapons of*

as will be discussed in the first chapter. But recently this lacuna has be-gun to be addressed. Scholars such as Jack Downey, Lance Richey, and Charles Strauss are critically examining the retreat and its influence, as well as some of the figures who surrounded it. Indeed, Downey's *The Bread of the Strong*—unfortunately, published too late to be discussed here—offers the first book-length scholarly treatment of the retreat and its historical and sociological context.[3] I can only hope that my project will also contribute something to this growing recognition of the role that the retreat and its theology play in understanding Day.

As a student in historical theology at the University of Dayton, I was taught early and often that "chronology matters." That is never tru-er then when acknowledging the many folks who have contributed to a project like this. I have been fortunate in my life to have had many wonderful teachers, guides, and communities who have helped me.

My first teachers were my parents, Joe and Jan Peters, who brought me into the Catholic community and introduced me to its rich in-tellectual tradition. And my mom, in particular, deserves thanks for her invaluable work in transcribing Dorothy's retreat notebooks which appear in the appendix. I have also been blessed a wonderful wife and a family that has steadily grown over the years alongside this project. My wife Liza has been a constant support and companion, encourag-ing me at times to simply "get that thing done!" My kids Samuel, Ruth, Mary, and Thomas—to whom this book is dedicated—have not only provided much needed distractions over the years, but have also en-abled me to see that the call to holiness can and must entail the day-to-day life of a parent.

I was also lucky to have spent three years in the St. Peter Claver Catholic Worker community in South Bend, Indiana, where I was not only formed in the Worker's tradition of gospel radicalism, but was also first introduced to the writings of John Hugo by his nephew Michael Hugo. It was in South Bend that I also got to know Michael Baxter, initially while taking his courses at Notre Dame, but since as a collaborator and good friend. This project would never have begun without his guidance and encouragement—"Hugo, now there's an in-teresting topic."

---

the Spirit: Selected Writings of Father John Hugo, edited by Mike Aquila and David Scott (Huntington, IN: Our Sunday Visitor Press, 1997), 11-21.

3   Jack Lee Downey, *The Bread of the Strong: Lacouturisme and the Folly of the Cross, 1910-1985* (New York: Fordham University Press, 2015).

I was also very fortunate to land in the "U.S. Catholic Experience" Ph.D. program at the University of Dayton where I was immersed in a true community of scholars. In particular, Sandra Yocum, Kelly Johnson, and Dennis Doyle helped me formulate and articulate many of the arguments in this book. At UD, I was able to work with William Portier, a great teacher and mentor, who continues to be my model for what it means to be a theologian.

During my doctoral research, I met Brigid O'Shea Merriman, OSF, who shared with me much of her research, as well as some one-of-a-kind sources on Hugo and the retreat. I also received a great deal assistance and support from Phillip Runkel at the Dorothy Day-Catholic Worker archives at Marquette University—Phil was particularly gracious in allowing for Day's retreat notebooks to be published in the appendix.

Over the last five years, I have also been blessed to be part of the Department of Religious Studies and Theology at the University of Saint Joseph, where I have received support and encouragement from my colleagues Ann Caron, RSM, Joseph Cheah, OSM, and Judith Perkins. Judith, especially, has been a wise and patient guide through this process.

Finally, I want to thank Andrew Tallon and Maureen Kondrick at Marquette University Press for all their help and work in bringing this project to publication.

INTRODUCTION

J. F. Powers, winner of the National Book Award in 1963 for *Morte d'Urban*, met Father John Hugo in the 1940s. A Catholic conscientious objector in World War II, Powers had attended a retreat led by Hugo just before his imprisonment for draft resistance.[1] In a letter written decades later, this is how Powers described Hugo:

> ...Fr. Hugo's writings in the Catholic Worker were influential in my decision to be a conscientious objector, but this would've happened anyway because of an instinct I had then and still have at times to say <u>Shit, no</u>. I say it nowadays when I see newscasters, oh so serious, wearing striped shirts and floral neckties...

> ...I first saw Father Hugo at a priests' retreat, preached by him, in the summer of 1943 at St. John's Abbey, Collegeville, to which I'd received an invitation and train fare from an old friend, a priest in the St. Paul diocese. I knew I was going to prison and so I was in the mood for Fr. Hugo (unlike one elderly retreatant, I remember, who, on learning there would be no group picture, checked out). I remember seeing Fr. Hugo off at the Minneapolis-St. Paul airport, all of us kneeling on the tarmac for his blessing. I seem to remember seeing him again when I made a private retreat at the orphanage in Oakmont with Fr Farina. I admired and liked Father Hugo, his mind, heart, wit, courage...

---

1 Powers was one of 15 Catholic COs whose sentence at the Danbury Federal Prison was eventually commuted through the efforts of Arthur Sheehan and the Association of Catholic Conscientious Objectors (a group started by Catholic Workers). Powers and the other COs were assigned to work at hospitals in New Haven, Boston, and Baltimore. McNeal, "Catholic Conscientious Objection During World War II" *The Catholic Historical Review* (April 1975, vol. 61, no. 2): 233.

... there were a few in fairly high places who stood up for Fr. Hugo. In general, though, it was, to quote from my story "The Forks": "'If that fellow's right, Father, I'm'—his voice cracked at the idea—'wrong!'"[2]

Hugo is best remembered for his association with Dorothy Day (1897-1980) and the Catholic Worker movement. But Powers' letter suggests that Hugo was important beyond that relatively limited circle of so-called Catholic radicals. Indeed, he offered a theological perspective that, while somewhat unique in American Catholicism of the day, shared a great deal in common with several of the more important impulses emerging within early twentieth-century Catholic theology. In this way, John Hugo was—and continues to be—significant within the broader scope of U.S. Catholicism.

MY BOOK

Hugo's life was certainly a full one. This book will capture the sweep of it by focusing on the decade or so between when he attended his first Lacouture retreat in 1938 and the "retreat controversy" at the end of the 1940s. This was indeed an interesting period of time with the Second World War as certainly the defining event. But this was also an important period for Day and the Catholic Worker. Day's embrace of the Hugo retreat and her introduction of it into the Catholic Worker movement coincided with her public pacifist stand in World War II which had had a deeply disruptive—and transforming—effect on the Catholic Worker and on Day herself. Within Catholic theology, these were also the years just before the promulgation of *Humani Generis* in 1950, with its attempt to bring the nature-grace debates of the previous decades to some sort of conclusion. And it was also the time that would mark the beginning of the end of a theological perspective that had profoundly shaped Catholic thinking at least since the turn-of-the-century—a form of neo-Thomism that some called "strict observance Thomism."[3] Needless to say, a lot was going on during the time

---

2   This quote is taken from a letter (dated August 22, 1994) written by Powers to Mike Aquilina who co-edited, with David Scott, *Weapons of the Spirit: Selected Writings of Father John Hugo* (Huntington, IN: Our Sunday Visitor Publishing Division, 1997).

3   The terms "neo-Thomism" and "neoscholasticism" have often been used somewhat interchangeably. In his helpful study, Gerald McCool, S.J. explained that while neoscholasticism referred to the theological tradition

Hugo was giving the retreat and defending its theology and his work should be understood within this theological and historical context.

In this book, I will present three main arguments. First, the perception in much of American Catholic scholarship that Hugo was a rigorist and the retreat theology tended toward a world-denying Jansenism is mistaken. It certainly is not the way Day and many others who made the retreat understood its theology—indeed Day provided a beautiful illustration of that theology in *The Long Loneliness*. Not only are such depictions a caricature, but they are based on a reading of Hugo's theology rooted in the neo-Thomism of the first half of the twentieth-century.

Second, while Hugo's theology of nature and grace was not Jansenist—in fact Hugo asserted that it was rooted in Ignatian spirituality—it did have many similarities with some of the major emerging currents in Catholic theology at the time, particularly the work being done by Henri de Lubac, S.J. (1896-1991). These similarities included Hugo's understanding of the nature-supernatural relationship, his efforts at a *ressourcement* theology, and his challenge to the dominant theological perspective of the day. Hugo's work and the reaction to it, therefore, can be better appreciated in light of these broader theological movements developing in Catholicism.

Finally, it will be argued that Hugo's theological argument remains relevant to contemporary Catholic discourse, particularly in discussions of Catholic engagement with American society and culture. I will argue that Hugo's theology offers a corrective to the dominant perspective on such engagement today—Catholic "public theology"—as it once did for a perhaps not so different neo-Thomist stance that prevailed in American Catholicism over seven decades ago. And I will also suggest that charges made against more recent American Catholics who are influenced by Day and the Catholic Worker are very similar to the charges made against Hugo in the 1940s and that all these charges seem to be based on shared theological assumptions.

These arguments are presented in six chapters. Chapter one presents a survey of how Hugo has been remembered in American Catholic history. While not exhaustive, this survey, which includes Day's

---

rooted in scholastic thinkers broadly understood, neo-Thomism was based in the writings of Aquinas and the tradition of "Thomistic" commentators. Gerald McCool *Catholic Theology in the Nineteenth Century: The Quest for a Unitary Method* (New York: Seabury Press, 1977), 29.

description of Hugo and the retreat, highlights some of the main ways in which Hugo has been depicted. The second chapter then provides a day-by-day account of the Hugo retreat, with descriptions of each of the twenty-six sessions based on Hugo's *Applied Christianity* as well as Day's own unpublished retreat notes. This account gives a sense of what an actual retreat entailed and how its theology was presented and received. In chapter three, I focus on Hugo's assertion that the theological roots of the retreat are found chiefly in the *Spiritual Exercises* of Ignatius of Loyola. I also describe Hugo's attempt to place Lacouture's reading of the *Exercises* within a long but sometimes overlooked strain of Jesuit spiritual writers. This was Hugo's attempt to "return to the sources" in order to justify his theological arguments—his own self-styled *ressourcement*. Next, chapter four looks at the historical and theological context within which Hugo was working. As noted earlier, this was an important time not only in the Catholic Worker movement, but also within Catholic theology in general and Hugo should be understood within that context. Chapter five will then examine the controversy that surrounded the Hugo retreat, particularly the back and forth between Hugo and several prominent American theologians. And the final chapter looks at the ways in which Hugo's theology remains relevant in Catholic theological discourse today.

Over the course of this research project, an image of Hugo came into focus that was not always flattering. Hugo had his detractors and he often seemed to do little to discourage them from not liking him. At times, he even came across as uncharitable. Also, the way in which he presented his theology was sometimes mechanical and even heavy-handed. Despite this, Hugo did seem to have grasped (or at least had been grasping at) some very important theological truths particularly regarding human nature and its relationship to grace. And for this reason, he was somewhat unique in the American Catholicism of his time and is significant for American Catholicism today.

CHAPTER I

FATHER HUGO FROM PITTSBURGH

Dorothy's introduction to Fr. Hugo, a young priest from Pittsburgh,
was among the most important encounters of her life.

☞ Robert Ellsberg[1]

In this first chapter, a picture of Hugo will begin to be sketched with an examination of how Hugo has been remembered by both Catholic Workers who knew him and by scholars who have written about him. This examination will not only fill out the image of Hugo, but it will also show something of his legacy within American Catholic studies. As we will see, while not in all cases, very often the depiction of Hugo is not flattering and his theology is described in terms of perfectionism, rigorism, and Jansenism. One of the main of arguments of this book is to show that such portrayals are simplistic caricatures. As later chapters will show, these depictions of Hugo originated from critics in the 1940s who were working out of a certain "two-tiered" theology which prevailed in early twentieth-century Catholic thought. That this depiction of Hugo is rooted in such a theology has been missed by contemporary scholars even as they have continued to propagate similar depictions themselves. And such accounts of Hugo and the retreat theology are significant, as it will be later pointed out, since they contribute to the continued marginalization of the radical Christianity put forth by Day and other Catholic radicals as "perfectionism" and "apocalyptic sectarianism" or even as "irrelevant."

But a very different account of Hugo is presented by Dorothy Day. Hugo's importance for Day was as her chief resource for the theology of the retreat—a theological vision which Hugo did not limit to the retreat itself, but brought into discussions of social issues including

---

1   Ellsberg, ed., *All the Way to Heaven: The Selected Letters of Dorothy Day*, ed. Robert Ellsberg (Milwaukee: Marquette University Press, 2010), 134.

Catholics participation in war. While she peppered her writings with quotes from Hugo, Day's description of him in *The Long Loneliness* (1952) was brief. Despite this, I would argue that it is the way Day structured her autobiography itself that reveals the true influence of Hugo. For Day wrote the story of her life—a life that has been described as "the most significant, interesting, and influential" in American Catholicism—as an illustration of the retreat theology at work.[2] Recognizing the influence Hugo had on her is necessary, therefore, not only for understanding Hugo, but for better understanding Day herself.

WHO WAS FR. HUGO?

John Jacob Hugo was born in McKeesport, Pennsylvania in 1911. After studying at St. Vincent's College in Latrobe, he was ordained a priest in the diocese of Pittsburgh by Bishop Hugh Boyle (1873-1950) in 1936 and was then assigned to teach Sociology at Seton Hill College in Greensburg, Pennsylvania.

In September 1938, after having missed the annual priests' retreat in the diocese, Hugo attended a retreat at St. Mary's seminary in Baltimore led by a French-Canadian Jesuit named Onesimus Lacouture, S.J. (1881-1951). Hugo was greatly moved by the retreat and attended a second Lacouture led retreat held in September of the following year. That fall, Hugo was also transferred from Seton Hill to Mount Mary College (now Carlow College) in Pittsburgh where he worked as the chaplain for the women's college run by the Sisters of Mercy. In the summer of 1940, he and Fr. Louis Farina, another Pittsburgh priest who had attended a Lacouture retreat, began leading Lacouture inspired retreats at St. Anthony Orphanage in Oakmont, Pennsylvania where Fr. Farina was director at the time. While Lacouture's retreats were mainly offered to clergy, Hugo and Farina opened their retreats to the laity as well.

Dorothy Day attended her first Hugo retreat in July 1941; she was encouraged to do so by several friends. Day was so inspired by the retreat that she asked Hugo to lead the second annual Catholic Worker retreat to be held at Maryfarm in Easton, Pennsylvania two months later. Day promoted the retreat enthusiastically and over the next decade

---

2   Quote taken from David O'Brien, "The Pilgrimage of Dorothy Day," *Commonweal* 107 (1980): 71.

Hugo became a regular contributor to *The Catholic Worker*, writing several articles which—as Powers noted—had defended American Catholic conscientious objectors in World War II. Because of Day, the founder and matriarch of the Catholic Worker, Hugo enjoyed a fixed place as the theological and spiritual leader of the movement.

But not everyone in the Catholic Worker appreciated Day's introduction of Hugo and the retreat, and indeed real divisions emerged within the Catholic Worker over the retreat. And more formal opposition to Hugo and the retreat also existed. In 1942, responding to complaints from clergy in Pittsburgh, Hugo's bishop transferred him to a rural parish, effectively ending his ability to regularly lead retreats. In response to this criticism, Hugo wrote *Applied Christianity* in order to present the retreat and its theology. It was published by The Catholic Worker Press (an in-house operation) in 1944 with illustrations by Ade Bethune (1914-2002) and an imprimatur from New York's Francis Cardinal Spellman (1889-1967). Starting in 1945, a series of articles by several influential American Catholic theologians like Francis Connell C.Ss.R. and Joseph Clifford Fenton began to appear in prominent journals like the *American Ecclesiastical Review* criticizing the theology in *Applied Christianity*. Hugo responded to this criticism, leading to what Fenton labeled as the "retreat controversy."[3] And this controversy was itself predated by an earlier one surrounding Lacouture in Canada in which charges of "Lacouturism" appeared and led to Lacouture being banned from leading retreats by his Jesuit superiors in 1939.

During what he termed his "exile"—the years during which he was transferred to various assignments throughout the diocese that prohibited his leading retreats—Hugo continued to write articles for *The Catholic Worker* along with several books and pamphlets which both expanded the theological themes in the retreat and employed this theology in discussing issues of war and economics. He also continued to request an assignment from his bishop—now John Dearden (1907-1988)—that would allow him time to resume leading retreats.[4]

---

3 Joseph Clifford Fenton, "Nature and the Supernatural Life" *American Ecclesiastical Review* 114 (January 1946): 54-68.

4 According to Hugo, he and Farina even traveled to Rome in the early 1950s to "appeal" their case to Cardinal Ottaviani (1890-1979), only to be turned away by his secretary. Hugo later recalled that they had not realized

In 1959, Hugo was finally able to resume leading retreats with the blessing of his new bishop, John J. Wright (1909-1979). Hugo had been made pastor of a suburban parish and was thus able to take the time necessary to lead retreats. Wright was clearly a supporter of Hugo and appointed him the founding director of the Diocesan Theological Commission. And in the midst of the build-up to *Humanae Vitae,* Wright even asked Hugo to write a defense of the Catholic teaching on artificial birth control, which was published in 1968 under the title *St. Augustine on Nature, Sex, and Marriage.*[5] Hugo was also invited by Wright's successor in Pittsburgh, Bishop Donald W. Wuerl, to contribute to a catechism for adults titled *The Teaching of Christ* which Wuerl edited.[6]

For a short time starting in 1964, Hugo also resumed giving the annual Catholic Worker retreat then held at Tivoli farm in upstate New York. He led one each of the following two summers, but cancelled the 1967 retreat claiming to be too engaged in writing his book on birth control. Late the following year, *The Catholic Worker* began printing a series of chapters from another of Hugo's forthcoming books, *Love Strong as Death.*[7] Day included an editorial comment highlighting his work during World War II in which she stated that Hugo had "led the way among Catholics in the struggle for peace."[8] In 1976, Day made what would be her final retreat with Hugo at a convent outside of

that "there was no such thing as recourse to Rome." Hugo, *Your Ways are not My Ways,* volume 1 (Pittsburgh: Encounter with Silence, 1986), 179.

5   In his "Introduction," Wright wrote: "Comes now Father Hugo, a student of St. Augustine during all the years of his life as a scholar, retreat director and thoroughly pastoral priest... In this scholarly work he has successfully (indeed, at times heroically!) met the trial of contradiction and the testing by that magisterial criticism which forces on the intellectually honest a careful weighing of their conclusions and leads to the kind of results reflected in this book." Hugo, *St. Augustine on Nature, Sex, and Marriage* (Chicago: Scepter Press, 1968).

6   Ronald Lawler, OFM, Cap., Thomas Comerford Lawler, and Donald Wuerl, eds., *The Teaching of Christ: A Catechism for Adults* (Huntington, IN: Our Sunday Visitor Press, 1976).

7   John Hugo, *Love Strong as Death: A Study of Christian Ethics* (published by author, 1969). Hugo dedicated the book to Onesimus Lacouture, S.J. The articles in *The Catholic Worker* appeared from October 1968-June 1969.

8   *The Catholic Worker* (December 1968): 4.

Pittsburgh, an experience that she later recalled had left her "refreshed and strengthened."[9] And in 1981, Hugo delivered the homily at a Memorial Mass for Dorothy Day celebrated at Marquette University, which he titled: "Dorothy Day: Driven by Love."

Hugo spent the last few years of his life as chaplain to a community of sisters writing a two-volume work on the retreat. Indeed, he was still editing the second volume of *Your Ways Are Not My Ways: The Radical Christianity of the Gospel* when he died in a car accident on October 1, 1985—he had just finished giving a retreat two days earlier.[10] Hugo was buried on the grounds of the convent of the Sisters of the Holy Family of Nazareth in Bellevue, Pennsylvania, where he had been chaplain.[11]

HOW HUGO HAS BEEN REMEMBERED

Father Harvey Egan, who lived in a Catholic Worker house in Minneapolis as a seminarian in the 1940s and attended a Hugo retreat, remembered the retreat as having had a deeply profound effect on Day. He even suggested that it had brought about something of a "second conversion" in her life:

> Dorothy really had two conversions. Her second conversion, after she started making the retreat, added the interior life to her exterior life, I guess you'd say. She had been in her first conversion from 1933, when the Worker was established, until she made the retreat. What she was doing was the works of mercy, the exterior life. After she made the retreat, she continued with that. She did not diminish, didn't become the solitary or live aloof from the house. But she began to read the scriptures everyday. She loved the word of God. She went to Mass, read the lives of the saints, really latched onto the traditional religious experiences.[12]

---

9   Day, "On Pilgrimage" *The Catholic Worker* (September 1976): 2.

10   Aquilina and Scott, *Weapons*, 22.

11   Hugo reported that Father H.A. Reinhold—a leading figure in the Catholic liturgical movement—had served as the previous chaplain there. Hugo, *Your Ways Are Not My Ways: The Radical Christianity of the Gospel*, vol.1 (Pittsburgh: Encounter With Silence, 1986), 37.

12   Riegle, *Dorothy Day: Portraits by Those Who Knew Her* (Maryknoll, NY: Orbis Press, 2003)84.

It is important to note that Day's encounter with the retreat and this "second conversion" it brought about took place in the aftermath of her declaration that the Catholic Worker was pacifist in World War II, an extremely painful and disruptive moment in Day's life and in the history of the young Catholic Worker movement. In this context, the retreat can be seen as also having offered her the theological resources she needed to understand and articulate such difficulties as a necessary part of a life of holiness.

And it was this desire for holiness that Dorothy Gauchat, a Catholic Worker from Cleveland who also attended Hugo retreats, remembered as being central to Hugo's preaching. She recalled that while a lot of people got "carried away on the cigarette thing"—the retreat's suggestion that attachments to cigarette smoking could become impediments to holiness and therefore should be given up—she recounted that Hugo's discussion of smoking was always within the context of his broader description of created goods as "samples."[13] While things like cigarettes were described as good (this was the 1940s after all!), she remembered Hugo explaining that they were still only "samples" of God and that the desire for such things was a distraction.[14] For Gauchat, the portrayal of Hugo's teachings as "Jansenistic" probably had more to do with the way some retreatants responded to his retreat, rather than with what the retreat theology actually taught. She recalled once sitting down to a delicious meal during a retreat and seeing many of her fellow retreatants refusing to eat the more delectable of the foods offered. Gauchat remembered Hugo sitting at the table saying, "Hey! That's not the message. If somebody puts a good steak in front of you, you don't say you can't eat it. You eat it."[15] While Hugo stressed that attachment to such things as good food could—and usually did—become obstacles to loving God, steaks and other "beautiful things" were regarded as good and could be seen as samples of something infinitely better. Gauchat recalled Day as saying: "You must receive as humbly as you give. If somebody puts a steak in front of you,

---

13   Riegle Troester, *Voices*, 19.

14   She recalled Hugo preaching: "We can use them, you know, to reach the goal of really living the way Christ wanted us to live. Living the Sermon of the Mount. Not let those things get in the way. That's all." Riegle Troester, *Voices*, 19.

15   Riegle Troester, *Voices*, 20.

you thank God. On the other hand, if having steaks every day and having all the extras and niceties in your life is your consuming drive, then you're on the wrong track."[16]

WILLIAM MILLER

Picking up on such recollections, William Miller—whose *Harsh and Dreadful Love* and *Dorothy Day: A Biography* are two of the earliest, most comprehensive, and most often cited of studies of Day and the early Catholic Worker—described Day as being attracted to the theology of the retreat because it presented the Gospels in the fullness of their "radical and uncompromising spirituality."[17] He portrayed this theology as having greatly influenced Day and suggested that she understood it as giving new meaning to what Maurin had taught her earlier, emphasizing the more "transcendent sense of the worth of man's nature."[18] Through the retreat, Day's vision was lifted "more fixedly on the supernatural and with a new strength it revivified for her the meaning of love" and she came to see Christ "not primarily as a social reformer but as the exemplar of all-sufficient love."[19] And because of this, Day came to realize the necessity of *all* Christians to strive to live a life of holiness—what the Second Vatican Council would refer to as "the universal call to holiness"—and Miller quoted her as saying, "We are put here to become saints...We must combat the idea that only a few are called to sanctity."[20]

According to Miller, attending these retreats also seemed to have "settled" Day more securely in some of her positions regarding the Catholic Worker movement.[21] He wrote that early on Day had been very sensitive to the Marxist critique of religious charity and often questioned her own motives for performing the works of mercy, wondering if these motives were not somewhat disingenuous, "the

---

16   Riegle Troester, *Voices*, 20.

17   William Miller, *Dorothy Day: A Biography* (San Francisco: Harper & Row, 1982), 340.

18   William Miller, *A Harsh and Dreadful Love* (Milwaukee, WI: Marquette University Press, 1973), 188.

19   Miller, *Harsh*, 189-190.

20   Miller, *Dorothy*, 363.

21   Miller, *Harsh*, 189.

pandering to the weakness of others in order to build up one's own holiness."[22] But in the theology articulated in the retreat an answer was provided to her self-doubt, for if "the charity of the Workers was through supernatural love—love of God—then all natural motives, all vainglory, would be weeded out and only then would the object of the charity be truly influenced toward good."[23] And in a more mundane key, Miller also noted that after her initial encounter with the retreat Day lost "something about her that might be called brassiness"; she stopped smoking and drinking and her speech became "less salty."[24]

Acknowledging some of the division that the retreat brought to the Catholic Worker movement, Miller stated that while some of the younger Catholic Worker's chafed at the austerity of the retreat, "Dorothy found it good" and called the six days of silence "manna from heaven." [25] The idea that Day embraced the retreat while other Catholic Workers resisted it reflects the importance the retreat had for Day. As evidence of this, Miller reported that Day took over 300 pages of retreat notes, and that up until her death she talked of editing these notes into a book titled *All is Grace*.[26]

In Miller's accounts, Hugo is depicted as "the master of the Catholic Worker retreats," someone who possessed "the best understanding of Father Lacouture's message and methods."[27] He is portrayed as the best preacher and promulgator of the retreat theology in the United States. And after the two retreats in 1941, Hugo became Day's spiritual advisor—both "formally and informally"—for most of her life.[28]

---

22   Miller, *Harsh*, 190.

23   Miller, *Harsh*, 190.

24   Miller also suggested that after the 1941 Hugo-retreats, in particular, Day had a "new sensitivity" to what she viewed as the truth of the Gospels, and that it gave her "a reinforced spirituality." Miller, *Dorothy*, 341.

25   Miller, *Harsh*, 188; Miller, *Dorothy Day*, 340.

26   Miller, *Dorothy*, 362. In his edited volume of Day's retreat notes, *All is Grace*, Miller explained that Day never published the book, but gave Miller a folder of retreat notes that she titled, *All is Grace*. Miller edited the notes and included many of them in his book *All is Grace* (Garden City, NY: Doubleday & Company, 1987).

27   Miller, *Harsh*, 187.

28   Miller, *Dorothy*, 340. Miller recounted the story that in September, 1942 when the sixteen year old Tamar surprised Day with her plans to marry

While his influence came initially through leading retreats, the image of Hugo went beyond simply that of a "retreat-priest" with Miller
describing him as *The Catholic Worker's* "principal theological reference
for its positions on war and military conscription."[29] On this point,
Miller quoted a note Hugo sent Day soon after their initial meeting
regarding her pacifist stand in World War II:

> No doubt [pacifism] is all clear to you; but then you have not tried
> to work it out doctrinally. If you knew no theology, it would prob-
> ably be simpler to make a solution. Yet the decision must be based
> on doctrine. Pacifism must proceed from truth, or it cannot exist at
> all. And of course this attack on conscription is the most extreme
> form of pacifism.[30]

Prior to 1940, Miller suggested that Day and Maurin had been using
"history-based arguments" to justify their pacifist positions—for instance, arguing that the Treaty of Versailles was the primary cause of
World War II.[31] But by 1940, it had become clear to Day that such arguments had little direct meaning on the European situation and she
saw Hugo's critique as more accurate—her pacifism had to "proceed
from truth."[32]

In response, Day invited Hugo to write a series of articles in *The
Catholic Worker* on Christian participation in war. Miller described
Hugo's lengthy articles as calling for the use of the "weapons of the
spirit" (prayer, fasting, and almsgiving) in fighting what he argued was

---

David Hennessy, Day turned to Hugo for guidance: "Father Hugo said he
was greatly concerned and would like to help.'But humanly, there is so little
that one can do.'" While the conditions for such a marriage may have seemed
"unpropitious," Hugo counseled Day that her daughter would have to fashion her own destiny. Besides, he concluded, "if you forsee suffering for her,
that is no bad thing by the divine standard of things." Miller, *Dorothy*, 360.

29   Miller, *Harsh*, 187.

30   Miller, *Harsh*, 166. While many scholars have since quoted this note
and cite Miller as its source, unfortunately, Miller did not cite where this
note came from.

31   Miller, *Harsh*, 166.

32   Miller argued that "Nazi Germany was not the Weimar Republic, and
to continue to base her pacifism on the points made by the revisionist histo-
rians on the causes of World War I was obviously not a position that would
sustain her." Miller, *Harsh*, 166.

the real war—"history's movement toward a spiritless objectivization
and violence."[33] These articles (which will be looked in a later chapter) employed the retreat's theology of nature and grace and to argue
that war, even one that was deemed "just" through natural law reasoning, could be renounced in favor of a supernatural pacifism—what
Hugo termed as "the higher way of Jesus."[34] All of this led Miller to
conclude that Hugo—along with the Catholic University of America
philosopher Msgr. George Barry O'Toole—provided Day and *The
Catholic Worker* with much of the theological justification for a more
Gospel-based pacifism.[35] That Hugo could be remembered this way
by one Day's earliest biographers reveals something of the influence he
had on Day and the Catholic Worker even beyond the retreats. And
the fact that Day has been referred to as the "Mother of American
Catholic Pacifism" also points to Hugo's significance for American
Catholicism.[36]

   The extent of Hugo's influence was also seen in what Miller calls
the "changing prospect" of the Catholic Worker movement in the
years surrounding WWII.[37] Indeed, Day's attempt at a "year away"

---

33   Miller, *Harsh*, 164.

34   Miller noted that while some readers were turned off by "such weighty
fare," Day appreciated that *The Catholic Worker's* positions were being put
to "close theological analysis." He quoted Day as having written that, "Father
Hugo was a hard reasoner who, like Jonathan Edwards, found theology
sweet to his taste. When once in the *Worker* he asked the rhetorical question
why others in the clergy had not reached conclusions similar to his own, he
answered by saying that they had not thought enough about the subject."
Miller, *Harsh*, 183.

35   Miller, *Harsh*, 183. See also, Patricia McNeal's *Harder Than War* (New
Brunswick, NJ: Rutgers University Press, 1992), and *American Catholic
Pacifism* Anne Klejment and Nancy Roberts, eds. (Westport, CT: Praeger
Publishing Co., 1996).

36   McNeal called Day the "Mother of American Catholic Pacifism. "
Harder Than War, 29. And she noted that Paul Hanly Furfey also provid-
ed a "theological rationale that would eventually form the basis of Catholic
Worker pacifism." 38.

37   John Cogley pointed out that Hugo, along with Robert Ludlow and
Ammon Hennacy, were the main influences on Day's post-war reshaping of
the movement. John Cogley, "Harsh and Dreadful Love," *America* 127 (Nov.,
11, 1972). Hugo's influence was seen as having brought him into tension

in 1943 under the direction of Hugo followed by her desire to convert Maryfarm into a retreat center in 1944 were regarded as having
been largely shaped by Hugo.[38] Though the conversion of Maryfarm
was not welcomed by many others in the Catholic Worker, Miller explained that Day hoped to try to build a "training center for Catholic
Workers, for apostles, for followers of the Lord."[39] She even asked
Hugo to be the chaplain-in-residence and the retreat master, but he
was unable because of his "exile."[40]

Miller noted that Day made a final retreat with Hugo in July 1976—
what he called "a gesture to a meaningful part of her past."[41] And at its
conclusion, Day is reported to have asked Hugo to give the homily at
her funeral.[42] This request went unfulfilled.

BRIGID O'SHEA MERRIMAN

Recognition of Hugo's significance also emerged in Brigid O'Shea
Merriman's account of Hugo and the retreat in *Searching for Christ*.[43]

---

with others in the movement, in particular Ammon Hennacy. Miller noted
that Hugo was one of the many people associated with the Catholic Worker
concerned about Hennacy's effect on the movement. He quoted a note
Hugo wrote to Day in 1955 in which he stated that he was "concerned by the
direction the paper was taking…since Ammon became a definite member of
your staff" and that he was at first "puzzled, then disturbed" by discussions
of "Catholic anarchism." While he was sorry to have to write such a letter,
Hugo explained that "in departing from the truth, you depart also from genuine truth." Miller, *Dorothy*, 426.

38   Miller wrote of Day's stated wish to take a year off, "from all active work,
all responsibility." She also wanted to put herself under "complete obedience"
to the spiritual direction of Hugo. Miller, *Dorothy*, 367.

39   Miller, *Dorothy*, 384.

40   Pacifique Roy, SSJ, moved to Easton instead and retreats were given
there until 1946. In describing the retreat "controversy," which greatly affected both Lacouture and Hugo, Miller somewhat casually quipped that
"when the furor eventually subsided no one was burned at the stake." Miller,
Dorothy, 340.

41   Miller, *Dorothy*, 512.

42   Miller, *Dorothy*, 512.

43   Brigid O'Shea Merriman, O.S.F., *Searching For Christ: The Spirituality
of Dorothy Day* (Notre Dame, IN: University of Notre Dame Press, 1994).

She noted that while over the years there were various "retreat-priests," Hugo was considered its best articulator and the key figure in the promulgation of the retreat in the United States, as well as in the controversy that surrounded it.[44] This fact was especially evident after 1942 when he was no longer able to preach retreats. Despite the fact that other priests continued to lead the retreat, Merriman explained that the "largeness" of Hugo's presence in the retreat movement had been so important that his geographic removal caused Day to become uncertain about the movement's future.[45]

Merriman described Hugo's significance as being rooted in the impact his theology had on Day. In contrast to the earlier retreats which she regarded as "too rarified," Day stated that after encountering the retreat through Hugo and Roy she came to "see all things new."[46] Merriman pointed out that the July 1941 Hugo retreat had

I am grateful to Sister Merriman—who interviewed Hugo in 1984 and attended one his retreats—for generously donating a great deal of Hugo material, including her interview notes, to this research project.

44   Merriman pointed out that after attending the 1938 retreat led by Lacouture in Baltimore, Hugo felt that he had been given "a new perspective on Christian life." She wrote that Hugo "dreamt of being the counterpart of his adopted mentor, Lacouture"—but while Lacouture had been giving retreats exclusively to clergy, Hugo wanted to "devote his life to preaching the retreat doctrine to the laity." Hugo's emphasis was on the retreat's claim that supernatural holiness was central to lives of all Christians—not only spiritual elites. Merriman, 165, 141.

45   Merriman, 146. In the July-August 1947 issue of *The Catholic Worker*, Day highlighted three moments of conflict in the history of the Worker: the choices precedence gives to the works of mercy over indoctrination and organization, the fallout following Day's pacifist stand in WWII, and the retreat controversy. Day called the controversy "one of the wars in our midst." And it took a toll on Day, for while at first she regarded it as an opportunity "for clarification of thought," as the controversy continued her "assurance gave way to discouragement." Merriman suggested that Day became distressed that the retreat which had become so vital to her own spiritual growth was the cause of so much dissension both in and outside of the Catholic Worker. Merriman, 157.

46   Merriman took this quote from an obituary Day wrote for Roy in November 1954. 141. Merriman described several retreats Day made including ones led by a group of former Furfey students called the Campions, as well as ones led by Fulton Sheen in 1937, Missionary Servant Father

an almost immediate effect on Day, and that upon returning to New York she wrote to the other Catholic Worker houses stating that the annual Catholic Worker retreat would be a full week long retreat rather than just a weekend.[47] She also began to incorporate the language and terminology of the retreat into her writings and promulgate it in *The Catholic Worker*.[48] Merriman surmised that Day clearly accepted and employed the notions of renunciation and detachment preached by Hugo, but within a context that was "positive" for her own spiritual development.[49] And she concluded that Day's attraction to the Hugo retreat was based on the fact that it provided her with a larger theological vocabulary to express the beliefs and insights she already held.[50] In this way, the retreat theology offered Day "a practical body of instruction" which enabled her in her quest for continued growth in holiness. And it was this desire for holiness—for the supernatural life—that made Hugo and retreat so influential for Day. For the implications of this supernatural life was the chief focus of Hugo's preaching.[51] Absent from Merriman's account is any suggestion that Hugo promoted an extreme perfectionism or some sort of Jansenist theology. In fact, she pointed out that one of the concerns Day had with the retreat was that many of its promulgators—including Hugo

---

Joachim Benson from 1937-1939, and Furfey in 1940. Merriman, 138. Day also made a retreat led by Father Joseph Clifford Fenton, a later critic of the Hugo retreat, in 1938—the only year Fenton led retreats. J. Leon Hooper, "Murray and Day: A Common Enemy, A Common Cause?" *Theological Studies* 24 (Winter 2006): 56.

47   Merriman, 144. Merriman noted that Day specified that unlike the 1939 and 1940 Catholic Worker weekend retreats, the 1941 retreat would be a week long and held in strict silence. Merriman also noted that, contrary to Day's account in *The Long Loneliness*, Sister Peter Claver Fahy claimed that she introduced Day to Hugo.

48   Merriman, 144.

49   Merriman, 145.

50   Merriman, 165. Merriman quoted Sr. Peter Claver Fahey as saying that the retreat "only gave consent to all the things she had in her own heart." Merriman, 145.

51   Merriman, 166.

himself—did not always embody its call to holiness, especially in their responses to critics.[52]

ROSALIE RIEGLE

The impact that Hugo and the retreat had on Day is further highlighted in Rosalie Riegle's *Voices from the Catholic Worker* and *Dorothy Day: Portraits by Those Who Knew Her*.[53] In these collections of interviews, Hugo is described as providing Day with the "spiritual armor" that allowed her to continue even after the euphoria of the early years of the Catholic Worker faded.[54] For after meeting Maurin and starting the Catholic Worker, Day had forged a Catholic identity but, Riegle asserted, "it was not with joy and not with surety of faith and righteousness, in the best sense, that she needed to carry on through a long and productive life."[55] Instead it was Hugo who provided Day with exactly what she needed at the time, for his retreat "solidified [Day's] identity and gave her spiritual practices that delineated her relationship to a Christianity she deeply loved but whose compromises with the world she could not condone."[56] All this is to say that her encounter with Hugo and the retreat initiated a "second conversion" in Day's life.[57]

THOSE WHO WERE CRITICAL OF HUGO AND THE RETREAT

CATHOLIC WORKERS

But not everyone remembered Day's introduction of Hugo and the retreat into the Catholic Worker in such positive terms. Indeed, in his account of the Catholic Worker, *Wings of the Dawn*, Stanley Vishnewski, a long-time Catholic Worker, recalled Day's introduction of the "basic retreat" as an act which brought a great deal of conflict

---

52   Merriman, 283, fn.72.

53   *Voices from the Catholic Worker* (Philadelphia: Temple UP, 1993); *Dorothy Day: Portraits by Those Who Knew Her* (Maryknoll, NY: Orbis Press, 2003)

54   Riegle, *Portraits*, 86.

55   Riegle, *Portraits*, 86.

56   Riegle, *Portraits*, 86.

57   Riegle, *Portraits*, 83.

and tension to the movement.[58] He described the main argument of the retreat as the call for "a complete renunciation of everything that was in the natural order," an argument he understood as revolving around the idea of motives: "all our actions had to be done from a supernatural motive, otherwise, there was no merit for these actions in the sight of God."[59] Because of this he recalled that he began "to resent and envy pagans and the unbaptized" for they could "enjoy all the creatures and comforts of this world and enjoy their eternity in Limbo," while if Christians did not give up the things of this world "we were headed straight for hell."[60] To "live the retreat" meant that one had to give up "every natural affection and delight and pleasure as something alien and hostile to the love of God…to seek the will of God in all that one did, loved and thought."[61] Such a theological vision was not always appreciated.

According to Vishnewski, even before Hugo began giving Catholic Worker retreats, its theology had already "radiated out throughout the country and began to create dissension and disunity in many monasteries and convents."[62] He recalled that this divisiveness was so strong that in some seminaries all reference to the retreat was forbidden and any seminarian caught advocating the retreat doctrine was

---

58   Vishnewski was a member of the New York Catholic Worker until his death in 1979. *Wings of the Dawn* was published posthumously by the Catholic Worker Press in 1984.

59   Vishnewski, 214-215.

60   To illustrate this point, Vishnewski said that a retreat-priest once told him that if he were to kiss a girl—even one he was engaged to—and "felt any emotion other than that of kissing a doorknob" he was committing a mortal sin. He then recounted "I kissed a doorknob once in an effort to find out exactly what a sinless action of kissing would feel like—just in case…" Vishnewski, 214.

61   Vishnewski, 214. He described the retreat as originating in Canada: "The people who made the retreats would assemble in a church for a day of prayer and fasting. Two hour-long sermons on the love of God and detachment from creatures would be preached. The only book permitted to be read was the Bible. Bread and water were a concession to those who were not strong enough to keep the strict fast." Vishnewski, 209.

62   Vishnewski, 210.

subject to expulsion.[63] While Hugo was a "chaplain of a girl's school in Pittsburgh," Vishnewski recounted, he had also caused conflict, for the "girls as far as I could learn, did not like the idea of being told that it was wrong to use lipstick, to go dancing and to go to the movies."[64] And it was this sort of conflict that led Bishop Boyle to transfer Hugo to the chaplaincy of the prison system and forbid him the use of St. Anthony's Village for the retreat.[65]

Such division and controversy was brought to the Catholic Worker when Day invited Hugo to lead the Maryfarm retreat in 1941—an action Vishnewski did not support. Indeed, he recalled that it was this 1941 retreat that split the Catholic Worker into two camps: those who had made the retreat and those who had not. For the former, "no one could be a true Christian who did not live up to the teachings of the retreat," while for the latter "the retreat was nothing else but a revival of Jansenism in its worst form."[66] He wrote that this division was vividly

---

63   Such opposition, though, was seen as only affirming the retreatants' belief that "if they followed the teachings of the retreat that the world would hate them." Vishnewski did admit that the retreat did produce good for many people—particularly in priests who "gave up worldly goods and became spiritually oriented and ascetic." But even here, division followed the retreat as these priests "provoked scorn and opposition on the part of clerics who felt that these priests were a spiritual threat to them." Vishnewski, 210-212.

64   Interestingly, Vishnewski remembered that at first even Hugo himself had opposed much of the retreat theology and rejected the retreat's basic premise of "being completely detached from the things of this world." Soon enough, though, Hugo became "converted" to its basic doctrine and with "fervent zeal started to preach it in the United States." Vishnewski, 209.

65   Vishnewski, 210. Vishnewski said that when he was younger he felt grateful to grow up in a period of history when all theological or philosophical problems had been resolved. But then "I joined the Catholic Worker, a good Catholic boy from Brooklyn, and as a result found myself living right in the storm of theological controversy on the nature of Grace. Shades of St. Augustine." Vishnewski, 214.

66   Vishnewski. 211. While the term "Jansenism" continues to be thrown around quite a bit in descriptions of Hugo and the retreat, it should be remembered that it is a technical term referring the five propositions condemned in 1653 by Pope Innocent X in *Cum occasione*: 1. Some of God's precepts are impossible to the just, who wish and strive to keep them, according to the present powers which they have; the grace, by which they

illustrated in "the most controversial part of the retreat"—its call for retreatants to quit smoking. "Theological and abstract questions made little appeal to the average Catholic," Vishnewski stated, "but cigarettes were a concrete fact and could be touched and smoked."[67] Those who made the retreat and gave up smoking as a result became a kind of "spiritual policemen" persuading others to quit as well. Besides the obvious tension this caused, Vishnewski joked that the anti-smoking fervor meant that these retreats became good places to collect packs and even whole cartons of cigarettes.[68] He even suspected that many of the anti-smoking "police" were themselves in it for the free smokes.

But Vishnewski reported that even for those who initially embraced the retreat, difficulties in following its teachings emerged as the retreat produced "spiritual aberrations among lay people who could not handle the rather harsh and unyielding doctrine."[69] While many people finished the retreat in "a stage of spiritual exaltation"—giving up so-called worldly pleasures—they soon found that they could not "live the retreat" for any sustained period. As a result, Vishnewski remembered that some of these former retreatants became extremely critical of the retreat and argued that they had been "soul washed."[70]

---

are made possible, is also wanting. 2. In the state of fallen nature one never resists interior grace. 3. In order to merit or demerit in the state of fallen nature, freedom from necessity is not required in man, but freedom from external compulsion is sufficient. 4. The Semipelagians admitted the necessity of a prevenient interior grace for each act, even for the beginning of faith; and in this they were heretics, because they wished this grace to be such that the human will could either resistor obey. 5. It is Semipelagian to say that Christ died or shed His blood for all men without exception. Denzinger, *The Sources of Catholic Dogma* (1957), 1092-1096. For twentieth-century critics of the retreat, the label seemed to simply mean any theological tendency that appeared to disparage or denigrate the abilities and goodness of human nature.

67   Vishnewski, 211.

68   Vishnewski, 211.

69   "Most lay people," Vishnewski argued, "did not have the theological and philosophical knowledge to be able to find the spiritual loopholes that permitted one to enjoy life and also to enter heaven with a 'scorched behind.'" Vishnewski, 212.

70   He even remembered that a "young Benedictine was so embittered that he made it a personal crusade to travel around the country preaching against

Further division arrived when Day decided to transform Maryfarm from a farming commune into a center for preaching the retreat.[71] Vishnewski remembered that some of the Catholic Workers objected to the imposition of a retreat house on the farm, though Day argued that giving retreats was a spiritual work of mercy and fit into the larger Catholic Worker "program."[72] But Day's defense of the retreat did not end the criticism and Vishnewski noted that many Catholic Workers believed that her move had "perverted the original idea of the movement."[73]

Vishnewski's account highlights the degree to which Hugo and the retreat were divisive for the young Catholic Worker movement. It has been noted that the early 1940s were already a tense and difficult time for Day and the Catholic Worker, and so her continued support of Hugo and the retreat—despite this opposition—appears even more telling. Far from easing tension or reconciling the losses her pacifist declaration caused, Day's introduction and support of the retreat only seemed to increase. But Vishnewski's account also highlights the important fact that despite this opposition and division, Day continued to strongly embrace the retreat and defend its theological vision.

Vishnewski was by no means the only Catholic Worker to remember Hugo and the retreat in this manner. Indeed, Harvey Egan noted that those Catholic Workers who were attracted to the retreat were a clear minority.[74] For instance, Jim O'Gara, an early Catholic Worker from Chicago who attended the Hugo retreat at Maryfarm in 1941 and would go onto become an editor at *Commonweal*, described Hugo as "more of a Jansenist."[75] And Betty Doyle, a Catholic Worker from Minnesota, recalled that much of the division brought on by the retreat revolved around its the call give up attachments to created goods. "People were detachers" she said, and Hugo was "very much a detacher and a lot of us didn't think we should be detached from the world in

the harm caused by the retreat." Vishnewski, 213.

71   He also recounted that some in the movement felt that Roy and Hugo were "exerting undue influence on the thinking and direction of the Movement." Vishnewski, 210.

72   Vishnewski, 210.

73   Vishnewski, 210.

74   Riegle, *Portraits*, 84.

75   Riegle Troester, ed., *Voices*, 32.

that way, giving up all these beautiful things and living such a strict, bare kind of life."[76] Julian Pleasants, a long-time Catholic Worker from South Bend, who attended the Hugo retreat with Day in July 1941, recounted that while the retreat was impressive and helpful in encouraging his own prayer life, neither he nor Day accepted it wholeheartedly:

> I didn't agree with the giving up things at all. Father Hugo said that the best thing to do with good things was to give them up. And I just didn't think that was Dorothy's attitude at all. She didn't want to give them up, she wanted to give them away. It was a totally different approach. Dorothy liked her good literature, her good music, and she never really felt that obligated. I think she got out of the retreat only the notion that you had to be *ready* to give them up. She took what worked for her and hoped other people would take what worked for them.[77]

And Ruth Heaney, a Milwaukee Catholic Worker, also remembered the issue of "detachment"—particularly to cigarette-smoking—as being at the center of people's unease with the retreat,

> I remember once Father Hugo said, "If you smoke, you love God just this much—the length of a cigarette—if you won't quit smoking for his sake." Some of the healthier ones among us...well, they either had sufficient education or enough spiritual insight to recognize that this was another kind of spirituality and not one they wanted to buy into.[78]

Heaney also remembered, though, that Day was one of those drawn to this kind of "asceticism" and that she gave up smoking after her encounter with the retreat.[79]

---

76   Riegle, *Portraits*, 86.

77   Riegle Troester, *Voices, 20.*

78   Riegle Troester, *Voices, 19.*

79   Riegle Troester, *Voices, 19.* This notion of "detachment" was a popular one in certain mid-century American Catholic circles. Gary Wills has recently pointed out that J.F. Powers and his wife Betty, Robert Lowell and his wife Jean Stafford, as well as Eugene McCarthy and his wife Abigail were all at one time part of this "Detachment movement." Garry Wills, "Relicts of a Catholic Renaissance" *New York Review of Books* (October 10, 2013).

MEL PIEHL

Several scholars have followed in this more critical view of Hugo and the retreat. For example, in *Breaking Bread*, his early account of Day and the Catholic Worker, Mel Piehl described Hugo's influence as stemming from the fact that he "preached the doctrine of the Mystical Body, attacked society's individualism and materialism, and urged radical action to end race and class discrimination and war."[80] Hugo was "a dominant intellectual influence" on *The Catholic Worker* with regard to issues of war and pacifism, and the retreat was Day's first encounter with "the sort of radically inward Christianity" which up until that point she had known only in books.[81] Piehl wrote that Day found the retreat exhilarating—"what I expected when I became a Catholic"— and she appreciated its strong appeal to "sources" within the Catholic tradition which provided "applications of the radical Gospel."[82] For Piehl, it was these "applications of the radical Gospel" and "radically inward Christianity" that defined Hugo and the retreat theology, and it was this that Day embraced. But he also noted that the effects of the retreat were "complex" and that for a time its theology led Day into some "bewildering theological thickets" and sidetracked her with "some of the sumptuary moralist preachings" such as attacks on cigarettes and cosmetics.[83]

As Piehl told it, Day met Hugo during a time of "crisis and decline" for the Catholic Worker movement, when opposition to her pacifist stand in World War II caused subscriptions and financial support to wither and many Catholic Workers left in disagreement with Day.[84] That Day encountered Hugo and the retreat during this volatile period is important to understanding why Day embraced its theology.

---

80   Mel Piehl, *Breaking Bread: The Catholic Worker and The Origin of Catholic Radicalism in America*, (Philadelphia: Temple University Press, 1982), 88.

81   Piehl, 87.

82   Piehl, 88.

83   Piehl, 89. Piehl noted that Day was eventually able to sort out "these peripheral elements" from the valuable core of the retreat. Hugo read Piehl's book and was critical of this claim that the retreat caused "bewildering theological thickets" and "sumptuary moralist preachings." Hugo, *Your Ways*, vol.1, 242-244.

84   Piehl, 88.

Piehl argued that its theology allowed Day to interpret these painful experiences of division and loss in light of the Gospel paradoxes of "stripping of natural desires" and "taking up the Cross."[85] Day came to understand this time in terms of the renunciations and mortifications prescribed in the retreat theology.[86] The loss of people and support for the movement were understood as created goods "sown" in order that the supernatural life—which included the practice of Gospel nonviolence—could be embraced. According to Piehl, Day justified her pacifism and the division it brought with the retreat's theological terms and categories—what Piehl called its "radical Gospel perfectionism."[87] In short, Hugo was seen as offering Day a more a radical theology at the exact time she was becoming more radicalized in her own actions and beliefs.[88]

---

85   Piehl, 88.

86   For example, Day explained the Catholic Worker protests to the civil defense drill in the 1950s as acts of penance. Sandra Yocum argued that for Day the "arduous demands of the retreat provided clarification or at least reinforcement in her thinking through why those 'baptized in Christ's death' must be willing to assent to absolute pacifism. Yocum Mize, "We Are Still Pacifists: Dorothy Day's Pacifism During World War II" in *Dorothy Day and the Catholic Worker: Centenary Essays*, edited by Susan Mountin, et al. (Milwaukee: Marquette University Press, 2001) 471.

87   Piehl, 87.

88   Piehl suggested that after her encounter with Hugo, Day began turning towards the "passive" writings of Thérèse of Lisieux and away from her earlier attraction to the more "activist" Teresa of Avila. In the former, Day saw proof "that silence and inactivity were the sources of all right action." Piehl described Teresa of Avila as "intensely religious, but also bright, gay, intelligent, attractive, and a successful writer and activist," while the Little Flower was depicted as "a passive teenager who had suffered a debilitating illness and died in obscurity without accomplishing anything of consequences in the world." Day was quoted as saying, "I could see clearly the difference between the two Teresas and I came to the conclusion that St. Thérèse of Lisieux's was the loftier vocation, the harder and more intense life…From that year I spent away from my work I began to understand the greatness of the Little Flower…By doing nothing she did everything. She let loose powers, consolations, and streams of faith, hope, and love that will never cease to flow." Piehl, 89. Day's book on the Little Flower, *Therese*, was published in 1960.

JAMES T. FISHER

The timing of Day's encounter with Hugo and the retreat is also not overlooked by James Fisher in *The Catholic Counterculture in America, 1933-1962*, where he described Hugo as Day's "mentor" who directed her conversion toward its "final logic."[89] According to Fisher, the Hugo retreat introduced Day to "an interior landscape which vindicated her withdrawal from the American demand for measured productivity in the world" and guided her with "spiritual analogues to the deconstructivist ethos of the houses of hospitality." [90] More simply put, Hugo provided Day with the theological resources in what Fisher argued was her quest for a "downward path to salvation."[91] In this, Hugo is depicted as offering a "consistent jeremiad" against American Catholics' desire for middle-class materialism, and therefore comes across as sharing in Day's "bitter hostility to middle-class religiosity" and its exaltation of such worldly ambitions.[92]

For Fisher, the "controversy" surrounding the retreat in the United States was essentially Hugo's "private battle with the entire theology faculty of the Catholic University and their organ, the *American Ecclesiastical Review*."[93] Critiques of Hugo's theology were based on the perception that it smacked not only of "Jansenism," but of "Protestantism" in its imperative to live the supernatural life which was understood as expanding the definition of what it meant to be a Christian far beyond the largely juridical understanding assumed by his critics.[94] If nothing else, Fisher confirmed that Hugo was not insignificant in the American Catholic world of the 1940s.

89   James T. Fisher, *The Catholic Counterculture in America, 1933-1962*, (Chapel Hill, NC: University of North Carolina Press, 1989), 59.

90   Fisher, 56. For Fisher, this was all part of Day's "antitriumphalist" reversal of the Weberian Protestant work ethic which so dominated the American landscape. Fisher, 55

91   Hugo was portrayed as repeatedly driving home the point that "salvation would only come through an assent to the suffering and folly of the Cross." This is the essence of the Baudelarian "downward path to salvation" that figured prominently throughout Fisher's book. Fisher, 56.

92   Fisher, 56.

93   Fisher, 58.

94   Fisher argued the critics' primary concern was over the question of ecclesiastical authority. The retreat theology was described as confirming

But Fisher also described the retreat as central in "one of the most abject brands of self-abnegation in American religious history."[95] Hugo's theology was depicted as being excessively scrupulous and fostering "a radically personal spirituality" unlike anything ever encountered by the American laity.[96] Fisher described the theology Hugo learned from the French-Canadian Lacouture as a "bitterly mystical" and "gloomy Catholicism"—a combination of seventeenth-century "Jansenism of Port Royal" and "the harsh struggle for Catholic survival in Canada."[97] And he suggested that Day was attracted to this theology because its "ethnic Jansenism" blended well with her "aesthetic Jansenism."[98] This Jansenism was portrayed as being the source of her less than affirming view of the materialist American culture to which so many of her fellow Catholics were aspiring.[99] And indeed, building on Fisher's account, Eugene McCarraher has argued that a certain elitism existed in Day and other "Catholic radicals" that ultimately made them "irrelevant" to American Catholicism.[100]

Day's conviction that the Mystical Body of Christ was not only a "reality in the moral order, but a genuine reality," and this conviction was precisely the sort of "antinomianism over which barrels of theologians' ink had been spilled in dreaded anticipation." Thus, Fisher concluded, "Hugo had to be silenced, especially after 'Mystici Corporis' reaffirmed the priority of church membership to salvation." Fisher, 59.

95   Fisher, 1.

96   Fisher, 57, 63.

97   Fisher argued that like Peter Maurin, Hugo had an "intense hostility to Anglo-American liberalism, to the point of suggesting that the English (and now the heathen French) deserved the punishment of World War II because 'they had been faithless to Christ.'" Fisher, 60.

98   Fisher, 60. While the notion that Hugo's theology was Jansenist was not necessarily a negative perception within Fisher's broader narrative of certain American Catholics' embrace of the downward path, this idea that Hugo's theology was Jansenist reappears elsewhere in American Catholic studies. See, for example, J. Leon Hooper's "Dorothy Day's Transposition of Thérèse's 'Little Way'" in *Theological Studies* 63 (2002): 76, fn 23; and "Murray and Day: A Common Enemy, A Common Cause?" in *Theological Studies* 24 (Winter 2006): 57.

99   Fisher, 71-99.

100   Eugene B. McCarraher, "The Church Irrelevant: Paul Hanly Furfey and the Fortunes of American Catholic Radicalism" *Religion and American*

HOW DOROTHY DAY SAW THE RETREAT

What is most interesting about all of these accounts is that despite their more critical and even negative depictions of Hugo and the re-treat, they all note that Day did embrace the retreat and turned to Hugo as her spiritual guide. Whatever its critics saw as its shortcom-ings, the theology of the retreat is remembered as having profoundly influenced Dorothy Day. And it is this fact that is confirmed in Day's writings.

In 1933, under the encouragement of her spiritual director at the time, Paulist Father Joseph McSorley (1876-1963), Day began at-tending what were then known as "lay retreats."[101] Such retreats were part of the broader "retreat movement" that was fast emerging in the first half of the twentieth century.[102] Four years earlier, Pius X's en-cyclical *Mens Nostra* (1929) stressed the importance of retreats for the Christian life and described them as the "soul" of Catholic Action. "There is a need for elect groups of men, both of the secular and regu-lar clergy, who shall act as faithful dispensers of the mysteries of God," the Pope wrote, and "to these we must have compact companies of pious laymen, who united to the Apostolic Hierarchy by close bonds of charity, will actively aid this by devoting themselves to the manifold works and labors of Catholic Action."[103] As Joseph Chinnici has not-ed, these early twentieth-century lay retreats offered men and women a brief respite from the world, a chance to listen to speakers and relax in a quiet setting before they returned to the world.[104] The idea that

---

Culture 7 (Summer, 1997): 172, 176, 186.

101   William Portier, "Dorothy Day and her first spiritual director, Fr. Joseph McSorley, C.S.P." *Houston Catholic Worker*, (September-October 2002): 5.

102   Joseph Chinnici, O.F.M., *Living Stones* (Maryknoll, NY: Orbis Press, 1996), 166. In the growth of the lay retreat movement in America, Chinnici highlighted Terence Shealy (1863-1922), a New York Jesuit and first dean of Fordham's school of sociology and social science, who was instrumental in the Laymen's Retreat League which saw the lay retreat as a source of social reform. It is also important to note that in an apostolic constitution *Summorum Pontificem* (July 25, 1922), Pius X named St. Ignatius of Loyola the patron of retreats.

103   Pius X, *Mens Nostra* (8).

104   Chinnici, 167.

these retreats would cause some type of mystical or spiritual fervor and have some sort of practical implication in the lives of retreatants was not emphasized. The concrete activities of Catholic Action were seen as taking place outside of and separate from the spirituality of these retreats.[105]

What emerged, then, was a very clear separation between the lay retreat's focus upon the spiritual and Catholic Action's more worldly activities—a separation that reflected the "two-storied" view of the Christian life prevalent at the time.[106] For on the one hand, there was the extra-ordinary Christian life focused upon the mystical or supernatural—a life reserved to (or quarantined within) the cloister—while on the other hand, there was the more ordinary life of a Christian involved in the world and lived by both laity and secular clergy. This dualist conception of the Christian life was itself rooted in a "two-tiered" theology, a theology that saw the supernatural as "separated" from world and understood as building a kind of superstructure upon a largely self-contained nature. All of which led to the "separated theology" that existed throughout Catholicism in the first half of the twentieth-century. And despite this dualist theology—or perhaps because of it—Pius's endorsement of lay retreats was well received. In fact, by 1936, there were twenty-six permanent retreat houses in the United States which had hosted some 267 retreats to over 11,000 women; while in 1939, 59 of the 110 retreat houses for laymen reported that over the previous decade a total of 2,340 retreats had been given to some 131,000 men.[107]

Interestingly, Day was not impressed with the first such retreat she attended. She described it as "too rarified."[108] Nevertheless, she continued making other retreats in the years that followed. In July 1941, Day and a small group of Catholic Workers attended a retreat led by Father Hugo at St. Anthony's Village. Day was greatly moved by the week-long silent retreat. "I am completely sold on this retreat business," she proclaimed upon her return, "I think it will cure all ills, settle all problems, bind up all wounds, strengthen us, enlighten us,

---

105   Chinnici, 167.

106   Chinnici, 168.

107   Chinnici, 158.

108   Day, *Long Loneliness*, 244.

and in other words make us happy."[109] She immediately asked Hugo to lead what would be the second Catholic Worker annual retreat at Maryfarm the following month. Hugo readily agreed.

In *The Long Loneliness*, Day recalled that the first time she heard about "the retreat" was when her friend, the publisher Maisie Ward, informed her of a retreat given to workers in Montreal:

> They bring their own lunch and eat it right there in the church and share it with others who come. They spend the day in silence, walk the streets between conferences, go home at night, and come back the next day for more. People are thronging to it. It is an evangelical retreat.[110]

Day did not join Ward in Montreal, mainly because the retreat was given in French. But she was able to later read a copy of the notes from a different retreat—this one led by Onesimus Lacouture himself—which were given to her by another friend, Missionary Servant Sister Peter Claver Fahy, M.S.B.T.[111] After reading these notes, Day confessed that she was again not much impressed, explaining that "the written word did not have the life and vitality of the spoken word, and perhaps it was the personality of the retreat master that made the teaching so powerful."[112] Day recalled that Fahy, herself a devout follower of the retreat, soon brought such a retreat master to meet Day—Father Pacifique Roy, S.S.J. (d. 1954).[113]

Roy, a French-Canadian Josephite priest working in Baltimore at the time, was responsible for bringing Lacouture to Maryland to lead the priest-retreats in 1938 and 1939, both of which Hugo had attended.[114] After their initial meeting, Roy quickly became a feature in the

---

109   From a letter to Gerry Griffin dated June 18, 1941 in *All the Way to Heaven*, 125.

110   Day, *Long Loneliness*, 245.

111   Day, *Long Loneliness*, 245. According to Sr. Brigid O'Shea Merriman, Fahy had been given the notes by her confessor, Father Frank Giri, who attended a priest only retreat led by Lacouture in Baltimore either in September 1938 or 1939. Merriman, *Searching for Christ*, 140.

112   Day, *Long Loneliness*, 246. Merriman noted that Day was also not very impressed with Giri himself. Merriman, *Searching*, 140.

113   Merriman guesses that Roy came to New York in either 1938 or 1939.

114   Day, *Long Loneliness*, 246.

Catholic Worker and often came to the New York house to preach "the doctrine of the Lacouture retreat." Day remembered him sitting in the dining room talking all day long to anyone who would listen:

> Father Roy talked to us about nature and the supernatural, how God became man so that man might become God, and how we were under the obligation of putting off the old man and putting on Christ, how we had been made the sons of God, by the seed of the supernatural life planted in us at our baptism, and of the necessity we were under to see that the seed grew and flourished.[115]

Roy was also present at the first Catholic Worker annual retreat held at the Maryfarm over Labor Day weekend 1940.[116] This retreat was led by Father Paul Hanly Furfey (1896-1992), a professor of Sociology at The Catholic University of America as well as an early spiritual director to Day and frequent contributor to *The Catholic Worker*. But Day remembered Roy as a leading speaker at the event, in effect "giving a retreat within a retreat."[117]

Roy soon began leading Day and the Catholic Workers in days of recollection in Baltimore where he presented more of "the retreat doctrine." In *The Long Loneliness*, Day quoted her notes from these days: "We had to aim for perfection; we had to be guided by the folly of the Cross."[118] She recalled that Roy preached about "supernatural motives" as a means of "supernaturalizing all our actions of every day," and that by doing this Christians would follow their baptismal vows "to put off the world."[119] Day described these as "beautiful days" in which it was as though she were listening to the Gospel for the first time: "We saw all

---

115   Day, *Long Loneliness*, 246. Sandra Yocum noted that Day's recollections of the retreat were probably a blend of those given by Roy and Hugo. Yocum Mize, "We Are Still Pacifists": Dorothy Day's Pacifism During World War II" in *Dorothy Day and the Catholic Worker: Centenary Essays*, edited by Susan Mountin, et al. (Milwaukee: Marquette University Press, 2001): 469.

116   This was the retreat that Dorothy called after her declaration that the Catholic Worker was a pacifist movement in WWII, a move which many Workers disagreed with and which resulted in several houses closing and subscriptions lost.

117   Merriman, *Searching*, 140

118   Day, *Long Loneliness*, 247.

119   Day, *Long Loneliness*, 247.

things new. There was a freshness about everything as though we were in love, as indeed we were."[120] She called the theology presented in the retreat "bread for the strong."[121] And it was through these days of recollection with Roy that Day became attracted to the retreat theology.

While it was Roy who first articulated this theology to her, Day wrote that Roy was never satisfied with his presentation of what he simply called "the retreat." It is out of this dissatisfaction that he told Day that "the man who can really give this retreat is Father John J. Hugo."[122] Day recalled that at the time Hugo was a young priest "who had amplified the retreat notes of Father Lacouture into a book entitled *Applied Christianity*"—a book which she made sure to point out had been given an imprimatur by Cardinal Spellman himself.[123] Such ecclesiastical approval was significant, Day noted, since Hugo had written another book on the history of the retreat movement titled *A Sign of Contradiction: As the Master So the Disciple*, which she said had caused a stir in American clerical circles as it "was widely circulated among other priests and was regarded as an extreme example of self-criticism, that is criticism of the clergy in general."[124]

Day recalled that Hugo and Farina had been giving the retreat in an orphanage in Oakmont during the summers, "when the dormitories could be turned into classrooms and the gymnasium used as a conference room."[125] She remembered her first Hugo retreat as "a feast indeed" and described Hugo as "a brilliant teacher" who took great joy in his work.[126] Each day of the retreat was made up of five conferences, each lasting one hour, followed by prayer in the chapel. For Day, the

---

120   Day, *Long Loneliness*, 251.

121   Day, *Long Loneliness*, 263.

122   Day, *Long Loneliness*, 254.

123   Day, *Long Loneliness*, 254. In a 1941 letter to Gerry Griffin, Day, describing Hugo, remarked that there was "nothing namby-pamby about him." *All the Way to Heaven*, 125.

124   Day, *Long Loneliness*, 254. Day wrote this description as a defense of Hugo in the midst of the controversy surrounding his theology.

125   She also recalled that the sisters operating the orphanage were "quite as enthusiastic as the priests and willing to take care of the retreatants in addition to the hundred and fifty children who were in their care." Day, *Long Loneliness*, 254.

126   Day, *Long Loneliness*, 255.

Hugo retreat was unlike any she had ever attended. There was not much discussion of sin, she recalled, but there was a lot of talk on "the good and the better."[127] Alluding to the theology of nature and grace at the heart of the retreat, Day wrote that emphasis was placed on the choice one had to make—a choice not between good and evil, but rather between a natural happiness and a happiness that was super-natural: "We have been given a share in the divine life; we have been raised to a supernatural level; we have been given power to become the sons of God."[128] Recounting all of this in her autobiography, published in 1952, eleven years after making her initial Hugo retreat, Day acknowledged that she still had her notes from this retreat and enjoyed reading them over for mediation.[129]

In the July-August, 1941 issue of *The Catholic Worker*, printed immediately following her attendance at her first Hugo retreat, Day described the experience,

> We spent this period in complete silence, the day beginning at six and ending at ten. For spiritual reading at meals, we had the entire life of St. Francis by Jorgensen, and there were five conferences a day. These were so stimulating that not a moment dragged. We read nothing but the New Testament, and we all took copious notes. It was a time of real study, to put off the old man and on the new, and we came out with a real sense of renewal, a feeling that we had obtained a perspective, a point of view that gave balance to our outlook.[130]

And so while Day's first encounter with "the retreat doctrine" was through Roy and she would later attend other Lacouture inspired retreats led by various "retreat priests," she clearly preferred Hugo and considered him to be the best articulator of the retreat and her primary source for its theology.

---

127 Day, *Long Loneliness*. 256.

128 Day, *Long Loneliness*, 256.

129 Day, *Long Loneliness*, 255.

130 Day, "Day After Day," *The Catholic Worker* (July-August 1941). The Pauline image of putting off the old and putting on the new man was one of the many scriptural images employed in the retreat to illustrate its theology of nature and grace—the idea that the natural was put off or renounced so that the supernatural could be put on. The Gospel image of a seed falling to the ground and dying was also often used to explain this idea.

Day also alluded to the "controversy" which surrounded the retreat in both Canada and the United States. She wrote that Lacouture was charged with "inexactitude of expression" which brought division among the clergy and caused people to go to extremes in "the business of mortification."[131] As a result of these charges, Lacouture was forbidden from giving the retreat and sent to an Indian reservation where Day described him as happy and at peace "sowing, as he terms it, his own interior senses, the memory, the understanding, the will."[132] She also noted that a few years later, Hugo lost permission to give the retreat from his bishop Hugh Boyle.[133]

Day described the issues surrounding the charges against Lacouture and Hugo as "the old controversy of nature and grace," and she recalled that some theologians had also labeled the teaching on nature and grace in *The Imitation of Christ* as "dangerous" even while Pope Pius XI had called it "that incomparable work."[134] She reported that the retreat controversy began to spread in the U.S. through a series of articles written in *The Ecclesiastical Review* "attacking" Hugo's teaching.[135] And she pointed out that a similar "controversy" was taking place in Europe surrounding the work of Henri de Lubac, S.J., whose books she had enjoyed.[136] Glossing over the problems it brought to Lacouture, Hugo,

---

131   Day, *Long Loneliness*, 258,

132   Day, *Long Loneliness*, 259. Lacouture died in "exile" in 1951. Day reported that she was the only U.S. citizen to attend his funeral. Hugo was denied permission to attend.

133   Over the next decade, Day would make continual appeals to Boyle on behalf of Hugo. Prior to the Hugo controversy, Day knew Boyle having dealt with him on labor issues in Pittsburgh. Kenneth Heineman, *A Catholic New Deal: Religion and Reform in Depression Pittsburgh.* (University Park, PA: Pennsylvania State University Press, 1999).

134   Day, *Long Loneliness*, 258. *The Imitation of Christ* was an important text in "the retreat," particularly the discussion of nature and grace in Book Three, chapter 54: "The divers moving between nature and grace."

135   Day, *Long Loneliness*, 258. In her diary entry for January 15, 1946, Day wrote "Attack in *Ecclesiastical Review*," a reference to an article by Joseph Clifford Fenton critical of Hugo that recently appeared. Day, *The Duty of Delight: The Diaries of Dorothy Day*, Robert Ellsberg, ed. (Milwaukee: Marquette University Press, 2008), 100.

136   Day, *Long Loneliness*, 258.

and de Lubac, Day described these controversies as "a wonderful thing" for it revealed that Catholics could still become excited about points of doctrine concerning nature and the supernatural—"forces, spiritual capacities far more powerful than the atom bomb."[137]

Despite her claims to being unqualified to comment on these often technical theological disputes, Day appeared to have a significant grasp of the issues. This was particularly apparent in her suggestion that the controversy surrounding Hugo was similar to that surrounding de Lubac. Day seemed to recognize that the debates surrounding the retreat taking place in North America were part of the larger nature-grace debates taking place within Catholic theology at the middle of the twentieth-century. And it is important to remember that *The Long Loneliness* was written in the wake of *Humani Generis* (1950)—an encyclical Pius XII wrote in hopes of bringing such debates to an end.

THE STRUCTURE OF *THE LONG LONELINESS*

While evidence of the influence Hugo and the retreat had on Day appeared throughout her writings in the 1940s and 50s, it is in the way she structured *The Long Loneliness*—her most important and well-known piece of writing—that such influence can be most profoundly seen. For in her autobiography, Day presented the story of her conversion around the idea that in becoming Catholic she had renounced much more than simply a life of sin. As she told it, she gave up *the good* so that she could choose *the better*: "It is a choice, a preference. If we love God with our whole hearts, how much heart have we left?"[138] Unlike many other conversion stories, Day was deliberate in not presenting her pre-conversion life as one simply of sin and misery, but rather she described it as a life that was in many ways good and even joyful. For Day, her conversion meant leaving behind this good life for something better, something more—a life of a saint.

In telling this story, Day divided her autobiography into three parts. In Part I, "Searching," Day described her life in the Old Left, a movement she called one of her "two great loves."[139] Her radical friends were presented as good, though clearly lacking. Writing decades after her

---

137   Day, *Long Loneliness*, 259.

138   Day, *Long Loneliness*, 256.

139   Day, *Long Loneliness*, 149.

conversion in the 1920s, she still remembered her old comrades with admiration for dedicating their lives to heroically caring for and fighting for the poor and disenfranchised:

> ...the Marxists, the I.W.W.'s who looked upon religion as the opiate of the people, who thought they had only this one life to live and then oblivion—they were the ones who were eager to sacrifice themselves here and now, thus doing without now and for all eternity the good things of the world which they were fighting to obtain for their brothers. It was then, and still is, a paradox that confounds me. God love them![140]

Her description of these radicals was indeed positive and she saw her years with them as having been, in many ways, a good thing—something she still very much admired and even wished her fellow Christians would imitate.[141] Yet, it was this life—this in many ways good life—that she left behind in favor of a new life she regarded as far better.

This idea of leaving behind the good in favor of the better was illustrated even more vividly in "Natural Happiness"—the second and pivotal part of the story—which contains Day's account of the period surrounding her becoming a Catholic. In presenting her life leading up to her conversion, she recounted the happiness that she experienced with her other "great love," her common-law husband Forster Batterham. And the idea that clearly dominates Day's description of her marriage to Forster is, again, that there was real goodness in this life and that she did not simply regard it as sinful. For, far from quickly noting a past which she was ashamed of, Day wrote a great deal about her life with Forster and its simplicity and joy: "Because I feel that this period of my life was so joyous and lovely, I want to write at length about it, giving the flavor, the atmosphere, the mood of those days."[142] And her autobiography makes it clear that she was very much in love with Forster:

> I loved him in every way, as a wife, as a mother even. I loved him for all he knew and pitied him for all he didn't know...I loved his

---

140　Day, *Long Loneliness*, 63.

141　As we will see, this notion that these radicals sacrificed "the good things of the world" resonated with the retreat's notion that "the best thing to do with the best things is give them up."

142　Day, *Long Loneliness*, 116.

lean cold body as he got into bed smelling of the sea, and I loved his integrity and stubborn pride.[143]

That these lines were written some twenty-five years after her marriage to Forster ended is evidence of the extent of Day's love for him—a love that she still regarded as good, though insufficient. Her time with Forster was presented as being filled with happiness and joy, and Day found herself praying in the midst of this life—particularly when she learned she was pregnant. And she was explicit as to the reason: "I did not turn to God in unhappiness, in grief, in despair—to get consolation, to get something from Him...I am praying because I am happy, not because I am unhappy."[144] Again, Day makes it clear that her life at this time was good, her happiness was genuine.

Yet at the same time, she also wanted to make clear that this very happiness—what she called "natural happiness"—was lacking: "I was happy but my very happiness made me know that there was a greater happiness to be obtained from life than any I had ever known."[145] In one sense, this recognition that it was joy, not sorrow, which led her to God can be understood as Day's response to her old Marxist friends' view of religion as an opiate, as she explained:

> I had known enough of love to know that a good healthy family life was as near to heaven as one could get in this life. There was another sample of heaven, of the enjoyment of God. The very sexual act itself was used again and again in Scripture as a figure of the beatific vision...It was not because I was tired of sex, satiated, disillusioned, that I turned to God. Radical friends used to insinuate this. It was because through a whole love, both physical and spiritual, I came to know God.[146]

It was out of a joyful love, not suffering, that she turned to God.

But in another sense, Day can be read here as recounting one of the most painful experiences of her life in terms of the theology of nature and grace which she learned from Hugo and the retreat. The goodness

143   Day, *Long Loneliness*, 148.

144   Day, *Long Loneliness*, 132.

145   Day, *Long Loneliness*, 116. "I have always felt that it was life with him [Forster] that brought me natural happiness, that brought me to God." Day, *Long Loneliness*, 134. Day titled Part Two of *The Long Loneliness* "Natural Happiness."

146   Day, *Long Loneliness*, 140.

of her "natural happiness" was understood as a "sample"—good but insufficient—of the infinitely better "supernatural happiness" offered by God. And it was that "sample of heaven" which had led her to God.

It was through this theological perspective—the preference for the supernatural over the merely natural—that Day interpreted and described her decision to end her relationship with Forster. She knew she wanted Tamar baptized, to plant that seed within her. But this would mean the loss of her life together with Forster and the "natural happiness" that it brought.[147] She saw her conversion as a preference for the better over the good.[148] And this choice was not an easy one: "I felt all along that when I took the irrevocable step it would mean that Tamar and I would be alone, and I did not want to be alone. I did not want to give up human love when it was dearest and tenderest."[149] For Day, the difficulty was rooted in the fact that in choosing supernatural happiness over the merely natural she was indeed going against—like Ignatius of Loyola's *agere contra*—her natural inclination:

> God always gives us a chance to show our preference for Him. With Abraham it was to sacrifice his only son. With me it was to give up my married life with Forster. You do these things blindly, not because it is your natural inclination—you are going against nature when you do them—but because you wish to live in conformity with the will of God.[150]

---

147   Day wrote that "Forster, the inarticulate, became garrulous only in wrath. And his wrath, he said, was caused by my absorption in the supernatural rather than the natural." Day, *Long Loneliness*, 120.

148   She wrote, "To become a Catholic meant for me to give up a mate with whom I was much in love. It got to the point where it was a simple question of whether I chose God or man." Day, *Long Loneliness*, 145. The analogy of marriage was used often in the retreat as a metaphor for this choice, and as a married woman, Day employed it to describe her decision, "I loved... and like all women in love, I wanted to be united to my love. Why should Forster not be jealous? Any man who did not participate in this love would, of course, realize my infidelity, my adultery. In the eyes of God, any turning toward creatures to the exclusion of Him is adultery and so it is termed over and over again in Scripture." *The Long Loneliness*, 149.

149   Day, *Long Loneliness*, 145.

150   Day, *Long Loneliness*, 256.

Clearly this was not a simple or easy decision and Day did not hide the pain she felt while agonizing over it. "I became so oppressed I could not breathe and I woke at night choking…my heart was breaking with my own determination to make an end, once and for all, to the torture we were undergoing."[151] That she remembered the difficulty leaving Forster had caused and the suffering that accompanied it only further affirms the notion that Day's love for Forster was something that even decades later she still considered to be real and good. And to give up or renounce such a good thing was not a simple matter. "It was years before I awakened without that longing for a face pressed against my breast, an arm about my shoulder. The sense of loss was there. It was a price I had paid. I was Abraham who had sacrificed Isaac."[152] For Day, to go against your natural inclination was painful—a mortification even—and that pain was genuine.

In the third and final part of her story, "Love is the Measure," Day offered an illustration of this life of supernatural happiness which she had chosen, a life lived with clear focus on the beatific vision.[153] Her description of this life is one of ongoing discernment and the daily renunciation of that which did not lead to God. As Sandra Yocum has pointed out, the smells, sights and sounds in the Catholic Worker house where Day lived for some fifty years, the constant harassment by mentally unstable guests, and even the very act of living in a slum were all portrayed by Day in terms of Christian renunciation—a way of giving up habitual attachments to the good things of this world out of a longing for something much greater.[154] While Day understood the supernatural life as one that entailed renunciation of more than that which was sinful—what the retreat termed as "sowing"—she also recognized that giving up these created goods was not always done

---

151 Day, *Long Loneliness*, 148.

152 Day, *Long Loneliness*, 236.

153 "Love is the measure" is a quote taken from St. John of the Cross and was used in the retreat.

154 Yocum noted that Day thought that mortification was a way of life in the Catholic Worker: "A Worker mortifies the body through exposure to vermin, cold and dirt; sight by 'bodily excertions, diseased limbs, eyes, noses, mouth, the nose with 'smells of sewage, decay, and rotten flesh;' the ears 'by harsh and screaming voices;' and taste 'by insufficient food cooked in huge quantities." Sandra Yocum Mize, "We are Still Pacifists": 472.

voluntarily. Indeed, Day described such involuntary renunciation as God's act of cutting away or "pruning" attachments to the world so that a more supernatural love could flourish.

These notions of "sowing" and "pruning" can be seen in Day's account of Peter Maurin's final days:

> The fact was he had been stripped of all. He had stripped himself throughout life; he had put off the old man in order to put on the new. He had done all that he could do to denude himself of the world...He had stripped himself, but there remained work for God to do. We are to be pruned as the vine is pruned so that it can bear fruit, and this we cannot do ourselves. God did it for him. He took from him his mind, the one thing he had left, the one thing perhaps he took delight in.[155]

In the same way she described her life with Forster, Day portrayed Maurin, who she claimed had had the most influence on her and the Catholic Worker, in the theological language of the retreat. For her, Maurin was an example of a Christian who had given up much that was good—and had much that was good taken away—out of a deep preference for that which he regarded as something better.

The retreat theology she learned from Hugo had a lasting effect on Dorothy Day. References and allusions to the retreat dot her published writings, as well as her recently published diaries and letters. In fact, in recalling her final visit just before Day's death in 1980, Sister Peter Claver Fahy remembered reminiscing with her long-time friend about the retreat, after which Day pointed to some flowers on the table and softly proclaimed that she was still "sowing."[156]

AN IMAGE OF HUGO

A few points regarding Hugo and the retreat have emerged thus far. The first is that the theological vision Hugo preached was a formative influence on Day. This is particularly true in how she interpreted and presented her story in *The Long Loneliness*. Any reading of her autobiography must take the retreat's theology into account. And Hugo was the crucial figure in Day's embrace of that theology. While he was not the originator of the retreat, Hugo was certainly the most prominent and theologically articulate of its promulgators in the United States

---

155   Day, *Long Loneliness*, 274.

156   Miller, *Dorothy*, 517.

and he employed its theology beyond the retreat itself to discussions of war and pacifism.

It is also the case that Day's introduction of Hugo and the retreat into the Catholic Worker movement was far from benign. The division that the Hugo brought within an already divided movement was real and painful. Furthermore, the "controversy" that surrounded Hugo's writings was not insignificant. It dealt with serious theological issues that were also being discussed in the larger Catholic world and it involved some of the most eminent theologians in America. From all of this, it can be concluded that Hugo was not only important for Day and the early Catholic Worker movement, but that he was also a significant figure in American Catholicism more broadly understood. But the legacy and image of Father John Hugo and the retreat remains contested and debate over how to portray Hugo and interpret the retreat theology continues. Some scholars, like Piehl and Fisher, have promoted the image of Hugo as a rigorist, perfectionist and Jansenist—a view that finds support in Vishnewski's recollections as well as those of the other early Catholic Workers. At the same time, other scholars like Miller, O'Shea Merriman, and Riegle have presented the retreat in terms of its universal call to holiness and portrayed Hugo as a key figure in Day's life as well as in the development of the theological foundations for *The Catholic Worker*'s pacifism. Was Hugo a rigorist or radical perfectionist preaching a Jansenist theology in the retreat? If this was not the case—as Day certainly insisted it was not—then from where do these charges stem? Opposition to Hugo and the retreat was genuine, both within the Catholic Worker and within the major Catholic theological journals. Many intelligent and holy people had serious problems with what Hugo was preaching. The question is to what extent was this criticism valid and within what theological context was this criticism being made? One of the arguments of this book is that these charges emerged out of a very particular theological and historical context—early twentieth-century neo-Thomism. But before any of these questions can be addressed, the Hugo retreat itself must be looked at—not only to understand the theological perspective it offered, but also to get some idea of to what Day and others were so attracted. What was "the retreat"? It is to this question that we will now turn.

CHAPTER II

"THE RETREAT"

Unless a grain of wheat falls to ground and dies, it remains just a grain of wheat; but if it dies, it produces much fruit.

☞ John 12:24

In the Dorothy Day-Catholic Worker Collection held at Marquette University, there are two small, well-thumbed notebooks. These "little notebooks," as they were described in *The Long Loneliness*, contain the notes Day recorded from a Hugo retreat in August, 1942.[1] These notes were handwritten and their fragmented form indicate the fact that they were written quickly—the jotting down of main thoughts and examples as the retreat was taking place. Day opened these notes with the following description of the location of the retreat, St. Anthony's Village in Oakmont, Pennsylvania:

> St. Anthony's Village is in Oakmont, an hour's ride by bus northeast of Pittsburgh. You get off the bus and walk a mile or so uphill—a long climb on a hot day.
> The Village is one of children, and nuns, and in the summer a few visiting priests and forty or so retreatants. It is here members of the CW groups also had their retreat this summer. There are 10 acres of grounds, a salad and herb garden a little orchard—and many weeping willow trees. They are the kind of trees neither goats not children can hurt. Down one side of the grounds there is even a hedge of these trees.

---

1 In *The Long Loneliness*, Day wrote, "I have the retreat notes in two little notebooks and I still enjoy taking them to church with me and reading them over for meditation." Day, *Long Loneliness*, 255. These notebooks are published in the Appendix.

Surrounding a statue of St. Anthony in the center of the front
lawn are flowers, at his feet in boxes and at the foot of the pedestal
in a circular bed—a border of some fragrant herb, petunias, geraniums. There is nicotincana and phlox in other beds around the
grounds and at night the fragrance comes into the chapel during
night prayers. Small boys were cutting grass and there were additional smells of cut grass and the exhaust from the gasoline motor.
There was also the smell of Italian cooking which reminded us of
Mott St.

Where St. Anthony's once stood, today stands luxury condomini-
ums and the Oakmont Country Club where the U.S. Open is rou-
tinely played. But in the 1940s, when Day wrote her description, the
Village was an orphanage staffed by a community of sisters called the
Missionary Zelatrices of the Sacred Heart—now the Apostles of the
Sacred Heart of Jesus. Beginning in 1940, it was also the place where
Hugo and Father Louis Farina led "the retreat."

The retreat which Onesimus Lacouture, S.J. developed in the
1930s was based on the *Spiritual Exercises* of St. Ignatius of Loyola.
The French-Canadian Jesuit condensed the thirty-day *Exercises* into
a series of three, one-week retreats.[2] For various reasons, the first retreat in this series was the one preached the vast majority of times by
Lacouture and the other "retreat priests," including Hugo.[3] This "first
series" retreat was centered on the first week of the *Exercises* and so
devoted primarily to the purification of the retreatant and reorienting
his life toward God.[4] This was the retreat that Hugo wrote about in
Applied Christianity and therefore was the material which his critics
would later attack.[5] It was also *"the retreat"* Day recorded in the two

2   Merriman, *Searching for Christ: The Spirituality of Dorothy Day* (Notre
Dame, IN: University of Notre Dame Press, 1994). 133.

3   Merriman suggested that reasons for this were that Lacouture favored
the first series, that most retreatants were attending their first such retreat,
and that the first series was very popular making it impossible to schedule
the next two. Merriman, *Searching*, 133.

4   Merriman noted that the second and third weeks of the *Exercises* comprised the "second series" of the retreat, while week four formed the basis of
the "third series" of the retreat. She pointed out that out of 142 retreats he
led, Lacouture appeared to have led the second series only thirteen times
and the third series not at all. Merriman, *Searching*, 133.

5   Hugo, *Applied Christianity*, (New York: Catholic Worker Press, 1944).

little, red notebooks. And these notebooks provide some of the earliest records of Hugo's version of the Lacouture retreat—how it was structured, preached, and received.[6]

As the previous chapter pointed out, differing portrayals of the retreat and Hugo have been made. These various accounts have raised questions regarding its theological perspective as well as the theological perspective of those who, like Day, embraced it. But to understand the theology of the retreat and its advocates, some understanding of what the retreat actually entailed becomes necessary. This chapter will provide such an understanding by presenting the retreat itself as it was articulated by Hugo in *Applied Christianity* and recorded by Day in her "little" notebooks. Because Day's notes recount the daily schedule Hugo employed to structure his retreat, they will form the basis for the following description of the retreat. Day's notes were sporadic, though, written quickly during the conferences or at the end of very full days, and so much of the content of the retreat conferences will be gleaned from Hugo's book. While similarities can be recognized between Day's 1942 retreat notes and the chapters in *Applied Christianity* written two years later, Hugo did add some material and rearranged the order of the material in his book.

"THE RETREAT"

According to Day's notebooks the retreat opened with a conference on Sunday evening and ended with conferences the following Saturday. Each day began with Mass at 8:30am in the morning followed by breakfast and then a conference at 9:45am and another at 11:45am. After lunch and time for private reflection, Farina gave a series of conferences on prayer at 3pm. Hugo then led a conference at 5pm followed by Benediction and supper. The day ended with a final conference by Hugo at 8:30pm. It was a full day and one in which silence was maintained throughout—Hugo and Farina did all the talking.[7] Day noted that the sisters had turned classrooms into

---

6   Day also wrote a 300-page yet unpublished manuscript, titled "All is Grace," that recounts a series of retreats she made in 1943. Hugo provides another, later version of the retreat in *Your Ways are Not My Ways*, vol.1 (1984).

7   Early in Day's notes she described the conditions for a good retreat: "1. Silence. The Holy Ghost, Retreat Master, 'I will lead you into the desert and then I will speak to you.' 2. Solitude. In the desert. Physical. Ten acres here.

dormitories for the retreatants to sleep and prepared delicious Italian meals throughout the week.[8]

I. NATURAL AND THE SUPERNATURAL[9]

SUNDAY EVENING, CONFERENCE I:
"THE TWO PRINCIPLES OF ACTIVITY"[10]

The retreat opened with a Sunday evening conference in which an understanding of nature and grace was introduced which formed the basis of the entire retreat theology.[11] In the coinciding chapter in *Applied Christianity*, Hugo presented the idea that in every person there is a "twofold principle of activity"—the natural and the supernatural—each of which corresponds to a particular way of life.[12] A "natural life" is lived in accord to what is known from reason alone and so proceeds from "purely natural powers."[13] In contrast, a "supernatural life" is lived

---

Interior. Put aside secular activities. Even from thoughts. 3. Prayer. Lifting of mind and hearts to God. Walk with him."

8   According to Day, a free will offering was requested from the retreatants, with some contributing enough to pay for those that who could not afford it. Interestingly, she also noted the names of some of those from New York who were also making the 1942 retreat, including her daughter Tamar and Fr. Roy.

9   Hugo divided *Applied Christianity* into five parts. This examination of the retreat will follow Hugo's division.

10   In Day's notes, this conference was titled "Two Ways of Life."

11   In her notes on this conference, Day began to describe something of this distinction between the natural and the supernatural: "How shall we enter, live in the Kingdom of God? We must be born again. Born again of water spirit. Physical—human birth. Rebirth—baptism. New creature. Share divine life. Regeneration. Now we have natural life and supernatural. Unless you live [supernatural] life we cannot enter Kingdom of God. Grace is share of divine life. Cornerstone of retreat. Baptism is like blood transfusion. I possess blood of my parents, their life. So also children of God, heirs of Heaven. Last Gospel. John 1. Sons of God. Raised up to supernatural plane. Natural. Conforming to human powers. Supernatural. What we cannot do by ourselves. We are given powers to become sons of God."

12   Hugo, *Applied*, 10.

13   Hugo explained that "Purely natural powers" included: senses, bodily powers, will, imagination, reason. Hugo, *Applied*, 10.

in accord with what is known from divine revelation and empowered by "supernatural means" that exceed all human powers.[14]

Hugo explained that a natural life can be distinguished from one that is supernatural life in terms of what it entails, what guides it, and its final end.[15] For instance, a natural life is made up of "natural actions," actions performed through a person's "purely natural powers" and motivated by "natural motives"—desires for worldly or created goods. In contrast, a supernatural life is composed of "supernatural actions," actions that require correspondence with grace. Such correspondence occurs when one acts out of a "supernatural motive"—a desire for or love of God.[16] No action, Hugo stated, no matter how good, which is not motivated by love of God—and thus corresponding with grace—could be considered "supernatural."[17] Furthermore, while unaided human reason is a capable enough guide for a natural life, faith is needed as a guide for the supernatural life.[18] In this sense, Hugo pointed out, faith "is the headlight of the supernatural, as charity is its

---

14   "Supernatural means" were charity, faith, grace. In other words, a natural life was "proportioned to man's natural abilities" while a supernatural life was "simply beyond all human ability and would be completely impossible without God, who gives us both the knowledge of this higher way and the necessary means to pursue it." Hugo, *Applied*, 10.

15   Hugo, *Applied*, 10.

16   Hugo, *Applied*, 11. While natural actions were good because they proceeded from human nature, Hugo wrote, "we are not to leave this natural activity on the merely natural level...we must graft our natural activity on to the supernatural life; so that the latter, animating our natural activity, will enable us to produce supernatural works." Hugo, *Applied*, 26.

17   Hugo argued that "An action is supernatural when grace is its principle; and grace becomes operative in faith and charity. Nature, even at its best, cannot merit supernatural happiness apart from grace." *Applied*, 12.

18   Hugo qualified this idea; to live by faith did not mean to abandon reason but instead it meant "follow reason illuminated by faith; i.e. no longer does our reason depend on purely natural principles, arrived at by study, but on principles and truths revealed by God." Hugo, *Applied*, 11. Although there is no contradiction between the truths of faith and those of reason, Hugo explained, nevertheless, the former truths were "much higher" than the latter; and when we live by faith "we break away, as it were, from our human moorings and follow a line of conduct that we cannot understand." An example of this would be when, instead of defending oneself against injury,

engine."[19] And finally, while the final end of a natural life is "merely" natural happiness—the satisfaction of the natural powers, such as the senses, the intellect, and the will—the ultimate destiny of the supernatural life is a supernatural final end: the beatific vision.[20] For Hugo, this supernatural final end of human nature meant that all Christians are called to live a supernatural life—a life of holiness. He referred to this as the "continuity of the Christian life."[21] In her notes, Day wrote, "Unless [we] live the supernatural life, we cannot enter the Kingdom of God."

Even though the natural life was recognized as being distinct from—and indeed infinitely less than—the supernatural life, Hugo clearly affirmed its goodness and distinguished it from that which is sinful. Hugo presented these distinctions in a graphic of the "three possible levels of life."[22]

---

one practiced Christ's injunction to "turn the other cheek." Hugo, *Applied,* 26.

19   Hugo, *Applied,* 11.

20   Hugo, *Applied,* 11. Hugo explained that while "the full fruition of the supernatural life" belonged in the next world, the grace and the life of grace on earth are "a beginning of the life of glory in heaven." For in this life God already invites us to correspond with grace—to enter into "the friendship of the Trinity." Hugo, *Applied,* 10.

21   Hugo listed various passages from scripture to support this understanding of humanity's supernatural destiny: John 1:12, John 3:5, John 12:46, Romans 8:14-18, Ephesians 1:11-14. "By grace we are deified, divinized," Hugo stated, "and, once baptized, God expects us to act as divinized beings and no longer as mere men." He turned to the biblical notion of putting off the old man and putting on the new (Eph.4:22). Hugo, *Applied,* 13.

22   Hugo, *Applied,* 14. "In each of us, therefore," Hugo asserted, "there are three possibilities of action: one may act as an angel, a pagan (a natural human being), or a devil. We can act in any of these three ways. To go to heaven, we must act as angels. But, even though baptized, we are still capable of acting like pagans; when we do so, our actions do not reach heaven, although there may be no sin in them." Hugo further clarified these distinctions by saying that "of course, there is in each of us only one soul, one life, one person. But this person is free to conduct himself in any of these three ways. The reason is that grace, nature, and concupiscence— though on different levels and in differing ways— are all distinct principles of activity." Hugo, *Applied,* 14.

	I	II	III
	Make–Up	Guide	Destination
Supernatural	Charity	Faith	Heaven
Natural	Natural Activity	Reason	Natural Happiness (limbo)
Sin	Disobedience to God	Appetite	Hell

Such distinctions between the supernatural, the natural, and the sinful are at the core of the retreat theology and Hugo would employ them in support of various theological positions, such as his defense of American Catholic conscientious objectors in World War II. Central is the idea that human nature and the natural life exist apart from both what is supernatural and what is sinful. Human nature was recognized as good, but inherently insufficient in its ability to attain its ultimate destiny.[23] This understanding of human nature as good but unstable and so always in need of grace—as distinct but not separate from the supernatural—set the retreat theology apart from the more dualist account of nature and grace prevalent in much of early twentieth-century Catholic theology.

Fundamental to Hugo's explanation here is the idea that something like a natural end or natural happiness is only "a theoretical possibility," for human nature is called to a supernatural final end far beyond such a "merely" natural end. Nevertheless, the idea of such a hypothetical natural end is theologically very necessary in order to recognize the distinction between the sinful, the natural, and the supernatural. Hugo noted that the error of the fifth-century Pelagians was to forget this distinction and so to blur or confuse nature with the supernatural—believing that humans could live holy lives on their own. [24] As

---

23   While human nature itself was from God and therefore good, it was limited in that it could not attain supernatural happiness—its final end. In order to attain our destiny, our nature must be penetrated by grace or "divinized" and thus perfected. Hugo noted that this divinization transformed human nature, making it ready to follow the impulses of grace. Hugo, *Applied*, 25.

24   Hugo, *Applied*, 16. Hugo paraphrased Pius XI in *Miserentissimus Redemptor* (1928), where the pope argued that a resurgence of Pelagianism was taking place in the modern world; "men have become again so confident

a result of such blurring, the supereminence of the supernatural was lost and heaven became regarded as "just beyond" hell.[25] And so, the importance of a hypothetical natural happiness is to illustrate the fact that while a natural life is good and not sinful, at its best it could only attain an end far less than that which is supernatural.[26]

Hugo further pointed out that without some recognition of the theoretical possibility of natural happiness, the rest of the natural life is also forgotten. For without a proper recognition of what is "natural," only two "levels of life"—the sinful and the supernatural—would remain. And as a result, living a holy life would become understood as simply a life spent avoiding sin—something which Hugo asserted to be the mark of a natural life at its best.[27] In other words, because it helped to recognize that there is something that exists between that which is sinful and that which is supernatural, an accurate account of the natural illustrated a central tenet in the retreat theology: that a Christian life entails something much more than simply not sinning.

MONDAY, CONFERENCE 2:
"THE TWO PRINCIPLES OF ACTIVITY: PRACTICAL IMPLICATIONS"

Monday morning opened with a conference (*Applied Christianity,* chapter 2: "The Two Principles of Activity: Practical Implications") which presented the implications of this understanding of the nature-supernatural relationship laid out the previous evening.[28] Here Hugo argued that the distinction between a supernatural and a natural life implied that the supernatural life could not be lived by "the

of their human powers, so little appreciative of the incomparable dignity conferred on them by divine grace, that they think to obtain eternal happiness by their own human efforts and their own native goodness." Hugo, *Applied,* 14. See Pius XI, *Miserentissimus Redemptor,* 8.

25   Hugo, *Applied,* 15.

26   Hugo wrote that to put natural happiness "into our thinking gives us a true picture of the immense height of heaven." Hugo, *Applied,* 16.

27   He argued that in order to attain that holiness one must "rise above nature, that is, above natural standards of conduct"—beyond simply following the natural law. Hugo, *Applied,* 15.

28   Hugo explained that Lacouture structured the retreat in such a way that a doctrine was presented in one conference, followed by a conference describing the implications of that particular doctrine. Hugo seemed to employ a similar structure throughout his retreat and in *Applied Christianity.*

mere avoidance of sin"—what he described as a "natural action" which could be practiced by simply following the natural law.[29] But the "mere obedience to the commandments of the natural law" did not make one a Christian, Hugo explained, for if a person seeks "only to avoid sin and aim at nothing higher, ignoring the requirements of charity and the impulse of grace," then he or she lives as "a pagan rather than as a Christian—a good pagan, no doubt, such as described by Aristotle, but a pagan, nevertheless, having a natural and rational standard of conduct."[30] Rather, Christian life takes "natural morality" as a starting point and then goes far beyond—for it is "essentially a supernatural religion."[31] Indeed, more than simply avoiding sin, Hugo claimed that indifference to the world or "spiritual detachment" is at the heart of the Christian life.[32] Such indifference—or even contempt—for the things of the world is necessary, not because the world is evil, but because detachment from these things helps to remove distractions to loving God and obstacles to the correspondence with grace needed to reach union with God.[33] This kind of Christian indifference or detachment was presented as a "practical implication" of the retreat theology.

---

29   Hugo, *Applied*, 18.

30   Hugo, *Applied*, 18.

31   Hugo, *Applied*, 18-19.

32   Hugo wrote: "It is only by raising ourselves above the whole natural order that we become Christians." Hugo, *Applied*, 19.

33   Hugo acknowledged that the idea of contempt for created goods could be problematic, but he asserted that this contempt did not imply these goods were evil or that love of them was sinful; in fact their very goodness and attractiveness made indifference to them even more imperative for Christians. Rather, it implied that, "since we must love God wholly, we ought to rid ourselves of all sensual, selfish and merely natural love for creatures apart from God." He pointed out that Aquinas had defined sin as an aversion from God and a conversion to creatures (*ST*, II II, 104,3,c), and that contempt for creatures was a sign that one's soul was in a state of grace (*ST*, I II,112,5). Hugo, *Applied*, 20.

In the next conference, this notion of detachment from created goods was further developed in terms of "dying" to habitual attachment to these goods through mortification. Hugo explained that because human nature has a supernatural final end, "we are called by God to leave the plane of natural living; we are to give up the merely human way of life and act henceforth in accordance with our now divinized humanity."[34] For Hugo, this giving up of the "merely human way of life" was a form of dying to oneself, and he made it clear that the need for such renunciation did not simply stem from some notion that human nature is corrupt or sinful. Rather, this kind of mortification is done fundamentally out of recognition that human nature is lacking in its ability to attain the supernatural beatitude to which it is called.[35] "Dying to oneself" removes the obstacles to correspondence with grace and thereby perfects nature. Hugo called this the "process of divinization."[36]

Sin is a reality, though, and to understand its effects on human nature another important distinction was highlighted in the retreat: the distinction between human nature in the abstract and in the concrete. For in the abstract, human nature is considered in itself (*in se*)—"in its essential stuff and properties" which are from God and so therefore good.[37] But even in the abstract, human nature still has a need to correspond with grace.[38] In other words, human nature is inherently insufficient and has never been capable of reaching its supernatural destiny without the assistance of grace and therefore sin is not the primary cause of human nature's need for grace. And so correspondence with grace requires living beyond a "merely human way of life"—even

---

34   Hugo also clarified that to mortify "the natural" did not mean destroying our entire human nature, but only those elements of our nature in conflict with our supernatural destiny. Hugo, *Applied*, 24.

35   Hugo, *Applied*, 24.

36   Hugo, *Applied*, 25.

37   Hugo, *Applied*, 25.

38   Hugo, *Applied*, 25.

in the abstract.[39] But, as Hugo pointed out, human nature does not actually exist in the abstract, instead it exists in the concrete (*in re*) with the historical reality of sin and its consequences.[40] In this sense, an inherently insufficient human nature is further hindered by the historical effects of sin and so needs to be perfected even more.[41]

Again—as with the idea of natural happiness—this kind of distinction was important for Hugo. While human nature does not exist in the abstract, the discussion of a human nature *per se* helped to recognize the practical implications of human nature's supernatural final end apart from sin—to recognize that the need to give up or rise above a merely natural life is not simply because such a life is sinful. For even apart from sin, dying to oneself is necessary. This distinction also helped to reveal that while sin is not the primary reason for Christian renunciation, concupiscence does indeed have a disordering effect on human nature and so the need to give up or renounce attachments to created goods becomes more necessary as a result of the Fall. Thus, Hugo asserted that a Christian life—a life called to holiness—entailed giving up attachments to the things of this world in order "to rise above nature" both in the abstract and concrete.

To justify the need for this kind of detachment, Hugo turned to St. John of the Cross and his description of habitual attachments as being like a string around a bird's leg:

> It makes little difference whether a bird is tied by a thin thread or by a cord. For even if tied by thread, the bird will be prevented from taking off just as surely as if it were tied by cord—that is, it will be impeded from flight as long as it does not break the thread. Admittedly, the thread is easier to rend, but no matter how easily this may be done, the bird will not fly away without first doing so.[42]

---

39   Hugo argued that: "Of itself human nature, although good, cannot merit supernatural happiness; for this it must be penetrated by a higher principle." Hugo, *Applied*, 25.

40   Hugo, *Applied*, 25.

41   Hugo explained that while the guilt and the punishment of original sin were removed by baptism, the effects remain: "And if these do not injure the substance and powers of human nature, nevertheless the damage that they do is real and serious, wounding all its activities." Hugo, *Applied*, 25.

42   Hugo, *Applied*, 121. John of the Cross, *The Ascent to Mount Carmel*, in *The Collected Works of St. John of the Cross*, trans. Kieran Kavanaugh, O.C.D.

For the seventeenth-century Carmelite mystic and Doctor of the Church, the same holds true for a person with attachments to created goods, for any such attachments—no matter how few or how minor—are obstacles or impediments to one's pursuit of God. On this point, Day wrote in her notes: "Keystone of retreat. Raised above ourselves. Heart of the supernatural life is love. Most important commandment. Love demands renunciation. Official meditation during the paschal season: Seek things that are above. Col:3.... All this is the starting point of Christianity."

MONDAY, CONFERENCE 4:
"THE CONFLICT BETWEEN THE NATURAL AND THE SUPERNATURAL"

In the following conference (*Applied Christianity*, chapter 4), retreatants were introduced to the "two principles of sanctification" which are necessary to live a supernatural life: grace and the human will. Grace is the chief means of sanctification, it is superabundant and always available to those who desire it for God is good and generous.[43] Hugo preached that retreatants should not worry about the availability of grace, but rather they should be concerned as to whether they are acting out of a desire to correspond with it—whether they are acting out of a "supernatural motive."[44] He taught that a practical implication of

and Otilio Rodriguez, O.C.D.(Washington, DC: ICS Publications, 1979) Bk 1, ch.11, 97.

43   Hugo pointed out that in *Mystici Corporis* (1943), Pius XII condemned certain tendencies of contemporary Christians ("a certain unhealthy quietism") to be so preoccupied with the efficacy of grace that they forget and almost deny their need to correspond with that grace. Hugo argued, "Many people excuse their own mediocrity by doubting whether the Holy Ghost is there to help them, instead of blaming the deficiencies of their own wills. Others, who are sincere in their quest for knowledge concerning the spiritual life, nevertheless occupy their attention too much with the work of grace and not enough with the work that they have to do." Hugo, *Applied*, 37.

44   Hugo explained that, on our part, progress in holiness revolved around our motives: "God the Holy Ghost, of course, sanctifies us, but He does not do so without our cooperation; and there is no other way that we can cooperate except by the supernatural motive. Of the two principles of sanctification—God and our own will—God is far and away the more important; but our part is indispensable. The supernatural motive is like the contact of wires effected by an electrician—it does not create the current, but it is indispensable for the passage of the current." Hugo, Applied, 33.

their supernatural destiny is that they are called and even expected by God to act in accordance with grace, particularly the elevating action of grace which he would later distinguish as *"gratia elevans."* But since grace does not destroy human freedom, one can choose whether or not to act in accordance with it.[45] To act out of supernatural motives—the love of God—is to act freely in correspondence with grace and to thus "supernaturalize" one's actions. To act out of any other motive—the love of anything other than God—is not necessarily sinful, but neither is it acting in accord with grace. The desire to correspond with grace and act out of supernatural motives is crucial for living a holy life.[46] It was described as the human component in the process of sanctification.

According to Hugo, when a person acts out of a supernatural motive, harmony exists between her nature and the supernatural destiny to which she is called.[47] But conflict arises when a person acts out of natural motives not in accord with grace.[48] For to act out of a natural motive is to act for love of something other than God and this places a person in conflict with her final end. The love of God must be exclusive.[49] Natural motives, even at their best, desire worldly things and not the beatific vision. And so to act out of such motives, even in an abstract sense, is to act in conflict with the supernatural. Hugo explained:

> God has raised us to the supernatural plane; and now He wants us to live there and to leave the natural plane of life. It is not that the natural life is evil—it is good and created by God. But it is not supernatural, and God wants us to be supernatural. Accordingly,

---

45   Hugo argued that grace leaves us free: "By grace God has given wings to our nature; and we can still refuse to use these wings. Raised to the supernatural, we can still live on the natural plane, as pagans." Hugo, *Applied*, 31.

46   Hugo, *Applied*, 33.

47   *Applied*, 31. He explained that supernatural motives clear "imperfection from our heart and our intention, thereby allowing the divine grace to provide the impulse for our actions." Hugo noted that for spiritual writers such as St. Alphonsus Liguori the purity of supernatural motives is more important than their frequency. Hugo, *Applied*, 28.

48   Hugo, *Applied*, 31.

49   Hugo likened this exclusive love to marital love: "When John marries Martha, he must relinquish his affection for Mary." Hugo, *Applied*, 34.

when we live natural lives, even though they may be naturally good,
we are in conflict with our supernatural destiny. Natural motives
at best—i.e., even if they are purified of the sensuality and egotism
which spoils them in all except perfect souls—are infinitely lower
than the supernatural order.[50]

In the concrete or historical reality of sin, this conflict only deepens
as natural motives now "habitually bear the taint of concupiscence."[51]
As Day wrote, "To enjoy things of this world and try to avoid mortal
sin as impossible as to jump from the Empire State and expect to stop
before we get hurt."

MONDAY, CONFERENCE 5: "THE PAGAN MENTALITY"

In the fifth conference (*Applied Christianity*, chapter 5) it was pointed
out that while acting out of natural motives is not itself sinful, it did
pose a real obstacle to living a supernatural life. For Hugo contended
that a "pagan mentality" emerges from the habitual acting out of natural motives or intentions.[52] He listed several "worldly maxims" that,
when accepted, would develop such a mentality—for instance, that
natural actions performed in a state of grace were meritorious. Hugo
argued that while this was a common interpretation of the "Thomistic
view" on these issues, it was in fact a misinterpretation of Thomas
Aquinas and had led to the belief that all actions which are not sinful
are good enough.[53] It was this belief that led to the minimalist notion
of the Christian life that Hugo characterized with the axiom: "Eat,
drink, be merry...as long as you avoid mortal sin."[54]

In addition to charging that Thomas had been misinterpreted by
his twentieth-century neo-Thomist interpreters, Hugo also contrasted Aquinas's own teaching on this point with that of St. Alphonsus
de Liguori. In fact, Hugo even argued that Liguori presented a clearer
and more accurate account of natural actions than did Aquinas.[55] That

---

50   Hugo, *Applied*, 34.

51   Hugo, *Applied*, 34.

52   Hugo, *Applied*, 37.

53   Hugo, *Applied*, 39.

54   Hugo, *Nature*, 49.

55   Hugo dedicated an entire appendix to the question "Are Natural
     Actions Meritorius?" In it, he explained that Aquinas had taught that in
     the abstract (or formally) a good natural motive—something possible only

Hugo would question Aquinas's theology—let alone suggest that the teaching of another Doctor of the Church might be preferable to the Angelic Doctor—is noteworthy given the central place that Thomas held in Catholic thinking, at least since Leo XIII's encyclical *Aeterni Patris* in 1879. And so Hugo's critique of Thomas—as well as his much harsher critique of the modern "Thomistic view"—should be understood as part of Hugo's broader challenge to the particular form of neo-Thomism that dominated Catholic thought at the time. This challenge will be looked at more closely in a later chapter.

Hugo also listed other "worldly maxims" such as that a single discreet action performed with natural motives was not problematic;[56] that not all natural motives led to sin;[57] and that all actions could be viewed abstractly (in themselves) and thus that all actions which in themselves were morally indifferent would also be permissible.[58] He argued that theological assertions like these diluted the supernatural character of the Christian life and thus led to a pagan mentality or

---

for saints—was enough for an action to be meritorious. But Liguori had contended that a supernatural motive was necessary for an action to be meritorious. Hugo *Applied*, 208.

56 While he acknowledged that in one sense this assertion is true, Hugo stated that the problem is that "such acts of self-indulgence" are not performed individually, but habitually. And such "Habitual indulgence in sensuality nourishes concupiscence and lessens the influence of grace." Hugo, *Applied*, 39.

57 Hugo argued that just as it would be impossible to breath in only good germs in a room recently vacated by a tuberculosis patient, so also it would be "impossible to distinguish good from selfish natural motives in practice" and so it is best "to get rid of them all." He quoted the modern Irish spiritual writer Blessed Columba Marmion, O.S.B. (1858-1923): "to remove from our actions not only every culpable motive, but even every motive that is merely natural; to keep our hearts free, with a spiritual freedom, from all that is created and earthly: such is the first element of our holiness." Abbot Columba Marmion, *Christ in His Mysteries* (St. Louis: B. Herder Book Co., 1939), 291. Hugo, *Applied*, 39.

58 Hugo countered that in the concrete sense no action could be morally indifferent, since if "the morality of an action is not determined by its object, like theft or murder, then its morality is determined by its end (motive) and circumstances." In the concrete sense, every action "takes us either closer to God, or further away from Him." Hugo, *Applied*, 40.

"naturalism."[59] And as a result, the central importance of the gratuitous gift of grace was forgotten.

MONDAY, CONFERENCE 6:
"JESUS SPEAKS OF THE SUPERNATURAL LIFE"

Monday closed with a conference (*Applied Christianity*, chapter 7)
in which it was suggested that the Sermon on the Mount is itself a
Gospel call to renounce a natural life.[60] For Hugo argued that it is
natural actions that are rejected in the admonitions: "Blessed are the
poor in spirit,"[61] "Blessed are the meek,"[62] and "Blessed are those that
mourn."[63] Furthermore, natural motives are renounced when Jesus
states, "When you give alms, do not sound a trumpet before you, as
the hypocrites do..." (Matt.6). And renunciation of the natural life in
general can be found in the declaration, "Unless your justice abound
more than that of the Scribes and Pharisees, you shall not enter into
the Kingdom of God" (Matt.5:20), for while the scribes and Pharisees
were good men, their goodness was "natural"—following only the
commandments of the natural law—and therefore did not merit

---

59   Interestingly, Hugo turned to Archbishop John Ireland—the late
archbishop of St. Paul and a central figure in the late nineteenth-century
"Americanism" controversy—to sum up this notion: "There is not much
practical Christianity in the world. The danger of today is that of living
a purely natural life as the good old pagans did. Naturalism, materialism,
worldliness possess the world. Everything is done for fame or money or the
honor that is in it, else you are a fool and have no purpose in life. We should
lead a supernatural life. Our works are dead and have no merit unless we are
in the state of sanctifying grace and do them from a supernatural motive. On
the supernatural plane elevated above the natural the just man lives by faith.
We should have a supernatural motive in all that we do. The true happiness
of the Christian soul lies in the heavenly regions on the supernatural plane
above the merely natural life." [Hugo cited Ireland's quote from an article
by John F. Duggan, in *The Ecclesiastical Review*, (December, 1939)] Hugo,
Applied, 38.

60   Hugo, *Applied*, 49.

61   (Matt.5:3) Here, Jesus was seen as condemning goods or ends pursued
by pagans.

62   (Matt.5:4) Here, he was seen as condemning bodily goods.

63   (Matt.5:5) Here, he was seen as condemning the goods of the mind.

entrance into the Kingdom of God.[64] Far beyond such a natural life, Jesus' followers are called to live a life of holiness, to "Be perfect, as your heavenly Father is perfect"—a perfection not merely of the saints but of God. [65] Hugo explained that, in this way, Jesus sets up "an absolute and divine standard of sanctity...addressed to all."[66] And in her notes Day wrote that the Sermon on the Mount, "Does not institute sacraments, does not talk about Mass." Rather, she stated that it is a "Christian Manifesto, elementary statement, basic principle. Like Communist Manifesto, Constitution. Summed up in one sentence, You must cease to be human, begin to be divine."

TUESDAY, CONFERENCE 7: "THE LAW OF THE FLESH"

Tuesday morning opened with the seventh conference of the retreat (*Applied Christianity*, chapter 6), during which the link between natural motives and sin was discussed. To do this, Hugo introduced the concept of "imperfect actions"—actions that are motivated by both the love of God and the love of created goods. Because these actions are motivated to some extent by natural motives, they are less than supernatural and therefore are lacking or imperfect.[67] While these imperfect actions are not in themselves sinful, they inevitably will become habitual and thus eventually will lead away from God and toward sin.[68] For Hugo, this idea of imperfect acts becoming habitual and ultimately leading to sin flowed out of the notion that living a holy life is a process

---

64   Hugo, *Applied*, 50.

65   Hugo, *Applied*, 51.

66   Hugo, *Applied*, 51.

67   Hugo described this lacking or "spiritual undernourishment" as similar to a man who decides only to eat one biscuit a day, and when told that because of this he will die soon, he protests that he is eating regularly. Hugo, *Applied*, 43.

68   For support, Hugo quoted Reginald Garrigou-LaGrange, O.P. as saying that such an act "which is too weak is an imperfection disposing to venial sin, as the latter disposes to mortal sin." Garrigou-LaGrange further described the weakness of imperfect acts: "these acts dispose us to positive retrogression, for by reason of their weakness they permit the rebirth of disordered inclinations which lead to venial sin, and may end by overcoming us or leading us to spiritual death." Reginald Garrigou-LaGrange, *Christian Perfection and Contemplation*, trans. Sr. M. Timothea Doyle, O.P. (St. Louis: B.Herder Book Co. 1937), 189. Hugo, *Applied*, 44.

in which there is "no standing still"—one either progresses or regress-es.[69] Thus, natural motives which motivate natural and imperfect ac-tions inevitably cause a person to turn away from God, or as Hugo put it they will "starve the supernatural life."[70] Natural motives were likened to termites which get into a house and undermine it. While the collapse of the house may be occasioned by a bad storm, the cause of the collapse was the fact that it had been weakened by the bugs. "So also sin may be sudden and violent," Hugo explained, "but it is nevertheless the result of a long process of undermining; and this has happened through pampering the appetites of fallen nature in little things."[71] Each natural action increases one's desire for created goods and in turn weakens the desire for the divine.[72] And so, in order to cultivate a desire for God, a person must give up acting out of natural or imperfect motives.[73]

TUESDAY, CONFERENCE 8: "THE CHRISTIAN MENTALITY"

Having earlier described the "pagan mentality," the eighth conference (*Applied Christianity*, chapter 8), defined the "Christian mentality" as one dominated by God: one's mind, will, and whole life permeated with

---

69   Hugo cited several passages from scripture to support this idea: James 1:14-15, James 4:4, Phil.3:18-19, Rom.8:5-14, Matt.7:24-27, Gal.5:16-17. Hugo, *Applied*, 45.

70   Hugo, *Applied*, 46.

71   Hugo, *Applied*, 46.

72   Paraphrasing a popular spiritual writer of the time, Hugo explained that, "According to St. Paul, there is a law working in us resulting in acts and desires which are not in themselves sinful, but which prepare the way for sin. We know well enough what is definitely right and what is wrong, but there is something else, in itself neither right nor wrong, belonging to a debatable land, the borderland between right and wrong. The region neither of light nor darkness, but twilight." B.W. Maturin, *Self-Knowledge and Self-Discipline* (Paterson, NJ: St. Anthony's Guild Press, 1939), 95. Hugo, *Applied*, 49.

73   Hugo, *Applied*, 47. Again, the reason for this opposition or conflict be-tween nature and the supernatural was the twofold insufficiency of human nature: in the abstract, even at its best, human nature was still inherently lacking and could only attain some sort of "natural happiness" on its own, while in the concrete, human nature was limited even more so by the histor-ical effects of concupiscence.

the idea of God.[74] Hugo described the development of this mentality as "the science of the supernatural" which he likened to the "science of architecture" using St. Paul's "temple of God" metaphor (1Cor.3:16). Just as an architect first had to decide to build a building, so too one must first decide to build a "temple of perfection"—one must want to be perfect.[75] Having made this decision, a person lays out plans for building such a temple, plans which Hugo suggested could be found in various sources within the tradition such as the works of various spiritual writers, as well as in the practice of contemplation itself.[76] With these plans in hand, one would then need to dig out "the sand of natural motives" in order to build a temple of perfection on "the rock of the supernatural."[77] Having thus set the supernatural foundation, a person could build the temple with "first rate" materials: supernatural actions.[78] And like a good architect, a Christian would have to keep

---

74 Hugo, *Applied*, 52.

75 Hugo suggested that no one would say, "first I will get rid of mortal sin, then venial sin; and finally, if I am successful so far, I will work to remove imperfections." Instead, a person must desire to be perfect first (in the order of intention) even though that perfection will be achieved last in the order of execution, directing all subsequent work. Hugo, *Applied*, 53.

76 Hugo noted that John of the Cross offered plans or rules for living a supernatural life of holiness: "First, let him have an habitual desire to imitate Christ in everything that he does, conforming himself to His life... Secondly, in order that he may be able to do this well, every pleasure that presents itself to the senses, if it is not purely for the honor and glory of God, must be renounced and completely rejected for the love of Jesus Christ... Strive always to choose, not that which is easiest, but that which is the most difficult...Strive thus to desire to enter into complete detachment and emptiness and poverty, with respect to that which is in the world, for Christ's sake." St. John of the Cross, *Ascent of Mount Carmel*, trans. E. Allison Peers (London: Burns, Oates & Washbourne, 1933) Bk I, ch.15. quoted in Hugo, *Applied*, 53.

77 Hugo, *Applied*, 53.

78 Hugo pointed out that it was not so much the frequency of supernatural motives that was important, as was their purity in perfecting one's actions, though the frequency of supernatural motives did help. For support, Hugo turned to St. Alphonsus de Liguori's *True Spouse of Christ*, trans. Fr. Eugene Grimm (Brooklyn: Redemptorist Fathers, 1929). Hugo also noted that Dom Chautard called for habitual vigilance of one's motives through

everything in her temple straight and "the plumb line" of the supernatural life is Christian perfection. The Christian mentality—the temple of perfection—therefore, did not develop chiefly through great acts, but rather by working to do as many things as possible out of a love of God.[79]

TUESDAY, CONFERENCE 9: "CHRISTIAN PERFECTION"

Having illustrated the development of this Christian mentality, the next conference (*Applied Christianity*, chapter nine)—which Day titled: "Obligation to be Saints"—began with the assertion that the mission of the Church is to make saints.[80] Building on the idea that all are called to the life of holiness presented in the Sermon on the Mount, Hugo argued that the Christian life was not two-tiered and so it made no distinction between the *extraordinary* life of a vowed religious and the *ordinary* Christian life of the laity. He explained that there was "just one kind of Christianity for all"—religious orders and congregations were human institutions and "the obligation to perfection [did] not come from them, but from Christ."[81] For Hugo, there was then nothing inferior or second rate about the lay Christian life, all are called to holiness.[82] And at this point in her notes Day wrote: "Jesus spoke in a scene of pastoral quietness, peacefully; he dismisses all our efforts to excuse ourselves. 'This is not for me.' Who was Jesus talking too. No Carmelites, no Carthusians. Ordinary people, fisherman, farmers, shepherds, housewives. This legislation was for all, lay people or religious."

Christians, then, are called to pursue perfection by the very fact that they are Christians.[83] The primary concern of the Christian, then,

---

"custody of the heart" in *Soul of the Apostolate*, Pt.5, sec. 4. Hugo, *Applied*, 54.

79   Hugo, *Applied*, 54.

80   Hugo highlighted Jesus' admonition in Matthew 5: "Be perfect as your heavenly Father is perfect." Hugo, Applied, 56.

81   Hugo, *Applied*, 56.

82   Hugo, *Applied*, 56.

83   Hugo pointed out that in *Rerum Ominium Perturbationem* (1923), Pius XI's encyclical marking the third centenary of St. Francis de Sales, Pius had stated: "Christ has constituted the Church as holy and the source of sanctity, and those who take her for guide and teacher must, by the divine will, tend

should be the desire to be perfect—to correspond with grace. With this intention, one would then seek the "proper means" for reaching this goal offered within the tradition: the precepts of charity and counsels of perfection.[84] And by employing these means, one could begin to live the life of a saint.[85]

SUMMARY

To sum up then, the first part of the retreat presented an understanding of the nature-supernatural relationship that formed its theological foundation—the natural life understood as distinct from both that which is supernatural and sinful. The implication of this understanding is that all Christians should seek to detach as much as possible from the things of the world—to mortify their habitual attachments to created goods and the motives which these attachments informed. Hugo was clear that the necessity of this type of renunciation is twofold: first and foremost, because nature is inherently insufficient and so infinitely less than the supernatural destiny to which humanity is called; and secondarily because of the historical effects of sin on human nature. Motives are crucial for the life of holiness, and acting out of natural motives weakens one's desire for God and eventually even leads to sin. Natural motives, therefore, needed to be renounced and replaced with supernatural motives so that a person could begin to correspond with the ever-abundant grace needed to live a supernatural life of holiness.

---

to holiness of life...Let no one think that this is addressed to a select few and that others are permitted to remain in an inferior degree of virtue." Hugo, *Applied*, 58. In her notes, Day wrote that according to St. John Chrysostom, God will be more severe with lay people for not pursuing holiness because they have "natural supports."

84 As will be seen, critics of Hugo's theology later charged that he confused the precepts of charity with counsels of perfection. The precepts can be understood as either commandments from God that bind us under the pain of sin or, in a stricter sense, as conditions that are necessary for salvation. Because of this, Hugo argued that since "charity is a precept in this stricter sense, so also perfection can be no mere counsel, but is a precept, and that in the stricter sense likewise." All are called to seek perfection, and so the precept of charity was "universal, absolute, and equal." *Applied*, 59.

85 Day wrote in her notes, "Perfection is love. God is love...Perfection means love of God and love of neighbor."

Despite the sometimes tedious nature of these conferences, it must be recognized that in all of this a particular understanding of nature and grace—as distinct but not separate—was being articulated. This understanding made the retreat theology significant for its time, a point which will be visited in later chapters. While nature is not sinful and is indeed good, it is also not enough. And so a Christian life, one which recognizes the "practical implications" of grace, requires much more than simply avoiding sin—it necessitates the giving up of one's attachment to worldly things. And in the retreat Hugo offered what he believed was a blueprint for discerning how to do this.

II. THE SUPERNATURAL WORLD

TUESDAY, CONFERENCE 10: "THE GLORY OF GOD"

Tuesday night's final conference (*Applied Christianity*, Part Two, chapter one) presented one of the more central points in the retreat theology of nature and grace. This was the notion that "the divine motive" of creation is to communicate the goodness and glory of God, and therefore the final end or purpose of creation is to receive, possess, and manifest that goodness, and thereby to glorify God.[86] Since God has fixed this final end into the very being of human nature, Hugo explained, it is not an arbitrary or external end "imposed on us from above," but rather it fulfills "the deepest needs of human nature."[87] Thus to work toward any other final end is to act not only contrary to the will of God, but to act against "the deepest laws of [one's] own being."[88] And so while human nature is created with an ultimate destiny far beyond its ability to attain on its own, this is a final end that is not extrinsically placed upon human nature, but rather one intimately related to "the deepest needs of human nature." In short, the fulfillment of human nature is found only in the glorification of God.[89] As will

---

86   Hugo, *Applied*, 64.

87   Hugo, *Applied*, 68.

88   Hugo, *Applied*, 64. Day's notes quote the very Augustinian line from Francis Thompson's *Hound of Heaven*: "Our hearts were made for Thee O God, and never rest until they rest in Thee."

89   "In fulfilling God's purpose," Hugo wrote, "man likewise fulfills the deepest purpose of his own nature; he thus perfects his nature and achieves happiness." Hugo, *Applied*, 68.

be seen in later chapters, this theological perspective—which reflects the Ignatian roots of the retreat—not only distinguished Hugo from the "two-tiered" theology that prevailed in early twentieth-century Catholic theology, but it also shared a great deal in common with discussions on the "natural desire for God" being put forth by de Lubac, and others in Europe at the time.

WEDNESDAY, CONFERENCE 11: "THE DOCTRINE OF THE SAMPLES"[90]

The next morning's conference (*Applied Christianity*, Part 2, chapter 3), opened with a description of a means by which a retreatant could discern how to glorify God—the "Doctrine of the Samples."[91] Hugo's discussion of "samples" began with a description of the paradoxical condition which marks human nature: while we live in the world and have a "taste" for the things of the world, we also have an ultimate destiny that calls us to leave such things behind as we move toward union with God. But while the things of this world must inevitably be renounced, Hugo suggested that because they are created by God and so reflect God, they could properly—albeit temporarily—be used as "stepping stones" in our journey toward God.[92]

This idea that created goods could be properly used is "the doctrine of the samples." It is an idea that is significant, especially in light of the charges that the retreat theology smelled of world-denying Jansenism. For Hugo presents the samples as a very non-rigorist notion that the things of the world are not sinful and that therefore they need not be completely rejected. In fact, one could come to know something of God through these things, and so created goods could be understood as "samples" of God.[93] In a clear affirmation of the goodness of

---

90 Day titled this conference: "Means to Glorify God: The Samples."

91 Hugo, *Applied*, 70.

92 He explained: "For all creatures are made by God, all proceed from the divine mind, and, therefore, all represent in some degree the perfections of this mind." Hugo, *Applied*, 70. In her notes, Day wrote, "As an artist leaves mark of his genius on his work, creation bears mark of his divine perfection. Every creature reflects God."

93 Hugo noted that this notion was also found in scripture: Psalm 93, Wisdom 13, Romans 1:18-20. Hugo, *Applied*, 70.

creation, Hugo stated that it is only because they are good that these things can be understood as "samples."[94]

But like any other kind of sample of something else, these created goods are not meant to be enjoyed for themselves, but rather as images or reflections of a much better thing.[95] And indeed, when given the choice between a mere sample and the real thing, Hugo pointed out that one would be foolish not to choose the genuine article—something affirmed in Reginald Garrigou-LaGrange's oft-quoted admonition that, "The best thing that one can do with the best things is to sacrifice it."[96] While created goods could be properly used to come to a better knowledge of God, their use should only be temporary in order to avoid attachment to them.

WEDNESDAY, CONFERENCE 12:
"THE DOCTRINE OF THE SAMPLES APPLIED"

The concrete implications of this doctrine of the samples were laid out in the next conference (*Applied Christianity*, Part Two, chapter four). By understanding created goods as samples of God and not as ends in themselves, Hugo suggested that attachments to them would gradually lessen and giving up things would become easier. For in so doing, the exterior life of the senses would gradually "dry up" and the interior life of contemplation focused on the supernatural would blossom.[97] In her notes, Day vividly illustrated this process:

> Doctrine will help to dry up life of the senses…Whenever you love anything you become like unto it—or its slave: St. John of the Cross. Tyrannized over by our senses. Great difficulty is when we live in the world of senses. Hence difficulty! We are smothered by

---

94 Hugo, *Applied*, 73.

95 Day wrote, "More you get of natural pleasure less you want; more of spiritual you get, more you want. No satiety. No revulsion." Hugo referred to several Gospel passages which seem to demonstrate this idea of the samples: John 7:37, John 4: 34, John 6, Matthew 2:28, Luke 12:37. He also noted that John of the Cross spoke of creatures as mere crumbs that fall from the table of God in *Ascent to Mount Carmel*, I, 6.

96 Garrigou-Lagrange, *Christian Perfection*, 132. This, of course, was the quote that many critics of the retreat within the Catholic Worker, like Ade Bethune, Stanley Vishnewski, and Julian Pleasants often negatively referred to, but which Day often quoted approvingly.

97 Hugo, *Applied*, 76.

the world of senses, but the doctrine of samples shows us an escape. We are as though trapped in a submarine. Samples are like a submarine valve: where there is attachment there is union. Shows us these things are not to be used for our enjoyment but as a means of getting to God. [98]

For Hugo and Day, the doctrine of the samples offered a way to re-imagine the renunciation of created things not as a condemnation of these things, but as a way to live out a desire for God in one's daily life.[99]

In what was clearly part of a broader critique of what he saw as the minimalist theology of his day, Hugo asserted that the failure of Catholic Youth Organizations to bring forth "real spiritual fruit" was rooted in that fact that discussions on such matters of grace and holiness never appeared. Instead, the prevailing notion of "Catholic Action" consisted in sprinkling brief discussions of faith onto a full recreational program.[100] In this way, the supernatural character of Christianity was depicted as something that could be added—or not—onto a somewhat sufficient human nature. Lost was the centrality of grace and its practical implications for the Christian life.

---

98   Day also explained the benefits of this kind of detachment: "Develops life of spirit. Shows us how to meditate…Do we have to give up music etc. No, God [did] not put creatures here to give them up. No, to teach us about God. 'Best thing to do with the best things is to give them up.' St. John [of the] Cross: If anything leads you immediately to contemplation of God, go ahead. But if it causes you to become attached, give up."

99   Hugo, *Applied*, 79. Day further explained this in her notes, "Minimum degree of love: we must prefer him above every creature. Love of preference. Temptation is an opportunity to make an act of living love…We are in this world to be tried. Devil is like a general trying to take a city, St. Ignatius said. Watch and pray."

100   These organizations, he argued, were founded on the assumption that young people should be appealed to through worldly things like sports, dancing, and recreation— "everything except religion." Hugo, a college professor at the time, asserted that, in fact, "religion is one of the most discussed topics of college students." Hugo, *Applied*, 77.

WEDNESDAY, CONFERENCE 13:
"THE FOLLY OF THE CROSS DOCTRINE"[101]

The understanding of created goods as "mere samples" that enabled Christians to gradually leave them behind in the pursuit of their ultimate destiny was laid out in the "Folly of the Cross" introduced in the thirteenth conference (*Applied Christianity*, Part Two, chapter 7).[102] Hugo described the two main points that made up the Folly of the Cross:

> a. In order to possess ourselves of supernatural happiness, we must give up all natural affections; or, in other words, the supernatural rises out of the destruction and death of the natural man, just as the phoenix of old was said to arise out of its own ashes.

> b. This death of the natural takes place independently of sin, whether original or personal sin. The necessity of dying to nature derives from the very fact that we have a supernatural destiny. Our supernatural destiny requires that we abandon the merely natural plane of living.[103]

The idea of Folly of the Cross, then, centered on the renunciation of the "natural man"—specifically the natural motives and the natural life they informed—in order to correspond with grace.[104] Again, such renunciation was regarded as necessary even apart from sin, for Christ came not just to overcome sin, but to bring about holiness.[105] And so,

---

101   In Day's notes, she numbered this the fourteenth conference as she sometimes included Farina's prayer conferences in her numbering.

102   Hugo noted that while sacrifice for one's country is regarded as heroic, the sacrifice of created goods for God was considered foolish, hence "The Folly of the Cross." *Applied*, 88.

103   Hugo, *Applied*, 87.

104   Hugo clarified what he meant by our dying to the natural self: "The corruption that we must be rid of is that element in our nature which we have seen is in conflict with the supernatural; it includes not only sin, but love of creatures, the use of them for their own pleasure, and the egotistic pursuit of personal ends in preference to the glory of God." *Applied*, 89.

105   Hugo explained, "Even if there were no sin in us, we could not, by our natural powers, merit supernatural life. For supernatural life exceeds our greatest natural powers by an infinite distance. Before our actions could be meritorious on the supernatural plane, it was necessary for God Himself

the Folly of Cross reflected the practical implications of grace in the life of a Christian.[106]

Indeed, the Folly of the Cross was seen in the Gospel admonition: "If any man will be My disciple, let him deny himself and take up his cross daily and follow Me," (Luke 9:23)—a passage Day described in her notes as the "Best short summary Jesus gave of Christianity." For in this passage, Jesus was read as teaching renunciation—seemingly without limitation—as a daily and on-going process of discernment for his followers. For Hugo, this was scriptural confirmation that such renunciation is not to be considered an "occasional indulgence," but rather as "co-extensive with Christian life."[107] For in the Gospel, it was only after this call to daily renunciation that one could follow Jesus. From this, Hugo concluded that while the "essence" and final end of Christianity was the love of God, that love was only possible after denying oneself all other loves and taking up of one's cross daily.[108]

WEDNESDAY, CONFERENCE 14:
"THE FOLLY OF THE CROSS: APPLICATION"

The last conference on Wednesday ended with a discussion of what the Folly of Cross implied for the ordinary Christian life (*Applied Christianity*, Part Two, chapter eight). During this discussion, Hugo introduced two concepts gleaned from the Gospel of John which are key to the retreat theology. The first was the notion of being "pruned" (John 15:3)—the idea that just as a farmer pruned a living branch that is not bearing fruit, so too God prunes individuals through mortifications and afflictions, cutting away the natural self so that they may

---

to elevate them to that plane. Now God chose to do this through His Son Jesus Christ; so that our actions can be supernatural only if they are bathed in the blood of Jesus Christ. Therefore, if it had not been for the merits of Jesus, even if we lived the Folly of the Cross in the fullest measure, denying ourselves in all things, we could never merit supernatural happiness." Hugo, *Applied*, 91.

106   Hugo stated, "aside from sin, God planned to elevate man to the divine level. For this privilege, man would have to renounce a merely human happiness. This is why the practice of the Folly of the Cross is necessary apart from sin." Hugo, *Applied*, 91.

107   Hugo, *Applied*, 87.

108   Hugo, *Applied*, 89.

bear fruit.[109] This notion offered a way to see involuntary suffering as part of the Folly of the Cross. The second Johannine concept was that of "sowing" (John 12:24) our attachments to created goods and pleasures in order to live a supernatural life, just as a farmer sowed his seeds in order to reap a greater harvest in the future.[110] Hugo suggested that a person sow all her goods—including her time—with faith in a greater harvest in return.[111] Like a farmer who sowed his grain anticipating the harvest soon to be reaped, one should be cheerful—even joyful—about such "sowing."[112] In this sense, the Folly of the Cross is indeed to act contrary to "the dictates of mere human wisdom."[113]

III. THE SAMPLES

THURSDAY, CONFERENCE 15: "THE LOVE OF GOD"

While much of the previous discussions centered on the need to give up the love of created goods, Thursday morning's conference (*Applied Christianity*, Part Three, chapter 1) opened with the question of how to increase one's love of God.[114] Hugo answered that the first step in loving God came in knowing God, and that knowledge of God came through God's creation—"the samples"—particularly other people. In this way, one could come to know and love God by knowing and loving one's neighbors, or as Hugo put it, "the measure of the one love is the

---

109   Hugo, *Applied*, 94.

110   Hugo pointed out that while the farmer could keep his seeds and eat them, getting some pleasure from them, it is only when he sows them, casting them off to the field, that they will produce a much greater harvest. Hugo, *Applied*, 94.

111   Hugo saw prayer as a way to sow time, a practice modern society often regarded as wasting time. Hugo, *Applied*, 95. Commenting on this, Day wrote in her retreat notes, "Can you not spend one hour with me? St. Francis de Sales, 1hr. St. Teresa, minimum 1 hr. not including Mass, No Bible, no rosary, no stations, no prayer book. St. Ignatius says don't let devil cheat you out of one minute. Without prayer soldiers without weapons."

112   Hugo, *Applied*, 97.

113   In doing so, Hugo argued, "we must want very much to do the things that we don't want to do." Hugo, *Applied*, 97.

114   Hugo, *Applied*, 105.

measure of the other."[115] And as this love for God increases, desire
for created goods would decrease as God would be preferred to mere
samples.[116] Having turned aside from the love of samples, a person
could then turn to God more fully through charity and prayer. And
it was this supernatural love which Day described in her notes as "the
measure by which we shall be judged."

THURSDAY, CONFERENCE 16:
"THE CONTEMPT FOR THE WORLD: DOCTRINE"

Love for God is exclusive and the implications of that exclusivity were
the topic of the next conference (*Applied Christianity*, Part Three,
chapter 2). In her notes, Day wrote that the love of God implied "contempt of the world," which she described as the "Opposite to love of
God, like convex and concave go together cannot be separated. Must
have right idea of this harsh world. Holy indifference. *When we compare creatures to God, they are contemptible.*"[117] Hugo justified such language of "contempt of the world" as a notion found in sources throughout the Christian tradition and rooted in the idea that the love of God
involved a certain "withdrawal" of love for the world—an indifference

---

115   Hugo defined the reasons for this love of neighbor even further: "It is
not merely because man is an image of God that we must so love our neighbor. In addition to this we and our neighbors are members of the Mystical
Body of Jesus, living with His divine life; and he that hurts the member
hurts Jesus." Hugo, *Applied*, 103.

116   To justify this claim, Hugo turned to a quote from John Henry
Cardinal Newman: "A smooth and easy life, an uninterrupted enjoyment
of the goods of Providence, full meals, soft raiment, well-furnished homes,
the pleasures of sense, the feeling of security, the consciousness of wealth—
these, and the like, if we are not careful, choke up the avenues of the soul,
through which the light and breath of heaven might come to us. A hard life
is alas! no certain method of becoming spiritually minded, but it is one of
the means by which Almighty God makes us so." ("Love, the One Thing
Needful," *Parochial and Plain Sermons*, vol.V, 23), Hugo, *Applied*, 104.

117   Day's notes became even more pointed on the subject: "Adulterers. Do
you not know that friendship of this world is enmity with God. We are
adulterers when we love the world. Fornicators, idolators...Jesus used even
more vehement language: Unless a man hate his father, mother, sister, brother, children."

to worldly things. [118] For in comparison to the infinite excellence and "lovableness" of God, such worldly things would be seen as contemptible. As an embodiment of this kind of "contempt of the world" Hugo held up St. Francis of Assisi, for he said that while no one had ever loved the things of the world more, so too, no one had ever lived a more mortified life than the Poverello. [119]

And this contempt *of* the world, Hugo declared, would inevitably bring contempt *from* the world. [120] Day illustrated this point in her notes when she wrote that, "Our enemy is not sin, it is the world. The world will oppose you...When world no longer persecutes the church, the church is no longer preaching the truth." [121] Respect and acceptance by the world should be regarded as a warning sign for a Christian—a sign that one is marching in tune with the worldly preferences rather than God. Instead, Hugo urged his retreatants to try to become indifferent to their "place" in the world and to the opinions and respect of others. [122] Again, this was not because the world is evil, but rather because it is insufficient and lacking—both inherently and historically—and unable to bring about human fulfillment.

---

118   Hugo once again made clear that contempt of the world did not imply that the things of the world are evil, but rather that precisely because they are good and desirable they must be rejected; otherwise there would be no merit in renouncing. Hugo suggested that this notion of contempt for the world could be found in scripture: 1Cor.7:29-31, 1 John 2:15-16, James 4:4, Gal.6:14, Phil. 3:7. Hugo, *Applied*, 110.

119   Hugo, *Applied*, 111.

120   Hugo quoted the nineteenth-century English Catholic spiritual writer and member of Newman's Oratory, Frederick Faber (1814-1863): "To give ourselves up to the spiritual life is to put ourselves out of harmony with the world around us." Faber, *Growth in Holiness* (Baltimore: John Murphy [1854]) ch. 10. Hugo, *Applied*, 115.

121   Day attributed this quote to Newman.

122   Hugo wrote, paraphrasing B.W. Maturin, that "human respect was synonymous with moral cowardice." *Applied*, 116.

THURSDAY, CONFERENCES 17 AND 18:
"THE CONTEMPT OF THE WORLD: APPLICATION"

FRIDAY, CONFERENCE 19: "FORBIDDEN SAMPLES"

In the next three conferences (*Applied Christianity*, Part Three, chapter 3 and chapter 4), the idea of how this contempt of the world could
be practiced was laid out further by distinguishing four different types
of samples: those which are "necessary," "captivating," "indifferent," and
"forbidden." According to Hugo, "necessary samples" are those things
that a person could not completely live without—like food, clothing,
and shelter—and therefore are things which could not completely be
sown. However, he warned that one must not indulge too much in
such samples, but instead regard them as a farmer regarded the seeds
he did not sow—as being that much less that he will be able to harvest.[123] Beyond such things as food and shelter, each person also has
his or her own attraction to particular creatures and therefore each
person must sow or be pruned of these particular "captivating samples."[124] Hugo went on to explain that "indifferent samples," like imperfect actions, are not sinful in themselves, but their repeated use would
inevitably cause a person to become attached to that sample for its
own sake and thus ultimately away from God and toward sin.[125] Hugo
listed dancing, drinking, and smoking as examples of such samples
which when used too often would hinder the love for God. And as
will be noted in a later chapter, in his *Catholic Worker* articles written during World War II, Hugo described participation in a just-war
in similar terms. Finally, Hugo turned to "forbidden samples," created goods whose misuse is always forbidden. Sexual intercourse was
highlighted as a particular instance of such a sample that is good, but
whose misuse is prohibited.[126]

The point in making all of these distinctions was, in one sense, to
further illustrate that the Christian life is more than simply avoiding

---

123   Hugo, *Applied*, 117.

124   According to Hugo, being able to overcome the attachment to one's
captivating sample was particularly crucial to being filled with the love of
God. For example, it was only after Francis of Assisi overcame his aversion
to lepers that his conversion was complete. Hugo, *Applied*, 118.

125   Hugo, *Applied*, 119.

126   Hugo, *Applied*, 122.

sin.[127] Indeed, the Christian life is a supernatural life of holiness—a life of renunciation, charity, and prayer.[128] But in another sense, Hugo's account of the samples offered a very pastoral—non-rigorist—approach to discerning how to live such a life. For the retreat did not call for a blanket rejection of worldly pleasures out of some sense that they are all corrupt. Rather, the samples provided a constant and critical, yet flexible and even loving means for discerning what ordinary Christians encountered daily in American culture and society.

IV. THE SUPREME DOMINION OF GOD

FRIDAY, CONFERENCE 20:
"THE SUPREME DOMINION: GOD'S INTENTION"

Earlier in the retreat, Hugo had pointed out that the practice of the Folly of the Cross gives glory to God. In the twentieth conference (*Applied Christianity*, Part four, chapter 1), he suggested that God is further gloried through what he termed "The Supreme Dominion of God." Day described this as the acknowledgement that God governed "all things in the world that they may accomplish its purpose. God's providence is universal... Nothing happens except thru the providence of God."[129] According to Hugo, this notion of supreme dominion was essential, in that the Folly of Cross—the striving to die to one's "natural self"—could never be fully completed by human effort alone. [130] Ultimately, God intervenes and assists in this purification or pruning. And this pruning took place within a creation over which God holds supreme dominion.[131]

---

127 Hugo, *Applied*, 123.

128 Hugo, *Applied*, 130.

129 Day further wrote "God's providence is universal: birds of the air, grass of field, hairs of your head. Nothing too small. Every action in human life. All we need to know that it is universal. Very beautiful and consoling. It is efficacious, powerful. It is sweet. Does not force anyone. Does not destroy our freedom, intelligence."

130 Hugo argued that our self-love and unconscious imperfections prevented us from completely dying to our natural self on our own. Hugo, *Applied*, 141.

131 Hugo, *Applied*, 141.

This process of purification and its necessity was articulated within the "Doctrine of Assimilation"—the idea that all of creation comes from God and therefore tends by its very nature to return to God. [132] But only human nature is able to return to God directly, while all other creatures do so through humanity. [133] And, as the rest of creation has to become "assimilated" into humanity, humans have to ultimately become assimilated into the divine—to be "made like unto God"— in order to reach their ultimate destiny. [134] Just as the rest of creation becomes transformed into something greater through this process of assimilation, so too humans are perfected into "new creatures" as they become more fully assimilated into the divine through this process of purification. [135] Understood in this way, injustices, reproaches, humiliations, afflictions, and any other forms of suffering can be seen as potential means by which God brings about perfection and sanctification. [136] And in all this, retreatants were assured, the divine intention is always love. [137] Therefore, just as one sowed attachments to created

132   In Day's retreat notes she wrote that this "doctrine of assimilation" was from Thomas Aquinas's discussion of divination and deification. Day described assimilation in *The Long Loneliness*, 248.

133   Hugo, *Applied*, 142.

134   Hugo, *Applied*, 142.

135   Hugo continued, "In order that we may enter the divine companionship we must be wholly purged. We must be purged of the desires of the natural man (flesh and blood) with his merely human ambitions; we must be purged of the 'corruption' in us, that is, of egotism and the tendency to use creatures for ourselves." Hugo, *Applied*, 143

136   Hugo, *Applied*, 143. Hugo pointed out that St. John of the Cross compared the soul being sanctified in this way to a statue being carved by several workers: "So our neighbors have been selected by God as workmen to carve us into saints: one neighbor mortifies us in one way, another in another way; until we are wholly stripped of the Old Man and the life of Christ appears resplendent in us." According to Hugo, the Spanish saint also compared this divine action on the soul to fire that consumes wood: "So the divine love also burns the impurities from us, blackens us by suffering, then transforms us into itself, i.e., unites us to itself." Hugo, *Applied*, 145.

137   On this point, Day wrote, "'One reason why many souls do not become saints, no patience, generosity.' St. John of Cross. We struggle and complain too much."

goods with joy, one should also try to understand the process of being pruned with a sense of gratitude and even joy.[138]

And the tools which God uses to carry out this loving pruning were further described in conference twenty-one (*Applied Christianity,* Part Four, chapter 2). Here, Hugo suggested that people are the primary instruments—blind instruments with freedom intact—that God employs in this purification process.[139] Such purification is total in that it engages all human faculties: the lower appetites are pruned by physical afflictions;[140] reason by encounters with human foolishness;[141] memory through disappointments in other people;[142] and the will through the malice of others.[143] Despite the fact that such instruments of puri-

---

138   Hugo compared this divine pruning to a surgeon cutting out cancer from a body, and just as one would thank the surgeon for this work, so too one should thank God. Hugo, *Applied,* 151. He also cited scriptural support for this concept: Judith 8-10; Tobias 3:21, 12:13, 13:1; Ecclesiasticus 2:1-10; Hebrews 10:32-39; II Cor 12: 9. Hugo, *Applied,* 144.

139   Hugo pointed out that God is "closer to man than man is to himself" and thus there is "no difficulty in penetrating to the root of human will and freedom." While exactly how God used people as blind instruments without destroying their free will is ultimately a mystery, Hugo suggested that God could be understood as directing human actions through human "antecedents"—temperament, talents, sensibility, environment, background, opportunities and, thus, arrange every situation for the good. Hugo, *Applied,* 149.

140   These are "the desires of the flesh," which, as a consequence of concupiscence, tend toward creatures. Hugo argued that God purified these desires through afflictions and sickness—for instance, if a person was vain, God may send sickness or old age to spoil her beauty. Hugo, *Applied,* 146.

141   Hugo illustrated this idea by noting that while keeping the Israelites wandering in the desert for forty years seemed foolish, it was through that foolishness that God taught them about divine power. Hugo, *Applied,* 146.

142   Hugo suggested that memory is the "storehouse" in which we keep the pleasures of the world and therefore memory has to be emptied of these pleasures in order to make room for the hope of heavenly joys. Hugo, *Applied,* 147.

143   So that we may be filled with charity, God prunes us of creaturely love by allowing us to be surrounded by the malice and hatred of others. And

fication do not come directly *from* God, God's supreme dominion can and does employ them for bringing about sanctification.[144]

The human will, Hugo explained in the following conference (*Applied Christianity*, Part Four, chapter 3), is the final and most important aspect of one's self that needs to be pruned.[145] Our desire to love God is ultimately a desire to be in union with the divine will and so to attain this union our will also has to be purified.[146] No doubt in an allusion to his own struggles with ecclesial authorities, Hugo suggested that God's "favorite tool" for pruning a person's will is his or her superior.[147]

DUTY OF THE PRESENT MOMENT

Once purified in this way, Hugo points out, there are two main ways to enter into union with God. The first is directly through contemplative prayer which marks the contemplative Christian life. But a second

---

thus in our search for love, we will find only hatred in world and will begin to realize that true and lasting love can only be found in God. Hugo, *Applied*, 147.

144 Hugo, *Applied*, 151.

145 Again, Hugo turned to the Christian tradition for support, quoting St. Alphonsus de Liguori as stating: "They who give to the Lord their worldly goods by alms-deeds, their honor by embracing contempt, and their body by mortification, by fasts and by works of penance, make only a partial consecration of themselves to Him. But he that offers to God the sacrifice of his own will consecrates all that he possesses to God's glory, and can say: Lord, after having given to Thee my will, I have nothing more to present to Thee." Liguori, *The True Spouse*, quoted in Hugo, *Applied*, 154.

146 Hugo, *Applied*, 155. Hugo defined our will as "the rational appetite," which desires what the mind presented to it as the good. Both love of God and love of creatures proceeded from what the will desires, therefore making the purification of the will necessary in order to unite it with God. Hugo, *Applied*, 170.

147 To illustrate this point, Day wrote in her 1942 notes that if Catholics had followed Pius XI's call for peace in 1937, "there would be no war today." On the importance of such obedience, Hugo again quoted Liguori: "Obedience to rule and to the commands of superiors is the greatest sacrifice that a Christian can offer to God." Hugo, *Applied*, 154.

path is also available indirectly through the "duty of the present moment"—what the seventeenth-century Jesuit Jean-Pierre de Caussade
called "the sacrament of the present moment." And it was this second
path that Hugo saw as the one much more suited for the active life of
an ordinary Christian.[148] In making this distinction, Hugo was careful
not to fall into the dualist account of the Christian life which he criticized. So while these two paths to union with God are distinct, Hugo
was careful to note that they are not to be separated. For the more
indirect path through the "duty of the present moment" presupposed
some form of contemplative prayer. As Hugo explained, "the active life
is energized by prayer; and activity that is not so energized is supernaturally sterile."[149] Contemplative prayer could not be exiled or quarantined from the ordinary, "active" Christian life, for its focus on the
supernatural is a necessary aspect of every Christian life.

Having made its connection with contemplative prayer, Hugo presented "the duty of the present moment" as a viable way for his retreatants—ordinary Christians—to seek union with God. He described
this "duty" as twofold, involving both any command that proceeds from
"the signified will of God" and every event which emerged from "the
divine will of good pleasure.[150] In the "signified will of God," the divine will is revealed explicitly through direct precepts such as the commandments, the counsels of the Gospels, the precepts of the Church,
and "the duties of one's state in life."[151] By following these precepts and
commands, a person could begin to unite her will with that of God.

---

148   Pierre de Caussade, S.J. *Abandonment to Divine Providence*, ed. J.
Ramiere, S.J., trans. E.J. Strickland (St. Louis: B. Herder Book Co., 1921).
Hugo stated that Caussade's book, "a classic on the subject," which brought
together the thought of St. Francis de Sales (*Treatise on The Love of God*)
with that of "another important writer of self-abandonment"—and as
will be noted later, a central figure in the Quietist controversy—the seventeenth-century French bishop Bossuet. Hugo, *Applied*, 165. Day did not
record any of this in her retreat notes, though she did write about the duty
of the present moment elsewhere, having been introduced to Caussade
by Joseph McSorley. See, William Portier, "Dorothy Day and Her First
Spiritual Director, Fr. Joseph McSorley, C.S.P." *Houston Catholic Worker* 22
(September/October 2002), online edition.

149   Hugo, *Applied*, 169.

150   Hugo, *Applied*, 167.

151   Hugo, *Applied*, 167.

The "divine will of good pleasure," a concept similar to that of "the supreme dominion of God," is the notion that the will of God could be manifest in every event in creation. In this way, a person could unite her will with God "at every moment and in every occurrence" throughout her day-to-day life.[152] While obedience is the virtue exercised in following the "signified will," Hugo stated that self-abandonment must be exercised in response to the "divine will of good pleasure." And this form of self-abandonment takes place as one discerns throughout the day how to surrender her will to the divine—a discernment at the heart of the retreat.[153]

Hugo explained that this entire process of giving up habitual attachments to created things—both by sowing and being pruned—comes to a climax with this union of the human will with the divine. With the renunciation of one's will, the correspondence with grace is made full:

> By doing my present duty for the love of God I unite myself to His holy will and graces enter my soul. As we said when dealing explicitly with the subject of motives, the supernatural motive is the means by which the soul is nourished with grace; it is the point of contact at which grace enters the soul; it is the sole means of nourishing the supernatural life within us; it is the valve through which, alone, charity can enter into us. The practice of uniting one's self to the divine and keeping all motives supernatural thus finally resolves itself into the same thing.[154]

For Hugo, this was the Folly of the Cross.

---

152   Hugo further stated that such events could be "sickness and afflictions, consolations, criticism, interior trials, etc., -in a word, all events whether they happen in the interior of the soul or exteriorly." Hugo, *Applied*, 168.

153   Interestingly, Hugo also made clear that there is no taint of Quietism in self-abandonment: "by obedience to the signified will of God, the soul actively does all that is required of it for salvation; self-abandonment is practiced in regard to the will of good pleasure." Hugo, *Applied*, 168.

154   Hugo, *Applied*, 166.

V. THE FOLLY OF THE CROSS

SATURDAY, CONFERENCE 23, 24, 25: "ALMSGIVING,"
"MORTIFICATION," "DEATH"

The final three conferences of the retreat (*Applied Christianity*, Part
Five, chapters one, two, and four) left retreatants with some tangible
practices for living the Folly of the Cross. Almsgiving, for instance,
was described as the "sowing of external goods" by giving them to
the poor—Day wrote, "Poor are porters of the rich. Give them your
possessions. They will carry them into heaven for you."[155] As with all
forms of renunciation, Hugo argued that the measure to determine
how much should be sown was found in the Paul's admonition, "He
that sows sparingly reaps sparingly" (Romans 8:9).[156] Physical ail-
ments were presented as the sowing of bodily goods, and again it was
emphasized that these mortifications could be practiced with a sense
of joy.[157]

Finally, the retreat ended with the conference: "The Sowing of
Everything: Death." In it, Hugo suggested that Christians should regularly think about death.[158] Christians should prepare for death by
performing each action as though it were their last. And they could
even "rehearse for death" by practicing what in the Christian tradition
has been called a "mystical death"—to become completely detached
from the things of the world, particularly one's own selfishness and

---

155   Hugo noted that such almsgiving perfectly fulfills the duty of charity—a withdrawal of love for creatures and then union with God. Hugo,
Applied, 177.

156   Hugo, *Applied*, 178.

157   Hugo, *Applied*, 180. In her notes, Day described mortification of the
eyes: "most sins enter thru eye. Eye should be inward. We have a divine
guest" -the mortification of the ear: "not to listen to gossip. Practice interior
solitude" -the mortification of the tongue: "Let your speech be yea, yea, nay,
nay...Practice periods of silence and solitude" -the mortification of smell:
"Put up with offensive odors. Do not be fastidious: Sow perfume" -the mortification of taste: "Eat what is set before you. Jesus' rule"—and the mortification of one's imagination: "thru sight, hearing, seat of hope."

158   Throughout the retreat, Hugo emphasized the point that "death
changes nothing" in our spiritual quest, and therefore we must strive to live
a supernatural life before death.

egotism.[159] And in dying so completely, Hugo concluded, one became united with Christ, for, "even the greatest mortification is of no value except when it is joined to Christ's suffering and thereby made meritorious."[160]

CONCLUSION

As we saw in the previous chapter, many of those who attended Hugo's retreats did not like it. They heard its call for renunciation and dying to the "natural self" as rigorist and extreme. And the idea that the created things of the world should be given up as much as possible, struck many as denigrating to nature and smelling of Jansenism. Many smart, holy people saw the retreat in these terms. And the critiques of Hugo's theology that appeared in prominent American Catholic theological journals in the 1940s echoed these sentiments.

Yet this was not the way Hugo, Dorothy Day, and many others understood the theological vision presented in the retreat. For them it was "the bread of the strong" and "like hearing the Gospel for the first time."[161] Its theology was not seen as world-denying Jansenism, but rather it was understood as a theology which recognized that human nature is distinct from both that which is sinful and that which is supernatural. It recognized that human nature is good, but it is also both inherently (in the abstract) and historically (in the concrete) insufficient and unstable. The retreat theology recognized that while nature is distinct from grace, grace is not separated from nature but intimately connected to it as its inner dynamism and final end. This is the understanding of the nature-supernatural relationship at the heart of the retreat. Day and Hugo did not regard the retreat as rigorist or excessively perfectionist, but rather they saw it as a way to take seriously the "practical implications" of grace and holiness in the Christian life.

For those who embraced the retreat, it offered a way for ordinary Christians—laity and secular clergy alike—to strive to live a holy life in the context of early twentieth-century American culture and society. The retreat provided a means for discerning what is holy in the world and to perfect or renounce what is not, all in light of the beatific

---

159   Hugo, *Applied*, 193. Day described this death in her notes: "React to world, its joys, its sorrows, as dead men do. Indifferent. Mystical Death."

160   Hugo, *Applied*, 194.

161   Day, *The Long Loneliness*, 263

vision. In this way, the retreat can be seen as providing an ongoing and critical evaluation of what Christians encountered in American life—not to reject it outright, but to assess it in light of their ultimate destiny and to chart how to negotiate the complexities of their lives in that light. Hugo saw himself as a spiritual director pastorally assisting his retreatants in their daily engagement with society and culture. Understanding Hugo's retreat in these terms challenges oft-repeated caricatures of his theology. It also reveals something of why it was so influential for those who embraced it and why it is still relevant today.

In response to the criticisms of the retreat, Hugo argued that its theology is rooted in the Christian tradition and he justified it by highlighting the various sources from that tradition which formed the foundations for the retreat. Many of these sources, including Scripture, have already emerged in this presentation of the retreat: John of the Cross, Alphonsus de Liguori, Francis de Sales, Thomas Aquinas, Jean-Pierre de Caussade, and Francis of Assisi. But it is one source in particular—Ignatian spirituality—that Hugo held up as primary to the retreat. And so it is to Hugo's return to this source—his *ressourcement*—that we will now look.

CHAPTER III

IGNATIAN RADICALISM

...on my own part I ought not seek health rather than sickness, wealth rather than poverty, honor rather than dishonor, long life rather than a short one, and so on in all matters.

☞ St. Ignatius of Loyola[1]

I n the December 1951 issue of *The Catholic Worker*, Dorothy Day included an obituary for Onesimus Lacouture, S.J., in which she noted that the originator of the retreat was born in a little town north of Montreal called St. Ours on April 13, 1881 and was the nineteenth of twenty-one children—his father had married twice. With this, she stated,

> Doesn't that sound like the beginning of the life of a saint? Peter Maurin was one of twenty-three children. These two men who had most influence on my life (and so in a way on the life of the **Catholic Worker**) were both French peasants, of France and French Canada. They both knew the life of the land and of the city. Both were men of the poor.[2]

In his own account of the retreat, Hugo quoted Philippe Desranleau, the bishop of Sherbrooke in Quebec, who had described Lacouture's retreat as the "most supernatural and the most efficacious awakening of Christian and priestly life ever recorded in the religious history of

---

1   Ignatius of Loyola, "The Spiritual Exercises," (no.22) trans. George Ganss, S.J. in *Ignatius of Loyola: Spiritual Exercises and Selected Works*, ed. George Ganss (Mahwah, NJ: Paulist Press 1991), 130. All references to the *Exercises* in this book will come from this edition.

2   Dorothy Day, "Death of Father Onesimus Lacouture, S.J." *The Catholic Worker* (December 1951):1.

Canada."[3] And, indeed, between April 1931 and December 1939, Lacouture led some 142 retreats to over 6,000 participants—mainly priests, but also several bishops and even the cardinal-archbishop of Quebec.[4] These numbers led Hugo to declare that, "No comparable work has ever been done by any Jesuit, either in this country or in Canada, and scarcely by any priest anywhere."[5] Such hyperbole aside, it is clear that Lacouture's retreat made an impact.

To better understand this retreat, as well as Hugo's appropriation of its theology, the sources of its theological vision must be examined. To this end, three points will be looked at in this chapter. First, we will examine Hugo's assertion that Lacouture—a loyal son of St. Ignatius of Loyola—rooted his retreat in Ignatius's *Spiritual Exercises* and Jesuit spirituality. While Hugo turned to several sources from within the Christian tradition to justify the retreat theology, he argued that such sources were secondary to the influence the *Exercises* had on the retreat. Merriman has described the retreat as "one of the most noteworthy early twentieth-century developments of the Ignatian retreat in North America."[6] Therefore an understanding of Lacouture's reading of the *Exercises* is necessary to understand the retreat. Next, while

---

3   Hugo, *Your Ways Are Not My Ways: The Radical Christianity of the Gospel, Volume.1,* (Pittsburgh: Encounter With Silence, 1986), 4. This book was published after Hugo's death in 1985.

4   According to Merriman, the apostolic delegate to Canada, a dozen bishops, and Cardinal Rodrigue Villeneuve, the Archbishop of Quebec (1931-1947) attended Lacouture retreats. Some Canadian bishops even reportedly made attendance mandatory for the priests in their dioceses. Brigid O'Shea Merriman, O.S.F., *Searching for Christ,* (Notre Dame, IN: University of Notre Dame Press, 1994),136, fn16. Merriman also indicated that some laity may have attended Lacouture led retreats. Also see, Anselme Longpré, *Un Mouvement spiritual au Québec (1931-1962): au retour à l'Evangile* (Montreal: Fides, 1976) and Jean-Claude Drolet, "Un Mouvement de spiritualité sacerdotale au Québec au XXe siècle (1931-1965): Le Lacouturisme," *Canadian Catholic Historical Association: Study Sessions,* 1973 (Ottawa, 1974), 55-87.

5   Hugo went to write that "And yet the Society in Canada, celebrating an anniversary several years ago, and listing proudly all the great works they had undertaken, never mentioned this one!" Hugo, *A Sign of Contradiction: As the Master, So the Disciple* (published by author, 1947), 61.

6   Merriman, *Searching,* 132.

Lacouture's interpretation of Ignatius brought him into conflict with many of his twentieth-century contemporaries within the Society of Jesus, Hugo went to great lengths to show that this interpretation brought Lacouture into accord with many early modern Jesuit spiritual writers such as Louis Lallemant (1578-1635), Jean-Joseph Surin (1600-1665), as well as Caussade. And so this often overlooked "strain" of Jesuit spiritual writers will be identified, as will Hugo's attempt to locate Lacouture and the retreat within it. Finally, Hugo's own efforts at a *ressourcement* theology—his attempt to certify the theology of the retreat by turning to sources within early modern spiritual writing, particularly these sixteenth and seventeenth-century Jesuits—will be highlighted. For Hugo's "return to the sources" was noteworthy for an American Catholic at the time and should be understood within the context of other such efforts at *ressourcement* taking place in early twentieth-century Catholicism.

ONESIMUS LACOUTURE, S.J.

While Canadian by birth, Onesimus Lacouture moved with his family to the United States when he was six years old.[7] After graduating from Wayland High School in Massachusetts in 1900, Lacouture returned to Canada to attend *College de l'Assumption* near Montreal. And in 1902, he entered the Jesuit novitiate at Sault-aux-Recollets. After studying at the Jesuit seminary in Poughkeepsie, New York— St. Andrews-on-the-Hudson—and at Immaculate Conception Seminary in Montreal, Lacouture began four years of teaching Latin at St. Mary's College in Montreal followed by another three years teaching children on a Jesuit mission in Alaska. It was during his time in Alaska—an experience which he remembered as being initially a miserable one—that Lacouture began to develop what would become the retreat.[8]

In 1913, Lacouture left Alaska to resume his studies at Immaculate Conception and was ordained in 1916 on the feast of St. Ignatius. After various assignments, including as a chaplain in France during World War I and a Tertiary year in Belgium with Raoul Plus, Lacouture was made pastor of another Jesuit Indian mission—this time near

---

7   All biographical information on Lacouture comes from Hugo's *A Sign of Contradiction*, chapter 5.

8   Hugo, *Sign*, 55.

Montreal—where he began to give conferences on the spiritual life to local religious communities. The popularity of these conferences led to an assignment on a Jesuit mission band in 1927. And Lacouture was working on the mission band, headquartered at the novitiate in Sault-aux-Recollets, when he led his first retreat to fifteen priests in 1931.

Lacouture led retreats in various locations throughout Canada and the United States until December 1939, when his Jesuit superiors forbade him to continue this work and assigned him to posts on various missions. Lacouture eventually ended up at St. Regis, an Indian mission in Hogansburg, New York in 1942 where he died in November 1951. Day reported that the funeral Mass was said at St. Regis and that Lacouture's body was then driven back to Montreal in a procession of some thirty cars. She noted that it was "a small funeral, considering how great a man Fr. Lacouture was. Just a few years ago he was famous. Now he is anonymous."[9] Day was the only person from the United States to attend the funeral—Hugo was not able to attend.

THE ORIGINS OF THE RETREAT

In *A Sign of Contradiction: As the Master, So the Disciple* (1947), Hugo offered an account of the history and origins of Lacouture's retreat. This book is important not only because Lacouture left behind little published writing of his own, but also because this was Hugo's attempt to defend the retreat theology in the face of criticism by situating it within both the broader Christian tradition and the history of Jesuit spirituality.[10] In this sense, *A Sign of Contradiction* can be read as a work of *ressourcement* theology—an effort that was in many ways similar to that being done by other Catholic thinkers at the time, such as M-D Chenu, O.P. (1895-1990), Jean Daniélou, S.J. (1905-1974) and Henri de Lubac, S.J.

According to Hugo's account, the origins of the retreat dated back to Lacouture's time in the Jesuit missions in Alaska (1910-1913). Lacouture had had a difficult time upon his arrival in Alaska due to both the mission's rough conditions and something of an inhospitable

---

9   Dorothy Day, "Death of Father Onesimus Lacouture, S.J." *The Catholic Worker* (December 1951): 1. Day then quoted a passage from scripture that was central to the retreat: "Unless the seed fall into the ground and die, itself remaineth alone. But if it dies it beareth much fruit" (John 12:24).

10   For more on Lacouture, see Jack Lee Downey, *The Bread of the Strong: Lacouturisme and the Folly of the Cross, 1910-1985* (New York: Fordham University Press, 2015).

reception from his fellow Jesuits.[11] These factors only increased the disappointment that Lacouture—an aspiring academic—felt in not being sent to a teaching position at a Jesuit university. And it was in such a despondent state—having reportedly spent an entire day weeping in the woods—that Lacouture opened his copy of *The Imitation of Christ* and read:

> Every man naturally desireth to know, but what availeth knowledge without the fear of God? A meek husbandman that serveth God is more acceptable to Him than is a curious philosopher who, considering the course of heaven, willfully forgetteth himself...Let us therefore cease from the desire of such vain knowledge, for oft times is found therein great distraction and deceit of the enemy, whereby the soul is much hindered and withheld from the perfect and true love of God...The most high and the most profitable learning is this, that a man have a soothfast knowledge and a full despising of himself.[12]

Hugo described reading this passage as a moment of conversion for the young Onesimus. His desire for "secular and natural learning" dried up and a new passion began to rule his soul, Lacouture became a "new creature."[13] Upon leaving Alaska, Lacouture returned to Montreal for four years of theological studies, years marked by tensions between Lacouture and many of his professors who taught theology as "a system of abstractions rather than as an actual approach to a living God."[14]

While it was a passage from Thomas À Kempis that brought about Lacouture's initial "conversion," it was to the spiritual writings of Ignatius of Loyola that the young Jesuit quickly turned. Lacouture made Ignatius's *Spiritual Exercises* in the Alaskan wilderness twice after this "conversion" experience.[15] In the midst of these wilderness retreats, what would later become "the retreat" began to gradually emerge. And so it was while meditating on the Ignatian *Exercises* that

---

11   Hugo suggested that the fact that Lacouture—a French-Canadian—was stationed with three Italian Jesuits was a source of tension for Lacouture. Hugo, *Sign*, 57.

12   Thomas Á Kempis, *Imitation of Christ*, I, 2, in Hugo, *Sign*, 55.

13   Hugo, *Sign*, 55.

14   Hugo, *Sign*, 58.

15   Hugo, *Sign*, 56.

Lacouture began to develop his basic theological perspective. It is the *Exercises,* then, which form the primary theological foundation of the Lacouture retreat—"the guiding principle of [Lacouture's] life and the central point of his subsequent spiritual teaching."[16] And so whatever other theological influences came to bear on him, Hugo contended that Lacouture was above all "a true disciple of St. Ignatius" and his retreat clearly manifested the marks of Ignatian spirituality.[17]

JESUIT REACTION TO LACOUTURE

As was noted earlier, Lacouture led retreats from 1931 until 1939 when his superiors abruptly ordered him to stop. Hugo reported that because of the stir that the retreat was making, Lacouture was asked to write down his retreat notes and submit them for review by a Jesuit censor in Rome. In 1943, four years after Lacouture had already ceased giving retreats, the anonymous censor returned his report.[18]

This review opened by stating that having "maturely and most diligently" examined the retreat notes, it was clear that "the work labors under many and grave faults (*vitiis*), which so pervade and infect it that its emendation would be wholly impossible."[19] The censor then went on to identify several of these "grave faults," most prominent of which was that Lacouture had confused "evangelical counsels" with "precepts of charity" and that he misrepresented the relationship between nature and the supernatural.[20] All of this led the censor to conclude that ultimately Lacouture's reading of the *Exercises* had

---

16   Hugo, *Sign,* 57.

17   Hugo, *Sign,* 203. Also see Downey, 84.

18   Hugo printed the report, dated August 12, 1943, in *A Sign of Contradiction,* 67.

19   In reply to this charge, Hugo wrote, "Here is something amazing indeed—a situation worth looking into: that thirty-five hundred priests and bishops had been unable to detect these great and manifold errors! Only those who had not attended the retreat had the requisite perspicuity and critical acumen. Not a situation, surely, to inspire confidence in the many priests and members of the hierarchy in Canada, or the cross-section of the American clergy, who had made these retreats!" Hugo, *Sign,* 69. Throughout his responses to critics, Hugo pointed out that none of the retreat's critics had ever actually attended a retreat.

20   Hugo, *Sign,* 67.

incorrectly interpreted the thought of Ignatius, and had dismissed and even ridiculed "the deservedly proved writings of the commentators on the *Spiritual Exercises.*"[21] For Hugo, it was this final charge that was at the root of all the other criticisms of Lacouture coming from within the Society of Jesus.

As Hugo read it, the censor was essentially criticizing Lacouture for preaching the Folly of the Cross—the idea that the supernatural final end of human nature has practical implications for the "ordinary" Christian life.[22] Recognition of these implications meant the recognition of a "continuity" in the Christian life, that the supernatural destiny implies that all Christians—not just spiritual "elites" cloistered away somewhere—are called to live a life of holiness. But such continuity between nature and the supernatural was absent from the two-tiered notion of the Christian life that prevailed in early twentieth-century Catholicism and "the deservedly proved writings of the commentators on the *Spiritual Exercises.*" According to Hugo, the retreat was "attacked" for emphasizing the interior life of prayer and renunciation as essential practices of every Christian. But for critics, such claims were dangerous in that they would "tempt those in the active life to neglect their duty, by giving them doctrines that belong only to contemplatives."[23] In short, Hugo charged critics of the retreat with having quarantined the supernatural away into the arena of a few cloistered elites. But it is the supernatural life of holiness—a synthesis of the active and contemplative—that Lacouture recognized to be at the heart of the Ignatian *Exercises* and Jesuit spirituality.

THE SPIRITUAL EXERCISES
OF IGNATIUS OF LOYOLA

St. Ignatius of Loyola (1491-1556) put together the basic elements of his *Exercises* sometime during the year he spent at Manresa (1522-1523) following his conversion—a time spent in prayer, fasting, mortification, and reading, among other things, *The Imitation of Christ.*[24]

---

21   Hugo, *Sign*, 68.

22   Hugo, *Sign*, 132.

23   Hugo, *Sign*, 132.

24   Details on Ignatius and his writing the *Exercises* come fro~ O'Malley, *The First Jesuits*, (Cambridge, MA: Harvard Uni~ 1993) and John O'Malley, "Early Jesuit Spirituality: Spaiٖ

During this period, Ignatius reported experiencing temptations and desolation of spirit, as well as profound mystical insights, and he wrote the *Exercises* based upon this spiritual journey as a means to help others make a similar journey.[25] In the opening paragraph, Ignatius stated—in words later echoed in Lacouture's retreat—that the purpose of the *Exercises* was in "preparing and disposing our soul to rid itself of all its disordered affections and then, after their removal, of seeking and finding God's will in the ordering of our life for the salvation of our soul" (*SE*, 1). Upon leaving Manresa, Ignatius began guiding some of his fellow students through his *Exercises* during the years he studied theology in Spain and Paris (1524-1535). And in 1548, eight years after he officially recognized the Society of Jesus, Pope Paul III approved Ignatius's *Spiritual Exercises*.

Ignatius opened his *Exercises* with the "Principle and Foundation" which presents his thinking on the ultimate purpose of life and the created world—a discussion that was central to Lacouture's interpretation of the *Exercises*. Ignatius then divided the *Exercises* up into four Weeks. The first offers considerations on the evils of sin and the havoc it brings to the person and world, as well as the constant love of God. This First Week—at the end of which Ignatius recommends going to Confession—focuses on the necessity of turning from one's old ways toward union with God. While the word "conversion" does not appear in the *Exercises*, John O'Malley suggests that "it is a dynamic that underlies the First Week—a turning from a sinful life or, probably more often, a turning to a more devout life," what for Hugo and Lacouture was a supernatural life of holiness.[26] In many ways the focus of this

---

Christian Spirituality III, ed. Louis Dupre and Don E. Saliers (New York: Crossroad, 1989). O'Malley noted that most scholars believe that Ignatius was profoundly shaped by the *Imitation of Christ*. He also pointed out, though, that in "its concepts, images, and directives, the book of the *Exercises* stands squarely within the Christian spiritual tradition, so much so that the search for its sources has consistently been frustrated by the very commonplace nature of its ideas." O'Malley, "Early Spirituality," 5.

25 The *Exercises* have been described as "the systematized, de-mysticised quintessence of the process of Ignatius's own conversion and purposeful change of life, and they were intended to work a similar change in others." H. Outram Evennett, *The Spirit of the Counter Reformation*, (Cambridge: Cambridge University Press, 1968), 32.

26 O'Malley, *The First Jesuits*, 39.

First Week captures the essence of the entire *Exercises,* and O'Malley has even suggested that if for some reason a retreatant could not continue with the rest of the *Exercises,* "the better ordering" of his or her life—which the *Exercises* are primarily concerned—would have been essentially set in motion during the First Week.[27] For if the purpose of this Week is achieved, the retreatant would have found "a new and happier orientation at the very core of their being" and would be "thus set more firmly than before on the path to salvation."[28] Recognizing the centrality of the First Week for Ignatius's *Exercises* is important for our discussions here since, as we will see, Lacouture's retreat is based upon the First Week.

Ignatius structured the next three Weeks with a vision of confirming what is presented in the First Week.[29] At the core of these Weeks are a set of contemplations on the life of Christ, the goal of which, Ignatius wrote, is "an interior knowledge of our Lord...that I may love him more intensely and follow him more closely" (*SE,* 104).[30] With this in mind, the Second Week presents contemplations on "the life of Christ our Lord up to until the Last Supper. The Third Week begins with the Last Supper and ends with the death and burial of Jesus. And the Fourth Week focuses on the Resurrection and everything that followed, as well as a discussion of the three "Methods of Prayer." Ignatius also included a number of directives or guidelines for directors called "Annotations" or "Explanations" along with various "Rules" including one for "the discernment of spirits" (*SE,* 313-336) and another for "thinking with the Church" (*SE,* 352-370).

In looking at the *Exercises,* O'Malley highlighted two key features. The first is its clear design, aimed at carrying out Ignatius's stated purpose: "to overcome oneself, and to order one's life, without reaching a decision through some disordered affection" (*SE,* 21). He noted that with "an understated style and with a mass of seemingly disparate elements," Ignatius constructed a course of discernment and preparation for how to live in a new way in response to "an inner call for intimacy"

---

27 O'Malley, *The First Jesuits,* 40.

28 O'Malley, *The First Jesuits,* 40.

29 O'Malley, *The First Jesuits,* 40.

30 Matthew Ashley, "Ignacio Ellacuria and the *Spiritual* Ignatius of Loyola" *Theological Studies* 61.1 (March 2000): 1\

with God.[31] The *Exercises*, in other words, are a tool for discerning how to live a more holy life in union with the divine.

A second feature of the *Exercises* is its flexible and non-prescriptive character which allows "the Creator to deal immediately with the creature and the creature with its Creator and Lord" (*SE*, 15). O'Malley suggested that Ignatius had great confidence in the direct inspiration of God and his *Exercises* sought to facilitate the reception of that inspiration and its implications for the life of the retreatant.[32] In other words, Ignatius wanted to open the retreatant to "seeking and finding God's will" and so he allowed for as much "liberty of spirit" as possible.[33] And this quest to give oneself over to the will of God is perhaps best articulated in the prayer Ignatius placed at the conclusion of the Fourth Week's "Contemplation to Attain Love" (*SE*, 234):

> Take, Lord, and receive all my liberty, my memory, my understanding, and all my will—all that I have and possess. You, Lord, have given all that to me. I now give it back to You, O Lord. All of it is yours. Dispose of it according to your will. Give me your love and your grace, for this is enough for me.

For Ignatius, the *Exercises* were meant to enable retreatants to better correspond with grace and its implications in their lives. Indeed, O'Malley explained that "the fundamental premise" of the *Exercises* is the "immediate action of God on the individual" and "the continuous action of God in the whole process."[34]

But despite this clear orientation toward union with God, Ignatius seemed equally clear that he did not want the *Exercises* to form

---

31   John O'Malley, "Early Jesuit Spirituality: Spain and Italy," in *Christian Spirituality III*, ed. Louis Dupre and Don E. Saliers (New York: Crossroad, 1989), 5.

32   O'Malley, "Early Jesuit Spirituality," 6.

33   O'Malley summed up this somewhat paradoxical nature of the *Exercises*, "I would stress that the book, and with it Jesuit Spirituality, while being rationalistic in it language and arguments, is more profoundly concerned with right affectivity; while being logical in the organization of its parts, it is more profoundly psychological in its movement and design; and while being methodical in the aids it provides to prayer and spiritual discernment, it is more profoundly nonprescriptive in the outcome it foresees for the direct divine intervention that is its basic premise." O'Malley, "Early Jesuit Spirituality," 6.

34   O'Malley, *The First Jesuits*, 38, 43.

members of a monastic order. Instead, the *Exercises* sought to bring about an "election" or ordering of one's life "for the greater service and praise of God."[35] Service to the "active apostolate" thus became an essential component of Ignatian spirituality—making it, in a sense, a "spirituality of service."[36] For Ignatius, the spirituality of the Jesuits was to be "ordered" to the active ministry and anything that would interfere with that ordering was removed.[37] Indeed, the *Exercises* themselves consist of various meditations—active, discursive, mental prayer—in which the retreatant was an active participant.[38] Through these Ignatius wanted to get his Jesuits to use their imagination (their memory) to place themselves within the events of the life of Christ or the reality of the divine order of the world.[39] They were then to use their mind (their understanding) to reflect on what they were imagining in order to bring their active life in accord with the divine will. And the retreatant was to try to motivate his will to carry out the activities that God wanted him to undertake. In such a way, this method of discursive prayer in the *Exercises* became regarded as the foundation for the apostolic life of the Jesuits.

It is important to note that Ignatius's insistence on what has been referred to as his "activist piety" had roots in the historical context of early sixteenth-century Spain in which he was writing.[40] For Spanish

---

35   O'Malley, "Early Jesuit Spirituality," 6.

36   Joseph de Guibert, *The Jesuits: Their Spiritual Doctrine and Practice*, (Institute of Jesuit Sources, 1964), 176-181.

37   Ignatius's refusal to allow Jesuits to pray the Office in choir was an example of this "ordering," as time for prayer and ascetical practices was limited so as not to interfere with the Jesuit's ministry. O'Malley, "Early Jesuit Spirituality," 7.

38   McKeon, Robert, "Introduction" in Jean Pierre Caussade, S.J., *A Treatise on Prayer from the Heart* trans. Robert McKeon (St. Louis: The Institute of Jesuit Sources, 1998), 10.

39   McKeon, 10.

40   O'Malley, "Early Jesuit Spirituality," 7. This piety can be understood as part of its historical context: "The spirituality of the Counter-Reformation sprang from a triple alliance, as it were, between the Tridentine clarificati͠ of the orthodox teaching on Grace and Justification, the practical urg͠ day towards active works, and certain new developments in asc͠ ing and practice which promoted this outlook." Evennett, 32.

Catholicism at the time was flooded with an indigenous mystical movement whose followers were known as *Alumbrados* or *Illuminati*.[41] Emerging in the previous century, this movement advocated a method of prayer consisting in "abandonment to the love God"—a method which claimed to offer the safest and quickest means to achieve union with God.[42] The *Alumbrados* charged that Christian practices of vocal prayer, meditation, fasting, penances, rituals, images, and the vowed religious life in general were all useless hindrances to achieving this state of Christian perfection—charges which led to their condemnation in 1525.[43] In the heightened vigilance brought about by the Inquisition in Spain, Ignatius himself spent time in jail while being investigated for *Alumbrados* tendencies and was even forbidden from preaching for three years.[44] Such events stuck with Ignatius, making him careful to distance himself from any sense of this kind of false mysticism.[45]

---

41   Kieran Kavanaugh has pointed out that as Lutheranism quickly spread through Germany, the Inquisition sought to uncover it in Spain. Inquisitors suspected that Lutheranism and Illuminism were closely connected in that both emphasized internal religion at the expense of outward ceremony. In 1525, forty-eight *Illuminati* propositions were condemned. In 1559, the Inquisitor General published an extremely severe index of forbidden books which included works by Tauler, John of Avila, and Francisco de Osuna— mystical writers who greatly influenced Jesuit writers such as Balthasar Alvarez and Louis Lallemant. Kieran Kavanaugh, "Spanish Sixteenth Century: Carmel And Surrounding Movements," in *Christian Spirituality III*, ed. Louis Dupre and Don E. Saliers (New York: Crossroad, 1989), 73.

42   Kavanaugh, 73.

43   Kavanaugh, 73. Their critics perceived them as giving undue prominence to visions, raptures, and revelations. O'Malley, "Early Jesuit Spirituality," 15.

44   Kavanaugh, 73.

45   O'Malley suggested that Ignatius's exhortation that Jesuits "find God in all things" (*Constitutions* 288) and not just in quiet prayer or the solitude of their rooms could be seen as coming out of this fear of false mysticism. O'Malley, "Early Jesuit Spirituality," 15.

TWO WINGS OF JESUIT SPIRITUALITY

At the center of Ignatius's spirituality, then, is a synthesis of contemplation and action.[46] Cardinal Avery Dulles, S.J. called this the "practical mysticism" of Ignatius who was sensitive to the "interior leading of the Holy Spirit" while at the same time was dedicated "unswervingly to the service of the Church militant."[47] And indeed, as another scholar has pointed out, Ignatius's *Exercises* have the unique ability to hold such paradoxical notions together,

> Tensions and dialectics that conceptual systems almost inevitably elide, dichotomize, or conflate, are preserved and resolved in the *Spiritual Exercises* because they are not thought, but enacted so as to draw the person into the mystery of God's love, a mystery which, when expressed in act or articulated in concept and system, unfolds in terms of these dialectical tensions.[48]

Not long after Ignatius's death, though, this synthesis began to break apart within Jesuit spiritual writing. For instance, in 1609, a Spanish Jesuit named Alonso Rodriguez (1526-1617) published *Ejercicio de perfecccion y virtutes cristianas*, a book that was extremely influential within the Society of Jesus and quickly became a standard in

46   Avery Dulles, "Jesuits and Theology: Yesterday and Today" *Theological Studies* 52. 3 (September, 1991): 525.

47   Dulles noted that this synthesis had its roots squarely in the *Exercises*: "'The rules laid down in the *Spiritual Exercises* on the discernment of spirits (*SE* 313-36) and on the choice of a state of life (*SE* 169-89) have given Jesuits a sense of the immediate presence of God, who calls each individual to union with Himself. The director of the *Exercises* is admonished to let 'the Creator and Lord in person communicate Himself to the devout soul' and 'permit the Creator to deal directly with the creature' (*SE* 15). But this personal mysticism was balanced in the case of Ignatius by intense devotion to the institutional Church. For him it was axiomatic that 'In Christ our Lord, the bridegroom, and in His spouse the Church, only one Spirit holds sway, which governs and rules for the salvation of souls' (*SE* 365). In the *Constitutions of the Society of Jesus* and in the 'Rules of Thinking with the Church' (*SE* 352-70) he stressed the need for unquestioning obedience to the hierarchy and especially to the pope as vicar of Christ on earth. In the *Spiritual Exercises* Ignatius wrote affectionately of the 'hierarchical Church' (*SE* 170, 353, 355)—a term which he apparently was the first to Dulles, 525.

48   Ashley, 19.

Jesuit houses of formation.[49] In this work, Rodriguez emphasized Ignatius's more "activist" insistence that "love ought to manifest itself in deeds" (*SE*, 230). And while appreciative of "higher forms of prayer," Rodriguez insisted that any interior inspiration must be tested by the deeds it produced—if the deeds were virtuous, the inspiration was holy. And thus, the highest states of "mystical" prayer were regarded as suspect and even unacceptable if they did not pass this test.[50] What was not seen as suspect, and therefore what was considered truly authentic, was the observance of the duties of one's state in life, the adherence to the traditions of the Church, and respect for authority.[51] In other words, the avoidance of sin and the following of the natural law. Following Rodriguez, a great deal of Jesuit spirituality soon became reduced to this kind of "conventional practicality."[52] And while Rodriguez certainly did not represent the entirety of Jesuit spirituality, his influence and legacy did much to de-emphasize those more mystical tendencies within the *Exercises*.[53]

And such a de-emphasis certainly had an effect. Indeed, O'Malley pointed out that already by the seventeenth-century two "strains" in Jesuit spirituality could be distinguished. From writers like Rodriguez emerged a strain that could be described as "cautious and soberly ascetical, favorable almost exclusively to a methodical and even moralistic style of prayer."[54] This strain was "suspicious of contemplation and other higher forms of prayer as inimical to the active ministry"

---

49   By 1626, there were seven Spanish editions of Rodriguez's book, as well as translations in English (partial, 1612), French (1617), Italian (1617). Latin (1621), German (1623), and Dutch (1626). The book continued to be printed well into the twentieth century, and has gone through three hundred editions in twenty-three languages. O'Malley, "Early Jesuit Spirituality," 14.

50   O'Malley, "Early Jesuit Spirituality," 15.

51   O'Malley, "Early Jesuit Spirituality," 15.

52   O'Malley highlighted Jerome Nadal, S.J. (1507-1580) as a rare example of an early Jesuit who had correctly articulated Ignatius's spiritual synthesis. O'Malley, "Early Jesuit Spirituality," 7, 14.

53   O'Malley, "Early Jesuit Spirituality," 17.

54   O'Malley pointed out that "the insistence on the practice of the virtues, the importance attached to sacramental confession of sins and the 'reform of life,' and the insistence in Ignatius's writings to his fellow Jesuits on the practice of obedience could easily lead, in less expansive minds, to moralism and

to which the *Compagnia di Gesù* was committed.[55] But while this was the view that would come to prevail in much of Jesuit spirituality, an alternative perspective also existed. This strain was "more expansive" and "more syncretistic" within the broad tradition of Christian spirituality" and was intent on developing "the implications of the affective and even mystical elements" in the life of Ignatius.[56]

It is important to note that both of these "strains" remained operative within Jesuit spirituality well into the twentieth-century. And in fact, following along these same lines, Dulles suggested that by "the age of Vatican I" two major tendencies existed within Jesuit spirituality with adherents of each considering themselves faithful to Ignatius.[57] The first of these favored a preference for the "Rules of Thinking with the Church" found in the *Exercises* (*SE* 352-370) and certain passages from the *Constitutions* which stressed obedience to the hierarchical Church. This tendency was generally embraced by certain late nineteenth and early twentieth-century neo-Thomist Jesuits who continued in the long tradition of Counter-Reformation dogmatics by basing their theology on "natural reason and on the authority of the papal and conciliar documents."[58] As was the case with O'Malley's "more cautious and soberly ascetical" strain, this tendency was the dominant way through which the *Exercises* were read in the early twentieth-century and in the "deservedly proven writing" of Jesuit commentators that Lacouture was accused of ignoring.

The second tendency Dulles highlighted, out of favor in Rome at the time, preferred "The Rules for the Discernment of Spirits" (*SE* 313-336) and the more mystical aspects of Ignatius's thought.[59] Jesuits

---

a behavioralism that were far from the true intent of the saint." O'Malley, "Early Jesuit Spirituality," 14.

55 O'Malley asserted that this strain "ran the danger of reducing Loyola to a small-minded master of hackneyed precepts." O'Malley, "Early Jesuit Spirituality," 17.

56 O'Malley pointed out that this strain "bordered at times on the Illuminism that Loyola had so emphatically eschewed and wanted to exclude among his followers." O'Malley, "Early Jesuit Spirituality," 17.

57 Dulles, 531.

58 Dulles included Jesuits like Luigi Taparelli d'Azeglio, Matteo Liberaʳ Joseph Kleutgen, and Louis Billot. Dulles, 531.

59 Dulles, 531.

operating out of this tendency "sought to connect theology more intimately with prayer and the experience of the Holy Spirit"—to connect theology with spirituality.[60] Lacouture was clearly operating out of this tendency and so the controversy surrounding his reading of the *Exercises* should be placed within the context of this longer history of tension over how to read Ignatius within the Society of Jesus.

HOW LACOUTURE READ IGNATIUS

I. THE STRUCTURE OF THE RETREAT

As noted earlier, the retreat was based primarily on the First Week of the *Exercises*, though Lacouture seemed to have planned other retreats focusing on the remaining three weeks. Hugo explained that the reason for this emphasis was that the truths learned in this First Week through the contemplation of sin and reorienting of one's life were necessary before any consideration of the life of Christ could be made. [61] These lessons were so necessary, especially in the twentieth-century, that they not only warranted a full week-long retreat, but that that retreat could—and generally should—be made several times.[62] And it is important to remember that such a focus on the First Week of the *Exercises* was not contrary to Ignatius's thinking. Indeed, as was highlighted earlier, the essential concern of the *Exercises*—the "better ordering" of one's life—is laid out in this First Week, with the remaining Weeks confirming that concern.[63]

---

60   Included here were George Tyrrell, Henri Bremond, and Pierre Rousselot. Dulles, 531.

61   Hugo explained that for Lacouture this focus on sin was necessary at the present time because of the prevalence of a pagan mentality, a spirit of naturalism among Catholics. Therefore, retreatants must be led to, "meditate seriously on the fundamental maxims and rules of the Christian mentality, in order that they may have *the mind of Christ*; then, and only then, will they be ready to study the life of Christ with some insight." Hugo, *Sign*, 96.

62   According to Hugo, Lacouture's reason for this recommendation was that he did not consider one retreat enough for "fully assimilating all the elementary truths it contains." With only one retreat, the retreatant was still "insufficiently disposed to go on to the study of Our Lord's life." Hugo, *Sign*, 97.

63   O'Malley, *The First Jesuits*, 40.

Hugo explained that Lacouture saw himself as empowered to structure his retreat this way because of the freedom Ignatius had given directors in the various "Annotations" or "Explanations" at the beginning of the *Exercises*.[64] With such passages as justification, Hugo contended that Lacouture had not strayed from Ignatius's intention for it seemed clear that Ignatius allowed such adaptation.[65] Here again, Hugo seemed to be on solid ground, for in the "Fourth Explanation" (*SE*, 4) Ignatius insisted that the one giving the retreat should focus on the needs of the retreatant and should not move a retreatant from one Week before they are ready. From this pastoral concern, Matthew Ashley has suggested that a "hermeneutical extrapolation" emerges: any "theological interpretation of the *Exercises* will revolve, either implicitly or explicitly, around one particular part of the Exercises," for instance, on one particular Week or accompanying sets of reflections such as the "rules for discerning spirits."[66] As we will see, Lacouture's theological interpretation revolved around the "Principle and Foundation" that opens the *Exercises*.

But while he may have been within Ignatius's proscriptions for focusing the retreat the way he did, Lacouture was not in line with the way most of his fellow Jesuits were leading the *Exercises* at the time. Indeed, Hugo noted that it was not an uncommon practice to lead a retreatant through all of the *Exercises* over the course of just one week, or often even over just the course of a few days. Hugo suggested that one of the reasons why the Jesuit censor had charged Lacouture with departing from the "deservedly proven writings" of Jesuit commentaries on the *Exercises* was that he ignored such a practice—"and of

---

64 At the beginning of the *Exercises*, before the opening of the "Principle and Foundation" and the First Week, these twenty Annotations were offered in order, Ignatius wrote, "to gain some understanding of the spiritual exercises which follow, and to aid both the one who gives them and the one who receives them" (*SE*, 1). Hugo highlighted Explanations 14, 16, and 18 in particular. Hugo, *Sign*, 97.

65 Hugo stated that Lacouture had indeed obeyed Ignatius both in spirit and according to the letter, "whereas his brethren [critics]...are really ignoring the prescriptions of St. Ignatius and are giving a rigid, material obedience to a custom that has grown up contrary to the mind of the saint." H-, *Sign*, 97.

66 Ashley, 20.

course his persistent policy of ignoring it lends color to their charge."[67] But it was this modern practice of leading the entirety of the *Exercises* in just one week, Hugo argued—not Lacouture's concentration on the First Week—that was contrary to the mind of Ignatius.[68]

2. THE "PRINCIPLE AND FOUNDATION"

While the structure of his retreat may have broken with what was common practice at the time, it was Lacouture's interpretation of Ignatius—his "hermeneutical focus"—that truly separated him from the "deservedly proved writings of the commentators" on the *Exercises*. And while the retreat's emphasis on dying to one's self certainly shares much in common with Ignatius's notion of *agere contra*—"to act against" one's natural inclinations (*SE* 13, 322)—Hugo explained that Lacouture's reading of the *Exercises* revolved around the "Principle and Foundation" with which Ignatius opened the First Week. Hugo called this the "Principle and Foundation of Father Lacouture's Exercises."[69]

---

67   Hugo, *Sign*, 95.

68   Hugo argued that such a practice made a "hodge-podge" of a retreat: "In St. Ignatius' plan the weeks are divided logically, and there is a visible unity dominating the whole design. Each week marks off a particular subject matter as its own. But when the meditations of all four weeks are thrown together in a few days, the divisions are obscured, the plan is lost, the unity disappears; and the retreat is simply a jumble of conferences without any discernible connection—unless one has privately studied the *Exercises*. So that, in fact, preaching the *Exercises*, as this duty is materialistically interpreted, means simply that the preacher rifles the treasures of the *Exercises* to put together a series of conferences of his own, a procedure that does not carry out the intent of St. Ignatius or accomplish the purpose that the *Exercises*, rightly handled, are capable of realizing. No doubt, the saint, in the passage quoted above [Annotation 18], allows the First Week to be shortened as well as lengthened where circumstances suggest such a policy. But it would be shortened in favor of well-disposed or advanced souls. In the case of most groups—of beginners, imperfect souls, or those who are unmistakably worldlings—it would rather have to be lengthened. And, in any case, there is nothing in St. Ignatius' words to suggest that all the *Exercises* may be compressed with profit to a retreat of a few days." Hugo, *Sign*, 98.

69   Hugo, *Sign*, 203. Lacouture focused over half his retreat -sixteen conferences over four days—upon the theological truths found in this four-sentence paragraph. For a discussion of the somewhat contested nature of Jesuit interpretation of the "Principle and Foundation," see Ashley, 28 fn.41.

For Lacouture, the importance of the Principle lay in the two fundamental points which it presented: first, that humanity has a distinct
supernatural purpose corresponding to its supernatural final end; and
second, that the implication of that supernatural purpose is detachment from created goods. Lacouture regarded these "truths" as the basis of the *Exercises* and so as the heart of his retreat.[70]

a. Nature and the Supernatural

The "Principle and Foundation" begins with the lines: "Human beings
are created to praise, reverence, and serve God our Lord, and by this
means to save their souls" (SE, 23). Hugo explained that Lacouture
read these lines as clearly indicating that salvation is humanity's final
end and that that final end is indeed supernatural—for to save one's
soul was "to enter into supernatural happiness with God."[71] With this
simple acknowledgement, Ignatius was seen as making explicit the
fact that while the supernatural is distinct from nature, it is not separate from it—an understanding of nature and grace that was key to
Lacouture's interpretation of the *Exercises*.[72]

Having established that human nature has a supernatural final end
distinct but not separated from itself, Ignatius was then read as indicating that the means by which that final end could be attained—"to
praise, reverence and serve God"—are also supernatural.[73] Therefore,
humanity is called to praise, reverence and serve God, not according
to "the dictates of reason or of a merely natural religion," but because
these actions are supernatural and in correspondence with humanity's final end.[74] Such correspondence is what Hugo identified as the
"continuity" in the Christian life, and he explained this continuity in
a way—as will be later shown—that closely resembled the arguments
theologians like de Lubac were making at the same time in France.
Indeed, for Hugo,

---

70 According to Hugo, they became "a rock that steadied him and a beacon
    that guided him in the midst of the doctrinal difficulties proposed and the
    numerous criticisms fiercely made." Hugo, *Sign*, 203.

71 Hugo, *Sign*, 110.

72 Hugo, *Sign*, 104.

73 Hugo, *Sign*, 110.

74 Hugo, *Sign*, 104.

Man was not merely created and left in the order of nature; he was re-created and raised to the order of grace. Man does not live and never has lived, in the state of nature. The state of pure nature is a hypothesis, an abstraction. Although in his present state man retains his human nature and all his natural activity, *he does not retain his purely human or purely natural end: this has been replaced by a supernatural end.* Now an end determines the means that are needed to attain it...So, the fact that man has a supernatural end, determines that the means for attaining this end must also be supernatural. A natural end of man—which does not exist, having been replaced by another—cannot be the Principle and Foundation for Christian living, which is an immediate and urgent duty.[75]

Through the theology presented in these opening lines of the Principle, Hugo explained that Lacouture read the rest of the *Exercises* as an effort to help retreatants live out the practical implications of this account of nature and grace in the Christian life.[76] In short, for Lacouture, the *Exercises* offered training and guidance for discerning how to live a life of holiness—the life of a saint. And so, while Lacouture may indeed have been inconsistent with "deservedly proved writings" of Jesuit commentators, Hugo argued again that he was in line with Ignatius.[77]

b. Detachment

Hugo explained that for Lacouture, a crucial implication of this account of nature and grace is that in order to live a holy life it is necessary to detach from the things of the world, an idea also articulated in the "Principle and Foundation" when Ignatius stated,

The other things on the face of the earth are created for human beings, to help them in working toward the end for which they are created

From this it follows that I should use these things to the extent that they help me toward my end, and rid myself of them to the extent that they hinder me.

To do this, I must make myself indifferent to all created things, in regard to everything which is left to my freedom of will and is not forbidden. Consequently, on my own part I ought not to seek health rather than sickness, wealth rather than poverty, honor rather than

75   Hugo, *Sign*, 104.

76   Hugo, *Sign*, 107.

77   Hugo, *Sign*, 107.

dishonor, a long life rather than a short one, and so on in all other matters.

I ought to desire and elect only the thing which is more conducive to the end for which I am created (SE, 23).

Lacouture understood these lines as Ignatius describing the proper use of the created things of this world. God made the things of this world to assist humanity in pursuing its ultimate end and therefore these things should be used only in so far as they help this purpose and rejected when they become a hindrance, a process which required on-going discernment.

In all this, Ignatius was read as affirming the idea that Christian detachment must be more than simply detachment from what is sinful, for, as Hugo observed, all the things Ignatius highlighted to be renounced—riches, health, honor, and even one's life—are good.[78] But while the desire for riches or health or honor or life is not sinful, Ignatius seemed to recognize that desires for such created things become "disordered tendencies" when they are not properly ordered— when their use is not motivated by the love of God.[79] And so sin is

---

78   Hugo, *Sign*, 117.

79   Hugo, *Sign*, 118. Hugo pointed out that Ignatius made similar descriptions of created goods throughout the *Exercises*. For instance, in the "Prelude for Making Election" (SE, 169) in the Second Week, Ignatius discussed choosing a state of life and wrote that "In every good election, as far as it depends on us, the eye of our intention ought to be simple, only looking at what we are created for, namely, the praise of God our Lord and the salvation of our soul. And so I ought to choose whatever I do, that it may help me for the end for which I am created, not ordering or bringing the end to the means, but the means to the end: as it happens that many choose first to marry—which is a means—and secondarily to serve God our Lord in married life—which service of God is the end. So, too, there are others who first want to have benefices, and then to serve God in them. *So that those do not go straight to God, but want God to come straight to their disordered tendencies, and consequently they make a means of the end, and an end of the means.* So that what they had to take first, they take last; because first we have to set as our aim the wanting to serve God—which is the end—and secondarily, to take a benefice, or to marry, if it is more suitable to us, -which is the means for the end. So, nothing ought to move me to take such means or to deprive myself of them, except only the service and praise of God our Lord and the eternal salvation of my soul." Other examples of this idea of detachment in the *Exercises*: The Sixteenth Annotation (SE, 16), a Note attached to the

not the primary reason for detachment and indifference in Ignatius's thinking, but rather Hugo explained that such detachment is motivated by "the transcendence of nature by the supernatural" and "the nothingness of the creature before the Creator."[80] In other words, Ignatius was understood as calling retreatants to renounce their attachments to things which are good out of a desire for that which is super-eminently better.

OTHER JESUIT READINGS

As was the case with how he structured his retreat, Lacouture's interpretation of the "Principle and Foundation" differed from many other Jesuit commentators at the time. For instance, Hugo highlighted the work of the French Jesuit H. Pinard de la Boulaye, S.J., who wrote extensively on the *Exercises* and had identified three main ways in which the "Principle and Foundation" had been understood. One way was to read Ignatius as taking for his point of departure "some truths of natural philosophy" and therefore as intending to base the Christian life "primarily on rational evidence."[81] Another way understood the Principle as presenting the basis of the *Exercises* as "the first certain truths of reason regarding the origin and end of man" and such truths, Boulaye explained, are also confirmed by faith or "what amounts to the same thing, the first truths of faith on these essential points, truths also immediately justifiable by reason."[82] According to Boulaye, this was the "best founded" reading of the Principle.[83]

But Hugo argued that such interpretations regarded the "Principle and Foundation" as articulating simply that which could be known from "certain truths of reason" and then only later—if at all—confirmed by faith. And therefore, such readings did not take into account,

---

Fourth Day of the Second Week (*SE*, 157), the First Rule (*SE* 338) and the Fifth Rule "In the Ministry of Distributing Alms" (*SE*, 342). Hugo, *Sign*, 117.

80   Hugo wrote that "nature is in the first place to be mortified—and annihilated—quite apart from all sin, because it is the design of God that Christians should live on the supernatural plane." Hugo, *Sign*, 193-194.

81   H.Pinard de la Boulaye, S.J., *Exercices spirituels selon la methode de saint Ignace*, (Paris, 1944), 45-47, translated in Hugo, *Sign*, 105

82   Hugo, *Sign*, 106.

83   Hugo, *Sign*, 106.

"the specifically supernatural character of the Christian life, its supernatural end, [and] the supernatural means necessary to realize this
end."[84] In short, such interpretations did not recognize the practical implications of the supernatural in the Christian life—Ignatius's
"practical mysticism."

As a specific example of such a reading of Ignatius, Hugo pointed
to the English Jesuit Joseph Rickaby, S.J,, whose commentary on the
Exercises stated that on reading the "Principle and Foundation," "your
natural impulse, and impulse which years of acquaintance will not ob-
viate, is to cry Impossible!...No man is bound to the impossible."[85] But,
Rickaby cautioned, such an understanding is to take the Principle too
far, for Ignatius simply,

> follows logically from a truth of natural reason, the existence of God,
> our Creator and Lord... It is a theory of natural religion. But nature
> of itself, in our present state, cannot carry into effect all its own
> prescriptions, even of commandment, still less of counsel, without
> the aid of grace.[86]

But such a reading, Hugo argued, seemed to regard the Principle as
simply "a theory of natural religion"— "Grace is mentioned, but not its
specifically supernatural character; from this account we might easily

---

84   Hugo, Sign, 106.

85   Joseph Rickaby, S.J., The Spiritual Exercises of St. Ignatius Loyola: Spanish
and English, with a Continuous Commentary , (London, Burns Oates, 1915),
19. Hugo provided other examples of Jesuit commentaries on the Exercises
that made similar emphases. Pierre Bouvier, S.J., for instance, had argued
that "the Foundation supposes neither our elevation to the supernatural order, nor the degradation and disorder resulting from the Fall, nor
the teachings, examples, and sacrifice of Jesus Christ." Pierre Bouvier, S.J.
L'interpretation authentique de la Meditation fondamentale dans les Exercices
spirituels de saint Ignace, (Bourges, 1922), 77,[translated in Hugo, Sign,
111]. Other examples included: Aloysius Bellecio, S.J., Spiritual Exercises,
According to the Method of St. Ignatius Loyola, trans. Wm. Hutch, (London:
Burns Oates, 1883), Hugo Hunter, S.J., Sketches for the Exercises of an Eight
Days' Retreat, trans. John B. Kokenge, S.J. (St. Louis: Herder, 1919). Hugo
Sign, 103.

86   Rickaby, 19.

infer that the only function of grace is to help nature to keep the commandments of the natural law."[87]

Put differently, in these commentaries grace is seen as simply *building on* a somewhat self-sufficient nature. Any acknowledgement of *gratia elevans*—the action of grace which Aquinas described as that which perfects human nature by elevating it beyond itself—is missing.[88] Thus, Hugo saw Ignatius's admonition to praise, reverence and serve God as being depicted in these early twentieth-century Jesuit commentaries as a duty "already enjoined by reason" and thus as merely "natural actions." Lost, was any focus on the supernatural—that which is far beyond human nature.[89] Hugo saw such avoidance of the supernatural as stemming from overly apologetical concerns on the part of these Jesuit interpreters. And while these arguments may indeed have had some apologetic value, he saw them as having "little value in showing a Christian his supernatural duties as a son of God"—in short, they did nothing to inspire holiness.[90]

As a result of such interpretations, the rest of the *Exercises* was read as "a merely natural standard of conduct" rather than as a tool for discerning a path to Christian perfection. For Hugo, the problem was not that the existence of the supernatural was denied, but rather that grace—specifically *gratia elevans*—was not recognized as central to the Christian life,

> Man's supernatural elevation must not merely be dutifully mentioned and praised; it must be taken as the decisive fact in determining the meaning of the Christian life and the manner of living it. It is man's elevation to grace that fixes his end—a supernatural end; and this end in turn prescribes that the praise, reverence, and service due to God must be performed in the supernatural order:

---

87   Hugo, *Sign*, 103.

88   Thomas Aquinas, (*ST*, I,1,8).

89   Hugo stated that "No doubt, natural religion is all well and good in its own order. God *might* have been content with it. But in fact He was not. He raised us to a supernatural plane, has given us, in His grace, a share in His own divine life, has placed before us the privilege of supernatural union with Himself, and requires of us supernatural holiness as the condition of realizing this privilege." Hugo, *Sign*, 102.

90   Hugo, *Sign*, 102.

-otherwise there is no proportion between end and means. To do less than this is to misrepresent the Christian life.[91]

And so by not emphasizing the supernatural, these commentaries not only relegated the *Exercises* to that which was "merely natural," they also blurred nature with the supernatural—ignoring what Hugo asserted is a basic distinction in Christian theology.[92] For, the most wonderful thing about a Christian, he argued, is not that she is "created in the order of nature," but that she is "*re-created* in the order of grace."[93] And it is the practical implications of this re-creation by grace—grace perfecting an insufficient nature—that is central to the Ignatian *Exercises*.

HUGO'S APPEAL TO THE TRADITION

For Hugo, then, the theological vision presented in the retreat was firmly rooted in the *Exercises*. The Folly of the Cross—the notion of dying to one's self in order to live a life of holiness—emerged out of Ignatius's theological anthropology and its implications on the Christian life. As suggested earlier, this reading of Ignatius seemed to fall into one of the strains or tendencies through which the *Exercises* have been read by Jesuit spiritual writers, one with a long history. Hugo seemed to have recognized something of this—a fact which is itself significant—and he sought to defend and certify Lacouture's theological vision by looking to "sources" within Jesuit history who shared in this tendency. In sum, Hugo identified an often overlooked tradition of Jesuit spiritual writing—what Pope Francis has recently identified as the "mystical movement" in Jesuit history—and attempted to locate Lacouture within it.

91　Hugo, *Sign*, 105. Hugo pointed out that even though the commentators may mention the supernatural order, they failed to make the supernatural "the decisive function in our lives, the origin of our special duties as Christians, the basis of all spiritual effort and conduct." They missed the fact that the "determinant" of one's conduct was not the fact that one was created, but rather that one was elevated by grace -"the responsibilities of a prince are higher than those of a peasant. So the duties of a child of God are higher, holier, and more urgent than those of a child of nature." Hugo, *Sign*, 115.

92　Hugo pointed out that "the essential purpose of Christianity is to elevate man, by the grace of Jesus Christ, to participate supernaturally in the life of the Trinity." Hugo, *Sign*, 105.

93　Hugo, *Sign*, 104.

THE MYSTICAL MOVEMENT IN
JESUIT SPIRITUALITY

After first identifying similarities with the thinking of Ignatius him-self, Hugo turned to another sixteenth-century Spanish Jesuit for sup-port, Balthasar Alvarez, S.J. (1533-1580). In 1558, Alvarez became the confessor and spiritual director of Teresa of Avila, an assignment that introduced the twenty-five year old Jesuit to the methods of prayer he had not encountered during his years of formation.[94] And while at first opposing the practice of such contemplative or mystical forms of prayer, Alvarez gradually recognized their significance and soon began to encourage the future saint to continue in them. In 1567, Alvarez himself began to practice a type of contemplative prayer in which one remained in a state of quiet repose before the divine—a form of prayer which he reported had eventually allowed him to reach certain mystical states.[95] More importantly, he also began teaching this type of silent prayer to others in the Society.[96]

Such prayer, though, was seen as out of step with the more discursive method of meditative prayer which prevailed in Jesuit spiritual forma-tion at the time. And so from about 1573 on, Alvarez was repeated-ly scrutinized by Jesuit superiors suspicious that he was teaching a form of prayer which they regarded as deviating from the *Exercises*.[97] Alvarez's responses to this scrutiny did not satisfy Everard Mercurian S.J., the superior general of the Society (1573-1581), and in 1577, Alvarez was ordered to cease teaching such methods of prayer—an or-der to which he quickly submitted.[98] For Mercurian, the fear was that Alvarez would turn Jesuits away from the active apostolate and toward a more contemplative focus. Mercurian was no doubt also wary of the

---

94   Pierre Pourrat, S.S., *Christian Spirituality vol. III: From the Renaissance to Jansenism*, trans. W.H. Mitchell (London: Burns, Oates and Washbourne, Ltd. 1926), 113.

95   O'Malley, "Early Jesuit Spirituality," 16.

96   Alvarez was the rector and master of novices several times throughout his life and in the last year of his life was even named superior of the Aragon province. O'Malley, "Early Jesuit Spirituality," 16.

97   O'Mally, "Early Jesuit Spirituality," 16.

98   O'Malley, "Early Jesuit Spirituality," 16.

still lingering accusations linking Ignatius with the *Alumbrados*.[99] In 1578, Mercurian banned contemplative practices from the Society all together.[100] Thus discursive prayer—advocated by Rodriguez and others—was affirmed as *the* Jesuit method of prayer.[101]

Not surprisingly, none of Alvarez's writings were published during his lifetime, instead, it was his disciple (the Venerable) Luis de la Puente, S.J. who secured Alvarez's place in the history of Jesuit spiritual writing. In 1615, Puente published a biography of his teacher, *Vida del Padre Baltasar Alvarez*, which went on to become a classic spiritual work, influencing the likes of Augustine Baker (1588-1685) and St. Alphonso de Liguori (1696-1787).[102] Alvarez's biography also greatly influenced a seventeenth-century French Jesuit named Louis Lallemant (1587-1635).[103] And it was on this French Jesuit that Hugo focused a great deal of his attention, arguing that it was to Lallemant's particular "school" of Jesuit spirituality that Lacouture should be read as belonging.

Louis Lallemant entered the Society of Jesus in 1605 and spent almost his entire Jesuit life at the Jesuit College in Rouen in Northern France, where he served as spiritual director, rector, master of novices, and tertian-master.[104] Many young Jesuits passed under Lallemant's

99   Pourrat observed, "Did not prudence counsel this? There were so many and such dangerous errors about prayer, and they were to be met with... at every turn! Lastly the Inquisition was on the watch, and woe to anyone whom it set upon!" Pourrat, 118.

100   McKeon, 12. According to Pourrat, "The religious of the Society were bound still more firmly to the method of prayer of the *Exercises*, which many of them appeared to disdain. They were also forbidden to read certain mystics, and especially Tauler and Harphius, without special authorization." Pourrat, 118.

101   It should be noted that Mercurian's successor, Claudio Aquaviva, S.J. (1581-1606), lifted the ban in 1599 and tried to recover and give life to the more mystical strain in Ignatian spirituality—as did the future saint, Robert Bellarmine, S.J. (1542-1621) who around the same time had been speaking on the "liberty of the spirit." O'Malley, "Early Jesuit Spirituality," 17.

102   Modern editions of Alvarez's writings have since been published. O'Malley, "Early Jesuit Spirituality," 16.

103   O'Malley, "Early Jesuit Spirituality," 16.

104   Details of Lallemant's biography are taken from Michael Buckley, S.J., "Seventeenth-Century French Spirituality: Three Figures," in *Christian*

guidance at Rouen including Jean de Brebeuf, Antoine Daniel, and Isaac Jogues—three Jesuits who would go on to be martyred in the North American missions and then later canonized. Like Alvarez, Lallemant left no published materials behind after his death. But two of his former tertians, Jean Rigoleuc, S.J. (1595-1658) and Jean Joseph Surin, S.J. (1600-1665)[105] kept their notes from Lallemant's lectures.[106] And these notes eventually made their way to Pierre Champion, S.J. (1631-1701) who published them in 1694 under the title, *La vie et la doctrine spirituelle de Père Louis Lallemant.*[107]

Spirituality III , ed. Louis Dupre and Don E. Saliers (New York: Crossroad, 1989).

105   Surin was one of the more famous of Lallemant's "tertians." His legacy largely surrounded his involvement, beginning in 1635, with a community of Ursuline nuns in Loudon and the demonic possession believed to have occurred there. For the next twenty-five years, Surin suffered severe mental imbalances that he attributed to demonic possession. It was in this state that Surin also wrote one of the great classics in spiritual writing, the *Spiritual Catechism* (1657). The *Catechism*, which gained the approval of Bossuet in 1661, carried the influence of both Surin and Lallemant into the eighteenth century where it helped shape the spirituality of Jean Pierre Caussade, S.J. and Jean Grou, S.J. in the nineteenth-century. It was also claimed to have had a "decisive effect" on Raissa and Jacques Maritain. Buckley, 63. Surin's involvement at Loudon was memorialized in Aldous Huxley's *The Devils of Loudon* (1953).

106   François Courel has noted the significance of the audience for which Lallemant's teaching was aimed: young Jesuit priests in their third year of novitiate ("tertianship") which followed years of novitiate, studies, and ministry. Jesuits in this stage of formation would have been much more open to Lallemant's doctrine, Courel explained, since at " the heart of the Doctrine, in order to work that radical reform, there is the spiritual discernment which commands all of the thought of Lallemant, as it commands all the advance of the *Exercises*...One is not able to comprehend Lallemant, we believe, if one does not place at the center of every interpretation this discernment, this 'guidance of the Spirit,' which leads to the 'service of Christ.'" Francois Courel, "Introduction" *La vie et la doctrine spirituelle de Père Louis Lallemant* (nouvelle ed., Collection Christus 3; Paris: Desclée de Brouwer, 1979), 24 [trans. Buckley, 56].

107   Alan McDougall, ed., *The Spiritual Doctrine of Father Louis Lallemant of the Society of Jesus of the Society of Jesus, Preceded by an Account of his Life by Father Champion, S.J.* (Westminster, MD: The Newman Book Shop, 1946).

As was the case with Alvarez,[108] Lallemant was at the forefront of an incredible flourish of spiritual writing taking place during a time in Jesuit history not commonly associated with such writing, especially in France.[109] Indeed, writing on the significance of Lallemant's often overlooked "school" of spirituality, Henri Bremond—the sometimes Jesuit—wrote:

> More integral, more original, twenty times more sublime and twenty times more austere, more demanding than Port-Royal, the school which we are going to study made little noise. Its contemporaries scarcely suspected that it existed; Saint-Beuve did not speak of it; and for the most part, the Catholic of today knows nothing about it except its name. Its founder, the Jesuit Louis Lallemant died in 1635 without having written anything. Among the disciples of that great man, only one, Father Surin, has achieved recognition [*glorie*], but a recognition that was contested, for a long time suspect, and one of infinite sorrow.[110]

With such a legacy—or lack thereof—the fact that Hugo was even aware of Jesuits like Lallemant is noteworthy, as is his claim that Lacouture should be understood as part of Lallemant's "school."[111]

Buckley noted that a great deal of speculation surrounds the authorship of the *Spiritual Doctrine*, with many scholars believing it to have been largely written by Surin himself. Buckley, 55.

108 In the short biography he added to the *Spiritual Doctrine*, Champion wrote: "Some have considered with much reason that Fr. Louis Lallemant held the same place among the Jesuits of France which Fr. Alvarez occupied among those of Spain. He certainly united in an eminent degree, as did that celebrated director of St. Teresa, the knowledge and the practice of mystical theology, and like him, numbered among his disciples the most spiritual and interior men whom the Society has ever had amongst us." Champion, 17.

109 On the Society of Jesus in seventeenth-century France, Buckley observed, "Moralists, educators, savants, Molinists, and, yes, missionaries. Such is the constellation of the French Jesuits of the period, one dipped in blood through the martyrdoms in North America and in poison through the devastating satire of Pascal." Buckely, 54.

110 Henri Bremond, *Histoire*, v 5, 4 [trans. Buckely, 54].

111 The bulk of Hugo's familiarity with Lallemant and these other Jesuits seems to have come from Bremond's *Histoire*, Pourrat's *Christian Spirituality*, and Lallemant's *The Spiritual Doctrine* itself. Dorothy Day also had a familiarity with Lallemant, and credited her first spiritual director, Joseph

THE *SPIRITUAL DOCTRINE* OF
FATHER LOUIS LALLEMANT

Following the layout of Ignatius's *Exercises*, Lallemant's *Spiritual Doctrine* opened with a discussion of human nature:

> There is a void in our heart which all creatures united would be unable to fill. God alone can fill it; for he is our beginning and our end. The possession of God fills up this void, and makes us happy. The privation of God leaves in us this void, and is the cause of our wretchedness.
>
> Before God fills up this void, he puts us in the way of faith; with this condition, that if we never cease to regard him as our last end, if we use creatures with moderation, and refer to his service the use we make of them, at the same time contributing faithfully to the glory which it is his will to draw from all created beings, he will give himself to us to fill up the void within us, and make us happy. But if we are wanting in fidelity, he will leave in us that void which, left unfilled, will cause our supreme misery.[112]

Commenting on this, Michael Buckley, S.J. noted that Lallemant's spiritual doctrine centered on a particular theological anthropology—one of human emptiness seeking the fullness of God.[113] Thus, like Ignatius, Lallemant presented nature and grace not in terms of incompatibility or separation, but rather as a dynamic progression from void and fulfillment—the emptiness of human nature and the plenitude of God. And so human nature itself is recognized as being marked by a longing emptiness distinct from the fullness of the supernatural. Yet at the same time, human nature is not separated from the supernatural, but rather is intimately and dynamically connected with it as its final destiny and fulfillment.

Starting with these distinctions, Lallemant cautioned that the things of this world, while good, often worked to distract a person

---

McSorley, with introducing her to Lallemant's writings. See, William Portier, "Dorothy Day and her first spiritual director, Fr. Joseph McSorley, C.S.P." *Houston Catholic Worker*, (September-October 2002): 5.

112   McDougall, 28.

113   As Buckley noted: "The spirituality of Lallemant opens with an antithetical dynamic contrast. It is not that of contradiction but of privation and its fulfillment." Buckley, 56.

from God.[114] For the habitual attachment to these created goods, particularly to oneself ("we desire to be our own last end") deceives and eventually diverts a person from union with God.[115] Again like Ignatius, these created goods were not regarded as sinful, but neither were they supernatural, and so detachment from them becomes necessary. Lallemant's *Spiritual Doctrine* taught the renunciation of all interests, satisfactions, designs, and choices in order to be dependent only on "the good pleasure of God" and to be resigned "entirely into his hands."[116]

All of this took shape in what Lallemant called *la vie spirituelle*—a life made up of a twofold path along which Christian perfection could be reached: the purification of the heart and the guidance of the Holy Spirit.[117] In this, Lallemant's account of nature and grace again becomes apparent: the call for purification implies the emptiness of human nature, while the need to correspond with the Spirit reveals the fullness of grace.[118] For Lallemant, this purification was a gradual process that included the purification of a person's motives and consciousness in order to ultimately become the work of God. [119]

114 (*SD* I.1.2) McDougall, 28.

115 (*SD*, II.1.1.2.3) McDougall, 37.

116 (*SD*, II.1.1.2.3) McDougall, 37. Also see (*SD*. I.1.5) McDougall, 29.

117 (*SD*, IV.2.1.1) Buckely, 57.

118 Buckley, 57.

119 (*SD*, III.1.3.2) McDougall, 83. The first degree was attained mainly through penance which freed one from actual sins and the penalty due to them. The next degree was reached through mortification and the virtues and rid the person of evil habits and disordered attachments or affections. The third, attained in the sacraments, delivered a person from the "tinder" of sin—*fomes peccati*. And the final degree, reached through contemplative or mystical union with God, removed that "weakness which is natural to us" as creatures taken out of nothingness—what he termed human nature's "defectibility." Buckely, 59.

In *The Devils of Loudun*, Aldous Huxley included a lengthy section on Lallemant, as Surin was one of the main characters of the book. Huxley wrote that "Purification of the heart is to be achieved by intense devotion, by frequent communion and by an unsleeping self-awareness, aimed at the detection and mortification of every impulse to sensuality, pride and self-love...In this place our themes are the process of mortification and the 'natural man,' who has to be mortified. The corollary of "Thy kingdom

And such purity of heart sought to remove any obstacles to grace and restore the emptiness that marked human nature—what Lallemant called *la parfaite nudité d'esprit* ("the perfect nudity of the soul")—so that it could be filled with the superabundance of grace.[120] In short, grace was understood as always available, waiting to take possession of and correspond with a "purified soul." The task of the *vie spirituelle*, then, was to remove any obstacles to this correspondence and the perfection it would bring about. When a person had given himself up to grace, the Holy Spirit would then guide him gradually by an "interior light."[121] Lallemant described the guidance attained through this process of docility in terms of "the gifts of the Holy Spirit."[122]

But for all his teaching on purification and "the perfect nudity of the soul" it must be remembered that Lallemant spent his life working primarily in the formation of young Jesuits like St. Isaac Jogues— men very much engaged in the active life. In fact, Buckley has noted that Lallemant's *vie spirituelle* composed a life given over in apostolic service—a "service whose underlying determination [is] toward God as motive and in union with the Spirit as configuring guide."[123] And so, far from inhibiting such ministry, Lallemant saw his spiritual doctrine—and the mystical or supernatural union to which it sought—as

---

come' is 'our kingdom go." Huxley, *The Devils of Loudun* (New York: Harper Brothers, 1953), 77.

120   (*SD*, II.1.1.2.3) McDougall, 37. When thoroughly cleansed, "God fills the soul and all its powers, memory, understanding, will—with His holy presence and His love." (*SD*, III. 1.2. 1) McDougall, 81.

121   (*SD*, IV.1.1.1) McDougall, 108. As with the process of purification, the steps by which one developed the "docility" necessary for this guidance were spelled out: first, by being faithful to this guidance as it was offered; then, through the purification of sin and imperfections which "clouded" one's view of the Spirit's working; next, by not allowing oneself to be governed by "exterior senses" so that the "interior senses" could be opened instead; fourth, through an "awareness" of one's interior life and its movements; and finally, in the consistent use of spiritual direction. (*SD*, IV.1.3.5) McDougall, 112, Buckley, 59.

122   (*SD*, IV.3.2.1) Buckley, 60. (*SD*, VII. 1.4. 2) McDougall, 264. According to Pourrat, Lallemant's use of a theology of the gifts of the Holy Spirit" to explain contemplation was from the Rhenish and Flemish mystics like Tauler and Ruysbroeck. Pourrat, 55.

123   Buckley, 60.

necessary for such work. [124] In this way, Lallemant can be seen as trying to hold together Ignatius's "practical mysticism" in the spirituality
he taught to the young Jesuits at Rouen. [125]

LACOUTURE AND THE MYSTICAL MOVEMENT

Jesuits like Lallemant and Alvarez were clearly part of a tradition of
Ignatian spiritual writers that seemed to fit with O'Malley's "more expansive and more syncretistic" strain in Jesuit spirituality, as well as
with the tendency for thinking with the "rules for the discernment of
spirits" which Dulles highlighted. [126] What is interesting is that Hugo
seemed to recognize something of the significance of these often forgotten—at least in the 1940s—Jesuits when he argued that it was
through their spiritual vision that Lacouture should be understood
as "their heir, related at least by affinity, their son, begotten through

---

124   (*SD*, VII.4.5.1) Buckley, 61. Lallemant wrote that without contemplation, "we shall never make much progress in virtue, and shall never be fitted
to make others advance therein. We shall never entirely rid ourselves of our
weaknesses and imperfections. We shall remain always bound to earth, and
shall never rise much above mere natural feelings. We shall never be able to
render to God a perfect service. But with it we shall effect more, both for
ourselves and for others, in a month, than without it we should accomplish
in ten years." (*SD*, VII.4.4.2) McDougall, 264.

125   The rapid expansion of Jesuit colleges in France at the time demanded
so much active ministry that it threatened the interior life which Ignatius
saw as necessary to sustain such work. Buckley suggested that therefore
one must presuppose "the dominant experience behind the *Doctrine spirituelle* to be that of apostolic call, and the rest of Lallemant falls easily into
place." Buckley, 62. Louis Cognet noted that Lallemant's teaching did not
go without controversy, for in 1629, Mutius Vitelleschi, the Jesuit superior
general, censured Lallemant's spirituality as being contrary to the "spirit of
the Society." Louis Cognet, *Post-Reformation Spirituality* trans. P. Hepburne
Scott (New York: Hawthorne Books, 1959), 85.

126   In his list of seventeenth-century Jesuit disciples of Lallemant, Cognet
included, in addition to Rigoleuc, Surin and Champion: Jean-Baptiste
Saint-Jure (1588-1657), Jacques Nouet (1605-1680), Vincent Huby (1603-
1693), Julien Maunoir (1606-1683), Francois Guillore (1615-1684), Jean
Crasset (1618-1692), and Claude de la Colombiere (1641-1682) who was
the spiritual director of St. Mary Margaret Alacoque (1647-1690). Cognet,
107.

a mysterious spiritual atavism."[127] For like Lacouture, these Jesuits sought to somehow maintain the "practical mysticism" of Ignatius, recognizing that the supernatural had practical implications for the Christian life—implications that involved something much more than simply avoiding sin by following the natural law. They also recognized and emphasized that all Christians—not just spiritual elites—were called to live such a life of holiness.[128]

Despite its popularity in the seventeenth-century, by the late eighteenth-century Lallemant and his "school" were largely forgotten or ignored within the Society of Jesus.[129] Hugo suggested that this neglect of Lallemant was a primary reason for why so many of "the modern Commentators" have removed any emphasis on the supernatural from their readings of the *Exercises*, for,

> when essential elements of the supernatural order are lost—liberty of spirit, the unity of prayer, the continuity of the Christian life, the doctrine that all may aspire to the highest perfection, which is mystical union with God—the others are likely to go also.[130]

For Hugo, the criticism and opposition to Lacouture's retreat should be read within the context of this broader Jesuit history.

But while Hugo's assertion of deliberate neglect by the Society of Jesus may have some validity, it must also be acknowledged that Lallemant was part of a group of spiritual writers—including St. Teresa of Avila, St. John of the Cross, Cardinal Pierre Berulle, and St. Frances de Sales—who wrote from the time just after the Protestant Reformation until the controversy surrounding Quietism at the end of the seventeenth-century.[131] And in fact it was the Quietist contro-

---

127   See Hugo, *Sign*, 163.

128   Hugo wrote that Lacouture knew "the school of Lallemant" and that it was "perhaps from their teaching that he had learned that all may desire and dispose themselves to mystical graces." Hugo, *Sign*, 164.

129   Hugo explained that it was Rodriguez's interpretation of the *Exercises*, and not that of Lallemant, which were placed in hands of Jesuit novices and on the shelves of Jesuit libraries. Hugo, *Sign*, 155.

130   Hugo, *Sign*, 163.

131   In his volume on the period, Bremond used the term "Berullian Jesuits" to categorize many of these Jesuits including Lallemant. Pourrat disputed this claim, arguing that themes of mysticism and detachment are in fact Ignatian. Cognet and Buckley both seem to agree that Lallemant, though

versy which brought about the abrupt end of this amazing flourish of
spiritual writing. That Hugo would turn to early modern pre-Qui-
etist writers like Lallemant, as well as John of the Cross and Frances
de Sales, is therefore significant. For it was in the aftermath of the
Quietist controversy that such writers became suspect, as a particular
view of all things mystical or supernatural descended upon Catholic
thinking—a view which endured up to the time when Lacouture and
Hugo were giving their retreats and facing criticism. And so, to understand the criticism of the retreat as well as the significance of Hugo's
efforts at *ressourcement* to defend it, an understanding of the Quietist
controversy and its legacy is important.

QUIETISM

The Quietist controversy emerged in the latter half of the seven-
teenth-century with the growing popularity of the teachings of a
Spanish priest and doctor of theology at the Univeristy of Coimbra,
Miguel de Molinos (1628-1696).[132] In his extremely popular *Spiritual
Guide*, Molinos argued that only purely passive, contemplative prayer
lead to spiritual perfection and to attain it one had to concentrate

---

sharing much in common with Berulle, was essentially Ignatian at heart.
Perhaps more interesting is the Ignatian influence on Berulle. For Berulle
was a student at the Jesuit College of Clermont and made the *Spiritual
Exercises* in 1602 in Verdun. One of Berulle's earliest spiritual writings
was *Bref discours de l'abnegation interieure* (1597) which was a "translation"
of an Italian work *Breve compendio intorno alla perfezione cristiana*, a work
attributed to the visionary and mystic Isabella Bellinzaga, but whose true
author was understood to be her spiritual director, the Italian Jesuit Achille
Gagliardi (1537-1607). Gagliardi wrote one of the earliest commentaries
on the *Spiritual Exercises*. Gagliardi's writings led to him being charged with
introducing a monastic spirit into the Society of Jesus, and the controversy that followed required Claudio Aquaviva (the Jesuit superior general) as
well as Pope Clement VIII to intervene on Gagliardi's behalf. O'Malley, 21.
For more on Berulle, see Raymond Deville, *The French School of Spirituality*
trans. Agnes Cunningham (Pittsburgh: Duquesne University Press, 1994)
and *Berulle and the French School: Selected Writings* trans. Lowell Glendon,
S.S., William Thompson ed. (Mahwah, NJ: Paulist Press, 1989).

132   Molinos's *Spiritual Guide* was printed in both Spanish and Italian.
Dupré, 133. For an account of "pre-quietists" and their influence on Molinos
and , see Pourrat chapters 5-7.

entirely on an inner quiet.[133] Once in this state of disinterested or "pure love" (*pur amour*), a person would become totally passive or "quiet" and thus completely opened to the workings of God. Molinos asserted that human activity—particularly strenuous ascetical practices—would disturb that spiritual quiet and thereby become an obstacle to divine action.[134] As a result of such teachings, many of Molinos's disciples began to regard liturgical practices and sacraments as somewhat pointless—if not detrimental—for those in a state of *pur amour*.[135] They also taught that a person in this state should give up any resistance to sin. Not surprisingly, then, in 1687, sixty-eight propositions taken from Molinos's writings were condemned by Innocent XI in *Coelestis Pastor*.[136] Molinos admitted guilt to all charges and was imprisoned for nine years in the papal jail where he died.[137] And any teachings associated with the condemned proposals soon began to be labeled as "Quietist." Interestingly for our discussions here, Louis Dupré has pointed out that while it was Jesuits who first attacked Molinos's teachings for what they regarded as its threat to their more discursive method of prayer, it was also in the writings of an Italian Jesuit named Achille Gagliardi that the first identifiable—and orthodox—notions of "Quietism" emerged in the late sixteenth-century.[138]

Two years prior to the promulgation of *Coelestis Pastor*, a French mystic and lay woman named Madame Jeanne Guyon (1648-1717)

---

133   Louis Dupré, "Jansenism and Quietism," *Christian Spirituality: Post-Reformation and Modern* (New York: Crossroads Publishing, 1991): 121-142 at 133.

134   Dupré, 133.

135   William Portier and C.J.T. Talar, "Mystical Element of Modernist Crisis," in *Modernists & Mystics*, ed. C.J.T. Talar (Washington, DC: CUA Press, 2009), 3.

136   Innocent summarized the condemned "Quietist" teachings as: "God allows and wills the Devil to violate the bodies of some perfected souls and make them do wicked things, with all their wits about them and without feeling any scruple." *Coelestis Pastor*, Proposition 41, trans. Pourrat, 167.

137   Dupré, 134.

138   Gagliardi's book *Breve compendio intorno alla perfezione critiana* began circulating sometime before 1596 and was published in 1611 and was very influential for writers such as Bérulle and Surin, and was even paraphrased by Albert Camus. Dupré, 133.

published *A Short and Easy Method of Prayer* (*Moyen court et facile de faire oraison*) (1685).[139] In it, she instructed her readers on how to "quiet" their emotions and other mental faculties through contemplative prayer in order to grow in union with God in a state of "pure love," a love so pure that even love of one's self faded away—including the love of one's own salvation.[140] Guyon's book and teachings soon became very popular throughout elite circles in France and attracted many disciples, most notably François Fénelon (1651-1715), a member of the royal court and the future archbishop of Cambrai.[141] Appearing as it did in the midst of the controversy surrounding Molinos's teachings, many in France saw Guyon's advocacy of quiet abandonment to the divine as leading down the same path as the propositions condemned by Innocent XI. Chief among Guyon's critics was Jacques-Bénigne Bossuet (1627-1704), bishop of Meaux. While Bossuet did recognize that the mystical writing had a long history within the Christian tradition, he was suspicious of it and regarded it as being largely the

---

139   Pourrat suggests that one of the concerns with the teachings of Guyon and Molinos was not that it pointed to the possibility that such mystical states could be achieved in contemplative prayer, but that such states could be achieved rather easily and even quickly.

140   Talar has described this kind of love: "The mystical language of self-abandonment, death to self, and allied terms form a matrix for understanding disinterested love. Spiritual death does not occur without mortification. But asceticism remains rigorously a means. A desire to derive satisfaction for its successful exercise can paradoxically lead to a more subtle form of self-attachment just as one may become attached to consolations that can accompany prayer, and mistake those for love of God. Hence the experience of aridity, even to the point of feeling abandoned by God, that emerges with advancing stages of prayer. In these respects disinterested love stands in continuity with the spiritual tradition...When joined with an Augustinian anthropology that gives primacy to the will, such love entails radical adherence to the will of God, the replacement of the self-will by the divine will, and the forgetfulness of self, of all that prevents or hinders becoming one with God." C.J.T. Talar, "Prayer at Twilight: Henri Bremond's *Apologie pour Fénelon*," in *Modernists & Mystics*, ed. C.J.T. Talar (Washington, DC: CUA Press, 2009), 58.

141   For a time Madame de Maintenon, wife of Louis XIV, was enamored with Guyon's teachings. In fact, in *Apologie pour Fenelon*, Henri Bremond placed Maintenon at the center of a conspiracy that led to the Quietist controversy. Talar, 50.

exclusive concern of cloistered monks and nuns—the Church's spiritual elites. [142] And so, working out of such a "two-tiered" notion of the Christian life, Bossuet saw quiet contemplative prayer and the desire for mystical union with God as something that was not a part of the life of an "ordinary" Christian—laity and secular clergy alike.

In 1695, at Guyon's request, Bossuet called together a conference at Issy, outside of Paris, to evaluate her spiritual teachings. Fénelon attended to defend Guyon. Despite such a defense, the conference issued the "Articles of Issy" which condemned thirty-four propositions in Guyon's writings having to do with disinterested love and contemplative prayer—propositions considered to be similar to those of Molinos. [143] Though Guyon—like Molinos—submitted to this ecclesiastical censure, she would nevertheless later be imprisoned at various times throughout her life because of her teachings. [144]

In response to Issy and what he perceived to be Bossuet's direct attack on the Christian mystical tradition, Fénelon—recently installed as archbishop of Cambrai—published *The Maxims of the Saints* (*Explication des maxims des saints sur la vie intérieure*) (1697), which highlighted various mystical writers within the Christian tradition in order to justify Guyon's teachings. For Fénelon, at issue was not so much the particularities of Guyon's teachings, but rather the basic soundness of the theology expressed by early-modern spiritual writers like Francis de Sales, Teresa of Avila, Pierre Berulle, John of the Cross,

---

142   Talar, 41. Talar has noted that Bossuet's concern over the teachings of Guyon and Fénelon were twofold. First, unlike Fénelon, Bossuet did not believe that such love could be truly distinterested—i.e. purified of all self-interest. For Bossuet, "to acknowledge and affirm God as good in himself necessarily encompassed loving God as good for the self." Bossuet also thought that Guyon and Fénelon had taken the idea of pure love to the point were holy indifference could become holy passivity: "so great becomes the emphasis on God's work in the soul that the active exercise of virtue can become lost to view." Talar, 60.

143   Portier and Talar, 3.

144   William James, in *The Varieties of Religious Experience* (New York: New York American Library, 1958), 227, held up Madam Guyon's apparent indifference to her imprisonment as an example of what an active form of "resignation" can take in more optimistic religious temperaments.

Catherine of Genoa, as well as Guyon. [145] Indeed, it was this tradition of mystical writing itself that Fénelon regarded as having been
condemned at Issy. A literary back and forth ensued between Fénelon
and Bossuet, ending with Pope Innocent XII censuring twenty-three
propositions in *Explication des maxims* in 1699.[146] And that, followed
by Fénelon's quick submission, brought the Quietist controversy to an
end.

THE LEGACY OF THE QUIETIST CONTROVERSY

But while this Quietist controversy was itself relatively small—taking
place within a span of a dozen years (1687-1699) and mainly involving French ecclesiastical elites—its repercussions were much more
broadly felt. For almost immediately afterward, an "anti-mystical" attitude descended upon Catholic thought and more mystical spiritual
teaching—already in decline by this time—largely disappeared from
the public arena.[147] This decline left a clear void in Christian spirituality and not surprisingly the period following the Quietist controversy was marked by a vigorous resurgence of Jansenism through the
writings of Pasquier Quesnel (1634-1719) and others. Indeed, this
eighteenth-century Jansenist revival was in many ways brought on and
enabled by the Quietist controversy, filling as it did the spiritual void
left in its aftermath.[148] And this revived form of Jansenism—which

145   Talar, 52. English translation in *Fénelon: Selected Writings* trans. Chad
Helms (Mahwah, NJ: Paulist Press, 2006).

146   Six weeks after *Explication des maximes* was published, Bossuet published *Instruction sur le les états d'oraison*, a book he had, in fact, written before Fénelon's book and which Bossuet reportedly sent Fénelon a manuscript. Indeed, Pourrat suggested Fénelon's view that Bossuet disregarded
mystical writers was influenced by what Fénelon read in Bossuet's book. In
response, Fénelon wrote *Instruction pastorale* in September, 1697 in defense
of the criticized passages in his book. Bossuet replied in February, 1698 with
Préface sur l'Instruction pastorale and again in June, 1698 with *Rélation sur le
quiétisme*. In this second statement Bossuet openly ridiculed Fénelon, calling
him "the Montanus of this new Priscilla." Pourrat, 217.

147   Talar, 39.

148   For, as one scholar of the period explained, "It was the right moment
for [Jansenism] to come back and give free reign to its hostility to mysticism,
confounding true and false in a single reprobation. The Jansenists had been
most violent in their criticism of the Quietists, who had dared claim that

strongly promoted a rigorist asceticism coupled with the notion that only a few predestined souls would ever be able to attain mystical union—thrived in the anti-mystical atmosphere that the censure of Fénelon had engendered.[149] Following this Jansenist resurgence, the emphasis on the love of God—seen in the writings of Lallemant—quickly gave way in popular spiritual writings to an emphasis on the fear of God.[150]

The upshot of all this is that in reaction to Quietism, more mystical forms of spiritual writing became suspect. As Michel de Certeau, S.J. pointed out in *The Mystic Fable*, by the end of the seventeenth-century, the adjective "mystical" (*mystique*) had become the noun "mysticism" (*la mystique*).[151] And packaged as such, the mystical or supernatural

---

they provided an easy way for everybody to attain a close and happy union with God." Pourrat, 265.

149   In their introduction to Maurice Blondel's *The Letter on Apologetics and History and Dogma*, Alexander Dru and Illtyd Trethowan summarized this important moment in Catholic theology: "And if, as Claudel says, the influence of Jansenism persisted—surviving a persecution which did not stop at desecrating the graves of Port-Royal—and if its spirit pervaded the theological manuals of the nineteenth century, this was because, once the true spiritual tradition had been driven underground and silenced, the choice lay between an official religion, l'hyocrisie majestueuse (Maritain) of the Gallican Church, relying on the secular arm, and, on the other hand, a private, puritanical, and anti-mystical religion reacting against it—the religion of the Jansenists, the declared enemies of Fénelon. Alexandare Dru and Illtyd Trethowan, "Introduction" in Maurice Blondel, *The Letter on Apologetics and History and Dogma* trans. Alexander Dru and Illtyd Trethowan (New York: Holt, Rinehart and Winston, 1964), 23.

150   Robert McKeon described this legacy as being that "mysticism seemed like something remote from what ordinary Christians could aspire to. Inner peace and intimacy with God, which are achieved through prayer from the heart, just don't fit the pessimistic view of the human being who always re-mains unsure of where he stands in God's eyes." Robert McKeon, ed. Pierre Caussade, *A treatise on prayer from the heart: A Christian mystical tradition recovered for all* (St. Louis: The Institute of Jesuit Sources, 1998), 28.

151   Michel de Certeau, *The Mystic Fable*, vol.1, *The Sixteenth and Seventeenth Centuries*, trans. Michael B. Smith (Chicago: University of Chicago Press, 1992), 16, 76-77, 107-113.

became neatly marginalized and quarantined within the tradition.[152] Thus, within Catholicism, the prevailing understanding of mystical prayer largely followed Bossuet's notion that it was an extraordinary phenomenon reserved for the spiritually elite monitored in far-off cloisters.[153] Desire for union with God quickly came to be seen as something outside of the life of "ordinary" Christians.[154] And with this, the renaissance of spiritual writing that Lallemant was a part of and which flourished at the start of the seventeenth-century—with its emphasis on the implications of mystical or supernatural in the life of *all* Christians—all but slipped away by the end of that century.

Recognition that this legacy of the Quietist controversy and the revived Jansenism which resulted lingered on well into the twentieth century is important. If nothing else, it puts to question the assertions made by both Hugo's critics and by many contemporary scholars that the retreat theology was in some way "Jansenist." For the retreat—with its call to holiness for ordinary Christians—falls more on the side of Fénelon and Guyon in the Quietism-Jansenism divide.

JEAN PIERRE DE CAUSSADE, S.J. (1675-1751)

While the anti-mystical repercussions of the Quietist controversy were broad, a few spiritual writers continued to emphasize that union with God was a necessary part of the Christian life and was accessible to ordinary Christians. In noting this fact, Hugo highlighted Jean Pierre de Caussade, S.J. as an example of a Jesuit writer who continued the tradition of Ignatian mystical writing—that of Alvarez and Lallemant—into the eighteenth century. Hugo even placed Caussade within Lallemant's "school," portraying him as one of the few

---

152   William Portier and C.J.T. Talar, "Mystical Element of the Modernist Crisis" in *Modernists & Mystics*, ed. C.J.T. Talar (Washington, DC: CUA Press, 2009), 17.

153   According to C.J.T. Talar, "Though mystical experience could not be denied, forming as it did part of the accepted tradition of the Church, still there was the sense that it needed to be kept under surveillance, subject to theological scrutiny and supervision. Certainly, mystical experience continued within Catholicism but it was largely confined to convent and cloister and so remained for the most part hidden, a marginal phenomenon." Talar, 42.

154   McKeon, 28.

Jesuits, along with Jean Nicholas Grou, S.J. (1731-1803), to extend Lallemant's theological vision into the eighteenth-century.[155]

The bulk of Caussade's surviving work is from the years 1730-39, when he served as spiritual director for the sisters of the Order of the Visitation of the Blessed Virgin Mary in Nancy in the Northeast of France—most of Caussade's writings were copied and compiled by the sisters.[156] Throughout these writings, Caussade looked to restore and preserve contemplative prayer—what he called "prayer from the heart"—as a practice to which all Christians were called.[157] And such prayer required silence or "attentive pauses" as well as purification in order to attain union with God. Caussade taught that one of the major concerns of this type of prayer consisted in working to renounce merely "natural activity" which would become a "great imperfection" when it begins to oppose "the gentle peace of the Spirit of God."[158]

In the face of suspicion and opposition from within the Society of Jesus, Caussade sought to certify the worth of this kind of prayer by turning not only to spiritual giants like Teresa of Avila, John of the Cross, and Frances de Sales, but also to his fellow Jesuits Lallemant, Rigoleuc and Surin.[159] For all of these writers identified what Hugo called the "continuity in the Christian life"—one's supernatural destiny implied that one was called to live a supernatural life. And such a life required giving up "natural activity" so that one could abandon oneself to the divine will. Indeed renunciation of one's self was central to Caussade's notion of the "sacrament of the present moment"—the notion of letting God control one's life by letting the present moment govern one's life, as he explained,

---

155   According to Hugo, these Jesuits, "bear the same characteristics as their spiritual ancestors in the Society... [and] suffer the same trials." Hugo, *Sign*, 161. As was noted, much of Caussade's knowledge of Lallemant's teaching has been credited to his reading of Surin's *Spiritual Catechism*.

156   Scholars have classified Caussade's writings into three main clusters: his letters, mostly written to the sisters at Nancy, his *Treatise in Which One Finds the True Doctrine of Perfect Salvation*, and his *Treatise on Prayer from the Heart*. McKeon, 32.

157   McKeon, 6. Caussade described purity of conscience, of mind, of heart, and of action. McKeon, 7.

158   McKeon, 103.

159   McKeon, 15.

It is necessary to be detached from all that one feels, and from all that one does, to follow this method, by which one subsists in God alone, and in the present duty. All regard to what is beyond this should be cut off as superfluous. One must restrict oneself to the present duty without thinking of the preceding one, or of the one which is to follow...In the state of abandonment the only rule is the duty of the present moment...Yes! give to God what belongs to Him, and remain lovingly passive in his hands. [160]

In terms echoed by all the Jesuit writers in this mystical movement, Caussade stated that through this kind of renunciation to the present moment the heart would become free from attachment not only to that which is sinful, but to any created good, "because in truth these never can be fully innocent, since the heart, which is only made for God, leaves room for creatures."[161] And so like Ignatius and Lallemant before him—and Lacouture and Hugo after—Caussade recognized that the Christian life entailed something much more than simply avoiding sin.

But Caussade's teachings were not entirely welcomed within the Society of Jesus. A draft of *Prayer from the Heart* was submitted to two Jesuit censors at the Collegium Romanum in 1737 for review and while they generally approved Caussade's work, they were wary of the importance he gave to "attentive pauses." [162] They also encouraged

---

160   Caussade, *Abandonment to Divine Providence*, trans. Ramière, 58.

161   Caussade, *Prayer from the Heart* in McKeon, 133.

162   While no copies of this draft have been found, the censor's letters indicate that it contained two dialogues on prayer. This text was further reworked by Caussade's colleague, Paul-Gabriel Antoine, and was allowed to be published (under Antoine's authorship) in 1741 under the title, *Instructions spirituelles en forme de dialogues sur les divers états d'oraison suivant la doctrine de M. Bossuet, évêque de Meaux.* Henri Bremond published the *Instructions* under the title *Bossuet, maître d'oraison,* and it was republished in 1891 and again in 1895. The 1895 version was published in English in 1931, *On Prayer: Spiritual Instruction on the Various States of Prayer According to the Doctrine of Bossuet, Bishop of Meaux,* trans. Algar Thorold. McKeon, 34. Joseph McSorley, who was fluent in French, published a critical edition of Caussade's *Instructions* in 1904 as: *Progress in Prayer, translated from Instructions spirituelles, par le R.P. Caussade, S.J.* by L.V. Sheehan. Adapted and edited, with an Introduction by Joseph McSorley, C.S.P. (St. Louis: B. Herder, 1904). In his introduction, McSorley casts Caussade as trying to

Caussade to promote the practice of discursive meditation found in the *Exercises* rather than such "silent" prayer.[163] And they directed him to clearly state upfront that the form of prayer he taught was only for those whom God had called to a higher level of prayer.[164] And thus the legacy of Bossuet lived on.[165]

And so the controversy surrounding Quietism marks a significant turning point in the Catholic tradition.[166] For in its aftermath, "a narrowing, suffocating, and hyper-intellectualization" of the tradition began.[167] All of which, as Maurice Blondel suggested, culminated in the form of neo-Thomism that came to dominate Catholic thinking in the late nineteenth and early twentieth-century with its two-tiered theological perspective.[168] Thus the legacy of Quietism can be seen as

preserve "the finest flower of Catholic spirituality" which "lay in danger of being crushed utterly out of existence." McSorley, 11.

163   McKeon, 34.

164   McKeon, 34.

165   Scholars have noted that despite this opposition, mysticism did not disappear within the Church, for "mystics were left to their spiritual directors, and the study of their experiences to a restricted circle of specialist theologians." And outside of Catholicism, "mysticism tended to be identified with abnormality or assimilated to the occult." Portier and Talar, 9.

166   Alexander Dru noted that in philosophy, "the victory of Bosseut (who was no philosopher as Bremond points out) led to what Blondel calls Extrinsicism, to an utter contempt for *le fait intérieur*, to a fear and suspicion of Pascal himself, to the divorce between thought and feeling and will which explains the impotent rationalism of nineteenth-century scholasticism: the scholasticism Blondel rightly regarded as the *lingua franca* of official theology." Alexander Dru, "Introduction" in Maurice Blondel, *The Letter on Apologetics and History of Dogma*, 24.

167   Portier and Talar, 4.

168   Dru pointed out that for Blondel "two Catholic mentalities" emerged from the Bossuet-Fénelon dispute—mentalities that set the positions in the major conflicts within nineteenth and early twentieth-century Catholicism. "The two parties make their first appearance in the struggle between the theocrats and classicists (Bonald, Maistre) and the romatic liberals (Chateaubriand, Balanche), the former harking back to Bossuet, the latter to Fénelon; but they soon narrowed and hardened into the Ultramontane party (Veuillot) and the liberal Catholics (Acton, Montalembert). As long as the intellectual life of Catholicism was dormant, the conflict was insoluble

helping to foster the quarantining of anything mystical from the life of ordinary Christians—let alone from "serious theology"—as well as the "exile" the supernatural from the modern world, something Henri de Lubac and others would lament at the time.

RESSOURCEMENT THEOLOGY IN THE
EARLY TWENTIETH-CENTURY

It was in response to this that some early twentieth-century Catholic thinkers began to look back into the Christian tradition in order to find examples of orthodox writings which emphasized the mystical or supernatural in a more integrated way. Prominent among these was Henri Bremond's eleven-volume work, *Histoire Litteraire du Sentiment Religieux en France depuis la Fin des Guerres de Religion jusqu'à Nos Jours*, which sought to recover and reclaim the mystical tradition which "an overly intellectualized theology" had obscured.[169] Bremond certainly recognized the importance of reclaiming this tradition and highlighted numerous "sources" in this tradition such as Catherine of Genoa and François Fénelon, as well as Lallemant, Surin, and Caussade.

Bremond's work is important, not only in that it initiated a renewed interest in Catholic mystical writers in the twentieth century, but also because it challenged the overly objective and often ahistorical theology of the period. It did this by appealing to particular "sources" within the Christian tradition. Scholars like William Portier and C.J.T. Talar have noted that Bremond's appeal to these "sources" sought to recover a fuller and deeper Catholicism than the "rigidities" neo-Thomism allowed and that this desire led to "serious spiritual *ressourcement*"—the

---

because it remained superficial and appeared to be a matter of *policy*—the participants were yet unconscious of the philosophical and theological problems it concealed. By the end of the reign of Leo XIII...the conflict spread to every sphere and led to a crisis without precedent...The 'diplomacy' of Leo XIII had been as ineffectual in dealing with the situation as the intransigence of Pio Nono, and he left the 'crisis' to explode in the inexperienced hands of his successor, Pius X." Blondel saw this crisis as also having emerged in both the Modernism controversy and debate over Catholic participation in *Action Française*. Dru, 25.

169   Portier and Talar, 20. Bremond published works on Jane de Chantal (*Sainte Chantal* in 1912), Fenelon (*Apologie pour Fenelon* in 1910) and the concept of "pure love" (*La querelle du Pur Amour au temps de Louis XIII* in 1932).

turning to particular early-modern writers rather than a "vacuous, universal mystic essence."[170] While this effort at *ressourcement* began with the work of writers like Bremond, it was passed onto Henri de Lubac and thereby into one of the main currents of the "rich and fruitful renaissance of Catholic life, thought, and spirituality" that occurred in the mid-twentieth-century.[171]

John Hugo's work to situate the Lacouture-retreat within the Jesuit mystical movement of Alvarez, Lallemant, Surin, and Caussade was also an effort at such *ressourcement*. In fact, in describing Lacouture's retreat, Hugo made clear that his French Canadian mentor did not *discover* anything new, but rather that "he *recovered* something—something, indeed, that ought never to have been lost but has in fact been lost to many through the treacherous entrance of modern paganism into the Church, yes, in the very sanctuary of the Church." [172] And in his work, Hugo relied heavily on Bremond—not an unimportant detail given Bremond's connection with the Catholic modernist controversy which had led to the "Oath against Modernism" that Hugo himself had taken.[173] Like Bremond, Hugo appealed to writers from the early-modern period to defend the retreat theology in the face of criticism.[174] Writing in the period between *Pascendi* (1907) and *Humani Generis* (1950), Hugo's appeal to these sources—while by no means as sophisticated as that of Bremond or de Lubac—must be seen within the context of this broader *ressourcement* taking place in Catholic theology in the first half of the century. And while such efforts have generally been associated with European theologians like de Lubac, Yves Congar, O.P., and Karl Rahner, S.J., Hugo's work

---

170   Portier and Talar, 22.

171   Portier and Talar, 22.

172   Hugo, *Sign*, 15 (italics in original).

173   Bremond presided at George Tyrrell's gravesite burial.

174   Hugo accused his critics of supporting their arguments with "textbooks," while he relied on sources within the tradition such as St. Francis de Sales, St. John of the Cross and St. Thomas Aquinas, as well as "stars of secondary magnitude" such as Lallemant, Caussade and à Kempis. These spiritual masters, he proclaimed, understood "not only the structure of Christianity, but its dynamism." Hugo, *Nature*. 162.

highlights the fact that such work was also taking place in the United States.[175]

CONCLUSION

A few points, then, are worth noting here. First, the theological roots of the retreat run deep into the Christian tradition. The sources of its theology are not found in the Jansenism of Port Royal, but rather within Jesuit history. Indeed, Lacouture's reading of Ignatius placed him within a strain of Jesuit writing that dated back to the sixteenth century. And criticism of the retreat theology—which will be examined more fully in the later chapters—can also be seen as coming out of this history. The arguments employed to critique Lacouture's reading of Ignatius stemmed from a particular strain or tendency that had long prevailed within Jesuit spirituality. Criticism was also fueled by a suspicion of any emphasis on the supernatural which existed within the broader Catholic psyche since at least the end of the seventeenth-century. In short, criticism of the retreat was—and continues to be—shaped by all of this history.

It is worth noting that Hugo, in his attempt to defend and justify the theology of the retreat, provided a mid-century American Catholic example of *ressourcement* theology. While Hugo was not in league with Bremond, Blondel or de Lubac, he was certainly making similar efforts at "returning to the sources" in the tradition—and in fact returned to some of the same early modern sources. This final point helps to further highlight the significance of Hugo beyond Day and the Catholic Worker, for Hugo clearly seemed to be someone in tune with some of the more important emerging currents in Catholic theology at the time. Indeed, Hugo can be seen as offering a critique and even a

---

175 Indeed, similar work had been done by the Paulist writer—another of Day's early spiritual directors—Joseph McSorley, C.S.P. In fact, already in the nineteenth-century, Isaac Hecker had made Lallemant and Caussade staples of his own spiritual life and his spiritual direction. McSorley was introduced to these writers by Hecker, through Walter Elliot's 1891 biography of Hecker, and in turn passed them to Day. Day recounted that McSorley had given her texts from Lallemant and Caussade to read. Day, *Houses of Hospitality* (New York: Sheed and Ward, 1939), 103. For more on McSorley, see William Portier, "Dorothy Day and her first spiritual director, Fr. Joseph McSorley, C.S.P." *Houston Catholic Worker*, (September-October 2002), online edition.

challenge to the neo-Thomist theological perspective that dominated Catholicism at the time. And like his efforts at *ressourcement*, this challenge brought Hugo into a growing and important discourse within Catholic theology. Therefore, to recognize the broader significance of Hugo's work, an understanding of how and where he fit into the larger context of mid-century Catholic theology is necessary. And so, it is to an examination of that context that we now turn.

CHAPTER IV

KINDRED SPIRITS

> It seemed a wonderful thing to me that priests and laity could still become excited about points of doctrine, about nature and the supernatural, nature and grace, about forces, spiritual capacities far more powerful than the atom bomb.
>
> Dorothy Day[1]

T he decade or so within which Hugo was preaching the retreat and developing and defending its theology was an eventful one. This was a period largely defined by the Second World War. Within the particular context of Catholic theology, though, these were also years that saw a great deal of often contentious discussion over issues of nature and grace—discussions which were not at all disconnected from the war as *theological* opponents were often also *political* opponents. Pius XII's 1950 encyclical *Humani Generis* can be seen as an effort to bring some sort of conclusion to these debates which had persisted for decades.

Despite the plurality of views these debates suggest, this was also a time when Catholic theological discourse was largely directed by one particular theological perspective: a "two-storied" account of nature and grace which saw grace as building a kind of superstructure upon a somewhat self-contained and self-sufficient nature.[2] Shaped by this understanding, early twentieth-century Catholic theology tended to separate nature and grace—a tendency which led to the development

---

1   Dorothy Day, *The Long Loneliness*, 258.

2   Gerald McCool, S.J., *Catholic Theology in the Nineteenth Century: The Quest for a Unitary Method* (New York: Seabury Press, 1977) offered an account of the role this account of nature and the supernatural played in the nineteenth century neo-Thomist revival.

of a "separated theology" paralleled with a "separated philosophy."[3]
And this kind of separation had real implications on Catholic political and social thought. For, as David Schindler recounted, this "double
separation both promoted and confirmed a growing remoteness of the
inner realities of faith from the ordinary—'worldly'—concerns of daily life."[4] And this was a remoteness acutely felt by many like Day and
Hugo during the war years. While this dualist theology dominated
Catholic teaching during this period, it did not go unchallenged, and
by the 1940s its influence could even be seen as beginning to wane.
Indeed, these years surrounding Hugo and the retreat mark the moment just before the abrupt collapse of this theology in the 1960s.[5]

It is within this historical and theological context that Hugo and
the retreat must be understood. It is one of the arguments of this
book that Hugo is significant beyond his connection with Day and
the Catholic Worker in that he was clearly challenging this prevailing theological perspective and was trying to articulate an alternative
theology of nature and grace. Hugo did not go unnoticed in his efforts, and the critical—and sometimes heated—reaction of prominent American theologians, most of whom were on the faculty at The
Catholic University of America, provides evidence of the significance
of Hugo's challenge. Hugo was not ignored.

And Hugo was certainly not alone in this challenge. In fact, as Day
herself suggested, Hugo's theological writings and the "controversy"
they fostered shared a great deal in common with the theology being
articulated at the same time by the French theologian Henri de Lubac,
S.J. and the controversy surrounding him a continent away:

> On this side of the Atlantic controversy began and spread through
> articles in the *Ecclesiastical Review* attacking Father Hugo's teach-
> ing. In France there was controversy about the teaching of another
> Jesuit, Father de Lubac, whom we had read with enthusiasm as a

---

3   Rudolf Voderholzer has pointed out that this idea of "separation" in
Catholic theological thinking was only encouraged by the complete "separation" of Church and State brought about by the French "Law of Separation"
passed in 1905. Voderholzer, 30.

4   David L. Schindler, "Introduction" in Henri de Lubac, *The Mystery of the
Supernatural* (New York: The Crossroad Publishing Co., 1998), xvi.

5   For more on this collapse, see Phillip Gleason, *Contending with Modernity*
(New York: Oxford University Press, 1995).

biographer of Proudhon, *The UnMarxian Socialist*, and the author of *The Drama of Atheist Humanism.*[6]

Though she claimed otherwise, the fact that Day made this connection in 1952—two years after the promulgation of *Humani Generis*—reveals something of her theological sophistication and understanding of these often technical debates.

And clearly Day was on to something in making this connection between the French Jesuit and Pittsburgh priest, for the similarities between Hugo and de Lubac are striking. Both were writing at the same time, *Applied Christianity* appeared in 1944, *Surnaturel* in 1946; both were criticized by prominent mid-century Catholic theologians, Hugo by Joseph Clifford Fenton and Francis Connell, de Lubac by Reginald Garrigou-LaGrange; both were effectively "silenced" by ecclesiastical authorities, Hugo in 1944, de Lubac in 1950—both submitted. And their theological perspectives also reveal some vivid commonalities.[7] Both presented a view of human nature as being marked or defined primarily by its capacity and longing for something greater

---

6   Day, *The Long Loneliness*, 258.

7   Some scholars have argued that de Lubac's theology changed over the course of his life: either taking a conservative turn following what he regarded as excesses following Vatican II or, as John Milbank has contended, "substantially" and "crucially" modifying his argument "under pressure in the aftermath of *Humani Generis*." Indeed, Milbank suggested that in the wake of *Humani Generis*, de Lubac "comes across as a stuttering, somewhat traumatized theologian, only able to articulate his convictions in somewhat oblique fragments." Milbank, *Suspended Middle* (Grand Rapids, MI: Eerdmans, 2005), 7. However, Susan Wood has pointed out that over the course of his scholarly life, de Lubac's writings maintained a unity and "betrayed no shifts in theological positions or fundamental convictions." Instead, Wood noted, it was his conversation partners who changed: from the neo-Thomists in the early twentieth-century to reformers like Edward Schillebeeckx in the latter half of the century. She asserted that "If Schillebeeckx was a fair representative, the fundamental differences between de Lubac and his later interlocutors lie in their theologies of history and the necessity of Christ and the church to mediate grace." The fundamental issue for de Lubac was always how grace was present in the world: was it present in nature by creation or was it made present through Christ mediated through the sacraments and preaching of the Church. Susan Wood, "Lubac, Henri de" in *Biographical Dictionary of Christian Theologians*, Patrick Carey and Joseph Lienhard (eds.) (Peabody MA: Hendrickson Publishers, 2002), 333.

than itself. For both, human nature—even prior to the Fall—is inherently unstable and insufficient, with the historical consequences of
sin having only exacerbated this insufficiency, and so nature was seen
as distinct from both that which is sinful and supernatural.[8] While
both de Lubac and Hugo affirmed the intimate connection between
human nature and its supernatural final end, they also maintained the
distinction between nature and the supernatural—nature is distinct
but not separate from grace. Both saw the gratuitous and supernatural
gift of grace as bringing about the perfection of human nature, not
as some kind of an extrinsic "super-addition," but rather as something
very much intrinsic to nature—an inner dynamism of sorts. In their
challenges to the prevailing early twentieth-century account of nature
and grace, each sought to "return to sources"—*ressourcement*—within
the Christian tradition to justify their arguments. And finally, both
Hugo and de Lubac can be seen as working out of the same tendency
within Ignatian spirituality as did Lallemant and Caussade and the
other Jesuits within the "mystical movement" before them.

Of course, none of this is to suggest that Hugo's work was on par
with de Lubac's or that Hugo had even read any of his French counterpart's writings. Hugo's work is clearly less theologically sophisticated
and his sources much more limited. What these similarities do suggest,
though, is a kind of synchronicity that existed in the theology Hugo
was struggling to articulate in America and the theology de Lubac and
others were putting forth at the same time in Europe. That the work
of de Lubac would go on to profoundly shape Catholic thinking in the
second half of the century implies that Hugo's work tapped into some
important theological currents and so was significant for an American
Catholic at the time. All of this also means that an understanding of
what theologians like de Lubac were doing during these years will
shed light on the historical and theological context of Hugo.

---

8   On maintaining this twofold distinction, de Lubac wrote that "this effort
     should consist particularly, in relation to Augustinianism, in better assur-
     ing the real consistency of the natural order in all its degrees as well as in
     better distinguishing this natural order from the order of sin. With respect
     to Thomism, it might consist in showing more explicitly that the kind of
     continuity shown in summary by the axiom *Gratia perficit naturam* does not
     exclude, from another point of view, the total transcendence and heteroge-
     neity of the supernatural." De Lubac, "Mystery," 287.

HENRI DE LUBAC, S.J.

Around the time Hugo was leading retreats at St. Anthony's in Oakmont, Pennsylvania, de Lubac was on the run from the Gestapo in France.[9] And it was during this time that the young Jesuit worked on a number of his most important theological works concerning nature and grace, including most significantly *Surnaturel*—drafts of which he remembered carrying with him while in hiding. Throughout these writings, de Lubac's theme was the "frightful lack of the sacred" that marked the modern understanding of the world.[10] And for de Lubac, the underlying cause of this loss was theological—an understanding of nature-supernatural relationship at the root of what he termed the "new theology" prevalent in early twentieth-century Catholicism. This was a perspective which had "brushed aside all the supernatural...all the sacred" and thus relegated it to "some distant corner where it could only remain sterile."[11] With the supernatural viewed as extrinsically separated from nature—marginalized to some kind of a parallel do-main—de Lubac argued that Christian belief and tradition had exiled itself from the modern world and into "a separate province...leaving it to die little by little under our care."[12] And with Christianity in this self-imposed exile, modern secular thinkers quickly began to organize, explore, and build a modern world in a "wholly secular spirit."[13] In

---

9   De Lubac was not a supporter of the Vichy and took a very active—and dangerous—part in the spiritual and theological *Résistance*. He took an ac-tive roll in founding, directing and contributing to the clandestine journal *Témoignage chrétienne*. And he served as a liaison between Cardinals Gerlier and Saliege, a role that put him in serious danger and led to his eventu-al flight from the Gestapo in 1943. Komonchak, "Theology and Culture at Mid-Century: The Example of Henri de Lubac," *Theological Studies* 51 (December, 1990): 598.

10   De Lubac, "The Internal Causes of the Attenuation and Disappearance of the Sense of the Sacred," in *Theology in History* trans. Anne Englund Nash (San Francisco: Ignatius Press, 1996), 224.

11   De Lubac, "The Internal Causes," 232.

12   De Lubac, "The Internal Causes," 232.

13   For de Lubac, this modern theological perspective which "hoped to pre-serve the supernatural with such jealous care was, in fact, a banishment. The most confirmed secularists found in it, in spite of itself, an ally." De Lubac, *Catholicism*, 313.

short, de Lubac made the bold assertion that modern Catholic theology had brought about and enabled the growth of modern secularism.[14] The result of this loss of any sense of the sacred in the world—along with any recognition of the practical implications of the supernatural for Christian life—was that instead of "impregnating the world with God" Christians had come to

> restrict themselves to superimposing God on the world, and as a result of this split between the secular and the sacred, the things of heaven, deprived of concrete ties, slide over the surface of formalism or of dreams, while the things of earth, cut off from their eternal source, find themselves handed over to all ravages of corruption and anarchy.[15]

Christians in the first half of the twentieth-century seemed largely unable to speak to the concerns and problems of the world—problems which were all too clear for de Lubac on the run from the Nazis.[16] And so in order to remedy this self-imposed exile and enable Christians to once again live out the implications of the supernatural—and "impregnate the world with God"—de Lubac spent much of the 1930s and 1940s both charting the history of this marginalization, as well as mining the tradition for more accurate and orthodox understandings of nature's relationship with grace.

With regard to this first task, de Lubac's research led him to the nature-grace debates in the sixteenth and seventeenth-centuries brought on by two theologians at Louvain, Michel du Bay (Baius) (1513-1589) and Cornelius Jansen (1585-1638). De Lubac saw these debates as having profoundly altered Catholic theology.[17] For central to the theological work of both Baius and Jansen was belief that human

---

14   De Lubac described modern theologians as "museum curators" who can take inventory, arrange and label everything, and have answers to all objections, but who have also lost sight of the "mystery of the Lord." De Lubac, Internal Causes," 233-34.

15   De Lubac, "The Internal Causes," 232.

16   "In the face of powerful movements that present themselves as totalitarian conceptions of the world and systems of life," de Lubac asked, "is a theory that tends to separate the supernatural from nature a suitable instrument for penetrating the whole reality and life of the authentically sacred?" De Lubac, "The Internal Cause," 236.

17   Volderholzer, 63.

nature had been thoroughly corrupted by the Fall, a belief based on
their understanding of humanity's claim on the "original justice" that
ordered human faculties prior to the Fall and which was lost afterward.[18] In order to illustrate the depravity of post-lapsarian "fallen nature," Baius and Jansen argued that in its pre-lapsarian state humanity
existed in a state of "perfect nature" able to attain its ultimate destiny
without supernatural assistance—de Lubac called this the "optimistic
idea of human nature" at the heart of Bainism and Jansenism.[19] De
Lubac pointed out that while the Christian tradition had long regarded "original justice" as a divinely given and gratuitous gift, Baius contended that it was simply part of human nature from creation, while
Jansen asserted that it was somehow owed to human nature by God.[20]
In either sense, the loss of "original justice" was described by both
Louvain theologians as a fall from this state of "perfect nature" and in
this way human nature was understood as changed and corrupted by
original sin.

In response, other early modern theologians charged that in their
account of "perfect nature," Bauis and Jansen had confused or even
blurred nature with the supernatural.[21] And to refute this problematic
blurring, de Lubac described sixteenth and seventeenth-century theologians as having developed the notion of a "pure nature" as a way of
protecting the distinctiveness and gratuity of the supernatural.[22] But

18   Louis Dupré, "Jansenism and Quietism" in *Christian Spirituality: Post
Reformation and Modern* edited by Louis Dupré and Don E. Saliers (New
York: Crossroad Publishing, 1991): 121-142.

19   De Lubac, "Mystery of the Supernatural," in *Theology in History*, trans.
Anne Englund Nash (San Francisco: Ignatius Press, 1996), 284.

20   De Lubac, "Mystery of the Supernatural," 284.

21   De Lubac, "Mystery of the Supernatural," 284.

22   De Lubac, *Mystery of the Supernatural*, 149. On this notion of pure nature, Robert Spaemann later explained,
    All the Thomists of the sixteenth century cite Aristotle in this context:
'If nature had given the heavenly bodies the inclination to linear motion,
she would also have given them the means for it.' [*De Caelo*, II, 290a] ...the
thought of a '*desiderium naturale*,' which points in nature beyond nature,
would, according to the theologians of the sixteenth century, make salvation a right, and grace would cease to be a gift. The consequence of this was
that one superimposed a hypothetical purely natural destiny to man, a '*finis
naturalis*,' onto the actual destiny given in salvation history; and thus the

de Lubac asserted that it was this idea of "pure nature"—which would develop over the course of the next four centuries—that lead to the dualist account on nature and grace and the "separated theology" of the early twentieth-century.[23]

As Schindler and others have pointed out, de Lubac saw the transformation of the idea of "pure nature" from a hypothetical notion (and admittedly a helpful one) to a belief in a self-contained nature as based primarily in a misreading of Thomas Aquinas's account of the twofold beatitudes of human nature (*duplex hominis beatitudo*)—a misreading which had developed over the course of the long history of commentaries on Thomas that emerged following the Thomist revival of sixteenth-century.[24] And at the forefront of this history of misreading of Thomas, de Lubac placed the commentaries of Thomas de Vio Cajetan, O.P. (1469-1534)—perhaps the most important

---

fateful construction of a '*nature pura*' came into being. God, so the theory goes, could have created man also '*in puris naturalibus*.' The destiny of salvation is purely accidental in relation to human nature. The ordering of nature to this destiny consists solely in the so-called '*potentia oboedientialis*,' a passive capacity to be taken up into this new destiny by divine omnipotence... The system of '*natura pura*' then became dominant in the disputations with Baius in Catholic theology. For the sake of the gratuity of grace, the theologians made the autonomy of nature a postulate, in relation to which grace has the character of s '*superadditum*.' Robert Spaemann, *Philosophische Essays* (Stuttgart Reclam, 1983), 26-27, trans. Nicholas J. Healy, "Henri de Lubac on Nature and Grace: A Note on Some Recent Contributions to the Debate" *Communio* (Winter 2008): 543.

23   Voderholzer, 31. Though much has been written in support of de Lubac's historical sketch, it should be noted that a growing number of scholars are attempting to nuance claims of the degree to which this dualism existed in theology. See Ralph McInerny, *Praeambula fidei: Thomism and the God of the Philosophers* (Washington, DC: The Catholic University of America Press, 2006), Lawrence Feingold, *The Natural Desire to See God According to St. Thomas Aquinas and His Interpreters* (Ave Maria, FL: Sapientia Press, 2010). For more on these scholars, see William L. Portier, "Thomist Resurgence" *Communio* 35, (Fall 2008): 494-504. But while this contemporary debate is important, for our study here, it is important to remember that Hugo—along with many others at the time—clearly understood this dualist account as the dominating theological perspective.

24   Schindler, "Introduction to 1998 Edition," xviii.

early modern Catholic theologian.[25] Indeed, so influential was this sixteenth-century Dominican, that following the promulgation of Leo XIII's encyclical *Aeternis Patris* in 1897—with its attempt to place

25   The argument that Cajetan played a central role in the Thomistic tradition which eventually led to the two-tiered neo-Thomism of the early twentieth-century was prominently made by Henri de Lubac in *Surnaturel* (1946). But de Lubac's historical analysis has been challenged recently, particularly by the so-called "Ressourcement Thomists." Many of these twenty-first century Thomist thinkers have sought to distinguish the form of Thomism rooted in Cajetan's commentaries and that of Francisco Suarez, S.J. (1548-1617) in the seventeenth-century. They argue that it was "Suarezarian Thomism" that took on the more two-tiered qualities that many in the twentieth-century, including de Lubac and Hugo, were reacting against. Such a distinction is important for these Ressourcement Thomists, since they want to read Aquinas through commentaries like those of Cajetan, John of St. Thomas, and others, and thus want to salvage them from de Lubac's critique. In this sense, the Ressourcement Thomists are similar to the nineteenth and early twentieth-century Thomists in that both groups read Thomas "forward" through Thomistic commentaries: the former, through the sixteenth- and seventeenth-century commentaries of Cajetan, et al., while the latter read Aquinas through the nineteenth- and early twentieth-century commentaries of the manuals. Both groups, therefore, differ from the reading of Aquinas made by de Lubac and others which read the Angelic Doctor "back" through the Christian tradition to the Patristics. For more on "Ressourcement Thomism," see Reinhard Hütter and Matthew Levering, ed., *Ressourcement Thomism* (Washington, DC: Catholic University of America Press, 2010). At the same time, Peter Bernardi, S.J., has argued that Suarezarian Thomists, many of whom were Jesuits such as de Lubac's seminary professor Pedro Descoqs, S.J., were not really as two-tiered in their theology as de Lubac, and Maurice Blondel before him, had depicted them. Peter Bernardi, S.J., *Maurice Blondel, Social Catholicism, & Action Française* (Washington, DC: CUA Press, 2009). All of this having been said, like the other "traditional Thomists," these Suarezarian Thomists read Aquinas "forward" through later commentaries.

   While certainly important, this historical debate is somewhat secondary to the fact that such two-tiered theology did exist in early twentieth-century Catholic theology. The question of whether this theology was historically rooted in sixteenth century commentaries or was the result of a "watering down" process in its mass translation into the nineteenth- and twentieth-century manuals does not change the fact that it was very real and had very real implications for Catholicism at the time. And it was these implications that de Lubac, and Hugo saw as problematic.

Thomas's thinking at the center of Catholic teaching—there emerged a revival of the "Thomism of Cajetan" which David Grumett has noted was "presented uncritically as if it were identical to Aquinas's own."[26] And indeed, Gerald McCool even labeled the twentieth-century advocates of this form of Thomism "Cajetanian Thomists" and distinguished their "traditional Thomism" from both the "transcendental Thomism" of Joseph Maréchal and the more "historical" form espoused by Etienne Gilson.[27] De Lubac simply referred to these theologians as the "new Thomists."[28]

Of course de Lubac recognized that Cajetan was not the originator of this idea of "pure nature" that sees human nature "as a closed and self-sufficient whole," and he pointed out that Cajetan gleaned the idea from the fourteenth-century theologian Denis the Carthusian. And certainly Cajetan was not the only one developing this idea, as later theologians like Francisco Suaréz, S.J., greatly elaborated it.[29] Nevertheless, Cajetan was the "patron and leading authority" of this theory and de Lubac charged him with having introduced the concept of "pure nature" into Thomist thinking and—more importantly—into "the exegesis of St. Thomas himself," and thus conferring upon it "a kind of usurped authority."[30] And so, following Cajetan's reading, "new Thomists" came to develop a way of reading Thomas that justified the idea of a separate "natural" beatitude or final end for human nature—a reading that quickly became the basis of the idea of a "natural order" that is largely self-sufficient and related only extrinsically to a parallel

---

26   David Grumett, *De Lubac: A Guide for the Perplexed*, (New York: T&T Clark, 2007), 13.

27   McCool, S.J., *Catholic Theology in the Nineteenth Century* (New York: Seabury Press, 1977), 257-259. For an excellent review of the variety of early twentieth-century Thomism, see Fergus Kerr, *After Thomas* (Malden, MA: Blackwell, 2002) and Helen James John, S.N.D., *The Thomist Spectrum* (New York: Fordham University Press, 1966).

28   Grumett, 4.

29   De Lubac, *The Mystery of the Supernatural*, 146.

30   De Lubac pointed out that prior to Cajetan, theologians recognized that this idea of pure nature was contrary to Thomas's thinking, while Cajetan was the first to sanction pure nature as consistent with Aquinas. De Lubac, *The Mystery of the Supernatural*, 146.

"supernatural order."[31] And it was this, de Lubac argued, that led to the dualist account of nature and grace, a "separated theology," and ultimately the exiling of Christianity from the modern world.

For de Lubac, though, all of this was a modern theological innovation—he called it "the new doctrine" (*la nouvelle doctrine*)—and it was clearly "far from being wholly faithful" to Thomas's true thinking.[32] For while Aquinas recognized that their existed two ends of human nature (*duplex hominis beatitudo*), de Lubac pointed out that the Angelic Doctor never understood the end which he described as "proportionate to our nature" to be a "transcendent" or "definitive" end in some hypothetical state of pure nature.[33] Rather, Thomas regarded this beatitude as "imperfect," "terrestrial," "temporal," and "immanent to the world itself."[34] In other words, this "imperfect" beatitude of human nature is far from the final end for which it yearns—Aquinas even

---

31   As an example, de Lubac highlighted Victor Cathrein, S.J., in "*De naturali hominis beatitudine*," *Gregorianum* 11 (1930): "It is therefore inadmissible to think that St. Thomas judged a perfect natural blessedness of the state of pure nature to be impossible. That blessedness which is the ultimate end of the state of pure nature must perfectly satisfy the natural appetite of man, otherwise it is not the ultimate end of nature; and although this blessedness is imperfect in comparison with supernatural blessedness, it is nevertheless perfect, if the proportion is respected of human nature and the natural end to which man through the principle of his nature is able to attain." De Lubac, "*Duplex Hominis Beatitudo* (Saint Thomas, Ia 2ae, q62,a1)," *Recherches de science religieuse* 35 (1948): 290-99, trans. Aaron Riches and Peter M. Candler, Jr. in *Communio* 35 (Winter 2008): 600.

32   De Lubac, "*Duplex*," 600; De Lubac, *The Mystery of the Supernatural*, 146. In recounting the impact of this critique of mid-century Thomists, Serge-Thomas Bonino, O.P., wrote: "Fr. de Lubac came up with a master stroke. In *Surnaturel*, seizing the sword of Goliath, fatal to its possessor, he denounced the excess of modern Thomism, turning St. Thomas against the Thomists of his time. Going back to the texts themselves and exploiting the perspectives of the history of doctrines, he sapped the foundation of a certain neo-Thomism by undermining its Thomistic legitimacy...the very scale of the reactions aroused among Thomists—for *Surnaturel* caused 'a number of Scholastic eyebrows [to] pucker'—shows the thrust hit home." Bonino, *Surnaturel*, viii.

33   De Lubac, "*Duplex*," 603.

34   De Lubac, "*Duplex*," 603. [*ST* I-II, q3,a2,ad4; *ST* I-II, q5,a5,*co*; *ST* I-II, q5,a3,*co*; *ST* I-II,q3,a5,*co*; *ST* I,q62,1,*co*.]

described this natural end as "necessarily mixed, unstable, and transitory."[35] And Aquinas made it clear that humanity is called to a final beatitude beyond anything that "human fragility can experience in this life"—a supernatural final end which he called "perfect."[36] All to say that for Thomas, human nature is anything but self-contained, instead it is marked by an instability and a desire for something greater than its own "fragility."

More than simply a misreading of Thomas, though, de Lubac argued that this "new doctrine" espoused by these twentieth century Thomists also greatly deviated from the accounts of nature and grace found throughout the Christian tradition—accounts which recognized nature as distinct but not separate from that which is supernatural.[37] Indeed, de Lubac turned to sources within the broader tradition—beyond Aquinas—in order to both reveal how far these modern theologians had strayed and to highlight more traditional Catholic thinking on the subject. In doing this, de Lubac was at the center of a *ressourcement* movement emerging within Catholicism at the time—a fact particularly evident in his founding of the *Sources chrétiennes* in 1940 which he co-edited with Jean Daniélou, S.J.[38] In these efforts at *ressourcement*—or to "return to the sources"—de Lubac sought to trace the historical development of theological concepts and shifts in their meaning in order to engage them creatively and critically.[39] Grumett has described this work as de Lubac's response to "the attempt to impose a single normative pattern on Catholic theology

---

35   De Lubac, "*Duplex*," 609.

36   Aquinas, *Summa Contra Gentiles*, lib.1, cap.5, n.2. Also see, *ST* I-II, q5, a5. Many recent scholars have begun to question de Lubac's reading of Aquinas, see McInerny *Praeambula fidei* and Feingold, *The Natural Desire*. But while noteworthy, such analysis is, again, secondary to our discussion here which is focused on how the arguments Hugo was making shared much in common with those made by de Lubac at the same time.

37   De Lubac, "The Internal Cause," 231.

38   Grumett, 8. Also see, Robin Darling Young "A Soldier of the Great War: Henri de Lubac and the Patristic Sources for a Pre-Modern Theology" in *After Vatican II: Trajectories and Hermeneutics*, ed. James Heft and John O'Malley (Grand Rapids, MI: Eerdmans Publishing, 2012), 134-163.

39   Grumett, 8.

based on the new interpretation of Thomist philosophy."[40] In other words, de Lubac's historical theology sought to counter the ahistorical objectivity that marked the form of Thomism he was challenging—a Thomism that seemed to look to Aquinas and his later commentators as its primary source. And it was out of similar motives, I would argue, that Hugo appealed to early modern spiritual writers within the tradition in his own attempts at *ressourcement* theology.

It was from sources within the broader Christian tradition that de Lubac sought to justify his challenge to the neo-Thomists' account of nature and grace, and in doing so he highlighted the early Christian concept of the "twofold divine gift" of *datum optimum* and *donum perfectum*.[41] From the tradition, de Lubac explained that the *datum* is understood as the gift of created being marked by a "capacity" (*capacitas*) for something beyond itself—a capacity that it many ways defines nature.[42] And it is this capacity—what Hans Urs von Balthasar later described as an "*aptitudo passiva*" rather than the "*potentia oboedientialis*" proper to all creatures—that brings about what would later be referred to as the "desire of nature" (*naturae desideratum*) for God, a longing beyond even a "natural desire" (*desiderium naturale*) for God.[43]

---

40   Grumett, 8.

41   De Lubac, *The Mystery of the Supernatural*, 91.While he employed this formula, de Lubac recognized the unavoidable inadequacy of this analogy of gift, for it lacked "that element of interiority—one could just as well say transcendence—an attribute of the Creator God who 'is more interior to me than I am to myself.'" De Lubac made very clear that this gift was being itself, indeed no thing pre-existed this gift or received it: "through creation, God has given me to myself." De Lubac, "Mystery," 300-301.

42   For concise explanation of de Lubac's thinking here, see Hans Urs von Balthasar, *The Theology of Henri de Lubac: An Overview*, trans. Joseph Fessio and Michael M. Waldstein (San Francisco: Ignatius Press, 1991), 69-73.

43   Balthasar, 70. In describing this "natural desire," de Lubac wrote: "From the moment I exist, in fact, all indetermination is lifted, and whatever may have been 'before', no other end is henceforth possible for me except that which is now inscribed in my nature and for which, by the very fact, I carry within me, consciously or not, the natural desire. If I lack that, I lack everything." De Lubac, "Mystery", 293. For a full discussion of this natural desire for God, see de Lubac, *The Mystery*, 185-206. For the distinction between "desire of nature" and "natural desire" see Grumett, 20.

But throughout the tradition, de Lubac pointed out that the action of grace has been understood as not limited to only the gift of creation—God did not create humanity and then simply leave it to its own abilities. Rather, there is a second, "perfect gift" of grace—the *donum*—that is completely gratuitous and distinct from the *datum*, and which brings about the supernatural finality to human nature's capacity. De Lubac linked this second gift of grace to the "call to deification" that perfects human nature into "a new creature" by both directing its longing "capacity" toward union with God and by empowering it to attain that supernatural beatitude. [44] While distinct from the *datum*, the *donum* is not separated from the human nature, but rather the relationship is that of a "two-fold ontological passage," or as de Lubac put it: "on this being that he has given me, God has imprinted a supernatural finality; he has made resound in my nature a call to see him." [45] In short, the action of grace is twofold and paradoxical, both giving human nature its being and then calling that nature to something beyond itself—to perfection. [46] De Lubac described this as the "Christian Paradox of Man." [47]

It is in this discussion of the *datum* and the *donum* that de Lubac and Hugo start to sound similar. For both were articulating the idea that human nature is called to something more that God did not create

---

44   De Lubac, "Mystery," 300.

45   De Lubac, "The Mystery," 300.

46   It is important to note that, contrary to the recent assertions made by John Milbank, de Lubac was clear that nature (the *datum*) was distinct while not separate from the supernatural (the *donum*), see John Milbank, *The Suspended Middle: Henri de Lubac and the Debate concerning the Supernatural* (London: SCM Press, 2005), 32. Milbank argued that the idea that the *datum* was distinct from the *donum* was a later addition to de Lubac's thinking as a concession to *Humani Generis* (1950). But I would argue that Milbank is incorrect in this reading, for the idea that the *datum* was distinct but not separate from the *donum* is at the heart of the idea of the "Christian paradox" that was central to de Lubac's theological project at least since *Catholicism* which he wrote in 1938. This was the paradoxical understanding which he famously articulated: "unite in order to distinguish" and "distinguish in order to unite." De Lubac , *Catholicism*, trans. Lancelot C. Sheppard and Sr. Elizabeth Englund. (San Francisco: Ignatius Press, 1988), 328. For a more sympathetic reading of Milbank, see Bernardi's *Maurice Blondel*, chapter 8.

47   De Lubac, *The Mystery*, 101.

humanity and then leave it to some kind of "natural order," but rather that human nature is created with a void or capacity for something which only God can fulfill. The supernatural—whether in terms of *gratia elevans* or *donum perfectum*—is not an extrinsic super-addition built onto a largely self-contained human nature, but rather it is an inner dynamism bringing nature to its perfection. And so for both de Lubac and Hugo—as, indeed, it was for Ignatius and Lallemant—the need for this perfection is not merely the historical consequence of sin, but rather it is first and foremost in order to fulfill the emptiness or insufficiency inherent to human nature.

DE LUBAC'S "PRACTICAL MYSTICISM"

And de Lubac, like Hugo, recognized that the supernatural has practical implications for the Christian life and it was these implications—what can be seen as a twentieth-century articulation of Ignatius's "practical mysticism"—that de Lubac presented in his political writings and activities.[48] And indeed, de Lubac's theology has been described as "profoundly political"—though it has been these aspects of his theology which have been perhaps the most neglected.[49] On this point, Joseph Komonchak has stated that de Lubac's theology "became an expression of the Church's engagement with society, culture and history" and in this way regained "the genuinely catholic, integral character" Catholic theology had lost during the time when it was considered to be mainly for "domestic consumption within an alienated Church."[50] For de Lubac, the supernatural was anything but an "extra something" that may or may not be relevant to the political life of a Christian.

It was on the relevance of the supernatural that de Lubac focused his lectures to the *Semaines sociales* in the late 1930s—what he later

---

48   Several of de Lubac more political writings written during this time— such as "The Authority of the Church in Temporal Matters," "Political Augustinism," and Patriotism and Nationalism"—have been translated into English. See Henri de Lubac, *Theological Fragments* trans. Rebecca Howell Balinski (San Francisco: Ignatius Press, 1989); and *Theology in History*, trans. Anne Englund Nash (San Francisco: Ignatius Press, 1996).

49   Grumett, 25.

50   Joseph A. Komonchak, "Returning from Exile: Catholic Theology in the 1930s" in *The Twentieth Century: A Theological Overview*, edited by Gregory Baum (Maryknoll, NY: Orbis, 1999), 35-48 (45).

described as a "Catholic group interested in social issues."[51] Likewise, it motivated his critique of Catholic participation in *Action française* and cooperation with the Vichy in the 1940s. For de Lubac, Catholic involvement in such political groups reflected a modern theology which separated the Catholic theology of the supernatural from nature, the sacred from secular, and the Church from the world, with the result that the Church was unable to speak out against political oppression so long as its "purely spiritual" interests were respected—something both *Action française* and the Vichy appeared to offer.[52]

In contrast, de Lubac argued for a political stance that recognized the implications of the supernatural in the world rather than exiling it away. And Grumett has pointed out that while de Lubac based his political theology in a reading of Augustine's notion of the "two cities" in *City of God*, but it was a reading that was very different from the "political Augustinism" which separated the secular ("the earthly city") to the realm of the State and the sacred ("the heavenly city") to that of the Church.[53] Rather, de Lubac read Augustine through the lens of Ignatius of Loyola's meditation on the "Two Standards" in the *Exercises* (*SE*, 136-148) and indeed he argued that Ignatius offered an "authentic culmination" of Augustine's political thought.[54] For Ignatius, the two standards—the "Standard of Satan" and the "Standard of Christ"—are not two separated institutions of Church or State. Nor is there any sense of a third standard that could be described as "human, natural, moderate" which could peacefully preserve the "autonomy" of the human institutions, while entailing a Christian to do his "fair share for Lucifer as well as for God."[55] Rather, de Lubac

---

51　De Lubac, *At The Service of The Church: Henri de Lubac Reflects on the Circumstances That Occasioned His Writings* trans. Anne Elizabeth Englund (San Francisco: Ignatius Press, 1993), 27. For a concise description of the *Semaines sociales*, see Peter Bernardi, *Maurice Blondel, Social Catholicism, & Action Française* (Washington, DC: The Catholic Univeristy of America Press, 2009), 9.

52　Grumett, 38. Also see, Yves Simon, *Road to Vichy, 1918-1938*, trans. James Corbett and George McMorrow (New York: Sheed and Ward, 1942).

53　Grumett, 34.

54　De Lubac, "Political Augustinism?" *Theological Fragments* trans. Rebecca Howell Balinski (San Francisco: Ignatius Press, 1989), 266.

55　De Lubac, "Political Augustinism?", 266.

explained that these two standards exist together in the world and thus need to be distinguished:

> The weeds and the grain must always be separated, and that requires a constant struggle: either one joins the leader of the vast camp of Babylon, seated on his great throne of fire and smoke, or the leader of the vast camp of Jerusalem, "Christ our sovereign Captain and Lord, humbly seated, beautiful and gracious."[56]

In short, for de Lubac, Ignatian political and social engagement requires an ongoing discernment—"a constant struggle"—in order to recognize what is holy, what can be perfected, and what must renounced.

This was a very different approach to social engagement than the form taken by the "new Thomists," whose approach suggested that Catholic participation in *Action française* and the Vichy was justified in a separated natural sphere of politics. And so in criticizing Catholic cooperation with these groups, de Lubac was also challenging the dominant political stance taken by Catholics in France at the time. Indeed, at one point he was even criticized by a Jesuit superior for a lack of "loyalty" to the Vichy regime.[57] And so when Day reported that de Lubac's work met with controversy, that controversy—like that which surrounded Hugo—must be understood within its broader historical and political context. For as John Milbank has rightly highlighted, de Lubac's "*political* opponents—Catholic Rightists supporting the Vichy regime and collaborating with the occupying Germans were also [his] *theological* opponents."[58] And chief among these political and theological opponents was Reginald Garrigou-Lagrange, O.P.—the formidable Dominican theologian whom François Mauriac once labeled the "sacred monster of Thomism."[59]

From his position on the faculty at the *Angelicum* in Rome, Garrigou-Lagrange was a deeply influential theologian, particularly within ecclesiastical circles in Rome. Garrigou-Lagrange had also been a partisan of *Action française* until its condemnation in 1926, as well as an enthusiastic supporter of the Vichy—going so far as to once

---

56   De Lubac, "Political Augustinism?", 266.

57   Voderholzer, 60.

58   Milbank, *The Suspended Middle*, 3.

59   Richard Peddicord, O.P., *The Sacred Monster of Thomism, An Introduction to the Life and Legacy of Reginald Garrigou-LaGrange*, O.P. (South Bend, IN: St. Augustine's Press, 2005).

characterize support for Charles de Gaulle as sinful.[60] In his account of Garrigou-LaGrange, Aidan Nichols, O.P., called him a "Thomist of the strict observance," a form of early-twentieth century Thomism which Nichols described as having roots in the Thomist revival of the nineteenth-century that culminated in Leo XIII's *Aeterni Patris* in 1879. However, it was not until the controversy over Catholic modernism in the first decade of the twentieth-century that the Thomism of theologians like Garrigou-LaGrange and Louis Billot, S.J. (1846-1931) emerged in force.[61] For in the wake of *Pascendi Dominici Gregis*, Pius X's condemnation of "modernism" in 1907 and the "Oath Against Modernism" which all clerics were required to take after 1910, a new atmosphere descended upon Catholicism. And it was in this environment, Nichols explained, that this "strict observance Thomism"—with its Twenty-four Thomistic theses—began to truly dominate Catholic thinking.[62] This was the "new" Thomism that de Lubac criticized for having separated the supernatural from nature and Christianity from the modern world—exiling the former to irrelevance. For, as Gabriel Daly described, this kind of Thomism presupposed and promoted "a very strict parallelism" between nature and the supernatural.[63] Far from recognizing the inherent insufficiency that marked human nature and its longing for something beyond itself—an insufficiency central to the accounts of nature found in the spirituality of Ignatius, Lallemant, de Lubac and Hugo—these twentieth-century neo-Thomists presented human nature as largely self-contained.[64] Nature was

---

60   Voderholzer, 67. Komonchak, "Theology and Culture": 601.

61   Billot, who was made a cardinal in 1911, was also an active supporter of Catholic participation in *L'Action française*. In fact, after Pius XI forbade Catholic membership in the organization in 1926, Billot resigned from the college of cardinals and vowed to live out his days in silence. David G. Schultenover, "Billot, Louis" in *Biographical Dictionary of Christian Theologians*, ed. Patrick Carey and Joseph Lienhard (Peabody, MA: Hendrickson Publishers, 2002), 75.

62   Aidan Nichols, O.P., *Reason with Piety, Garrigou-LaGrange in the Service of Catholic Thought* (Ave Maria, FL: Sapientia Press, 2008), 2.

63   Gabriel Daly, O.S.A., *Transcendence and Immanence: A Study of Catholic Modernism and Integralism* (New York: Oxford University Press, 1980), 17.

64   Daly, 18.

seen as being related to the supernatural, but only extrinsically with grace *building on* or adding to nature.[65]

And it was through this theological lens that Garrigou-Lagrange himself read de Lubac as articulating a "new theology" (*nouvelle théologie*) rooted in the legacy of Catholic modernism.[66] And this controversy surrounding *nouvelle théologie* and its possible connection with modernism—of which de Lubac was the most prominent and articulate proponent—came to a head in 1950 with Pius XII's encyclical *Humani Generis*, an encyclical Garrigou-Lagrange played no small part in writing.[67] Although Pius did not mention de Lubac by name, the encyclical was seen by many at the time as a response to the perceived errors in the theological writings of de Lubac and others connected to the Jesuit theologate at Lyon-Fourvière.[68] Hans Urs

---

65   Joseph Komonchak provided an account of the emergence of this "modern Roman Catholicism" and its unique features in "The Enlightenment and the Construction of Roman Catholicism" in *Catholic Commission on Intellectual and Cultural Affairs Annual Volume* 1985: 31-59. It has been suggested that the long held institutional separation of the study of theology from other areas of study, especially philosophy, played a major role in maintaining this two-tiered understanding of the nature-supernatural relationship. As fewer and fewer students went on to study theology—something which was generally done in isolated seminaries rather than on university campuses—the significance of theology in the life of ordinary Catholics was gradually forgotten. See, Michael Baxter, "Notes on Catholic Americanism and Catholic Radicalism: Toward a Counter-Tradition of Catholic Social Ethics," in *American Catholic Traditions: Resources for Renewal*, ed. Sandra Yocum Mize and William Portier (Maryknoll, New York: Orbis, 1997), 53-71.

66   This was the argument Garrrigou-Lagrange made in a 1946 *Angelicum* article titled "Nouvelle Théologie, où va-t-elle?" Susan Wood noted that the term "New Theology" was first used by Msgr. Pietro Parente in *L'Osservatore Romano* in February, 1942 in reference to M.-D. Chenu, O.P., and L. Charlier, O.P. Susan Wood, "Lubac, Henri de" in *Biographical Dictionary of Christian Theologians*, ed. Patrick Carey and Joseph Lienhard (Peabody, MA: Hendrickson Publishers, 2000), 331-333.

67   Voderholzer, 64. For an historical account of this controversy, see Jürgen Mettepennigen, *Nouvelle Théologie—New Theology: Inheritor of Modernism, Precursor of Vatican II* (New York: T&T Clark, 2010).

68   Wood, 331. De Lubac later recalled reading *Humani Generis* "toward the end of the afternoon, in a dark, still room, in front of an open trunk..."

von Balthasar—de Lubac's friend and former student—later recounted that when *Humani Generis* appeared "a lightning bolt struck the
school of theology in Lyons and de Lubac was branded the principle
scapegoat."[69] Indeed, following Pius's encyclical, de Lubac was ordered
to leave his teaching position and his books were removed from Jesuit
houses of study.[70] De Lubac submitted to his superiors and began an
"exile" that would last until 1956. And so, much like Lacouture and
Hugo, de Lubac was made to feel the consequences of his theology
and the challenge it presented.

MAURICE BLONDEL (1861-1949)

In understanding all of this, it is important to remember that de Lubac
was not the first to make such of critique of this type of early twentieth-century Thomism and the politics it informed. Indeed, Garrigou-
LaGrange's criticism of de Lubac was largely based in the Dominican's
belief that the young Jesuit shared a great deal in common with
Maurice Blondel (1861-1949)—the French lay Catholic philosopher
who Garrigou-LaGrange pursued "both publicly and privately all his
life."[71] And the French Dominican was correct in his suspicions. For de
Lubac recounted that while studying philosophy at the Jesuit house of
studies in Jersey England (1920-1923) he had "read with enthusiasm
Maurice Blondel's *Action, Lettre* (on apologetics) and various other

---

and found it "rather curious" when he read "a phrase bearing on the question
of the supernatural...intending to recall the true doctrine on this subject."
At the time, de Lubac remembered that he wrote, "It reproduces exactly
what I said about it two years earlier in an article..." De Lubac, *At the Service
of the Church,* 71

69   Hans Urs von Balthasar, *The Theology of Henri de Lubac,* trans. Joseph
Fessio, S.J. and Michael Waldstein (San Francisco: Ignatius Press, 1991),
17.

70   Besides de Lubac, Emile Delaye, Henri Bouillard, Alexandre Durand
and Pierre Ganne were also ordered to leave the Jesuit house at Fourvière.
Voderholzer, 71. Balthasar described the next decade as a *"via crucis"* for his
mentor and friend. Balthasar, 17.

71   Olivia Blanchette, *Maurice Blondel: A Philosophical Life,* (Grand Rapids,
MI: Eerdmanns Publishing, 2010), 257. For the central place of Blondel
in twentieth-century Catholic theology, see William Portier, "Twentieth-
Century Catholic Theology and the Triumph of Maurice Blondel"
Communio 38, no.1 (Spring 2011).

studies"—this despite the fact that Blondel's writings had been prohibited from Jesuit houses of study because of his connection to the
modernist controversy.[72] De Lubac even met Blondel in 1922 during a
meeting arranged by Auguste Valesin, S.J. (1879-1953), a Jesuit teaching philosophy at the Catholic University of Lyons and a close friend
of Blondel.[73] And the young de Lubac quickly became a central figure
in a group of Jesuits Peter Henrici has identified as "les jesuites blondeli-
zants"—Blondelian Jesuits.[74] In short, de Lubac's theology was formed
through the lens of Blondel's philosophy.[75]

Blondel first articulated his philosophical vision with the publication of his dissertation L'Action in 1893, in which he challenged the
notion of a self-contained "separate philosophy."[76] Blondel recognized
that such an understanding of philosophy presupposed the dualism
that had become the norm within Catholic thinking—a dualism
he termed "extrinsicist monophorism."[77] Peter Bernardi, S.J. has described this "extrinsicist monophorism" as a view of nature as sufficient

---

72   De Lubac, At the Service of the Church, trans. Anne Elizabeth Englund
(San Francisco: Ignatius Press, 1993), 19.Volderholzer, 38.

73   De Lubac, At the Service, 19. De Lubac later edited a collection of correspondence between Blondel and Valesin.

74   Peter Henrici, "La descendance blondelienne parmi les jesuites francais,"
310, trans. in Portier, "Twentieth Century,"125.

75   Xavier Tilliette, "Le Père de Lubac et le débat de la philosophie chriéti-
enne," Les Études philosophiques 50 (1995): 193-203 at 193. Peter Henrici
has noted that in the 1920s, de Lubac had been encouraged by his teacher
Joseph Huby to "verify historically the theses of Blondel and Rousselot on
the supernatural while studying the same problem in St. Thomas" and suggested that de Lubac's studies of Baius and Jansen were inspired by a 1923
article by Blondel on Jansenism and anti-Jansenism in Pascal. Henrici, "La
descendance blondelienne," 312.

76   Oliva Blanchette noted that while writing his dissertation, Blondel
regularly practiced Ignatius's Spiritual Exercises. Oliva Blanchette, Maurice
Blondel: A Philosophical Life (Grand Rapids, MI: Eerdmans Publishing Co.
2010), 48.

77   Blanchette described Blondel's idea of "monophorism" as a view of the
supernatural that understood it as purely external. Blanchette, Maurice
Blondel, 246.

onto itself, which then unavoidably presented the supernatural as "a sort of counternature."[78]

In contrast to this, Blondel argued that human nature, and likewise reason and philosophical thought, is inherently lacking and open to something beyond itself—the supernatural.[79] He explained,

> Absolutely impossible and absolutely necessary for man, that is properly the notion of the supernatural. Man's action goes beyond man; and all the effort of his reason is to see that he cannot, that he must not restrict himself to it. A deeply felt expectation of an unknown messiah; a baptism of desire, which human science lacks the power to evoke, because the need itself is a gift.[80]

And this supernatural is not an arbitrary "something extra" built on to human nature, but rather,

> It is an adoption, an assimilation, an incorporation, a consortium, a transformation which through the bond of charity, insures both the union and the distinction of two incommensurables…[it is] intended to be in us, *in nobis*, without ever being on that account something coming from us, *ex nobis*.[81]

Blondel described the relationship of human nature to the supernatural in terms of an inexhaustible movement or "action" of humanity— what he called the "willing will" (*volonté voulue*).[82] As Michael Kerlin explained, Blondel's philosophy of "action" revealed,

---

78   Peter Bernardi, S.J., *Maurice Blondel, Social Catholicism, & Action Française* (Washington, DC: CUA Press, 2009), 86.

79   Blondel wrote that "It was impossible not to recognize the insufficiency of the natural order in its totality and not to feel an ulterior need." Blondel, *Action (1893)*, trans. Oliva Blanchette (Notre Dame: University of Notre Dame, 1984), 297. Blondel later wrote a two-volume work also titled *Action (1936-37)*, which was a new work and not simply a re-issuing of the 1893 book. Bernardi, 49.

80   Blondel, *Action*, 357.

81   Blondel, *Exigences philosophiques du christianisme* (Paris: O.U.F., 1950), cited in De Lubac, *Brief Catechesis on Nature and Grace*, 48.

82   Blondel wrote: "Between what I know, what I will and what I do, there is always an inexplicable and disconcerting disproportion. My decisions often go beyond my thoughts, my acts beyond my intentions." Blondel, *Action* (1893), 4. Bernardi described Blondel's idea of the "willing will" as the "inexhaustible aspiration to attain the infinite that is never permanently

the ways in which we move forward in semi-light by acts of natural faith through wider and wider circles of social involvement to form ourselves and our world. When we make any of these circles a final stopping point, we find ourselves pushed forward by the necessary logic of our situation and our analysis. It is a movement that can logically stop only with the alternative of affirming the possibility of 'one thing necessary' beyond all human creations, imaginings, and conceptions.[83]

Far from a self-contained "separate philosophy," Blondel argued that philosophical thinking must begin by recognizing human nature's inherent insufficiency and that such recognition was the mark of what he distinguished as "Catholic philosophy."[84]

And it was out of such a philosophical vision that de Lubac was able to articulate his understanding of nature and grace as being distinct, but not separate, which he expressed in the axiom: "distinguish in order to unite...unite in order to distinguish."[85] He credited this understanding to Blondel in a letter he wrote to the philosopher in 1932, in which he quoted Blondel as saying,

> There is a fear of mixing, confusing; there must be a fear of not uniting enough...It is in fact when one does not know how to unite things well that one particularly fears confusing them. If the general life of humanity today too often withdraws from Christianity, it is

---

quenched by the 'willed will,' that is, the specific, concrete instances of willing." Bernardi, 49.

83 Michael Kerlin, "Maurice Blondel, Philosophy, Prayer, and the Mystical," in C.J.T. Talar, ed. *Modernists and Mystics* (Washington, DC: CUA Press, 2009), 76.

84 Blondel employed the idea of "Catholic philosophy" in debates regarding the possibility of a Christian philosophy that took place in the 1930s. For an account of these discussions see Gregory Sadler, *Reason Fulfilled by Revelation: The 1930s Christian Philosophy Debates in France* (Washington, DC: The Catholic University of America Press, 2011) and Maurice Nédoncelle, *Is There a Christian Philosophy?* trans. Illtyd Trethowan (New York: Hawthorn Books, 1960).

85 De Lubac, *Catholicism: Christ and the Common Destiny of Man*, trans. Landelot Sheppard and Elizabeth Englund (San Francisco: Ignatius Press, 1988), 330.

perhaps because Christianity has too often been uprooted from the viscera of man.[86]

Central to the work of Blondel, then—as it was of de Lubac—was the effort to overcome the modern separation of philosophy from theology, nature from the supernatural, and thus Christianity from the world.[87]

BLONDEL AND SOCIAL CATHOLICISM

For Blondel—as it was for de Lubac and Hugo and Lacouture—these were not purely academic issues. To argue such an understanding of the nature-supernatural relationship was to also argue that the supernatural had practical and political implications in the life of an ordinary Christian. From his position at the University of Aix en Provence, Blondel sought to inspire his students to recognize these implications. And influenced by their teacher, many of Blondel's students became involved in various groups of "social Catholics" that were springing up in France at the turn-of-the-century.[88] For instance, Marc Sangier (1873-1950), who helped form *Le Sillon* ("The Furrow")—a group in which Peter Maurin was associated before coming to North America—was a student of Blondel.[89] Other former

---

86   De Lubac, *At the Service*, 183. The letter to Blondel is dated April 3, 1932.

87   According to Karl Neufeld, "All of de Lubac's theological work illustrates his effort to overcome a dualism and extrinsicism that artificially tears reality apart." Karl Neufeld, "Öffnung und Freiheit: Zum 90. Geburtstag von Kardinal Henri de Lubac, S.J." *Zeitschrift für Theologie und Kirche* 108 (1986) trans. in Volderholzer, 120.

88   Bernardi provides an excellent review of French social Catholicism, and quotes Jean-Marie Mayeur as stating that the "heart of social Catholicism resides in the affirmation that it is within the competence of the Church to speak about the problems of society. The specificity of social Catholicism is in its refusal of liberal 'separatism.'" Bernardi, 13.

89   *Le Sillon* was a French political and religious movement (1894-1910). Sangnier advocated the idea that democratic values were the evolutionary fruits of Christianity and that such democracy was the only political system in accord with the Gospel. Sangnier and his group were harshly criticized by Charles Maurras, and *Le Sillon* was eventually condemned by Pius X in 1910. Blondel supported the group, and included it among the social Catholics he defended in the *Testis* articles. Bernardi, 97.

students participated in the "*Semaines sociales*," gatherings of Catholics which meet periodically for a week to study the growing tradition of Catholic social thought and encyclicals—groups to whom de Lubac lectured.[90] Like the Catholic Worker movement in the United States, these French "social Catholics" can be seen as trying to take seriously the implications of grace in their lives and working to become a "leavening presence" in modern society.[91]

But not everybody welcomed this social Catholicism, and Blondel defended the *Semaines sociales* in a series of articles he published under the pseudonym "Testis."[92] In response to charges that such groups sought to involve the Church too heavily in matters of the world—and thus blur the supernatural with nature—Blondel argued that these Catholics were living out the implications of their supernatural destiny in their daily lives.[93]

And in his *Testis* articles, Blondel also challenged Catholic participation in the *Action française*—the right-wing political group led by a charismatic leader named Charles Maurras, whom many believed to be sympathetic to the political needs of the Church in France at the time but who was himself an avowed atheist. Blondel asserted that this kind of cooperation with such groups was based on an "extrinsicist" theology—a theology which enabled French Catholics to think they could be in common cause with Maurras in the natural realm of politics while at the same time disapproving of his atheism in the supernatural realm of faith. Blondel argued that such *extrinsicism* had led to an authoritarian use of violence to impose the faith—what he called "sacralized paganism."[94]

---

90   Blanchette, *Blondel*, 234. Bernardi described these groups: "Seeking to propagate Catholic social teaching beyond the urban centers of Paris and Lille, the *Semaines sociales* brought together for a week in a different city each summer a varied group of professionals, workers, clergy, and students. As many as two thousand participants followed courses given by experts on the Church's social doctrine and practice." Bernardi, 9.

91   Peter Bernardi even suggested a connection between Blondel and American Catholic radicals like Paul Hanly Furfey. Bernardi, 264.

92   These articles were published between October 1909 and May 1910. Blanchette, 235.

93   Critics charged social Catholics with "social modernism." Bernardi, 17.

94   Blanchette, 252.

In contrast to this, Blondel contended that the supernatural was not extrinsically added, but rather reaches souls "invisibly" by grace and— in words later echoed by Hugo—he explained that this grace enables humanity to

> break out of all the enclosures in which they would like to confine themselves, *to raise them above themselves, to burst every merely natural equilibrium*, to put them on a level, and require them to be in accord with the plan of providence.[95]

Blondel saw the *Semaines sociales* and other social Catholics as concrete examples of this kind of bursting out beyond the "merely natural."

But Blondel's critique of the theology that informed the political stance held by many French Catholics drew a response from Pedro Descoqs, S.J. (1877-1946)—another prominent supporter of *Action française*.[96] Even after Blondel's final *Testis* article appeared in May, 1910, Descoqs continued to defend Catholic participation in Maurras's movement and—with the help of *Pascendi* (1907), the condemnation of *Le Sillon* (1910), and the "Oath against Modernism" (1910)— Descoqs was able to paint Blondel with the dangerous label of "modernism."[97] And, as William Portier has suggested, to raise the specter of "modernism" in the overheated environment following *Pascendi* was to add "an ominous layer of meaning to Descoqs's arguments" as it was "more like a threat than a form of intellectual exchange."[98] Indeed, the characterization of Blondel as a controversial Catholic thinker has only very recently begun to fade.[99]

---

95   Second "Testis" essay: 33. Translated in Bernardi, 74, italics added.

96   De Lubac later recounted taking "some rather nonconformist notes" in Descoqs's class, which he said were "inspired more by Saint Thomas than by my Suarezian master, whose combative teaching was a perpetual invitation to react." De Lubac, *At the Service of the Church*. trans. Anne Elizabeth Englund (San Francisco: Ignatius Press, 1992), 42.

97   Portier "Twentieth Century," 30.

98   Portier, "Twentieth Century," 13.

99   Peter Henrici argued that Blondel's was the philosophical vision at work in John Paul II's *Fides et Ratio*, yet even in 1998, the French philosopher was still too controversial to be named in the encyclical. Peter Henrici, S.J., "The One Who Went Unnamed: Maurice Blondel in the Encyclical *Fides et Ratio*" *Communio* 26 (Fall 1999): 609-621. For a full account of this debate and its legacy, especially on how the understanding of the nature-supernatural

EARLY TWENTIETH-CENTURY CATHOLICISM

The examples of de Lubac and Blondel, then, offer some important points for our discussion of Hugo—as, indeed, a kind of synchronicity exists between them and Hugo. The first is that, like Hugo, both of these French Catholic intellectuals argued that the particular form of Thomism which had come to dominate Catholic thinking in the first half of the twentieth-century was one which espoused a "two-storied" account of nature and grace.[100] And that out of this theological perspective any emphasis on the supernatural and its implications for the Christian life was marginalized, if not completely removed. This marginalization of the supernatural was seen as enabling not only the emergence of modern secularism, but also a minimalist notion of what it meant to be Christian—a notion focused almost entirely on avoiding sin by following the tenets of the natural law, rather than on a Gospel life of "impregnating the world with grace." The fact that both de Lubac and Blondel—Catholic thinkers who would go on to profoundly shape Catholicism in the second half of the century—recognized the existence of such a problematic theological perspective offers support to Hugo's claims that such a perspective was at work in his critics and in American Catholic thinking in general.

De Lubac and Blondel also reveal that challenges were being put forth to this *extrinsicism* in Catholic thinking even before the turn of the century. While perhaps the two most influential Catholic thinkers to make such challenges, de Lubac and Blondel were certainly not the only individuals raising these kinds of concerns. Indeed, as the century wore on numerous heated debates over the relationship between nature and grace emerged, to which Pius XII sought to bring some kind of closure with *Humani Generis*. But it is important to note that these challenges and the controversies they brought about were not simply confined to academic circles, but rather the theological challenges to this neo-Thomism also critiqued the approach of social engagement

---

relationship informs discussions on Catholic social thought, see Bernardi's *Maurice Blondel, Social Catholicism, & Action Française*.

100   Again, while the contemporary debate over the extent to which this dualism existed in Catholic thinking at the time is important for our interests here, it is secondary to the fact that Hugo shared the same view as Blondel and de Lubac, that Catholicism at the time was heavily influenced by it. See fn 23.

that prevailed within Catholicism—a stance which critics like de Lubac and Blondel contended was based on a dualist theology. Of course, all this took place during years when much of the Catholic world was being torn apart by World War II—certainly a sensitive time for Catholics politically. The argument will be made in the next chapter that Hugo was likewise putting forth a challenge not only to a neo-Thomist theological vision, but also to the way in which that vision shaped how most Catholics had come to engage with American society and culture. And Hugo was doing this at a time when his fellow Catholics were being called upon to enthusiastically support the U.S. war effort.

And finally, both de Lubac and Blondel provide evidence of the price paid for challenging this type of early twentieth-century Catholic theology and politics. Both men, along with many others, suffered very real consequences for making the arguments they made. Those they were arguing with were some of the most prominent and influential Catholics at the time. In a similar way, Hugo and Lacouture also felt very real consequences for the theological vision they were putting forth and the challenge it presented.

All this, of course, is not to suggest that differences did not exist between de Lubac and Blondel, on the one hand, and Hugo on the other. Indeed, Hugo did not have the same extensive academic training—a fact often reflected in his work. Hugo's theological arguments were certainly not as sophisticated. For instance, there is no discussion or recognition of a "desire of nature" or for union with God in Hugo's arguments like there is in de Lubac. Instead, Hugo used much more mechanical terms like "supernatural motive" to explain human nature's longing for God. In many ways, Hugo continued to work with the theological categories he was challenging and therefore his arguments lacked the nuance and dynamism present in de Lubac's theology. This was especially the case as Hugo tried to incorporate sixteenth and seventeenth-century spiritual writers like Ignatius and Lallemant into the language of early twentieth-century neo-Thomism. And Hugo's effort at *ressourcement*—while noteworthy in itself—was also much less comprehensive than that of de Lubac or others. In other words, the originality and importance of the work of de Lubac or Blondel is only hinted at and suggested by Hugo. Nevertheless, Hugo was making many of the same essential theological points and should be recognized as part of the same emerging theological impulse that would go on to profoundly shape Catholicism in the second half of the century. And Hugo is one of the few examples of an American making these arguments.

This discussion of de Lubac and Blondel, then, provides some sense of the early twentieth-century Catholic context in which Hugo and the retreat existed. Hugo should be seen as a kindred spirit to these more recognizable Europeans thinkers. This discussion also helps to situate the "retreat controversy" that surrounded Hugo and his theology in the U.S. within the broader theological discourse taking place in Catholicism at the time.

CHAPTER V

THE "RETREAT CONTROVERSY": 1945-1948

> The main objection to *Applied Christianity* is the author's explanation of the relation between nature and grace, between the natural and the supernatural order, consequent on his teaching about original sin.
>
> Francis J. Connell, C.SS.R.[1]

> This refusal of my colleagues and me to take a "friendly smoke" or a "friendly drink" with our brethren is one of the chief reasons why we have antagonized many of them. In fact, I think this is the chief sore spot in the whole controversy... our attitude, they say—oh so often—is completely unCatholic: it is Manichean, Jansenistic, Puritanical.
>
> John Hugo[2]

In the October 1939 issue of *The Catholic Worker*, Father Paul Hanly Furfey, professor of Sociology at the Catholic University of America and an early collaborator of Dorothy Day and the Catholic Worker, wrote a letter to the editor in which he questioned the assertion, "there is no unemployment on the land"—which had appeared prominently in previous issues of *The Catholic Worker*.[3] Next to this letter, the editors wrote that Furfey had opened

---

1 Review of *Applied Christianity*, by Francis J. Connell, C.SS.R., *American Ecclesiastical Review*, (July 1945): 70.

2 John Hugo, *A Sign of Contradiction* (published by author, 1947), 32.

3 Paul Hanly Furfey, "Unemployment on the Land," *The Catholic Worker*, (October 1939): 8. In response to Furfey's suggestion that many agrarians desired a Utopia on the land, the editors wrote they had never seen the rural

"a controversy for the clarification of thought" and invited readers to respond. Several letters appeared in the following issue challenging Furfey's criticism of so-called Catholic agrarians, including one by Father John Hugo, who was then teaching sociology at Seton Hill College in Greensburg, Pennsylvania.[4] In response to these letters, Furfey wrote a much longer letter in which he distinguished between "Realist Agrarians" and "Romantic Agrarians," the latter of which did not base their view of the rural life on "facts" and "practical issues" as did the former, but rather based their understanding on their "dreams" of an ideal rural life in the future.[5] Hugo was then asked by the editors to write an article answering Furfey.[6] In his response, Hugo argued that it was Furfey's "Realist" position that, in fact, was unreal and that the position of the "Romantic agrarians" was based on their very realistic view that any true social reform had to offer a real alternative to "industrial capitalism"—the cause of both urban and rural unemployment.[7] He wrote that what Furfey had dismissed as dreams were the very active objectives that agrarians had set, objectives which any genuine social reformers needed to guide their purposes and actions.[8] Hinting at a more radical approach to social engagement, Hugo explained, "What

life as a Utopia and indeed recognized that their fellow workers on the farm were leading "a hard life and a poor life." But they also recognized and wanted to emphasize that these agrarians were "trying to rebuild within the shell of the old, a new society, wherein the dignity and freedom and responsibility of man is emphasized. And there is no place better to do it than on the land."

4   John Hugo, "Capitalism Impractical," *The Catholic Worker*, (November 1939): 8.

5   Furfey stated that for the romantic agrarians "the farm is a fetish." He also highlighted *Free America* magazine as an example of realistic agrarians. Paul Hanly Furfey, "There are Two Kinds of Agrarians," *The Catholic Worker*, VII, 4, (December, 1939): 7-8. Furfey's letter appeared under the headline "Controversy Continues In Re City Versus Land."

6   John Hugo, "In Defense of the Romantic Agrarians," *The Catholic Worker*, (January 1940): 8. Hugo's article appeared under the headline "There Is No Unemployment on the Land."

7   Hugo pointed out that *Free America* published its magazine and conducted its small-farm workshops in New York city. Hugo, "In Defense," 8.

8   Hugo wrote that it was lack of such clearly defined objectives that caused Catholics to "go around in circles, through grabbing hold of whatever any irresponsible person calls Catholic Action." He suggested that such actions

we need, even more than [Furfey's] sound, practical sense, is complete clarity *from the beginning* as to our *ultimate* objectives."[9]

This early and overlooked exchange between Hugo and Furfey is noteworthy for a couple of reasons. First, it reveals that Hugo was already in the Catholic Worker "world" even before he led his first Catholic Worker retreat in the summer of 1941.[10] But this debate can also be seen as something of a precursor to the "retreat controversy" that occurred a few years later in which Furfey was one of the prominent American Catholic thinkers to criticize Hugo.[11] This exchange with Furfey also further fills out the image of Hugo in the late 1930s, just before his work promoting and defending the retreat theology began. By the end of the 1930s, Father John Hugo was an aspiring young academic who was articulate and confident.

Hugo very much seemed to want to be a part of the American Catholic intellectual discourse of the time and was not afraid to challenge more established scholars.[12] He was a young and newly-ordained priest who had attended a retreat in the summer of 1938 that introduced him to a rich and deep theology he had not encountered before. He quickly recognized the uniqueness and worth of its vision and embraced it as his own. He not only went on to energetically promulgate the retreat itself, but he widely employed its theology within various discussions—particularly regarding Catholic engagement with various U.S. political and economic institutions. Hugo defended

---

often led to "collectivist measures" which the Social Encyclicals had warned against.

9 Hugo, "In Defense," 8 (italics in the original).

10 These articles appeared after Hugo had attended the two Lacouture-led retreats in Baltimore in the summers of 1938 and 1939. Hugo's discussion of ultimate objectives and their implications echoed the retreat's notions of the practical implications of one's supernatural final end.

11 This exchange also predated Hugo's replacing of Furfey as the leader of the annual Worker retreat in 1941.

12 In his account of American Catholicism at the time, William Halsey mentioned an article by Hugo that was published in the journal *Thought* while he was still a seminarian at St. Vincent's. Hugo was commenting on Realism within American Catholic novels. John Hugo, "The Realism of Values," *Thought* 9 (December, 1934). William M. Halsey, *The Survival of American Innocence: Catholicism in an Era of Disillusionment 1920-1940* (Notre Dame: University of Notre Dame Press, 1980), 111.

and justified the theology of the retreat, both by situating that theology within the broader Christian tradition and Jesuit history, but
also—as will be shown in this chapter—by challenging the dominant
theological view of early twentieth-century American neo-Thomists.
In doing this, Hugo, like de Lubac, tapped into theological currents
which had been strengthening within Catholicism for decades—currents that would largely shape Catholic theological discourse of the
second-half of the century. All this to again confirm that even beyond
his association with Day and the Catholic Worker, the young Father
Hugo was a significant and relevant figure within early twentieth-century American Catholicism.

In this chapter, this image of Hugo will be fleshed out further.
Beginning in 1942, when he was no longer able to lead retreats, a controversy emerged surrounding Hugo's writings that involved influential American theologians writing articles critical of Hugo's theology in
prominent journals like *The American Ecclesiastical Review* (*AER*) and
Orate Fratres. Hugo responded to these articles in *The Catholic Worker*
as well as in various self-published manuscripts.[13] It was within this
back and forth that the relevance of Hugo's argument becomes clearer.
And while this controversy largely took place in the years immediately
following the end of World War II, it was predated by earlier debates
Hugo had with other prominent American theologians over Catholic
participation in the American war effort. In the end, this examination
of the "retreat controversy" will reveal that the well-worn depiction of
Hugo and the retreat as rigorist and Jansenist—a depiction which remains operative in American Catholic studies and has lingering effects
on contemporary Catholic discourse—stems from these early twentieth-century critics who themselves were working out of what is now a
largely discredited theological vision.

---

13   *The American Ecclesiastical Review* was a monthly periodical for clergy
published by The Catholic University of America Press. It was published
under various titles. From 1889-June 1905 (volumes 1-32), it was printed under the title *American ecclesiastical review*. From July 1905-1943 (volumes 33-109) it was under the title *The Ecclesiastical Review*. After 1943,
it was titled *The American Ecclesiastical Review*. Joseph G. Hubbert, C.M.,
"American Ecclesiastical Review" in *The Encyclopedia of American Catholic
History*, Michael Glazier and Thomas J. Shelly, eds. (Collegeville, MN: The
Liturgical Press, 1997), 91.

AMERICAN NEO-THOMISM

While certainly rooted in the "strict observance Thomism" of Garrigou-LaGrange and others in Europe, the neo-Thomism that Hugo confronted did have some features unique to its American context.[14] For the rapid expansion of Catholic colleges and seminaries in 1920s caused this form of Thomism to be taught on a "mass basis," inevitably leading to it becoming somewhat "denatured in the process."[15] Indeed, for the great majority of American Catholics at the time, this neo-Thomism was simply a body of given content to be learned as well as possible. And as a result, Philip Gleason has described this American neo-Thomism more in terms of an "ideology" than a philosophy or theology, at the heart of which was the belief that Catholicism was rationally grounded.[16] But while such an assertion of rationality brought particular assurance to American Catholics—especially in the face of often hostile attacks from their fellow citizens—in fact, the vast majority of American Catholics had absolutely no idea how to actually make the step-by-step argumentation necessary to demonstrate the

---

14   One of Hugo chief critics, Joseph Clifford Fenton, was a former student of Garrigou-LaGrange at the *Angelicum*.

15   Philip Gleason, *Keeping the Faith: American Catholicism Past and Present* (Notre Dame, IN: Notre Dame University Press, 1987), 168. Gleason notes that the decade of the 1920s saw the emergence of various American neo-Scholastic journals: *The New Scholasticism* (1927), the journal of the American Catholic Philosophical Association; *The Modern Schoolman* (1925) out of St. Louis University, and *Thought* (1926) out of Fordham. By the 1930s, "Neoscholasticism reigned supreme in the philosophy departments of Catholic colleges and seminaries." Gleason, *Keeping*, 23. For more on the effect of neo-Thomism in Catholic higher education during this period, see Gleason, *Contending with Modernity* (New York: Oxford University Press, 1995).

16   As an ideology, Gleason explained that "it functioned primarily as an ensemble of agreed-upon answers to various kinds of speculative questions, the validity of which one accepted on authority, which provided a rational grounding for Catholic beliefs and attitudes and served as the source of organizing principles for practical action" Gleason clarified that he was not referring to the technical philosophical system of neo-Thomism, but rather to "the worldview or intellectual outlook its authoritative inculcation inspired." Gleason, *Keeping*, 168.

reasonableness of their faith.[17] Instead, most were comfortable simply holding the conviction that their faith was rationally grounded and that the necessary argumentation could be done by someone, somewhere. Gleason suggested that this conviction became "the hallmark of the American Catholic mind" in the early twentieth-century and that it even came to take on the quality of an article of faith itself, serving as the foundation for what came to be known as the "Thomistic synthesis."[18]

But while this "synthesis" was an attempt to keep the faith from being exiled from the daily life of American Catholics, it was nevertheless based upon the same theological assumptions that Hugo and de Lubac argued did not take seriously the implications of the supernatural in Christian life. With the desire to prove the rationality of the faith, the ability and sufficiency of human nature and reason were emphasized, while the instability and insufficiency which marked human nature and its desire for something beyond itself were largely overlooked. And as Hugo found, any emphasis on nature's instability and need to be perfected by grace was dismissed as "exaggerated supernaturalism" or Jansenism—a threat to this "ideology" of American neo-Thomism.

PRELUDE TO THE RETREAT CONTROVERSY

As already noted, Hugo's defense of the retreat and challenge to his critics occurred within the political and historical context of the Second World War, and in fact the retreat controversy can be traced back to Hugo's writings on Catholic participation in that war. For in February 1943, *The Ecclesiastical Review* published an article by Joseph Connor, S.J., a theologian teaching at the Jesuit theologate in Weston, Massachusetts, titled "The Catholic Conscientious Objector."[19] The

17   Gleason, *Keeping*, 171. Gleason explained that this rationality was premised on the "breath taking assertion" that human reason alone was sufficient to know the "preambles of the faith"—foremost of which was the certainty that God existed. Gleason, *Keeping*, 169.

18   According to Gleason, everything was tied up together in this synthesis and "it all rested on the assurance that human reason could establish the fact of God's existence and the implications of that fact for every sphere of life." Gleason, 171. On the extent of this Thomist synthesis in the American Catholic world, see William Halsey *The Survival of American Innocence.*

19   Joseph J. Connor, S.J., "The Catholic Conscientious Objector" *The Ecclesiastical Review* 108 (February 1943): 125-138.

article was intended to offer advice to Catholic clergy on what to do if asked to sign a military questionnaire attesting to the sincerity of belief held by a Catholic applying for conscientious objector status (CO).

Connor began his article by summing up what he saw as the present state of the question concerning American Catholic COs in World War II. He noted that in the First World War there was little movement to foster or support Catholic COs—though he did highlight the case of Benjamin Salmon, one of the four American Catholic COs in the war.[20] Following the "Great War," Connor noted that revulsion to the horrors of the trenches and the seeming futility of the conflict itself had led many Catholics to question whether such a war met the criteria of the just war theory. This examination by prominent and authoritative theologians took place mainly in pages of Catholic periodicals.[21] And as a result, a much more organized Catholic conscientious objector movement emerged between the wars, with many carefully articulated theological positions published.[22] For the most part, though, Connor noted that all of these discussions came to an abrupt end with the entrance of the U.S. into World War II and the American Catholic hierarchy's subsequently quick endorsement of the U.S. war effort. And with this, Connor reported that the conscientious objector position largely fell out of favor among American Catholics.[23]

---

20   Connor noted that Salmon was sentenced to 25 years in federal prison in 1917 after he was told that his Catholic religion could not have forbade him from participating since the Catholic hierarchy was actively supporting the war. Connor, 127. For more on Salmon see, Torin R.T. Finney, *Unsung Hero of the Great War: The Life and Witness of Ben Salmon* (Mahwah, NJ: Paulist Press, 1989). Salmon's story was featured prominently in *The Catholic Worker* during WWII.

21   An example of these critical pre-war Catholic discussions was the editorials written by Joachim V. Benson, M.S.Ss.T. (1904-1981) in the issues of *Preservation of the Faith* magazine between 1939-1941. William L. Portier, "'Good Friday in December,' World War II in the Editorials of *Preservation of the Faith* Magazine, 1939-1945," *U.S. Catholic Historian* 27.2 (Spring 2009): 25-44.

22   Connor, 127.

23   Connor noted that the "case for American Catholic conscientious objection seems to have been lost by default." He pointed out that any such movement would have been very difficult in the face of "modern society's high-pressure salesmanship of war." He also noted, though, that it appeared

Despite the loss of hierarchical and popular approval for conscientious objection, Connor reported that some American Catholics continued to object to World War II and turned to the pre-war literature for theological justification of their positions. Since the positions argued in this literature had never been "officially repudiated by the Church," Connor wrote that the use of these arguments during World War II had caused something of a "controversy" for the American Church—could a Catholic be a conscientious objector?[24] It was in the context of this "controversy" that Connor presented what he saw as the four main positions taken by Catholic writers in these discussions.

Of the four, Connor reported that the position which made up the largest party in the pre-war discussions held that Catholic conscripts should presume that the nation's cause was just and therefore should—and in "legal justice" must—enlist.[25] This position, he pointed out—apparently missing the irony—was the one taken not only by the U.S. bishops but also by the bishops in *all* the various countries fighting on both sides of the war in Europe.[26]

Connor pointed out other positions which questioned American Catholic participation in modern wars. Two of these "schools" of the pre-war discussions would fall into what could be called a "just war-pacifist" position, arguing that either World War II in particular

---

that American Catholicism had "not even wished to combat society on this issue," a fact he called significant to the present situation. Connor, 126.

24   Connor, 126.

25   Connor listed prominent neo-Thomist thinkers who supported this position: Vermeersch, Genicot, Davis, and Prümmer. He noted that Vermeersch had written that conscience objectors "take their stand upon a principle which is socially untenable, a principle which would give private persons the right to pass judgment upon public measures, a right which belongs to the sovereign power. At that rate there could be neither peace nor order in the internal affairs of the state. Everyone would manufacture his own opinions, whereas in things which are not evident, the presumption is in favor of the authorities." Connor cited Vermeersch's article in the *Modern Schoolman* (March, 1935), Connor, 137.

26   Connor, 135-137. Connor highlighted the U.S. Bishops' statement "Victory and Peace" which had appeared in the *New York Times* on November 15, 1942. For the full text, see "Victory and Peace," in *Pastoral Letters of the United States Catholic Bishops*, Hugo Nolan, ed. (Washington, DC: United States Catholic Conference, 1984), 2:38-43.

or modern war in general did not meet the criteria of a just war.[27] He also distinguished a fourth and much less commonly held position whose advocates, chiefly found in the pages of *The Catholic Worker*, he labeled as "Perfectionists."[28] And he summed up their stance toward the war as follows:

> I have an inalienable right to practice the counsels. Practice of the counsels includes non-resistance to an unjust aggressor. Therefore, even in a just war, I can, out of supernatural love of the enemy, refuse to resort to violence against him. Therefore I am exempt from military service, on the same grounds as the religious who practice Christian perfection.[29]

But Connor contended that the idea that an ordinary Catholic lay person would be called to follow the counsels of perfection out of a desire for Christian perfection was problematic and ultimately theologically impossible to justify. For obligations to family and citizenship severely restricted such a Catholic from practicing these counsels, as did the fact that American Catholics were "morally subject" to the State which itself did not practice the counsels.[30] Connor stated that this position also suggested "an air of exhilarating aloofness and detachment" and implied a desire to "dissociate" the Church from America life. Such detachment, which he likened to "Albigensian purism and

---

27   Connor argued that this was the position taken the "greater majority of the pre-war Catholic pacifist intellectuals" including Nicholas Berdyaev, E.I. Watkin, Donald Attwater, Eric Gill, and clergy like Luigi Sturzo, Vincent McNabb, O.P., James M. Gillis, C.S.P., as well as Franziscus Stratmann, O.P., Gerald Vann, O.P., Msgr. Barry O'Toole, and John K. Ryan, S.J. Despite this list of significant Catholic supporters, Connor argued that it did not include a sufficient number of "outstanding moral theologians" to warrant this position the technical note of "extrinsic probability." Connor,130.

28   Connor pointed out that adherents of this position often cited "ecclesiastical supporters" such as German exiled theologian Stratmann, British theologians Vann, and W.E. Orchard, and Catholic University of America faculty O'Toole and Ryan. However, after the start of World War II only Orchard still wrote in defense of this position in *The Catholic Worker*. Connor, 127.

29   Connor, 129.

30   Connor, 130.

Calvinist theocracy," was as foreign to Catholic dogma as Communist secularism.[31]

It is fair to say that Connor's argument was rooted in the two-tiered theology of the American neo-Thomists—a theology which in turn formed the basis for viewing the Christian life as itself two-tiered. For Connor, the life of holiness and Christian perfection was not something to which all Catholics were universally called, but rather such perfection seemed to be the arena of a select few spiritual elites. For most Catholics, both laity and secular clergy, the pursuit of perfection and holiness was offset by obligations to family and nation. And such obligations meant that the vast majority of American Catholics were not called to practice the counsels of perfection; indeed he appeared to suggest that they even had a duty *not* to perform them. To say otherwise was to be "perfectionist" and foreign to Catholic teaching properly understood.

In his study of American Catholic COs in World War II, Gordon Zahn (1918-2007) confirms Connor's assessment of the wartime situation, as well as the influence of Connor's argument. Zahn, who was himself one of only 135 American Catholic COs in World War II and a former graduate student of Paul Hanly Furfey at CUA, recounted the opposition he and other COs faced from the broader American Catholic community.[32] Bishops ignored the pleas of Catholics filing CO claims, priests angrily told draft boards that a Catholic could never be a conscientious objector, and a "hostile religious community" coldly confronted COs at Mass.[33] Zahn even quoted one priest at the time as having written that, "if a conscientious objector is found

---

31   Connor, 136.

32   It also must be noted that some 6,000 American men who did not receive CO exemptions in WWII went to prison for refusing to enlist. While the number of Catholics within this group is unknown, Zahn suggests that it was high. Gordon Zahn, *Another Part of the War* (Amherst, MA: University of Massachusetts Press, 1979), 28.

33   Zahn, 26. Zahn also seemed to confirm Connor's assessment of the various "schools" of Catholics who objected to the war: those COs who argued a "Thomistic pacifism" and objected either that WWII or any modern war had not met the criteria of a just-war, the "perfectionist" Catholic Workers who "called for nothing less than spiritual perfection," and the "Catholic liberals" like himself who recognized the "logical incompatibility between the spirit of the Gospels and the spirit of war." He also noted the followers of Fr.

among our Catholics, it is not because of the moral teachings of our Church but because he is afraid of his hide—he is a coward."[34]

It is worth noting that while opposition to American Catholic COs was clearly present and strong, Zahn did highlight Hugo among the very few American Catholic clergy who publicly defended and actively supported Catholic COs at the time.[35] Indeed, two months after Connor's article appeared in *The Ecclesiastical Review*, the first of Hugo's two-part reply: "Catholics Can Be Conscientious Objectors" was printed in *The Catholic Worker*. Though these were not the first articles Hugo had written about war in *The Catholic Worker*, they were some of his most important.[36] In fact, Day and the other editors of *The Catholic Worker* later described Hugo as providing "the definitive and

---

Charles Coughlin, though their objection was essentially based on political opposition to aiding the Communists. Zahn, 14.

34 Richard Klaver, O.S.C., in *Crozier Missionary* (July, 1941), Zahn, 25.

35 Zahn included CUA philosophy professor Barry O'Toole and Paul Hanly Furfey as the other two outspoken defenders of Catholic COs. Patricia McNeal also pointed out that a few U.S. bishops quietly supported Camp Simon, the work camp for Catholic COs under the auspices of the Catholic Worker. These included Archbishop John T. McNicholas of Cincinnati, who famously called for a "mighty league of Catholic noncombatants", Bishop Petersen of Manchester, New Hampshire, whose diocese hosted the camp, Bishop Shaughnessy of Seattle, Bishop Alter of Toledo, and Archbishop Bechman of Dubuque. Patricia McNeal, "Catholic Conscientious Objection During World War II" *The Catholic Historical Review* 61, 2 (April, 1975): 236.

36 At the time, *The Catholic Worker* had just finished printing a six-part article by Hugo titled "Weapons of the Spirit," which was later published by The Catholic Worker Press in book form, with an imprimatur from Cardinal Spellman—a point Day never tired of noting, John Hugo, *Weapons of the Spirit* (New York: The Catholic Worker Press, 1943). Ade Bethune illustrated the book. The articles appeared in *The Catholic Worker* between November, 1942 and April, 1943. The Catholic Worker Press had also published, with Spellman's imprimatur, *In the Vineyard* (1942) which was made up of ten Hugo articles that had appeared in *The Catholic Worker* between September, 1941 and July, 1942.

most forthright statement" on the subject of Catholic conscientious objection.[37]

"THE HIGHER WAY"

Hugo's articles were also significant in that—like the defense of the social Catholics in France offered by Blondel and de Lubac—Hugo's defense of American Catholic COs presented a direct challenge to neo-Thomist theology as well as to the approach toward Catholic engagement with American society and culture it informed, an approach which was held by most American Catholics at the time.[38] Relying heavily on the theological vision of the retreat, Hugo's articles presented a concrete application of its often abstract discussions of nature and grace. Indeed, Hugo portrayed American Catholic COs as examples of Christian renunciation in the pursuit of holiness.

Hugo began his reply to Connor by highlighting the shift that had occurred in American Catholicism with the U.S. entry into the war. A shift, he pointed out, which did not reflect any change or convergence in Church teaching on participation in war, but instead was the result of the "super-patriotism" that had encompassed Catholics during wartime.[39] But this submission by the majority of Catholics—including the hierarchy—to the American war-effort did not change Catholic teaching on war. And he argued that the scandal of the U.S. government's war propaganda and suppression of dissent was only surpassed by the American Catholic hierarchy's acquiescence to it.[40] Indeed, Hugo declared that the Church's rejection of its role as the sanctuary

---

37   This quote appeared in the November, 1944 issue of *The Catholic Worker*, in the editors' introduction to another Hugo article, "The Immorality of Conscription," *CW* (November 1944): 3.

38   For more on the Catholic hierarchy's response to the American entrance in WWII, see Patricia McNeal, *Harder Than War* (New Brunswick, NJ: Rutgers University Press, 1992) and O'Brien, *American Catholics and Social Reform: The New Deal Years*.

39   In "The Menace of Propaganda," Joachim Benson also criticized the "fever pitch of false patriotism and exaggerated Nationalism" that seemed to have overtaken many Americans by the late 1930s. Joachim Benson, M.S. SS.T., "The Menace of Propaganda," *Preservation of the Faith* 8.3 (June, 1939), as cited in Portier, "World War II," 34.

40   Hugo, "Catholics" (May 1943): 6.

of the conscience was the real "controversy" and it was "utterly prepos-
terous" for a theologian like Connor to invoke the Church's authority
in "refusing to accord the rights of conscience to any man."[41] Hugo was
clearly not pulling any punches.

As he would soon do in his defense of the retreat, Hugo looked to
sources within the Christian tradition to support the stance taken by
American Catholic COs and he noted that the tradition was full of
examples of seemingly solitary witnesses who had adhered to Church
teaching in the face overwhelming opposition and criticism from their
fellow Catholics—including their bishops. He highlighted Thomas
More was as one such example.[42] And like the sixteenth-century
English martyr, Catholics whose consciences led them to object to following their nation's leaders could look beyond their own local dioceses for support.[43] Furthermore, Catholic COs could ultimately appeal
to the Sermon on the Mount—what Hugo called "the Christian manifesto"—in which Jesus offered a "higher way" to bring about peace.

In contrast to the "higher way" of Jesus, Hugo read Connor as asserting that somehow the Gospel message was not opposed to participation in war. And even if it were, Connor seemed to suggest that
the entire debate over war should be discussed through natural law
reasoning, essentially making the Gospels irrelevant to the problem of
war. If theologians like Connor did not throw out the Gospel, Hugo
argued, "they at least reasoned as though it did not exist; they leave to

41   Hugo, "Catholics" (May 1943): 6.

42   Hugo called More a Catholic conscientious objector. For almost all
of Catholic England—except for More, one bishop, and a "handful of
Carthusians"—had accepted Henry VIII's innovations and had asserted in
the face of More's objections that it was inconceivable that everyone, including the priests and bishops, were wrong. Yet More's canonization four centuries later revealed that "all of Catholic England was actually wrong." Hugo,
"Catholics" (May 1943): 6.

43   Hugo, "Catholics" (May, 1943): 7. For instance, Hugo highlighted the
"Peace encyclicals" like Benedict XV's Ad Beatissimi (1914), Pius XI's
Caritate Christi Compulsi (1932), and Pius XII's various Christmas address-
es. Hugo also suggest that an American Catholic CO could ironically appeal
to the present-day German bishops "who in spite of repeated condemnation
of Nazi principles and practices, had never declared the German war effort
unjust and have given full support to their own soldiers." Hugo, "Catholics"
(May 1943): 8

one side all specifically Christian or supernatural principles, revelation, the evangelic law."[44] And in doing so, the practical implications
of the supernatural and the call to holiness were ignored. Connor presented the Gospel teachings regarding love of one's enemy as "counsels
of perfection" which ordinary Christians were not obligated to practice due to their "state in life." Packaged in this way, the more radical
teachings of the Gospel had become marginalized from the ordinary
Christian life—quarantined away for only those elites who were called
to seek such perfection.[45]

By depicting the more radical aspects of the Gospels as counsels
which ordinary Christians were not obligated to follow—and perhaps
even had a duty not to follow—Hugo asserted that Connor was separating grace from nature. As a result, Catholic participation in war
was typically discussed without reference to the supernatural, but
instead almost exclusively in terms of the natural law.[46] Hugo contended that while a Christian may not be obligated to always perform
the counsels of perfection, that did not mean that she should still not
strive—and indeed be encouraged to strive by theologians—to perform them whenever possible. It certainly did not mean that an ordinary Christian somehow had a duty not to perform them.[47] Hugo
wrote that living the Gospels and seeking Christian perfection was not
a "privilege" for a few "generous souls," but rather it was "God's eternal
and immutable decree, binding upon every last one of us."[48] For Hugo,
it was clear that all Christians were called to a life of holiness, and that
Catholic COs were responding to this call.

Hugo argued that this marginalization of the demands of the
Gospels also led to the view that those who did desire to live out
such demands were themselves dismissed as "extremists," "rigorists," or
"Perfectionists."[49] In this way, Connor and other American neo-Thomists "who claim the authority of moral theology for their views" had
declared that a Catholic could not refuse his duty to defend his

---

44   Hugo, "Catholics" (June 1943): 6.

45   Hugo, "Catholics" (June 1943): 6.

46   Hugo, "Catholics" (June, 1943): 7.

47   Hugo, "Catholics" (June 1943): 6.

48   Hugo, "Catholics" (June, 1943): 7.

49   Hugo, "Catholics" (June, 1943): 7.

country—a duty which according to natural law reasoning is rooted in his "state in life"—with an appeal to the Gospels. And so American Catholics were being told that not only were they under no obligation to follow the Gospel teachings on nonviolence, since such teachings were the counsels of perfection intended for the spiritual elite, but that in many cases they were not even permitted to follow such teachings.[50]

In all of this, Connor's argument provides an excellent example of how the "two-storied" account of nature and grace informed the prevailing stance of Catholic engagement toward American society and culture. And it was this form of engagement that Hugo was challenging with the theology of the retreat. For he explained that the American Catholic COs objection to war was not based on a belief that all war was necessarily unjust or evil, but instead on the notion that even a war determined to be "just" through natural law reasoning was at best a "natural action" and thus far less than "supernatural actions" which comprised the life of a saint.[51] As with the example of smoking cigarettes, Hugo argued that while participation in a war may indeed be "ethically justified"—and therefore not sinful—it was still not part of the way of life presented in the Gospels. Indeed, the "higher way" of Jesus—which involved loving one's enemies—did not imply that other "ways" are always sinful, just that they are not part of the life to which Christians are called.[52] In short, while fighting in a just war was not necessarily a sin, it was a failure to live a holy life.

In their contention that a Catholic could not in good conscience be a conscientious objector, Hugo saw American neo-Thomists like Connor denying that holiness was at least an option—if not an essential aspect—of the Christian life.[53] In his defense of American Catholic COs, Hugo contended that their objection to participating

---

50   Hugo, "Catholics" (June, 1943): 7.

51   Hugo, "Catholics" (June, 1943): 7.

52   Hugo, "Catholics" (June, 1943): 7.

53   According to Zahn, Dorothy Day once appeared before a Congressional panel alongside "a church dignitary" who had come to argue for military deferment for Catholic seminarians. Day suggested that laymen might also receive such an exemption. Zahn noted that Day was publicly berated by the Church official for making such an argument, and that it was in response to this episode that Msgr. Barry O'Toole committed his support to Day's position. Zahn, 33.

in war was a form of Christian renunciation done out of a desire for holiness.[54] These Catholics were striving to make real the implications of grace through living a "supernatural life"—a life they regarded as not being limited to only a select few. Hugo argued that a Catholic objecting to war was not working out of some "explicit regulation," but rather from an "interior compulsion" that comes from the "Spirit of Love."[55] Put in the theological terms of the retreat, the supernatural is not extrinsically *building on* a largely self-contained human nature, but rather it is an inner dynamism perfecting nature and bringing it to its fulfillment.

Hugo continued to make these arguments throughout the war years.[56] Zahn has noted the significance of his articles for American Catholic COs and Patricia McNeal has suggested that Hugo was one of the main influences on Dorothy Day's shift to more theological justifications of pacifism.[57] But these particular 1943 articles are especially noteworthy in that they reveal that Hugo already had a history with American neo-Thomists by the time Francis Connell—perhaps the most influential Catholic moral theologian at the time in America—published his review of *Applied Christianity* in 1945.[58] This was a

---

54   The influence of Hugo's argument can be seen in the statement of "Fundamental Principles," that Zahn reported was passed out to every new arrival at Camp Simon: "Conscientious objection for Catholics is a precept of perfection...Those who become objectors must earnestly strive after the perfection of love..." Zahn, *Another Part*, 47.

55   Hugo, "Catholics" (June, 1943): 9.

56   Later that year, Hugo wrote another series of articles on war titled "Gospel of Peace," which were later published as a book by The Catholic Worker Press. In 1944, he wrote "Immorality of Conscription" for *The Catholic Worker*, which was reprinted in 1948. In 1945, two more Hugo articles on war and peace appeared in *The Catholic Worker*, "Conscience Vindicated" in April, and "Peace Without Victory" in September.

57   Zahn, *Another Part*, 32; McNeal, *Harder Than War*, 41.

58   In *Nature and the Supernatural*, Hugo included a quotation that he attributed to Connell in reference to Hugo's writings during the war: "When, therefore, the bishops of an entire nation call Catholics to take part in a war and even pray for victory, etc., it is certainly rash for a private individual to declare the war unjust. This is a condemnation of the hierarchy, and (contrary to what the writer says) it does express a lack of respect and obedience to Episcopal authority." According to Hugo, this quote appeared in

history that included Hugo's criticism not only of these American neo-Thomists' theology, but—and perhaps more importantly—of their political stance toward U.S. war-making.

THE RETREAT CONTROVERSY

As has already been pointed out, Day noted the criticism faced by Hugo and Lacouture in her autobiography,

> In Canada, Father Lacouture was charged with inexactitude of expression, causing division among the clergy and causing people to go to extremes in the business of mortification...When this accusation was brought to the attention of Bishop Hugh Boyle in whose diocese Father Hugo and other young priests who gave the retreat belonged, he said glumly, "I wish someone around here were going to extremes." Nevertheless, within a few years Father Hugo and the others who gave the retreat were refused permission to give it any longer, and were told to take care of their parish duties.[59]

By the end of 1942, Hugo was no longer giving the retreat and would not resume doing so for another seventeen years.[60] In all likelihood, Hugo's "exile" was as much the result of complaints from his fellow priests as to any theological "inexactitudes." For, almost immediately after Hugo began giving the retreat at Oakmont, Bishop Boyle began to hear complaints of a certain rigorism appearing in seminarians and young clergy who attended these retreats. Stories spread of young clerics returning from Hugo-led retreats and becoming "detachers"—some were even called "Hugonuts" or "Lacouturemites." While still a young priest, Hugo was remembered by some Benedictines at St. Vincent College in Latrobe as the spiritual director to a group of seminarians who were known as the "Tanq Corps" and acted more

---

a mimeographed draft of Connell's critique of *Applied Christianity*, which would later be condensed into his 1945 *AER* book review. Hugo, *Nature*, 103.

59   Day, *The Long Loneliness*, 258.

60   Boyle transferred Hugo from Mt. Mercy College in Pittsburgh—where he was then an instructor and chaplain following his time teaching at Seton Hill College—to St. Mary's in Kittanning, Pennsylvania. With this transfer to a rural parish, Hugo's "exile" essentially began.

spiritually "serious" than others at St. Vincent.[61] Hugo dismissed such complaints, suggesting that they had more to do with his admonishing fellow clergy to give up smoking and drinking than any real theological concerns.[62] Nevertheless, as Day recounted, more serious criticism of Hugo also began to emerge.[63] And indeed the critiques of Hugo written by some of the most distinguished Catholic theologians in the U.S. soon began to appear. Again, if nothing else, Hugo did not go unnoticed in American Catholicism of the 1940s.

This "controversy" that surrounded Hugo is significant. For one, it calls into question the somewhat accepted view of Catholic theology in the America during the period between *Pascendi* (1907) and Vatican II as being uniform, bland, and without debate—a belief that all intellectual activity ceased after *Pascendi*.[64] The retreat controversy suggests that this was not the case. The often heated discussions

61   The "Tanq corps" was named after the author of a textbook of spirituality, Aldophe Tanquerey, then popular in seminaries. According to Nathan Munch, OSB, Theology professor at St. Vincent's College: "Hugo does not seem to have been held in high estimation by the St. Vincent's Benedictines who knew him." Email from Nathan Munsch (August 12, 2009).

62   For instance, Hugo described a typical gathering of his fellow priests as: "lavish feasts, the use of costly liquors and quantities of tobacco, attendance at 'exclusive' resorts and places of recreation; of luxurious apartments, private bars, costly furnishings, enervating softness, and extreme devotion to bodily comfort." Hugo, *Sign*, 34.

63   In a diary entry dated January 15, 1946, Day noted "Attack in Ecclesiastical Review," which Robert Ellsberg described as a reference to an article in AER that charged Hugo with "Jansenistic tendencies." Day, *The Duty of Delight: The Diaries of Dorothy Day*, edited Robert Ellsberg (Milwaukee: University of Marquette Press, 2008), 100. Also see, Day, *The Long Loneliness*, 258.

64   Peter Huff has noted that there remains a "lingering scholarly bias against the entire preconciliar period of twentieth-century Catholic history." Peter Huff, *Allen Tate and the Catholic Revival* (Mahwah, NJ: Paulist Press, 1996), 18. An example of this bias can be seen in Leslie Woodcock Tentler's description of early twentieth-century Catholicism in the U.S.: "It was—to exaggerate only slightly—a Catholicism almost bound to offend academic sensibilities, associated as it is likely to be with complacent anti-intellectualism, reflexive anticommunism, and a repressive sexual ethic." Leslie Woodcock Tentler, "On the Margins: The State of American Catholic History," *American Quarterly* 45 (March 1993): 113.

surrounding Hugo and the retreat theology highlight the fact that there was a lot up for debate before the Council and indeed a lot of theological discussion was occurring.[65] As with his defense of Catholic COs, the retreat controversy also reveals that Hugo was very clearly presenting a challenge to the dominant theological perspective in early twentieth-century American Catholicism.

THE CRITICS

FRANCIS CONNELL, C.SS.R (1888-1967)

The first published critique directed at Hugo was Connell's review of *Applied Christianity* that appeared in the July 1945 issue of *The American Ecclesiastical Review*.[66] The timing of Connell's review is noteworthy given Hugo's public stand defending Catholic COs in the war. By the summer of 1945, the U.S. war effort was all but victorious—the war in Europe had just ended in May and Japanese Emperor would surrender to the U.S. that August immediately after the dropping of atomic bombs on Hiroshima and Nagasaki. That Hugo's books warranted a review by Connell is also significant—Connell was the chair of moral theology at the Catholic University of America and "one of the most authoritative voices in moral theology in the United States" at the time. [67] His opinion carried weight.

---

65   J. Leon Hooper, S.J., likened the debates between Fenton, Connell and Hugo with those surrounding Fenton, Connell, and John Courtney Murray, S.J., which occurred during the same period and which eventually led to Murray being "silenced." J. Leon Hooper, S.J., "Murray and Day: A Common Enemy, A Common Cause?" *U.S. Catholic Historian* 24 (Winter 2006): 45-61. The debate surrounding Leonard Feeney, S.J., was another example of a theological debate taking place at the time.

66   Francis J. Connell, "Review of *Applied Christianity* by John J. Hugo," *The American Ecclesiastical Review* 113 (July, 1945): 69-72.   .

67   Terrence J. Moran, "Connell, Francis (1888-1967)" in *The Encyclopedia of American Catholic History*, Michael Glazier, Thomas J. Shelley, eds. (Collegeville, MN: The Liturgical Press, 1997), 371. According to Hugo's account, Connell's review was actually a condensed version of his criticisms of *Applied Christianity* which he had written earlier and then mimeographed and "passed around." Hugo explained that these unpublished criticisms had been categorized into five "General Comments" and 128 "Particular Comments." Hugo pointed out that "Such a long series of objections has the effect, apart from their intrinsic worth, of throwing suspicion and doubt on

Connell opened his brief review by charging Hugo with making statements which "if taken in their literal sense, bear a close resemblance to propositions condemned by the Church"—those of Bauis, the Jansenists, and the Manicheans.[68] While Connell listed a number of instances where he read Hugo as not conforming to Catholic teaching, his main objection was Hugo's description of the nature-supernatural relationship. For Connell, Hugo did not seem to affirm fully enough the goodness and ability of human nature.[69] The calls to renounce and give up natural motives and actions in *Applied Christianity* were perceived as being based upon a view of human nature as entirely corrupted by sin. While he noted that Christian asceticism called for renunciation "from time to time, of *some* lawful pleasures," that was very different from Hugo's call to give up created goods as far as possible.[70] Hugo was read as placing too much emphasis on grace, and

---

the competence or integrity of a writer. Superficial readers, not looking very carefully into the meaning of these criticisms, and not taking the trouble to study them in relation to the book, will be impressed, even convinced, by the sheer accumulation of 'evidence.'" Hugo, *Nature and the Supernatural: A Defense of the Evangelic Ideal* (published by author, 1949), 1 Before the publication of the *AER* review, Hugo had even written and mimeographed a response to Connell which he titled *Nature and the Supernatural: a reply to a critic*, the bulk of which he would later incorporate into book-form. Joseph Clifford Fenton later reported that this manuscript had been composed of 141 mimeographed pages bound together in book form, and had been "widely distributed to priests and seminarians along the eastern seaboard." Fenton, "Nature," 54, fn.2.

68   Connell, reflecting the heightened state of vigilance in American Catholic theological circles at the time, qualified his charges saying that it was not his intention nor within his competence to assert that Hugo's book deserved "ecclesiastical censure." Connell, "Review": 69.

69   Connell, "Review": 70. Hugo's other transgressions included his attitude toward natural pleasures as "samples" of the joys of heaven to be ultimately renounced. Connell, "Review": 72. Hugo would later call this idea of renunciation from time to time an example of the "minimalist Christianity" content with a Christian life as "eat, drink, and be merry...but avoid mortal sin." Hugo, *Nature*, 49.

70   Connell, "Review": 72.

Connell concluded by labeling Hugo's theology as a form of "exaggerated supernaturalism."[71]

PASCAL PARENTE (B.1890)

Connell acknowledged that he gleaned this term "exaggerated supernaturalism" from an earlier *AER* article—"Nature and Grace in Ascetical Theology"—written by his colleague at the Catholic University of America, Pascal Parente. Parente was a professor of ascetical theology and author of the widely-read text *The Ascetical Life*.[72] Though he mentioned neither Hugo nor *Applied Christianity* in his article, Parente did highlight an "exaggerated supernaturalism" which he saw appearing in some of the spiritual writings of the day. He described this as essentially a version of "an old heresy condemned many times in the past"—a heresy which asserted that whatever humans did without the assistance of grace or "without referring the action to the supernatural end" was sinful.[73] Like Connell, Parente stated that this was the heresy of the Manicheans, the Albigensians, as well as Luther, Baius, and the Jansenists. And Hugo noted that Parente's contribution to the "retreat controversy" was not limited to this article. For in *The Ascetical Life*, he mentioned that "a recent Catholic writer"—Hugo assumed it was him—was teaching that sin was "only a secondary reason for mortification and that mortification would be necessary even if there were no actual sin, for we must die, not merely to sin, but to the natural."[74] But Parente argued that the notion that sin is not the primary reason for Christian renunciation—that Christians are called to give up more than that which is sinful—implied that even apart from sin, human nature is corrupt. The need for renunciation is one of the historical consequences of the Fall and to suggest that a Christian must give up something beyond sin was seen as Jansenist.

---

71   Connell, "Review": 72.

72   Pascal P. Parente, "Nature and Grace in Ascetical Theology," *The Ecclesiastical Review* (June, 1943): 430-437. Pascal P. Parente *The Ascetical Life* (St. Louis: B. Herder Book Co., 1944).

73   Parente, "Nature," 434.

74   This quote was taken from a section subtitled: "Errors Regarding Mortification." Parente, *The Ascetical Life*, 94-95.

PAUL HANLY FURFEY (1896-1992)

Connell was not the only critic—or Catholic University of America (CUA) faculty for that matter—to employ Parente's notion of "exaggerated supernaturalism." In *The Mystery of Iniquity*, Paul Hanly Furfey had pointed out that some Catholics in Canada and the U.S. had fallen into "a sort of exaggerated supernaturalism" and in so doing seemed to deny the validity of created goods.[75] To illustrate this position, he quoted from a set of mimeographed retreat notes which he claimed "a friend kindly made available."[76] Furfey reported that according to these notes, an unnamed priest had preached, "Do not attack sin—attack the naturally good."[77] Following the lead of his CUA colleagues, Furfey suggested that such teachings had already been condemned as errors in the thinking of Bauis, Molinos, Jansen, and Quesnel.[78] Though Furfey did not name the priest he had quoted, stating that it seemed "to be the part of charity not to mention the name," Hugo read this as criticism of the theology he preached.[79]

Furfey's involvement in this controversy is certainly interesting in that he and Hugo already had something of a history even beyond their somewhat pointed exchange over Catholic agrarianism in the pages of *The Catholic Worker*. Both priests were closely associated with Day and the early Catholic Worker movement. Both—along with CUA philosophy professor George Barry O'Toole—were some of the very few American Catholic clerical voices publicly supporting the pacifist position in World War II and defending American Catholics conscientious objectors.[80] And so Furfey's critique of the Hugo-retreat—which coincided with Day's strong embrace of it—could be seen as an instance of the post-war break-up of the "New Social Catholics" or "the Catholic Front" which had thrived between the wars.[81] Hugo

75   Paul Hanly Furfey, *The Mystery of Iniquity*, (Milwaukee, Bruce Publishing Company, 1944), 43.

76   Furfey, *Mystery*, 43.

77   Furfey, *Mystery*, 43.

78   Furfey, *Mystery*, 43, fn. 2.

79   Hugo, *Nature*, 115, fn. 1.

80   McNeal, *Harder Than War*, 38.

81   In 1936, Furfey wrote a letter to Norman McKenna of the *Christian Front* in which he described a movement emerging in the Church that he

had replaced Furfey in leading the annual Catholic Worker retreat in 1941. Even before that, Furfey was not thrilled with Pacifique Roy's attendance at the 1940 retreat he led at Maryfarm—nor with Roy's insistence on "leading a retreat within a retreat." And so Day's turn toward Hugo and away from Furfey can be seen as an example of her increased radicalization during the post-war period.

JOSEPH CLIFFORD FENTON (1906-1969)

By 1946, this debate surrounding Hugo's writings (published or otherwise)—as well as the general stir within American Catholic circles caused by the retreat itself—was significant enough to warrant an article in the AER by Joseph Clifford Fenton.[82] Fenton was a priest from the Diocese of Springfield, Massachusetts, a professor of Dogmatic Theology at CUA and the editor of The American Ecclesiastical Review (1944-1963).[83] He was also a former student of Reginald Garrigou-Lagrange at the Angelicum where he wrote a dissertation under the French Dominican's direction.[84] All to say that in 1946, Fenton was perhaps the most influential and eminent Catholic theologian in America.[85]

---

called "New Social Catholicism." Representatives of this movement included: Day, Virgil Michel, O.S.B., John LaFarge, Joachim Benson, M.S.SS.T., as well as Furfey himself. William L. Portier, "Paul Hanly Furfey: Catholic Extremist and Supernatural Sociologist, 1935-1941," Josephinum 16.1 (Winter/Spring 2009): 34. Also see, Portier, "World War II," 28. Cultural historian Anthony Smith has called this pre-war Catholic movement the "Catholic Front." Anthony B. Smith, The Look of Catholics (Lawrence, KS: University of Kansas Press, 2010), ch.1.

82   Joseph Clifford Fenton, "Nature and the Supernatural Life," The American Ecclesiastical Review 113 (January, 1946): 544-568.

83   Joseph Komonchak, "Fenton, Joseph (1906-69)" in The Encyclopedia of American Catholic History, Michael Glazier, Thomas J. Shelley, eds. (Collegeville, MN: The Liturgical Press, 1997), 505.

84   Joseph Clifford Fenton, The Concept of Sacred Theology (Milwaukee: The Bruce Publishing Co., 1941), ix.

85   Fergus Kerr, O.P. described Fenton as "the most eminent American theologian" at Vatican II. Kerr, Twentieth-Century Catholic Theologians, (Malden, MA: Blackwell Publishing, 2007), 7. For more on the influence and power of both Fenton and Connell, see R. Scott Appleby and Jay Haas, "The

Fenton began his article by summarizing the history and significance of the discussions surrounding the retreat that had been taking
place, centering those discussions around Hugo:

> American priests have seen the rise and advance within our country
> of what must be described as an extraordinary school of Christian
> spirituality. Quite recently Fr. John J. Hugo has given literary ex-
> pression to the characteristic tenets of this school in his book
> *Applied Christianity*...Fr. Hugo's obviously high purpose and his no
> less patent forensic skill have contributed towards making his writ-
> ings decidedly influential. [86]

Fenton went on to point out that while these discussions were part of a
broader "lively discussion" that had been taking place over the past decade in Canada—one which had produced "some noteworthy" books
and articles—in the U.S. the best known statements on "this debat-
ed matter" were the written exchanges between Connell and Hugo. [87]
Fenton reported that most Americans who knew the retreat theology had learned it from Hugo and that the vast majority of the

---

Last of the Supernaturalists: Fenton, Connell, and the Threat of Catholic
Indifferentism" *U.S. Catholic Historian*, 13 (Spring 1995), 23-48.

86   Fenton, "Nature," 54.

87   Noting the controversy that surrounded Lacouture in Canada, Fenton
wrote that while Lacouture did not publish any writings, his student Fr.
Anselme Longpre had published *La folie de la croix* in 1938. In response,
a Sulpician theologian at the Grand Seminary in Montreal named Roland
Fournier had written an article, "Grâce et nature," (*Le seminaire*, August,
1941), which was critical of some of the key themes in Lacouture's theology
as they appeared in Longpre's book. Two replies to Fournier's article then
appeared in defense of the retreat: Dom Crenier's "Grâce et nature," (*Bulletin
de Saint Benoit*, September 29, 1941) and Canon Beaumier's pamphlet
"'Language Spirituel' dans la predication," which defended a Lacouture-
inspired retreat given by Abbé Saey in 1940. In *The Long Loneliness*, Day
mentioned that Maisie Ward had attended a retreat lead by Saey given
to workers in Montreal. Day, *The Long Loneliness*, 245. Fenton also noted *Synthèse théologique sur le renoucement chrétien* (Montreal: Grand
Séminaire de Montréal, 1945), by another Sulpician, Fernand Paradis, as a
valuable book which could help end what was a "singularly unfortunate controversy." Fenton, "Nature," 54-56. For more on the "controversy" surrounding Lacouture in Canada, see Downey, 80-116.

"often acrimonious" U.S. debate revolved around Hugo's writings.[88] As Fenton saw things, Hugo was not only at the center of the retreat movement in the United States with its "extraordinary school of Christian spirituality," but also of the "singularly unfortunate controversy" that had sprung up around it.

After briefly praising Hugo's book for its "ultimate purpose," Fenton asserted that Parente's 1943 article had provided an "obvious and forceful warning against the teaching presented in *Applied Christianity*."[89] He then presented a series of critiques of Hugo's theology, arguing that ultimately it denigrated human nature by suggesting that Christian renunciation meant that a Christian should strive to give up "natural motives" and attachments to created goods as much as possible. For Fenton, the motives or attachments that must be renounced were ones that are sinful. Natural motives that are not sinful are part of human nature and are good. He argued that such motives did not need to be renounced or perfected, but rather could remain as is, albeit "subordinated" under supernatural motives.[90] In short, as with his fellow American neo-Thomists, Fenton's view of human nature seems to be one that understood it to be largely sufficient as is, with the

---

88 Fenton seemed to want to rise above all of these debates when he stated that because of the interest and importance of the issues, it was important that American clergy should be well informed in this field and not get caught up in the acrimony: "If spiritual leaders of our people form inaccurate or confused judgments on the points involved in the controversy occasioned by these books, a situation seriously disadvantageous to Catholicism in the United States may well develop. Such inaccurate and confused judgments arise, for example, when opponents of Fr. Hugo's system condemn it as 'too strict,' and when advocates of this teaching claim that any objection to it involves an attack on the practice of Christian mortification. Such over-simplifications tend to obscure the paramount fact that our one concern in doctrine about the spiritual life must be to give our people exactly the teaching which God gave to the world through our Lord Jesus Christ and which He presents infallibly through the *magisterium* of the Catholic Church. The only test that matters for any book or any system dealing with doctrine of faith or of morals is that of conformity with the Catholic message. 'Strictness' and personalities have nothing to do with the case." Fenton, "Nature," 56.

89 Fenton, "Nature," 56.

90 Fenton, "Nature," 58.

supernatural building upon it a kind of superstructure—a self-contained nature "subordinated" under the supernatural.

Fenton also asserted that Hugo had fallen into the "central ecclesiological error of the Lutherans."[91] For, while in Catholic teaching a Christian was someone united in communion with the Church, Hugo appeared to suggest that a Christian was simply someone who practiced the supernatural virtues of faith, hope, and charity.[92] Fenton charged Hugo with setting forth an "invisible Church theory" and implied that his emphasis on the supernatural had a sectarian bent, separating Christians from the Church and the world.[93] This charge highlighted the particular emphasis on the juridical and external aspects of the Church in Fenton's thinking, along with a suspicion of any emphasis on the supernatural.[94]

GERALD VANN, O.P. (1906-1963) AND JOSEPH DONOVAN, C.M. (B.1880)

Two other prominent theologians also joined the discussions surrounding Hugo. The English Dominican, Gerald Vann, O.P. wrote "Nature and Grace" in *Orate Fratres* in 1947.[95] And Joseph Donovan, C.M., a theology professor at Kenrick Seminary in St. Louis, published "A Bit of Puritanical Catholicity" in *Homiletic and Pastoral Review* a year later.[96] In both pieces, Hugo's theology was portrayed as

---

91   Fenton, "Nature," 67.

92   Fenton, "Nature," 67.

93   Fenton, "Nature," 67.

94   Hugo later called Fenton's emphasis on the external, and not on the mystical or supernatural, "ecclesiastical materialism." Hugo, *Nature*, 176.

95   Gerald Vann, O.P., "Nature and Grace," *Orate Fratres* 21 (January 26, 1947): 97-105.

96   Joseph Donovan, C.M. "A Bit of Puritanical Catholicity," *Homiletic and Pastoral Review* 48 (August, 1948): 807-814. Donovan's article responded to an anonymously authored pamphlet titled "Brother Nathanial Has a Brainstorm" which bore a resemblance to Hugo's work. Hugo claimed that he did not write the pamphlet, but helped the author edit it. Donovan stated that after reading the pamphlet, he was struck by "a resemblance between the doctrine of this author and the early teachings and practices of that school of French thought and devotion that developed into Jansenism." And

viewing human nature as hopelessly corrupted.[97] With the publication of Donovan's article in 1948, the "retreat controversy" was brought to something of a conclusion—though Hugo's "exile" continued for almost another decade.

While all of Hugo's critics focused on slightly different aspects of the theology presented in *Applied Christianity*, there was clearly a certain unity in their criticism, with each critic basing his argument upon those made by previous critics. Their central focus was on the understanding of the nature-supernatural relationship which they read as being at the heart of Hugo's theology. Hugo was roundly accused of depicting human nature as corrupted and so as repeating the "old" heresies of the Jansenists and the Protestants. Hugo's account of nature was seen as both denigrating its goodness and exaggerating its reliance on the supernatural. Underlying this criticism were Hugo's assertions that the Christian life entailed the renunciation of more than what was sinful, and that the implications of human nature's supernatural final end meant that habitual attachments to created goods needed to be given up in order to live a holy life. For these twentieth-century U.S. theologians, operating out of a more extrinsicist account of nature and grace, such claims were read as confusing human nature with that which was sinful. And Hugo's emphasis on the supernatural and its implications for the ordinary Christian also sounded suspicious to a theological mindset still shaped by the legacy of Quietism.

HUGO'S REPLY

Hugo wrote *Nature and the Supernatural: A Defense of the Evangelical Ideal*, a self-published book that appeared in 1949, as a direct reply to these various critiques made by Connell, Fenton, and the others.

---

he ended his article stating that the author of the pamphlet was wooing a "straight-laced Jansenistic spirit." Donovan, 811, 814. See Downey, 162-164.

97   According to Vann, Hugo's view of human nature was "far nearer that of the Reformers who held it to be entirely corrupt than of Catholics who hold that, though sin has indeed 'wounded' it severely, it still remains essentially good." While Hugo was read as allowing this in the abstract, but denying it in the concrete, Vann explained that "by the abstract he really seems to mean nature as viewed apart from all question of sin. But it is of nature in the concrete that Catholicism holds this relatively optimistic view." Vann, "Nature," 101.

I.THE SPIRIT OF PIOUS NATURALISM AND
THE SIN MENTALITY

Throughout his response, Hugo maintained that his critics were caught up in a "spirit of pious naturalism" which placed more attention on human nature than to the exigencies of grace.[98] This naturalism led them to de-emphasize the instability that is both an inherent reality of human nature as well as the historical consequence of the Fall.[99] In short, Hugo argued that in this "spirit of pious naturalism," his critics tended to maintain an inaccurate view of human nature. Their over-emphasis on the sufficiency of human nature caused his critics to lose sight of the centrality of grace and its practical implications on the Christian life.

All of this, Hugo asserted, caused his critics to develop a "sin mentality" which only saw see things as either sinful or supernatural. And because of this mentality, they did not recognize nature as distinct from both that which is sin and the supernatural—as a created good that is inherently lacking.[100] The result of this view of human nature was to see the Christian life as focused primarily on avoiding sin. Apart from what is sinful—in violation of the natural law—all actions and attachments were generally seen as good enough as is and not in need of either being perfected or renounced. He argued that in all this, the supernatural became blurred with nature and seen as distinct only from that which was sinful.[101] And so, the Christian life had come to be regarded in a minimalistic fashion—or as Hugo summarized it: "Eat,

---

98   Hugo, *Nature*, 158. Hugo actually quoted Garrigou-Lagrange (whom he called "truly one of the greatest spiritual writers of our time as well as a great theologian") as stating that those who embraced this naturalism "will be more attentive to nature which must be perfected than to grace which should produce this transformation in us." Reginald Garrigou-Lagrange, O.P.'s *Christian Perfection and Contemplation*, trans. Sr. M. Timothea Doyle, O.P. (St. Louis: Herder, 1937), 54. Cited in Hugo, *Nature*, 222.

99   Hugo, *Nature*, 53.

100 Hugo, *Nature*, 8.

101 Hugo pointed out the similarities between this view and the one taken by the Jansenists, except that the latter blurred human nature with sin. In neither instance, though, was human nature regarded as distinct from both sin and the supernatural. Hugo, *Nature*, 11.

drink, and be merry…as long as you avoid mortal sin."[102] To say that such a life entailed anything more meant that you would be dismissed as a rigorist, perfectionist, or even a heretic. It was through the lens of this "sin mentality" that Hugo intended that his critics read his work.[103]

2. THE CRITIQUE OF "MODERN THEOLOGY"

For Hugo, this "sin mentality" and "pious naturalism" was the result of an underlying theological perspective. He labeled this as a "modern theology" which separated and even segregated belief from practice—the supernatural from its practical implications—with its rigid separation of dogmatic theology from moral theology.[104] For while distinguishing these two branches of theology was necessary, Hugo explained that this "modern" separation was problematic,

> By segregating dogmatic truth from moral teaching, the practical implications and corollaries of the former tend to be lost sight of and neglected. It is forgotten that such sublime mysteries as the Trinity and the Incarnation have immediate practical implications. They are studied speculatively, with the purpose of extending the horizons of the faith. Their relation to charity is forgotten or passed over. Moral theology, on its part, sets about its inquires independently of the great dogmatic truths: these being left to a separate sphere, lose their formative, practical, directing importance; and moral theology, as we shall see, seeks its norms elsewhere.[105]

Hugo saw these kinds of separations as the failure in the theology of his neo-Thomist critics. For the supernatural truths of revelation studied in dogmatic theology had become seen as largely irrelevant to discussions of the day-to-day life of a Christian that took place in

---

102   Hugo noted that proponents of this view could not imagine "any higher ideal of conduct than the avoidance of sin or allow that any actions are blameworthy, even in souls who have been divinized by grace, other than those that are clearly sinful." Hugo, *Nature*, 49, 7.

103   Hugo, *Nature*, 8.

104   Hugo observed that when such a theologian wrote a text, it was likely to be "either a *Summa Theologiae Moralis* or a *Summa Theologiae Dogmaticae*." And should the same theologian write two *Summas*, one of moral theology and one of dogmatic theology, he would still observe "the separation of these branches." Hugo, *Nature*, 190.

105   Hugo, *Nature*, 191.

moral theology—in this way, the practical implications of these theological truths were generally ignored.[106] Christian belief had become
seen as segregated from the Christian life, which in turn had become
guided almost exclusively by the natural law.

Hugo asserted that this loss was only exaggerated further by the
"modern" separation of moral theology from ascetical and mystical
theology.[107] This separation was destructive in that it removed any discussion of grace and holiness from moral theology.[108] As a result the
study of moral theology had become focused almost exclusively on casuistry rather than on what Hugo called a "positive moral theology."[109]
Indeed, he noted that Fenton himself had defined moral theology in
such terms in his book, *The Concept of Sacred Theology* (1941).[110] And
so moral theology was limited to discussions of what was sinful and
was not, missing was any concern with Christian perfection.[111] Indeed,
in his book, Fenton had written that any account of a higher ideal for
the Christian life would confuse the counsels of perfection with the

---

106   Hugo, *Nature*, 191.

107   Hugo continued, "And if one looks into the modern *Summas* of Moral
Theology, one finds that there has usually been removed from them most
of what pertains to ascetical and mystical theology, that is, the principles
that regulate the application of Christian truth to practice and to growth in
holiness." Hugo, *Nature*, 191.

108   In 1939, Hans Urs von Balthasar had made a very similar critique of
this separation of dogmatic theology from ascetical and mystical theology. For Balthasar, the result was the separation of a life of holiness from
the study of theology, and thus the absence in modern times of saints who
were also theologians. Hans Urs von Balthasar, "Theology and Sanctity," in
Essays in Theology: Word and Redemption, Bk 2, trans. A.V. Littledale, 49-86
(Montreal: Palm Publications, 1965).

109   Hugo, *Nature*, 197.

110   According to Fenton, moral theology "deals with the liceity and the il-
licit character of human acts. Because of its very nature the use of examples
or cases constitutes an excellent pedagogical means for learning and explaining this discipline. For this reason the subject itself is sometimes known as
casuistic moral." Fenton, *The Concept*, 214.

111   And Hugo noted that in practice, "this concern for sin is usually a
concern of mortal sin; venial sin is regarded as negligible; imperfections are
scarcely recognized at all." Hugo, *Nature*, 199.

commandments and natural law precepts.[112] Thus, any discussion of a holy life in correspondence with grace—what Hugo called, "the most important practical problem in the whole of theology"—was removed from moral theology and relegated to the confines of ascetical and mystical theology.[113] Hugo asserted that American neo-Thomists like Fenton and Connell were exiling what the Second Vatican Council would later term "the universal call to holiness" to the arena of the spiritual elites far beyond the life of "ordinary" Christians.[114]

With "modern" moral theology concerned almost exclusively with sin—particularly sins that violated the natural law rather than sins against charity—Hugo suggested that more ascetical and mystical theology had come to be understood as dealing with "supererogatory piety" rather than with integral and even essential aspects of theological study.[115] It was not surprising, then, that in American Catholic seminaries any interest in mystical theology was often considered a "sign of mental instability" and that when it was actually studied, the focus was typically on the accidental adjuncts of mysticism—"the mystical phenomena and charismata"—and not on the central and essential determinant of theology: union with God through love.[116] Hugo explained that,

> seminarians are usually taught not to regard such authors as St. John of the Cross and St. Frances de Sales as serious moral theologians…The greatest masters of applying the Christian teachings to the concrete problems of living, are neglected. Certainly their works are praised; but they are not used: they are honored and unread. The reading of such books is regarded as a commendable act of piety, although it is an act of piety that is usually not greatly emphasized; in any event they are not regarded or consulted as serious works of moral theology.[117]

---

112   Fenton, *The Concept*, 214.

113   Hugo, *Nature*, 201. To highlight this, Hugo described a three-volume, 1800 page manual of moral theology he owned that contained only nine pages on the subject of grace and treated "its practical problem in a footnote." Hugo, *Nature*, 201, fn 14.

114   Hugo, *Nature*, 204. See, *Lumen Gentium*, ch 5.

115   Hugo, *Nature*, 201.

116   Hugo, *Nature*, 200.

117   *Nature*, 200.

Likewise, ascetical theology usually carried with it certain "gloomy con-notations" and tended to be regarded as "a sort of hobby for spoilsports and misanthropes."[118] Lost was the notion that ascetical theology is "a practical discipline" concerned with the "dynamism of Christianity" and the "physiology of the Christian life."[119] Underlying all of this was a view of the supernatural further separated and exiled from nature.

3. "MODERN THEOLOGY" AND AQUINAS

Again, in much the same way as de Lubac, Hugo argued that the "modern theology" of American neo-Thomists like Fenton, Connell, and Connor had become far removed from the teaching of Thomas Aquinas—not a causal assertion to make in the 1940s. He pointed out that for Thomas, human nature's need to correspond with grace was a practical issue that was very much a part of his discussions of moral theology in the *Summa Theologica*.[120] Hugo explained that for Aquinas, "grace is an intrinsic principle of action and conduct; that is to say, it is the *inner dynamism* that impels supernatural conduct."[121] And to recognize grace as this "inner dynamism" is to recognize its prac-tical implications for the Christian life. For Thomas, grace is not sepa-rated from human nature—or merely related to it extrinsically—rather

118   Hugo, *Nature*, 200. Hugo pointed out an article in the May 1946 is-sue of *The American Ecclesiastical Review* which "hotly" disputed whether or not John of the Cross should be read by young seminarians or ordinary Catholics in general. Hugo *Nature*, 201, fn.13.

119   Hugo, *Nature*, 200.

120   Hugo noted that in the *Secunda Secundae* of the *Summa Theologica* which dealt with moral theology, Aquinas included not only a discus-sion of the virtues, but also of the active and contemplative life, the duty of Christian perfection, tracts on the Beatitudes and the gifts of the Holy Spirit in relation to the supernatural life and contemplative prayer, as well as a treatise on prayer. Thus, Hugo argued that the separations made by modern neo-Thomist did not exist in Aquinas, but instead there was unified theology. He pointed out that Aquinas's discussion of moral theology "devel-oped in close relation with his dogmatic teaching, all within the framework of a theology that he regards and treats as essentially one [and] includes, besides casuistry, the loftiest principles of ascetical and mystical theology, bringing all together in a unified system of spiritual doctrine." Hugo, *Nature*, 202.

121   Italics added. Hugo, *Nature*, 192.

it was intimately and intrinsically related to human nature as its final end and fulfillment. But in the "modern theology" of his critics, "this *intrinsic* principle of supernatural activity" that was central to Aquinas was largely ignored and instead the emphasis was placed on what Thomas had called "an *extrinsic* principle of action"—his discussion of law—which resulted in a tendency to "externalism and legalism."[122] In comparison with Thomas's more "unified system of spiritual doctrine," Hugo contended that the "modern theology" of his critics appeared rigidly separated and out of step with the Angelic Doctor.[123]

By claiming that mid-20th-century neo-Thomists had lost touch with the Angelic Doctor's more unified theological vision, Hugo was clearly onto something. For, more recently, Thomists like Leonard Boyle, O.P. have pointed out that Thomas wrote his *Summa Theologica* as guidance for Dominicans training for pastoral work.[124] And so, by "prefacing the *secunda* or "moral" part with the *prima pars* on God, Trinity and Creation, and then rounding it off with a *tertia pars* on the Son of God, Incarnation and the Sacraments," Boyle explained that Thomas "put practical theology, the study of Christian man, his virtues and vices, in a full theological context" firmly placed between the two mysteries of the faith: the Trinity and Incarnation.[125] And in doing so, Thomas can be read as trying to "deconstruct" the sin-focused casuistry which prevailed in the pastor's confessional handbooks of his day by dispersing his discussion of virtues and vices within a more systematic account of the final beatitude to which humans are called.[126] Indeed, Fergus Kerr, O.P. has explained that,

> Thomas offers a moral theology, a Christian ethics, centred on one's becoming the kind of person who would be fulfilled only in the promised bliss of face-to-face vision of God. It includes obedience

---

122   Hugo, *Nature*, 201.

123   Hugo wrote that "There is a need for someone to do for St. Thomas in theology what Cardinal Mercier did for him in philosophy, that is to restore him to the place of preeminence properly his, which the Church, as has been shown in many decrees, desires to have recognized." Hugo, *Nature*, 191.

124   Leonard Boyle, *The Setting of the* Summa Theologiae *of Saint Thomas*, (Toronto: Pontifical Institute of Mediaeval Studies, 1982).

125   Boyle, *Setting*, 16.

126   Fergus Kerr, *After Aquinas: Versions of Thomism*, (Malden, MA: Blackwell Publishing, 2002), 118.

to divine law, as a matter of course, but placed in the context of responding to the gift of divine beatitude.[127]

But as Kerr also noted, Thomas's hopes for such an integrated theology were quickly dashed as the discussions of moral theology in the *secunda secundae* soon became widely circulated apart from the rest of the *Summa*—disengaged from the *Summa* as a whole, thus "defeating Thomas's purpose of studying moral theology in the middle of the exposition of Christian doctrine."[128]

CONCLUSION

The upshot here is that Day appears to be correct in her suggestion that Hugo's theology and the controversy it caused shared similarities with that of de Lubac. Like debates taking place in Europe, the retreat controversy revolved around competing accounts of nature and grace. And like de Lubac and Blondel, Hugo's account of this relationship clearly challenged the understanding of the mid-century neo-Thomists. For Hugo, grace is not built onto a largely self-contained nature, but rather it was the inner dynamism of human nature bringing it fulfillment and perfection.

This American debate shared a similar dynamic with those involving de Lubac and Blondel. For at the time when Fenton and Connell were writing their critiques of *Applied Christianity*, Hugo was a parish curate in rural Pennsylvania. He had been ordained for less than ten years and had a master's degree in philosophy. He had been removed from his teaching positions and was no longer giving retreats. His responses were either printed by The Catholic Worker Press (at best a fly-by-night operation) or self-published. In stark contrast, Hugo's critics were some of the most important and influential Catholic theologians in the United States. From their faculty positions at The Catholic University of America and the editorial offices of *The American Ecclesiastical Review*, Fenton and Connell, in particular, had a great deal of influence in American Catholic theological and ecclesiastical circles. Their role in the "silencing" of John Courtney Murray, S.J. (1904-1967) in 1954 provided further evidence of this. [129] Fenton

127   Kerr, *After Aquinas*, 118.

128   Kerr, *After Aquinas*, 119.

129   See, J. Leon Hooper, "Murray and Day: Common Enemies, Common Cause?" *U.S. Catholic Historian* 24 (Winter 2006): 45-61.

and Connell were both working out of a theological perspective whose prevalence in American Catholic thought—while beginning to slip— was still very strong in the 1940s.[130] In short, the young Father Hugo's theological opponents were *the* American neo-Thomists of that period, tightly monitoring what Joseph Komonchak labeled a "domesticated theology."[131] And as was the case with Blondel and de Lubac, Hugo's retreat controversy was not a debate among peers, Fenton and Connell—like Descoqs and Garrigou-Lagrange—held a considerable advantage.

And Hugo's exchange with Connor over American Catholic COs reveals that—again like Blondel and de Lubac—Hugo's theological opponents were also his political opponents. For Hugo's public defense of American Catholic COs challenged the prevailing stance toward social engagement held in the Church. Indeed, his *Catholic Worker* articles questioned the basic assumptions of most American Catholics at the time—including most of the hierarchy and theological elites—that America was good for Catholicism and that Catholics were good for America.[132] For Hugo, while the United States was not evil, joining in its wars—even wars judged to be "just"—was by no means a pathway to holiness.

So, while the nature-supernatural relationship was very much at the center of Catholic theological discourse in general, it played a particularly crucial role in shaping Catholic engagement with particular cultures and societies—a fact highlighted by Blondel, de Lubac, and Hugo. The relevance of Hugo's theology today is that it continues to offer a corrective to much of the contemporary discussion of Catholic engagement with American society and culture. For these discussions have generally been dominated, as of late, by proponents of a

---

130   R. Scott Appleby and Jay Haas, "The Last of the Supernaturalists: Fenton, Connell, and the Threat of Catholic Indifferentism" *U.S. Catholic Historian*, 13 (Spring 1995): 39.

131   Komonchak noted that this theology was under the closest supervision and tightest control that theology had ever been in the history of the Church, and that it was taken seriously chiefly, if not exclusively, within the subculture of "modern Roman Catholicism." Komonchak, "Theology and Culture," 579.

132   For more on these assumptions, see Michael Baxter, "The Unsettling of Americanism: A Response to William Portier," *Communio* 27 (Spring 2000): 161-170.

Catholic "public theology"—in much the same way that neo-Thomism dominated such discussions two generations ago. And in fact, recent Catholics who have challenged this kind of public theology with a theological vision similar to Hugo have found themselves labeled by Catholic public theologians with many of the same charges that American neo-Thomists used to label Hugo in the 1940s. And so it is to these contemporary discussions and Hugo's relevance for them that we now turn.

CHAPTER VI

WHY HUGO STILL MATTERS

The general trend of Catholic theology in the twentieth century has been to seek a closer integration between nature
and grace, rejecting the "dualist" approach in which nature is
a self-enclosed structure upon which grace builds a kind of
superstructure, and to propose instead that grace is the fulfillment of nature's inner dynamism…However, having said
this one has not said a whole lot, because the vast majority of
theologians in the second half of the twentieth century would
say that they reject the dualist approach, that they believe that
grace and nature are integrally related, and that they believe
that holiness is not the special prerogative of the vowed religious. What matters is *how* one integrates nature and grace.

Frederick C. Bauerschmidt[1]

In 2004, Hugo's niece, Rosemary Fielding, wrote an article
about her uncle's theological vision titled: "Anti-Assimilationist
Retreat: Becoming Spiritually Inoculated Against
Americanism."[2] This provocatively titled article written in the
equally provocative *Culture Wars* magazine recounted Fielding's
spiritual journey which eventually led her to attend one of her uncle's retreats in 1981. She also described the "controversy" surrounding her uncle in the 1940s and likened it to contemporary depictions

---

1   Frederick C. Bauerschmidt, "Confessions of an Evangelical Catholic,"
Communio 31 (Spring 2004): 71.

2   Rosemary Fielding, "Anti-Assimilationist Retreat: Becoming Spiritually
Inoculated Against Americanism," *Culture Wars* (October 2004): 22-39.

of Hugo and the retreat.³ For Fielding, the opposition to her uncle stemmed from the fact that his theology challenged—both in the 1940s and today—Catholics' desire to fully assimilate into American society and culture. She recounted that her uncle often argued that Catholics should resist the temptation to divide themselves accord- ing to American political categories of "liberal" or "conservative" and instead think in terms of being either "superficial" or "radical." Fielding explained,

> Considering the muddying of the waters caused among Catholics by the new American ideology of 'neo-conservative/neo-liberalism' that supports the idea of an American empire, [Hugo's] aphorism about Christian social morality was somewhat prophetic of the way Roman Catholicism would be the casualty in the hardcore parti- san battles among Catholic thinkers at the turn of the millenni- um. The Retreat took arms against the reductionism that is forced upon Roman Catholicism by Americanism, the Procrustean bed on which American ideologies, liberal and conservative, repeatedly dismember the Church.⁴

For Fielding, the theology of the retreat had clear social and political implications for Catholics in the United States—implications which challenged the dominant approach to social engagement in American Catholicism both then and now.

This final chapter will examine the implications of Hugo's theolog- ical arguments for contemporary American Catholic social thought and will suggest that his arguments remain relevant today. For the charges leveled against Hugo by his neo-Thomist critics have a simi- lar ring to those that continue to be made against American Catholic radicals today by advocates of the theological perspective that has come to replace American neo-Thomism as the dominant approach to Catholic engagement with American society and culture—Catholic

---

3   Fielding pointed to Patrick Jordan's *Commonweal* review of an anthology of Hugo's writings, *Weapons of the Spirit*, edited by Michael Aquilina and David Scott. In it Jordan wrote that in reading Hugo he felt he had fallen into "a time warp." He called the retreat theology "harsh," "wooden" and hav- ing a "certain rigidity and literalness." Fielding also quoted a letter to the ed- itor from Mark and Louise Zwick, of the Houston Catholic Worker, which defended Hugo, arguing that he was "profoundly spiritual, full of wisdom, holy and holistic, totally unwooden and unrigid." Fielding, 33.

4   Fielding, 38.

"public theology." In fact, contemporary Catholic "public theologians" share some significant theological similarities with their now much maligned neo-Thomist predecessors—particularly in their view of human nature. All this to say that Hugo's theological vision and its challenge to the Thomism of the 1940s—while set in terms and categories somewhat removed from these contemporary conversations—continues to provide a much needed corrective and alternative to the Catholic public theology of today.

HUGO'S THEOLOGY

In order to appreciate its continued relevance, a summary of Hugo's theology is necessary. As preceding chapters have sought to reveal, Hugo's theological vision should be understood as having a much more nuanced account of nature and grace than his critics—both then and now—have recognized. Far from promoting an "exaggerated supernaturalism" that lead to a Jansenist denigration of human nature, Hugo recognized nature as good and yet as always insufficient. This insufficiency was twofold: *both* as inherent to a finite nature called to an infinite final end *and* as the historical result of original sin—concupiscence. His understanding of the nature-supernatural relationship, therefore, was one of distinction without separation: human nature was created with a supernatural final end far beyond its ability to attain on its own. In this sense, what Hugo was striving for was a more integrated view of nature and grace than his neo-Thomist contemporaries like Fenton, Connell, and even John Courtney Murray, S.J., were articulating—a view which emphasized the practical implications of the supernatural in the ordinary Christian life.

Such integration was clearly the theological thrust of the retreat, the notion that by virtue of their supernatural final end all Christians were called to live a life of holiness—the life of a saint.[5] At its core, such a life required correspondence with the grace necessary to perfect it. Beyond the gift of creation itself, Hugo understood that the action of grace was multiple and included not only healing the wounds of sin, but—even more fundamentally—elevating human nature beyond

---

5 For Hugo, "the fact that man has a supernatural end, determines that the means for attaining this end must also be supernatural." Hugo, *Sign*, 104.

that which was "merely natural."[6] The retreat focused on discerning how to live a life that corresponded with this grace. Over and over, Hugo assured his retreatants of the superabundance of this gratuitous gift from God and insisted that its availability should not be their concern, rather they should focus on how to correspond with it. And this correspondence with grace required that one focus on the love of God alone, while attachments to anything else would only present distractions. This required not only avoiding sin, but also breaking habitual attachments to created goods. For as Ignatius and the other Jesuit mystical writers made clear, while they were not evil, these goods could never fill the void that marks nature. This renunciation or "dying to self" was central to the retreat—the giving up of the merely good in favor of the infinitely better.

What Hugo offered, then, was an account of how to live a life of continual discernment which seeks to be in correspondence with the sanctifying action of grace—an account, he argued, which was deeply rooted in the Christian spiritual tradition. "The Folly of the Cross" was the name given to this constant assessment of one's life—the ongoing attempt to correspond with the actions of grace by examining one's own motives and actions to see if they are informed by the love of God. While this continual examination is a casuistry of sorts, it was not the rigid casuistry of the neo-Thomists and their manuals which Hugo had critiqued for separating the implications of grace from the ordinary day-to-day life of a Christian. Rather it is a flexible, alert, critical, yet loving assessment of the life of a Christian in light of his or her ultimate destiny. For while the call to die to oneself and renounce attachments to created goods often seemed harsh, Hugo was a spiritual director and retreat leader chiefly for lay people and he was aware that the life of these men and women inescapably involved some use of these goods. But he was also aware that attachment to these goods usually became habitual and could come to dominate their lives, becoming ends in themselves and detrimental to the Christian life. For these habitual attachments developed into the "natural motives"

---

6   Hugo explained that we have a twofold purpose in corresponding with grace: "first, that we may live on the supernatural plane; secondly, that we may overcome sin and its effects. And while these effects actually go on together in our souls, the limitations of human thought and speech compel it to distinguish them and treat of them separately." Hugo, *Nature*, 174.

which informed the "natural actions" that made up the "natural life." And again, Hugo was careful to explain,

> I do not say that it is necessary to give up morally good natural motives under pain of sin. I do not say that such motives are wholly without merit in a Christian (that is a doubtful matter). I simply say that it is better, more loving, more pleasing to God, to act out of love for Him than for any merely natural good.[7]

In short, a merely "natural life" is not the life to which Christians aspire.

Much of the discussion in the retreat, therefore, was devoted to how to use created goods without developing an attachment to them. In response to this largely pastoral and, indeed, un-rigorist concern for the proper use of the things of the world, Hugo offered the idea of the "samples." This is the notion that many of the goods of the world could be properly regarded as reflecting the goodness of God. Regarded as such, these samples were affirmed as good, necessary, and certainly distinct from what is sinful. But while samples are needed, the continual use of such goods could—and generally does—lead to developing an attachment to them. And so the more these samples can be renounced, the less likely they would become distractions and impediments to grace. These samples are sown not because they are spoiled or corrupt, but so that they will flourish into something much better. Like a farmer sowing seeds, the more samples that are sown, the greater the harvest that will be reaped. And just as the farmer did not mourn the loss of the seeds he sowed, so Hugo encouraged his re-treatants that their samples should be sown without regret but instead in joyful anticipation.

But this sort of renunciation is not always voluntary, for God will often cut away one's attachments to samples. In this way, Hugo suggested that hardship and suffering could be understood as the shears used by God to "prune" one's attachments—especially attachments to oneself. God is active in the world and this notion of pruning was seen as the will of God bringing a person closer to her ultimate destiny and so should also be regarded with a sense of gratitude and even joy.

Through this continual sowing and pruning, and the ongoing discernment of one's attachments and motives that it entailed, the daily

---

7   Hugo, *Nature*, 149.

life of a Christian could be made more perfect.[8] This was the notion
Hugo saw rooted in Caussade's "sacrament of the present moment"—
the idea that every moment of the day offers a chance to correspond
with the will of God. Such growth in perfection is the practical implication of grace. For grace is not remote from every day life, but
instead it is the inner dynamism of that life. As Hugo described it,
"the hurly-burly of every day" becomes holy through correspondence
with grace.[9] This was the integrated view of the Christian life that
Hugo proposed, what he called "the quintessential doctrine" of retreat
theology.

"MODERN THEOLOGY"

This notion that all Christians are called to holiness—a notion that
Hugo saw as so central to Ignatius, Lallemant, and many others within the tradition—had become lost to the theological perspective that
dominated Catholicism at mid-century. For instead of the more integrated account of the nature and grace that Hugo was attempting
to articulate, this theology separated and eventually exiled the supernatural from nature—and thus Christianity from the modern world.
Through this quarantining, the practical implications of grace were
overlooked and eventually forgotten. Correspondence with grace was
regarded as necessary only to the extent that it was needed to help
avoid sin. Lost was the idea that grace was necessary primarily—and
even apart from sin—to elevate human nature to its fulfillment and
perfection. For Hugo, this separation and exile of the implications of
grace could be seen in the separation of holiness or the supernatural
from discussions in the moral theology of his day. Instead of regarding the Christian life as one focused on seeking sanctity, this view of
Christian morality presented the Christian life as chiefly concerned
with following the tenets of the natural law.[10]

---

8   Hugo used the image of fire transforming steel to illustrate this action
of grace perfecting nature: "So must our human nature be transformed by
grace; it likewise will remain essentially the same; but when penetrated
through and through with divine action, it will be soft and pliant, readily
following the impulses of grace." Hugo, *Applied Christianity*, 25.

9   Hugo, *Nature*, 226.

10   Hugo suggested that while following the natural law and avoiding mortal sin certainly cleared away all that was wholly incompatible with the love

For Hugo, this "modern theology" produced a "spirit of pious naturalism" that overemphasized the sufficiency of nature, while at the same time it under-emphasized the need for grace.[11] And out of this naturalism emerged a "sin mentality" which no longer recognized human nature as distinct from both the sinful and the supernatural, but rather saw nature as either corrupted by sin or confused with the supernatural.[12] In either case, the loss of an accurate account of nature led many theologians to view the world exclusively in terms of sin and grace, with the result that the supernatural became regarded as simply that which is not sinful.[13] And with such a view, any sense of the supereminence of the supernatural was missed.

Hugo saw this "sin mentality" and its theological anthropology as a major factor in shaping how his critics could read the retreat theology as Jansenist.[14] And so, in response to his critics, he sought to recover a more accurate account of human nature from various sources in the tradition—particularly within Ignatian spirituality—and in this way to also recover a sense of the mystery of the supernatural.[15] For all the charges of denigrating nature and advocating an "exaggerated supernaturalism," then, Hugo was focused on restoring an understanding of human nature which he believed to have been lost—one rooted in the Christian tradition.

Indeed there is a clear recognition in Hugo's writings of the basic goodness in human nature—for again, if nature is seen as sinful, then the supernatural becomes merely that which is not sinful. This

---

of God, a Christian is called to "heights of love" beyond this. Hugo, *Nature*, 167.

11   Hugo, *Nature*, 77.

12   Hugo, *Nature*, 7.

13   Hugo, *Nature*, 7.

14   Hugo stated that for his critics, "as long as you observe the Mosaic code—which, they say, except for the third commandment, is the natural law imposed by reason—all will be well, nothing more required, and anyone who asks more of you is stricter than Christ Himself, is therefore a fanatic, a rigorist, an extremist." Hugo, *Nature*, 77.

15   Hugo wrote; "The reason why *Applied Christianity* is so interested in vindicating the goodness of nature is that only in this way is it possible to understand and define the supernatural order; and the task which *Applied Christianity* sets for itself is to describe the supernatural life." Hugo, *Nature*, 7.

goodness was particularly affirmed in his discussions of the "samples," for if they are not fundamentally good these samples could not function as reflections of the divine. Goodness is inherent to human nature and remained even after the Fall. Hugo was clear that the effect of original sin was not the loss or corruption of this goodness, but rather the removal of the "preternatural gift of integrity"—a divine gift given human nature to order its faculties to the love of God.[16] The "direct effect" of original sin, therefore, was to deprive human nature of this gratuitous gift—in effect to leave human nature on its own, but unchanged.[17]

In addition to this more direct effect of the Fall, Hugo pointed out that human nature was also affected more indirectly which prevented it from functioning properly and from fully accomplishing "even that justice which is connatural to it."[18] This was the "wound" brought on by concupiscence—the tendency of the human appetites to seek created goods rather than God.[19] While concupiscence is understood as not itself sinful, Hugo explained that it is an "inclination to sin" (*ad peccatum inclinat*): "prone to lead men astray and may even enter their good works, not of necessity ruining these in their substance, yet in

---

16   Hugo, *Nature*, 47.

17   Hugo likened this to descendants of a wealthy person losing the family's fortune. Hugo, *Nature*, 41.

18   Hugo, *Nature*, 43. Hugo explained that, while "in the long run" it is impossible to practice even the natural virtues without supernatural aid (i.e., without living a supernatural life) it is also indeed true that it is possible to perform "good natural actions" without the assistance of grace, "otherwise we would have to conclude that all the actions of pagans and infidels are sinful—a proposition that has been condemned by the Church." Hugo, *Applied Christianity*, 201.

19   Hugo described concupiscence as the natural appetites of human nature that are good. He explained that in itself, "concupiscence is simply the tendency of the human appetite to seek its own good, its own delight (*concupiscentia est appetitus delectabilis*)." Prior to original sin these appetites were regulated and ordered by the gift of original justice. But after the Fall, this gift was lost and concupiscence began to seek its own good immoderately and became—without any intrinsic change to itself and human nature—"an inclination" of our nature "to seek inordinately after corruptible goods." Hugo, *Nature*, 46.

some measure spoiling their goodness and diminishing their merit."[20] In short, Hugo did not view human nature as sinful or radically in-compatible with grace, but neither did he ignore its limitations and insufficiency.

"THOMISM IN ACTION"

Far from the Jansenism of Port Royal, Hugo argued that this theolog-ical anthropology was rooted in the thinking of Thomas Aquinas and that Thomas's teachings provided a "fundamental principle" to the re-treat's "practical spiritual doctrine."[21] Hugo even referred to the retreat as "Thomism in action."[22] Such a label is not without merit, for much of Hugo's thinking seems based in the theology and theological catego-ries of Aquinas. For instance, Thomas does clearly assert the goodness in human nature and even distinguishes it as threefold. First, there is a goodness intrinsic to human nature such as the body, the soul, and its various powers (reason, the will, and the irascible and concupiscible appetites).[23] Goodness is also present in the gratuitous "gift of origi-nal justice" (*donum originalis justitae*)—the only good aspect of human nature that is not intrinsic to it.[24] And finally, the goodness of human

20   Hugo, *Nature*, 48-49. Hugo wrote that "Everything in *Applied Christianity* that speaks of the influence of concupiscence is based on those words, *et ad peccatum inclinat*." Hugo, *Nature*, 41.

21   Hugo pointed out that while Baius and the Jansenists had held that all works of "infidels" are sinful because they regarded human nature as radi-cally corrupt, in contrast, *Applied Christianity* took "practical account of the disordered movements that result from concupiscence." He contended that the retreat theology asserted that natural actions are likely to be blemished, "not radically or necessarily as the Jansenists held, but as a matter of practi-cal experience and in the long run, as they habitually occur in one having a merely natural mentality." Hugo described his theology as taking seriously the effects of concupiscence—the fact that natural actions (imperfect ac-tions motivated by natural motives) are typically flawed because of concu-piscence. Hugo, *Nature*, 48-49.

22   Hugo, *Nature*, 45.

23   Aquinas, *ST* I-II, 85.1.

24   Aquinas, *ST* I-II, 85.5., *ST* I-II, 81.2. While in a very exact sense Aquinas called original justice a good of human nature, he nevertheless was clear that it was not intrinsic to human nature. For to view it as such would be to understand it as something owed to human beings rather than

nature is evident in its "inclination to virtue" (*inclinationem ad virtutem*).[25] Aquinas explained that after the Fall, the goodness intrinsic to human nature remained unchanged.[26] But what did change was that the gift of original justice was completely removed.[27] While the removal of this gratuitous gift did not change human nature intrinsically, the order and harmony it provided is no longer present—Aquinas described this as the direct effect of original sin.[28] Therefore, while the Fall did not change or corrupt human nature, it did result in the loss of this gift of original justice.[29]

For Aquinas, all other effects on human nature which follow from the Fall are a result of this privation of original justice and so are indirect effects. It is in this kind of indirect way that human nature's "inclination to virtue" becomes altered. For while the inclination to virtue remains in human nature after the Fall, it is lessened—not by original sin—but by the actual sins which occur as a result of the loss of original justice.[30] With this "wounding" of nature, its various faculties have trouble functioning properly. For instance, reason—especially

---

as a gratuitous gift. In contrast to Aquinas, the "perfect nature" of Baius and Jansen asserted that original justice was part of human nature and thus owed to human nature by God (Baius) or required by God (Jansen) as a part of human nature rather than a gratuitously given gift. T.C. O'Brien, "Appendix 2," *St. Thomas Aquinas Summa Theologiae, vol.26, Original Sin (Ia2ae. 81-85)* trans. T.C. O'Brien, O.P. (New York: Blackfriars/ McGraw-Hill Book Co.,1965), 113.

25   This inclination is an intrinsic part of human nature, deriving from the various aspects that comprise our nature. For example, Aquinas argued that our reason has a natural appetite for the truth, just as our will has for the good. In this way, both our reason and will incline our soul to satisfy these appetites by seeking their ends. This becomes an inclination to virtue, when for instance, in seeking the truth we practice the virtue of prudence and in seeking the good we practice justice. Aquinas, *ST* I-II, 51.1, *ST* I-II, 63.1, *ST* I-II, 85.1.

26   Human reason, for example, is not damaged or diminished by original sin, nor is our will. Aquinas, *ST* I-II, 85.1.

27   Aquinas, *ST* I-II, 85.1.

28   Aquinas, *ST* I-II, 85.3.

29   Aquinas, *ST* I-II, 85.1.

30   Aquinas, *ST* I-II, 85.1.

with regard to moral decision making—becomes "blunted" and the will becomes "hardened against the true good."[31] Thus, Thomas explained, "sustained virtuous activity" becomes increasingly difficult as concupiscence grows in ardor.[32] And so, an already insufficient human nature becomes even more limited following the Fall.

Due to their place in the "hierarchy" of human faculties, the wounding of the "concupiscible appetites" figures prominently in Aquinas's understanding of how the "inclination to virtue" becomes lessened. For these appetites are an intrinsic part of human nature and therefore are not sinful *per se*.[33] Indeed, when they were properly ordered by original justice these appetites supported "the inclination to virtue"— particularly the virtue of temperance.[34] But with the loss of original justice, Thomas described these now unchecked appetites as "straining towards" the various created goods they desire.[35] This is what Thomas means by "concupiscence." And with concupiscence, disorder and disharmony break out, for by straining or inclining toward worldly goods, concupiscence inclines human nature away from God. And in this way, Aquinas argued that concupiscence becomes an inclination *toward* sin.[36]

HUMAN NATURE "LEFT TO ITSELF"

In summing all of this up, T.C. O'Brien, O.P.—an editor and translator of the Blackfriars' edition of the *Summa Theologiae*—noted that for Aquinas original sin does not deprive human nature of anything that is strictly proper to itself.[37] Instead, it is the gratuitous gift of original justice that is lost. Following the Fall, human nature is simply "left to itself" and it is in this sense that Thomas understood human nature

---

31   Aquinas, *ST* I-II, 85.3.

32   Aquinas, *ST* I-II, 85.3.

33   Aquinas, *ST* I. 81.2.

34   This order, Aquinas explained, placed the concupiscible appetite under the control of our reason, and subjected to God as its final end. This order enabled the concupiscible appetite to temper its desire for created goods. Aquinas, *ST* I-II, 82.3.

35   Aquinas, *ST* I-II, 82.2.

36   Aquinas, *ST* I-II, 84.3.

37   O'Brien, 152.

as disordered—a disorder not caused by the corruption of sin, but by human nature's own "defectibility."[38] For Aquinas, then, "fallen nature" is human nature "left to itself" without divine assistance—or as O'Brien put it, human nature "stays itself, but forlorn."[39]

O'Brien pointed out that for Aquinas there are historically two "states" of human nature.[40] In "the state of original justice" before the Fall, original justice ordered human nature, while in "the state of fallen nature" human nature no longer has that assistance. In both states—before and after the Fall—grace is needed for human nature to function properly. In other words, human nature has never existed in either a self-sufficient state of "pure nature" nor in a state of "perfect nature" where grace was somehow a part of or blurred with human nature.[41] For Thomas, human nature—while good—has never been capable of much on its own.

Hugo pointed out that this view of human nature seemed to contradict many of the early-twentieth century neo-Thomist accounts which emphasized "the optimism inherent in the Thomistic conception" and thereby denied the need for renunciation of anything but sin: "since

---

38   O'Brien continued, "Original sin is not the addition of a positive inclination to moral evil; it is the loss, the lack of supernatural endowment that would have restrained the sources of moral defect in man." O'Brien, O.P., 152.

39   O'Brien stated: "As its description indicates, original justice preserved man from defects stemming from nature itself because of its 'composition' (Aquinas, *Compend. Theol.*195). The preventative power of original justice points to an innate defectibility in man's moral powers. This defectibility is not something added to nature, nor any positive obstacle or diminution of the inclination to virtue." For Aquinas, this inclination to virtue was 'not the actual possession of virtues, but a capacity for their acquisition, even as it is a capacity to receive a yet unrealized human perfection.'" O'Brien, 157-158.

40   O'Brien, 151.

41   According to O'Brien, "When St. Thomas speaks of nature 'in its integrity' or of what man can do in his initial condition 'by his natural powers alone' [I, 95,1; I-II, 109,3], he is speaking of the state of original justice, and of man's moral capacity for ends connatural to human nature, a capacity enjoyed because of the gift of original justice. He does not refer to an imaginary condition either of 'pure nature' or of a 'state of integrity.' He compares the natural power of man in original justice with the same powers in fallen nature." O'Brien, *St. Thomas*, 151.

nature is entirely good and uncorrupt both in itself and its activities, why—they ask—should it be mortified?"[42] Unfortunately, Thomas seems to be read in a similar fashion today. Indeed, Thomas's understanding of nature "left to itself" seems far removed from what many contemporary theologians have come to regard as the "Thomistic" view of human nature.[43] In fact, Aquinas's view of human nature seems closer to what is often termed an "Augustinian" anthropology, with its emphasis on the effects of sin and the need of grace—a view sometimes described as pessimistic of human nature in contrast to the optimism found in the Thomistic approach.[44]

ON BEHALF OF GRATIA ELEVANS

Just as he had turned to Ignatius, Lallemant, and the Jesuit mystical tradition to certify the retreat's emphasis on the supernatural, so Hugo turned to Aquinas to justify its account of human nature. [45] This anthropology recognizes that human nature is not the self-contained "pure nature" of neo-Thomists, and neither is it blurred with the supernatural into the "perfect nature" proposed by Baius and the Jansenists. Rather human nature is viewed as good, but inherently unstable.

---

42   Hugo concluded that the renunciation required by the supposedly more severe and gloomy Augustinian approach, which was practiced out of a conviction of personal sinfulness and corruption, was in fact "less strict, less thorough, less drastic" than that required by the Aquinas's doctrine "freely practiced, not in sorrow of being a sinner, though he will include this also, but in the joy of being a son of God, elevated by grace to the plane of the divine." Hugo, *Sign*, 196.

43   For an example of a recent use of these categories see, Richard Gaillardetz, "Ecclesiological Foundations of Modern Catholic Social Teaching" in *Modern Catholic Social Teaching*, Kenneth R. Himes, O.F.M., ed. (Washington, DC: Georgetown University Press 2004), 72-98. Also, Joseph Komonchak, "Vatican II and the Encounter between Catholicism and Liberalism" in *Catholicism and Liberalism: Contributions to American Public Philosophy* edited by R. Bruce. Douglass and David Hollenbach (New York: Cambridge University Press, 1994), 76-99.

44   Gaillardetz, 74.

45   Hugo wrote that Aquinas's account of human nature, "shows at once that nature is good and yet, in its present state, requires a purification." Hugo, *Nature*, 47

This account of human nature reveals that Hugo's theology is much more subtle than his critics—both then and now—have suggested. For the kind of renunciation Hugo called for is a much more radical process than simply seeking to remove the historical effects of the Fall, and Hugo was fond of pointing out that Latin word *radix* referred to "the root." Instead, Christian renunciation was "a disciplining of the natural faculties themselves, a restraint exercised on their natural activity, a curbing of it, even a breaking of it... that it may respond with immediate docility to the secret, unfelt control of grace."[46] In other words, Christian renunciation is not only about avoiding sin, but even more fundamentally and radically, it is about bringing human nature into correspondence with grace. And this is not a single action of grace, but rather it is twofold: acting to both heal the historical effects of sin (*gratia medicinalis*) and also to elevate human nature to perfection (*gratia elevans*).[47] While *gratia medicinalis* became historically necessary after the Fall, Hugo explained that *gratia elevans* was always a part of the economy of salvation—even prior to sin:

> sin is not the only or even the *primary* basis for mortification...there is *another* and a *prior* reason and motive... since man's elevation to the divine life is the primary element in the divine plan for the salvation of mankind, it is also the primary basis for the practices proper to the Christian life, which is essentially a supernatural life; hence it is the primary reason and motive for the practice of detachment and mortification...Sin is a contingent act on the part of man, not an essential element in the divine plan itself as originally conceived by God... Therefore, the need to do penance on account of sin, as a corrective and atonement, derives obviously from the contingent fact of sin and is therefore itself contingent, secondary, supplementary."[48]

---

46   Hugo explained that such mortification did not destroy human nature, but "break it, as we speak of a spirited horse being broken, that it may also be controlled by a rein held lightly in a child's hands." Hugo, *Sign*, 196.

47   According to Hugo, grace does not do these actions separately or at different times, "it does them at one and the same instant of time, and so long as it resides in us, it continuously produces these two effects in us: it acts medicinally to help us overcome sin, and at the same time it elevates us above nature." Hugo, *Nature*, 174.

48   Hugo, *Nature*, 105.

The necessity of grace is not simply a consequence of original sin, but rather it is inherent for an unstable human nature. For with the loss of original justice, "the Fall" was a fall from grace and not—as Baius and Jansen taught—a fall from a "perfect nature" with grace regarded as a corrective to simply restore this "perfect nature."[49]

To teach that Christian renunciation is necessary only for that which is sinful, as Hugo suggested his neo-Thomist critics did, was to fall into a similar theological trap as Baius and Jansen did and to limit the idea of Christian renunication far too narrowly.[50] For the whole "sacrificial element in Christianity" is not merely a historical consequence of original sin, but rather it is to raise one beyond her desires for the things of this world and to bring one's appetites, motives, and actions into correspondence with grace.[51] In this sense, far from a "Jansenist" over-emphasis on the effects of sin, Hugo's theological perspective viewed those effects as secondary.[52] Instead, its focus on the need to "die to oneself"—the Folly of the Cross—was centered first and foremost on human nature's ultimate destiny, a supernatural final end that it has longed for even prior to the Fall.

Hugo recognized *gratia elevans* as "the primary determinant" of the life of a Christian—proof of "the unity of the Christian life" as supernatural actions and their correspondence with grace perfect human nature into a "new creature."[53] He pointed out that this emphasis on the perfection brought about by grace is consistent with Aquinas's axiom: *cum enim gratia non tollat naturam, sed perficiat*—"grace does not destroy nature, but perfects it."[54] It also mirrored de Lubac's focus on the perfection brought about by *donum perfectum*, as well.

---

49   Hugo, *Nature*, 105.

50   Hugo called this a "gross naturalism." Hugo, *Nature*, 105.

51   According to Hugo, "This elevation to divine life is the primary reason for renouncing a merely natural mode of acting and living, because it is the primary fact and basis of the whole Christian religion." Hugo, *Nature*, 54.

52   While his view of the effects of original sin did not imply that human nature was intrinsically corrupted by the Fall, Hugo explained that it did "presuppose that there has been a Fall." Hugo, *Nature*, 54.

53   Hugo, *Nature*, 71, 204.

54   Aquinas, *ST* I, 1.8. Thomas Gilby, O.P., translated this famous axiom: "Since grace does not scrap nature but brings it to perfection," in *St. Thomas*

DISTINCT, BUT NOT SEPARATE

Underlying all of this is Hugo's theology of nature and grace, a theology which recognized the distinctions that exist between nature and that which is sinful or supernatural. Human nature is not sinful, but it is finite—both inherently and historically—and so it is distinct from the infiniteness and supereminence of the supernatural. But while distinct from nature, Hugo explained that grace is not separate from it, rather there is an "intimacy" that exists with grace as the inner dynamism and ultimate fulfillment of human nature.[55]

Nature and the supernatural are neither extrinsically related in the sense advocated by early twentieth-century Thomists, nor are they blurred together in the manner taught by Baius and Jansen. Nor are they are radically incompatible in the way Hugo's critics charged him with asserting. Grace has always been needed to bring a finite nature to its ultimate end.

Again, this was the theology that profoundly shaped Dorothy Day and structured her telling of her life story in *The Long Loneliness*.[56] For in her autobiography, Day clearly described giving up the "natural happiness" she found in her "two great loves"—her life with Forster and with her friends in the Old Left—in terms of choosing the better over the good. Day did not understand herself as simply renouncing something sinful, instead she saw herself as also giving up a life that

Aquinas *Summa Theologiae* vol.1 (New York: Blackfriars/ McGraw-Hill Book Company, 1963), 31.

55   According to Hugo: "Grace is in itself a principle of action wholly distinct from the human soul and infinitely above it. Grace is not merged with the soul, nor lost in it, nor does it become part of the soul. It is joined to the soul, closely indeed, but only in an accidental manner, as the philosophers put it. The intimacy of this union is sufficient to permit unity of action even when the soul acts on the supernatural plane; still, the distinction must be insisted upon to guard the supernatural character of grace and of actions impelled by grace. Hugo, *Nature*, 59, 192.

56   This theology is also evident throughout Day's recently published diaries and letters, see *The Duty of Delight*, Robert Ellsberg, ed. (Milwaukee: Marquette University Press, 2008); and *All the Way to Heaven*, Robert Ellsberg, ed. (Milwaukee: Marquette University Press, 2010). For some discussion of the significance of Hugo and the retreat as evidenced in Day's letters, see Michael Baxter's review of *All the Way to Heaven*, "The Long Correspondence," *America* (November 8. 2010).

was good and joy-filled in order to pursue what she regarded as something much greater—a supernatural life of holiness. And it was the natural happiness of her earlier life—in a sense a sample—which Day saw as leading her to this far better life.[57]

WHY HUGO STILL MATTERS

Hugo's theological perspective continues to be important for Catholic theological discourse today. For just as Hugo challenged the American neo-Thomists' stance toward Catholic engagement with American society and culture, so Hugo's theology offers an alternative to the public theology that is so influential in American Catholicism now. Not surprisingly, the charges leveled against Hugo by his neo-Thomist critics in the 1940s are very similar to contemporary charges made by "public" theologians against Catholics who have been shaped by Hugo's vision.[58]

David O'Brien, for instance, has argued that while the "evangelical Catholicism" practiced by Day and the Catholic Worker movement challenged the church, it also limited its audience, restricted its language, short-circuited its responsibility, and tended toward what he called "an apocalyptic sectarianism."[59] O'Brien asserted that by always questioning the legitimacy of secular institutions and policies, these Catholics "devalued" the demands of citizenship and "reduced" the moral significance of politics and the broader society.[60] This assertion

57   Day, *The Long Loneliness*, 134

58   As noted in Fielding's articles, Hugo wanted American Catholics to be *radical*. "Totalitarian Catholics" was a similar term he used to describe Day and other Catholic Workers: "men and women who accept in full the practical implications of the Gospel, are capable of creating a genuinely Christian society or could feel at ease in such a society should it ever be established." Hugo, *Sign*, 180. For more on the American Catholic radicalist tradition, see Michael Baxter, "Notes on Catholic Americanism and Catholic Radicalism: Toward a Counter-Tradition of Catholic Social Ethics," in *American Catholic Traditions: Resources for Renewal*, ed. Sandra Yocum Mize and William Portier (Maryknoll, New York: Orbis, 1997), 53-71.

59   David O'Brien, *Public Catholicism* (New York: Macmillan Publishing Co., 1989), 246.

60   O'Brien continued this critique, arguing that "by defining issues and responses in Christian terms, advocates [of this kind of "Evangelical Catholicism"] become marginalized in the larger public debate. Respected,

stems, at least in part, from a belief that the theology which informed their "Evangelical Catholicism" had itself devalued human nature and tended toward a world-denying and rigorist perfectionism.[61] And in much the same way, George Weigel has described Day as being rooted in "a radically eschatological view of history" with "apocalyptic overtones."[62] He argued that this view led Day to denigrate and ignore human history and thus the "world's demands in history."[63] Because of her "radically eschatological" perspective of history, Weigel asserted, Day maintained a kind of sectarian stance that was especially evident in her pacifism during in World War II.[64]

These charges of denigrating human history and devaluing citizenship by focusing too exclusively on an eschatological and apocalyptic final end, clearly mirror the charges of "exaggerated supernaturalism" made against Hugo decades earlier. And to fully understand the link between critiques made in the 1940s and these more recent ones, the paradigm out of which the more contemporary charges emerge must be recognized. This is the paradigm articulated by John Courtney Murray, S.J., in *We Hold These Truths*, published in 1960, in which he highlighted a particular response to the growing "*mystique de la terre*" in American society at mid-century.[65] He called this response a

---

even admired, they are not seen as offering an appropriate or reasonable way in which the American public as a whole can evaluate problems and formulate solutions. Only part of the problem is church and state. Rather, it is a problem of responsible citizenship." O'Brien, *Public Catholicism*, 246.

61   Hugo subtitled *Nature and the Supernatural*—"A Defense of the Evangelical Ideal."

62   George Weigel, *Tranquilitatis Ordinis* (New York: Oxford University Press, 1987), 150.

63   Weigel, 150.

64   Weigel wrote that her eschatology was especially influential: "Like the monk Father Zossima in *The Brothers Karamozov*, Day believed that 'the radicalism of love ignores time,' and thus the world's demands in history— even under Hitler. Dorothy Day did not flinch from the implications of this radically eschatological view of our present responsibilities in this world." Weigel, 151.

65   Murray explained that those making such a withdrawal regarding both human nature and history were "refused and denied," and their withdrawal was usually preceded by an "utter prophetic condemnation of the total *res*

Catholic temptation to "spiritually withdraw" from American culture and society, a temptation that had led to a "new American Catholic Right"—an "integrist" movement that regarded all of nature and history only as sources of corruption.[66] But such Catholics, Murray explained, tended toward an "eschatological humanism" which appealed heavily to Scripture and emphasized the fact that the final end of human nature was totally transcendent to human nature.[67] The supernatural final end was seen as a divine gift that is "radically discontinuous" with all human effort and history—thus the only human values worth affirming are those evoked by grace, the only true humanism is eschatological, and the only true human values are supernatural.[68] Since this account of human nature emphasized sin as a constant and permanent reality which darkened all human achievement, American social conditions, institutions, and ideals were regarded as "radically discontinuous" with grace—a "necessary evil" which meant that, at best, participation in American society and culture was as irrelevant as the basket-weaving of the Desert Fathers.[69]

As if referring to directly to Hugo, Murray argued that for these Catholics the "paradox of the Cross"—"he who would save his life must lose it"—was the central truth of Christianity.[70] For it was understood that through such renunciation, the dying to one's self as Christ died on the cross, that one's ultimate fulfillment could hope to

---

humana" which America represented. John Courtney Murray, S.J., *We Hold These Truths* (Kansas City, MO: Sheed and Ward, 1960), 184-185.

66 Unlike the "Old French Catholic Right" which firmly believed that the Church's fortunes were wedded to the fortunes of the monarchy, Murray pointed out, "The new American Catholic Right" believed that the fortunes of the Church and of the individual Catholics were "completely divorced from all manner of earthly fortunes." And this attitude had roots in the Catholic subculture—"the secular separation of Catholics from the main currents of national life." Murray, 185.

67 Murray explained that in this orientation, "The Kingdom is not built from below, nor does it repose upon any cornerstone laid by human hands. It is a divine act; it is an irruption from above." Murray, 185.

68 Murray, 185

69 Murray, 195.

70 Murray, 188.

226   *Peters* CALLED TO BE SAINTS

be attained.[71] Because of this, Murray concluded, this eschatological humanism led its adherents to hold a "contempt for the world." And he contrasted this eschatological humanism with a more "incarnational" form which he clearly preferred. This was a humanism that he depicted as having a more affirming approach to human nature and the world, and likewise to the structures and institutions of American society and culture.[72]

In his helpful account of Murray's argument here, Joseph Komonchak pointed out that Murray's discussion of eschatological and incarnational humanism emerged out of his debate with Paul Hanly Furfey over the issue of intercredal co-operation in the mid-1940s.[73] And in this sense, Murray's account of an eschatological humanism tempting certain Catholics to withdraw from American society can be seen, at least in part, as referring to Catholics like Furfey, Day, and the Catholic Worker. Murray saw these Catholics as being too focused on a supernatural final end that is "radically discontinuous" with human nature and history. And so, at the heart of what can be read as his critique of such American Catholic radicals, is what Murray regarded as their theological anthropology: human nature is sinful—radically discontinuous with grace—and thus viewed with contempt and renounced.

That Murray perceived Catholic radicals like Furfey in much the same way Fenton and Connell perceived Hugo's makes sense. For despite their many differences, Murray, Fenton, and Connell were all early twentieth-century American neo-Thomists operating out of a similar two-tiered account of nature and grace.[74] It was out of

71   Murray, 188.

72   Murray titled his section on "eschatological humanism" as "Contempt for the World." Murray, 189. This eschatological/incarnational distinction was already commonly used in regard to a debate going on in France in the time on which Murray had written. See Joseph Komonchak, "John Courtney Murray and the Redemption of History: Natural Law and Theology" in *John Courtney Murray & The Growth of Tradition*, ed. J. Leon Hooper, S.J., and Todd David Whitmore (Kansas City: Sheed & Ward, 1996), 76.

73   Komonchak, "John Courtney Murray," 74.

74   Michael J. Baxter, "'Blowing the Dynamite of the Church': Catholic Radicalism from a Catholic Radicalist Perspective" in *The Church as Counterculture*, ed. Michael L. Budde (Albany, NY: SUNY Press, 2000), 198.

this theological perspective that Murray read Catholics like Furfey as being too focused on a supernatural destiny radically discontinuous with human nature, just as Fenton and Connell had read Hugo as promoting an "exaggerated supernaturalism." I would argue that it is through this kind of incarnational-eschatological paradigm that many contemporary Catholic "public" theologians—successors of these American neo-Thomists—continue to read and critique those American Catholics who take a more "radical" theological stance. And in this sense, Hugo's challenge to his neo-Thomist critics remains relevant for discussions of Catholic engagement in American culture and society today.

CATHOLIC "PUBLIC" THEOLOGIANS

Like O'Brien and Weigel, Charles Curran's initial praise for Day and the Catholic Worker quickly turned critical as he charged them with espousing a "radical type of social ethics" emerging from a "gospel radicalism" that insisted that all Catholics are called to a life of holiness.[75] Curran saw this position clearly on display in the "absolutist" pacifist stance taken by Day during World War II, as well as Peter Maurin's "Green Revolution"—a "revolution that called for a return to the land, a withdrawal from the evil industrial society, and opposition to technology."[76] Just as Murray, Fenton, and Connell had done before him, Curran argued that these actions were based on the belief that a "radical incompatibility" existed between American culture and society on the one hand and Christian eschatological fullness on the other, a view which Curran argued inevitably led to sectarian withdrawal from American society and culture.[77] Like his neo-Thomist predecessors, Curran maintained that this incompatibility is grounded in a particular understanding of the nature-supernatural relationship that is also one of "radical incompatibility."[78] And he asserted that this is a theological perspective out of step with what he suggested has been the

---

75 Curran, *American Catholic Social Ethics*, 130.

76 Curran, 163.

77 Curran, 143, 165.

78 Curran, 168.

long held belief in "traditional" Catholic theology that "grace builds on nature."[79]

More recently, Kristen Heyer offered a similar reading in *Prophetic & Public: The Social Witness of U.S. Catholicism*, a book in which she claims to rely heavily on the work of both O'Brien and Curran.[80] For Heyer, contemporary Catholics such as Michael Baxter—like Day, Furfey, and Virgil Michel (1890-1938) two generations earlier—represent a "prophetic sect type" and "a rigorist, evangelical social ethic" which corresponds to O'Brien's "evangelical style" of Catholicism.[81] According to Heyer, all of this informs these Catholics' general non-participation in American society, including their refusal to support American war making, vote, pay taxes, or engage in public-policy debates. [82] In much the same way that Joseph Connor had criticized American Catholic COs non-participation in World War II, Heyer labeled such Catholics as "perfectionists" who advocate a theology of radical discontinuity between nature and grace. And like Curran, Heyer contended that such a perspective is in direct contrast to the notion that "grace builds on nature."[83]

For Heyer, these "perfectionists" should be contrasted with theologians who take a more "public" approach to engagement with American society and culture such as Curran, J. Bryan Hehir, David Hollenbach, and Kenneth and Michael Himes.[84] In a similar way, Richard Gaillardetz contrasted Curran, Hehir, Hollenbach, and the Himeses with Baxter, Michael Budde, and William Cavanaugh.[85] According

---

79   Curran, 158.

80   Kristen Heyer, *Prophetic & Public: The Social Witness of U.S. Catholicism* (Washington, DC: Georgetown University Press, 2006), 90.

81   Heyer, 70. For Baxter's "response" to Heyer, see Michael J. Baxter, "On Not Getting Lost in Translation: The Gospel, the Natural Law, and Public Theology" in *Translating Religion* ed. Mary Doak and Anita Houck, Annual Volume of the College Theology Society (Maryknoll, NY: Orbis Books, 2013): 137-151.

82   Heyer, 76.

83   Heyer quoted Curran: "traditional Catholic theology and ecclesiology cannot be consistently radical." Heyer, 90.

84   Heyer, 59.

85   Gaillardetz also included David Schindler and John Milbank in this group. Richard Gaillardetz, "Ecclesiological Foundations of Modern

to Gaillardetz, while the first group embodied a more "Thomistic" approach toward social engagement, the latter represents a more "Augustinian" theological framework which informs what Gaillardetz called their "radical cultural engagement"—a view of the Church's engagement with American society and culture inspired by the "radical social witness" of Day and the Catholic Worker.[86] Gaillardetz suggested that theologians like Baxter and Cavanaugh find inspiration in the "counterculturalism" and "commitment to fundamental gospel values" in the Catholic Worker and other "sources of Catholic radicalism" in the United States.[87]

THE "SACRAMENTAL" APPROACH

According to both Heyer and Gaillardetz, the Catholic "public" theology of theologians like Curran, Hehir, Hollenbach, and the Himeses largely affirms the goodness of human nature and therefore of the social, political, and economic aspects of American society and culture. And this affirmation is rooted in a "sacramental" approach in Catholic theology that emerged in the second half of the twentieth-century as one of the more common ways of integrating nature and grace, and so of overcoming the neo-Thomist dualism.[88] Advocates of this approach seem to suggest that all of created nature is the locus of grace, and so grace is always already present in the world which is itself the "primordial arena" in which grace is experienced.[89] In this sense, the sacred is seen as the secular in its "fullest depth"—every experience, act, and event has the potential for disclosing the sacredness of the

---

Catholic Social Teaching" in *Modern Catholic Social Teaching*, ed. Kenneth R. Himes, O.F.M. (Washington, DC: Georgetown University Press 2004), 77.

86   Gaillardetz, 78.

87   Gaillardetz, 77-78.

88   Richard Gaillardetz noted that this approach is the one taken by "the majority of Catholic moral theologians and ecclesiologists in North America." Gaillardetz, 79.

89   See, e.g., "Spirituality more easily found in the world than in churches," interview by Art Winter with Elizabeth Dreyer, *National Catholic Reporter*, 13 (December 1996): 9-10.

secular.[90] And all the world seems to be understood as graced everywhere and in the same basic way, whether it be a corporate boardroom, battlefield, or monastery.

But although the world is graced, proponents of this sacramental approach assert, the historical reality of sin prevents that world from recognizing its graced character and so the Church is needed in order to reveal or "thematize" grace in the world. Therefore, grace is not understood as entering into the world through the sacraments and preaching of the Church, but rather the Church uses its sacraments and preaching to "thematize" the grace already present.[91] For many "public" theologians, then, the tendency is to see the Church as engaging with American society and culture—or the "public"—not as a means of necessarily offering grace, but rather of making American society and culture aware of its graced character. Theologians like Kenneth and Michael Himes—whose theological perspective has greatly shaped Catholic "public" theology in the United States—have argued that this sacramental vision thus prevents Catholics from any type of "spiritual withdrawal" from American society. As they see it, Catholics *must* engage with the "public."[92]

Proponents of this notion that the Church's mission is to "thematize" grace have often been associated with the theology of Karl Rahner, S.J. (1904-1984).[93] Indeed, advocates of such a sacramental approach have even been labeled "American Rahnerians."[94] It should

90   A concise description of this sacramental approach and the way it can inform Catholic engagement with American society and culture is provided in Kenneth Himes and Michael Himes's influential book, *Fullness of Faith: The Public Significance of Theology* (Mahwah, NJ: Paulist Press, 1993).

91   According to the Himeses, the Church's sacraments are points at which "the depth of the secular is uncovered and revealed as grounded in grace." Himes, *Fullness of Faith*, 82. Dreyer contended that the purpose of the Church and its sacraments is to "name, symbolize and celebrate the grace we encounter in the world." Dreyer, "Spirituality," 9.

92   Himes, *Fullness of Faith*, 84. Heyer, *Prophetic & Public*, xix.

93   For instance, Rahner described the Church's preaching as "the awakening and making explicit what is already there in the depths of man, not by nature but by grace." Karl Rahner, *Nature and Grace: Dilemmas in the Modern Church*, trans. Dinah Wharton (New York: Sheed and Ward, 1964), 134.

94   Reinhard Hütter, "The Ruins of Discontinuity," *First Things* (January 2011): online edition.

be noted, though, that to support their account of "the Catholic sacramental tradition," the Himeses did not turn to the German Jesuit but rather relied heavily upon the work of Langdon Gilkey (1919-2004), the liberal Protestant theologian from the University of Chicago who they described as "an exceptionally knowledgeable and sympathetic observer of the Catholic tradition." Indeed, the Himeses employed Gilkey's argument that "religious symbols must provide shape and thematization to the patterns of ordinary life" to justify their assertions regarding the Church's thematizing role.[95]

Whatever its source, it is through the lens of this sacramental approach that many contemporary theologians like Curran, Heyer, and Gaillardetz appear to read and dismiss Catholic radicals. For if the world is always and already graced, sin is the only thing that must be renounced or given up, to say otherwise would be perfectionist or rigorist and reflect a theology of radical discontinuity between nature and grace. Despite their many differences, these "public" theologians seem to agree upon this view.

Now of course it is dualist theology of the early twentieth-century Thomists that contemporary "public" theologians desire to overcome.[96] And while their sacramental approach does differ in many ways from the now largely discredited neo-Thomist approach, it also shares some important theological claims—centering in particular on its understanding of human nature. Indeed, Frederick Bauerschmidt has pointed out that both the two-tiered and sacramental approaches regard human nature as having a kind of sufficiency "as is."[97] For in the neo-Thomist approach, human nature is understood as self-contained and largely able to function properly apart from the illumination of grace. While in the sacramental approach, human nature is understood to be sufficient "as is" due to the already present, albeit unthematized, illumination of grace. In short, the notion of a self-sufficient human nature appears to have been replaced by the notion of an always already graced and therefore always already sufficient human nature.

In either case, the idea that human nature needs to be continually transformed and perfected is de-emphasized, almost to the point

95   Langdon Gilkey, "Symbol, Meaning, and Divine Presence," *Theological Studies* 35 (1974): 261, quoted in Himes, *Fullness of Faith*, 83.

96   Himes, *Fullness of Faith*, 80.

97   Bauerschmidt, "Confessions of an Evangelical Catholic": 77.

of being forgotten. And here lies a crucial shortcoming of the sacramental approach used by Catholic "public" theologians: it puts forth a single notion of human instability—that which results from sin—and does not seem to acknowledge that human nature's insufficiency has long been understood within the Christian tradition as being beyond what is sinful. As Hugo pointed out, the traditional vision is that there is a two-fold insufficiency that marks human nature: *both* the historical consequence of sin *and* the inherent limitation of a human nature created and finite while at the same time called to share in the beatific vision. And as Thomas made clear, human nature "left to itself" is insufficient even prior to sin and so grace has always been a necessary part of the economy of salvation.

Unfortunately, neither the two-tiered nor sacramental approaches seem to seriously take into account this two-fold insufficiency, nor do they emphasize the necessity of *gratia elevans* or *donum perfectum* to bring about the perfection of human nature beyond overcoming sin. As a result, an always already graced human nature ends up looking a lot like one which is self-contained. For while the contemporary sacramental understanding is not the separated nature of the early twentieth-century neo-Thomists, nevertheless it so blurs nature with grace that recognition of human nature's ongoing need to be perfected tends to be lost. Absent from both the dualist and sacramental approaches is the more complex and more accurate account of human nature in which nature is understood as itself a gratuitous gift of grace, but also as marked by an ultimate destiny beyond its limited capabilities. Without such a paradoxical account of human nature, the mystery of the supernatural cannot be fully recognized and appreciated as both distinct from but necessary to our humanity.

Ultimately, then, the proponents of the sacramental approach appear to have failed to move beyond the two-storied model of their neo-Thomist predecessors. For the emphasis on the goodness and autonomy of human nature "as is," particularly as it is embodied in U.S institutions, seems to have caused them to have lapsed into the dualism that more recent Thomists have been trying to overcome. To take one example, Heyer, for instance, highlighted three organizations that she argued correctly incorporated theology into public-policy debates: Network, Pax Christi USA, and the United States Catholic Conference of Bishops.[98] But while all three of these organizations

98   Heyer, *Prophetic & Public*, 119-175.

have devoted much time to the reform of public policy, it is possible that this has come at the cost of making more in-depth critiques of U.S. political, economic, and social institutions. It can even seem, in some respects, that the emphasis on public policy is primary for these organizations while much less attention is paid to the insufficiencies of these U.S. institutions or of human nature itself.

Through their account of human nature, Catholic "public" theologians read the radical Christianity of Hugo, Day and others in much the same way as their neo-Thomist predecessors. If human nature and history is graced, then Hugo's notion of either perfecting or rejecting various aspects of American life appears rooted in a theology of radical discontinuity between nature and grace. And just as Murray, Fenton, Connell, and Connor marginalized Catholic radicals by depicting them as "perfectionists" rooted in an eschatological humanism or exaggerated supernaturalism, more recent critics like O'Brien, Curran, and Heyer continue to marginalize Catholic radicals by portraying them as sectarian or perfectionists, and so at variance with correct Catholic theological understanding.

But their view of human nature not only distorts the way these "public" theologians seem to read Catholic radicals, it also seems to make it difficult for them to maintain an integrated view of nature and grace that does not blur the two together. In short, the sacramental approach severely restricts the ability to identify what is *not* holy—beyond that which is sinful—in a graced world. As with the neo-Thomists two generations earlier, many Catholic "public" theologians today seem to largely affirm American society and culture "as is"—that is, its institutions must be reformed but the institutions themselves are viewed as fundamentally good and sufficient. Granted many "public" theologians offer criticism of U.S. political, economic, and social institutions, but this criticism remains largely superficial and almost entirely on an ideological level—criticizing or supporting particular "progressive" or "conservative" positions. Any more probing critique of the institutions themselves, however, would be very difficult for theologians operating out of a sacramental approach. For if such institutions are already graced, then only those aspects which are sinful would need to be denounced.

This difficulty can begin to be understood sociologically and historically by recognizing, as William Portier has pointed out, that many of these contemporary critics grew up within the "thick" American

Catholic subculture of the 1940s and 1950s.[99] What were taken to be
the workings of grace in American society and culture—and therefore
its graced character—were more often simply echoes of this rapidly
dissipating Catholic subculture. These theologians were so formed by
this subculture that certain attitudes, dispositions, and values became
seen as simply part of human nature, rather than as having been culti-
vated by the Church's teaching, preaching, and the grace of the sacraments.[100] And so what they perceived to be evidence of the sacredness
of the secular was in fact the leavening presence of the Church within
the United States.

Added to this historical shift, is the persistent tendency of many
Catholic "public" theologians to rely upon the axiom: grace *builds on*
nature. While Curran and Heyer attribute this idea vaguely to "traditional Catholic theology and ecclesiology" or "the Catholic tradition,"
when a specific citation is offered it is typically Thomas Aquinas's
quote: "*gratia non tollat naturam sed perficiat.*"[101] This passage is translated by the English Dominicans as "grace does not destroy nature,
but perfects it" and in the Blackfriars' edition of the *Summa* as "grace
does not scrap nature but brings it to perfection."[102] While *perficiat*
has been translated in different ways, "*builds on*" is not one of them.
Though its origins seem to be unclear, the much used and often repeated axiom "grace builds on nature" does suggest an understanding
of the nature-grace relationship very much like the two-tiered account
of the neo-Thomists. For the idea that grace *builds on* nature seems
to presuppose an understanding of nature as a self-contained structure to which grace *builds on* a kind of superstructure. Grace is not
portrayed as an inner dynamism transforming human nature toward

---

99   William L. Portier, "Here Come the Evangelical Catholics," *Communio*
31 (Spring, 2004): 35-66.

100   Bauerschmidt, "Confessions of an Evangelical Catholic": 73.

101   Thomas Aquinas, *ST* I 1, 8 ad. 2. Reference is also made to Aquinas,
ST I 2,2 ad 2: *fides praesupponit cognitionem naturalem, sicut gratia naturam,
et ut perfectio perfectible.* Also, Aquinas, *De ver* 14, 10 ad 9: *fides non destruit
rationem, sed excedit eam et perficit.*

102   St. Thomas Aquinas, *Summa Theologica*, trans. Fathers of the English
Dominican Province (New York: Benziger Bros., 1948). St. Thomas Aquinas
Summa Theologiae, trans. Thomas Gilby, O.P. (New York: Blackfriars and
McGraw-Hill Book Co., 1964).

perfection, but rather as a kind of super-addition extrinsically added onto a somewhat self-sufficient human nature. Again, lost is the two-fold insufficiency that marks Thomas's account of human nature, what Richard Schenk, O.P. has described as the Angelic Doctor's understanding that grace "deepens the natural awareness that we are anything but self-sufficient."[103] For Aquinas, nature is *perfected* by grace.

HUGO'S RADICAL CHRISTIANITY

Hugo was clearly aware of the dangers in both a separated nature and one blurred with the supernatural:

> The affirmation of an order of good natural activity midway between sin and grace is the means of avoiding the two great (and closely related) Jansenistic errors in this matter. It saves us from the error of believing that, since the Fall, all natural activity is evil; and at the same time, it prevents us from denying or underestimating the supernatural order, for it shows us that the effect of grace is to raise us above, *not sin merely*, but the divinely created natural plane itself.[104]

Because they did not maintain a proper account of human nature, Hugo saw the neo-Thomist theologians of his day as clearly "underestimating" the supernatural. The same can be said for Catholic "public" theologians today. So in this way, Hugo's critique of the American neo-Thomists can be applied to contemporary American Catholic "public" theologians. For in their attempt to defend the sacredness of human nature—and the American political and economic institutions they associate with human nature—these "public" theologians have tended to downplay and even ignore the instability of human nature that Hugo recognized as so important.

For Hugo, this kind of theology was a form of "pious naturalism"—similar to the "perfect nature" of Baius and Jansen—and perpetuated an inaccurate account of nature which had become "entirely merged with the supernatural."[105] And in this contemporary form of natural-

---

103   Richard Schenk, O.P., "Analogy as the *discrimen naturae et gratiae*: Thomism and Ecumenical Learning" in *The Analogy of Being: Invention of the Antichrist or Wisdom of God?*, ed. Thomas Joseph White, O.P. (Grand Rapids, MI: Eerdmans Publishing Co., 2011): 172-191.

104   Hugo, *Nature*, 5.

105   Hugo, *Nature*, 11.

ism, not only has a correct account of human nature been lost, but the supernatural—no longer regarded super-eminent—has become seen as simply that which is not sinful.[106] Missing from the more recent Catholic discourse on "public" theology is the idea that human nature, while itself a gratuitous gift of grace, is called to a destiny that is far beyond its limited abilities to attain.[107] Instead, the supernatural is portrayed as nature in its full depth.

This is the "sin mentality" that Hugo argued shaped his critics and which seems to also shape many of the "public" theologians' criticism of American Catholic radicals today. For without an accurate view of human nature—as good, but insufficient—these theologians tend to see the world exclusively in terms of the sinful on the one hand and blurred with the supernatural on the other. Accordingly, only attachments to what is sinful are rejected while everything else appears to be regarded as "graced." Any notion that Christians have been called to give up something more is rejected as perfectionism, sectarian, or world-denying Jansenism. This was the way Fenton and Connell read Hugo's calls for renunciation as rooted in an "exaggerated supernaturalism" and Murray read Catholics' withdrawal from American political institutions as rooted in their view of "radical discontinuity" between nature and grace. And it is the manner in which Curran, Heyer, and other "public" theologians read contemporary Catholic radicals as working out of a "radical incompatibility" between nature and grace. In

---

106   It is worth noting that Hugo critiqued a scheme—in many ways the reverse of this "naturalism"—that ended up looking very similar. Rather than merging natural actions with the supernatural, Hugo pointed out that Jansenists merged natural actions with sin, "regarding all natural actions as evil." Hugo argued that these Jansenists failed to recognize the reality of the natural (both historical and ontological), and therefore also blurred the nature-supernatural relationship. For in the Jansenists' emphasis on the sinfulness of human nature, the supernatural became understood as simply that which was not sinful human nature, with its mystery and supereminence lost. Hugo, *Nature*, iii, 5, 7.

107   Hugo explained that the graced character of human nature was not so much its created humanity, but its supernatural final end: "God gave us our human nature only that we might, through serving Him in it, come to possess supernatural happiness." Hugo, *Applied Christianity*, 200.

short, if the world is graced, then sin is considered the only thing that must be rejected.

As Hugo pointed out, for those operating out of such a "sin mentality," absent is any sense that Christians are called to live something beyond a natural—self-sufficient or always already graced—life. Gone too, is any sense that the supernatural final end has practical implications for human life, perfecting it into a "new creature"—making it holy.[108] He wrote that those working out of this mentality viewed holiness and perfection as a "work of supererorgation":

> limiting its pursuit to a small group of 'extraordinary souls,' while they encourage the devotees of their more cheering system to think that they may fulfill their highest Christian duties by the more pleasant method of practicing the natural virtues, say, at the movies or the baseball park.[109]

This criticism could be applied as well today to many contemporary theologians' affirmation of the "sacramentality" of American political, social, and economic institutions.

Indeed, in their attempt to articulate the integration of grace into the world—the sacred into the secular, theology into the "public"— theologians like Heyer and the Himeses have tended to uncritically affirm American society and culture.[110] Thus, in their attempt to make the call to holiness universal—to bring the idea of holiness out of its exile—these theologians have a difficult time identifying what is not holy in the world. While such "worldly" institutions and vocations may indeed offer a way to live a life of holiness, they cannot simply be affirmed as is.[111] Rather, Christians must discern what is holy in them and renounce or transform what is not in light of their ultimate destiny.

---

108   De Lubac seemed to make a similar point in his critique of Edward Schillebeeckx's description of the Church as *sacramentum mundi*. Henri de Lubac, *A Brief Catechesis on Nature and Grace*, trans. Brother Richard Arnandez, F.S.C. (San Francisco: Ignatius Press, 1984), 191-234.

109   Hugo, *Nature*, 78.

110   For instance, the Himeses argue that Christians "must engage in transformative conversation and action so that human political, social, and economic communities become what they are but so often obscure, the locus of the agape of God." Himeses, 84.

111   Bauerschmidt, 73.

It is such ongoing discernment, always in light of our final end, that Hugo advocated in the retreat and throughout his writings. For it is not simply sin that needs to be sown, but also that which is good but imperfect—that which does not lead to God. This can range from smoking cigarettes or watching cable TV, to voting or participating in a just war. Hugo's continual and critical evaluation of what Christians encountered in America was not done in order to reject it outright, but to assess it in light of their ultimate destiny and to chart how to negotiate the complexities of their lives in that light. Hugo was not a rigorist; he was a spiritual director offering a pastoral tool to lay people for their daily engagement with American life.

For all his supposed extremism, then, Hugo was actually occupying something of a middle ground. While he was not a Jansenist or a sectarian, he did not think that nature or the world was sufficient to fulfill human flourishing. Instead, he argued that attachments to created goods must be left behind so that one could live a supernatural life of holiness. From this theology, Day and others were able to put forth a radical Christianity without lapsing into either a blanket denial of the goodness of creation, or a wholesale affirmation of the world as the general site—a "primordial arena"—for grace. Human nature, politics, or the world are not inherently sinful or "radically discontinuous" with grace, but neither are they a sufficient locus for human flourishing.

Recognizing the theology of Hugo and the retreat as such, the way Catholics shaped by this theology have often been depicted by scholars can be seen as a caricature. Withdrawal from, and even rejection of, certain aspects of American life has not been done out of a view that human nature is corrupted by sin and radically incompatible with grace. Rather it is done out of the recognition that while these aspects may indeed be good, they often became obstacles in the daily, ongoing challenge of living a holy life. Human nature is not understood in terms of its always already graced character, but rather by its need for fulfillment—or in the Ignatian sense, its "emptiness."[112] Nature

---

112   Rahner also described this need in human nature: "We can only fully understand man in his 'undefinable' essence if we see him as *potentia obedienialis* for the divine life; this is his *nature*. His nature is such that its absolute fulfillment comes through grace, and so nature itself must reckon with the meaningful possibility of remaining without absolute fulfillment." Karl Rahner, S.J. *Nature and Grace*, trans., Dinah Wharton (New York: Sheed and Ward, 1964), 140.

encounters grace not as something completely alien or extrinsic to it, nor as something already possessed unthematically. Instead, grace is encountered as the ultimate destiny to which human nature longs. Hugo's approach affirmed the fundamental goodness of human nature, but it also recognized its inherent insufficiency.[113]

While not a "professional" theologian, Hugo is an example of an early twentieth-century American Catholic spiritual writer who wanted to integrate Christians' daily engagement in American life—their "social ethic"—into the broader vision of their journey to God. Like de Lubac and Blondel, though in a less nuanced and more mechanical way, Hugo proposed this vision of an integrated Christian life in response to a theological perspective which had exiled the supernatural and its implications away from the life of ordinary Christians. Like other early twentieth-century efforts at *ressourcement*, Hugo appealed to a broad tradition of spiritual writers to justify and support this vision. And all of this remains relevant today, as Hugo's vision of an integrated "supernatural life" continues to offer a corrective to the dominant accounts of the nature-supernatural relationship and the type of social engagement they inform.

113　Bauerschmidt affirmed this notion that the insufficiencies and limitations of human nature were not simply a result of sin. He described them as "constitutive of our nature as beings who are created and finite while at the same time called to share in the vision of God." And because of these inadequacies, human nature was an inherently unstable notion. He suggested, therefore, that, "Theological anthropology has its proper place, but that place is not as the basis for dialogue, if for no other reason than that thoroughly paradoxical character of human nature makes it an unstable and contested foundation." And like Hugo, one could affirm that there was "something like human nature distinct from the sinful and the supernatural—indeed, the doctrine of the Incarnation required it—without making it a category that was frozen in time or immediately accessible to our comprehension. Bauerschmidt called this an "Augustinian sensibility" with regard to human nature." Bauerschmidt, 76.

CONCLUSION

Though unable to lead retreats after 1942, Hugo continued to write articles, pamphlets, and books which proposed his vision for an integrated Christian life. But by 1959, when he was once again able to give retreats, the fervor of the early years of the retreat movement had died down. Despite all his efforts, Hugo's hopes for the retreat appeared to go unfulfilled as its categories and language appeared outdated. With the increasing influence of Ammon Hennacy and the Berrigans within the Catholic Worker, Hugo's radicalism seemed to lose its edge.[1] Strong memories remained of Father Hugo, many of which were not endearing. Both within the Catholic Worker and beyond, Hugo had his detractors. All this, coupled with the legacy of the "retreat controversy," meant that the depiction of Hugo that emerged was of a rigorist whose theology tended toward an extreme perfectionism. And it is this depiction that is often perpetuated in contemporary American Catholic studies—a depiction which I hope to have challenged in this study.

AND SO WHAT CAN WE SAY ABOUT FATHER JOHN J. HUGO?

First, it is clear that John Hugo had a profound influence on Dorothy Day as the primary source for a theological vision that shaped her life—one that brought about her "second conversion." After her encounter with Hugo and the retreat, Day came to see her life and work at the Catholic Worker in terms of the retreat theology: a journey from a good but "merely natural life" to one she regarded as much better—the supernatural life of a saint. For Day, the Christian life was

---

1 By the early 1980s, as Hugo was writing his two-volume account of the retreat, he could not get any interest in it from the Catholic Worker. The archives at Marquette contain letters Hugo sent to Sister Peter Claver Fahey in which he repeatedly asks her to intervene on his behalf with the editors at *The Catholic Worker* to help publish and promote his book.

more than a life spent avoiding sin, it was a life lived in the "higher way of Jesus." And her fifty years living in the Catholic Worker was an embodiment of this higher way.

Hugo's theology also offered Day a way to discern how to engage with American society and culture. For Day, selective non-participation in certain U.S. political, social, and economic institutions—like war-making or paying taxes or voting—was not done simply out of a view that these institutions were "radically incompatible" with grace. Instead, participation in these institutions was understood as avenues which, while possibly just, would make it difficult to live a holy life. Day was not a sectarian, nor are those who today have been shaped by the radical Christianity put forth by her and Hugo. Rather, she was an ordinary Christian discerning how to live a life of holiness in a social and culture context that did not always nurture such a life. By recognizing that the theology which Day was operating out of was not Jansenist, but rather to a large degree Ignatian, her approach to political, social, and economic engagement can be seen as offering a legitimate alternative to the "public" theology approach that prevails in American Catholicism today—an alternative approach that is not from the theological fringes, but rather one that is rooted within the Christian tradition.

Recognition of the significance of Hugo's theological perspective, then, is crucial for understanding the life and work of Dorothy Day. This is particularly important at a time when Day's cause for canonization has been renewed. Such interest has meant that sometimes her conversion has been portrayed as a journey from sin to sanctity and her rejection of certain U.S. institutions was done chiefly out of a view that they were corrupt.[2] Seeing Day through the lens of Hugo's theology offers a corrective to this kind of portrayal.

Furthermore, we can see Hugo's significance beyond his association with Day and the Catholic Worker movement. For Hugo presents an example of an American Catholic who challenged the dualism prevalent in so much of early-twentieth century Catholicism. And indeed, Hugo's challenge placed him in concert with some of the major impulses emerging within Catholic theology—impulses that would profoundly shape Catholicism in the second half of the century. Too often, scholarship on these theological movements has focused almost

2   Sharon Otterman, "In Hero of the Catholic Left, a Conservative Cardinal Sees a Saint" *New York Times* (November 26, 2012).

exclusively on European theologians, while American Catholicism is depicted as uniform and void of any real debate. While certainly not as theologically sophisticated as his European counterparts, Hugo should be seen as making—or at least attempting to make—very similar arguments which brought about real debate in American Catholic theological circles.

So again, far from the fringe character he is often portrayed as, Hugo's theological vision and its challenge to the "modern theology" of his day was rooted in sources from within the Christian tradition. Perhaps even more significant than his challenge to the American neo-Thomists, was Hugo's effort at a *ressourcement* theology—his return to often overlooked sources within Jesuit spirituality, like Lallemant, Surin, and Caussade. Significant too, was Hugo's attempt to apply this Ignatian spirituality to Catholic engagement with American society and culture. And so, while perhaps somewhat dated, Hugo's radical Christianity can be seen as providing a means for ordinary Christians today to seek holiness in their daily lives—to live the life of a saint.

BIBLIOGRAPHY

Appleby, R. Scott and Jay Haas. "The Last Supernaturalists: Fenton, Connell, and the Threat of Catholic Indifferentism." *U.S. Catholic Historian* 13.2 (Winter 1995): 23-48.

Aquilina, Michael and David Scott, eds. *Weapons of the Spirit: Selected Writings of Father John Hugo.* Huntington, IN: Our Sunday Visitor Publishing Division, 1997.

Balmes, Jaime. *Protestantism and Catholicity compared in their Effects of the Civilization of Europe.* Translated by C.J. Hanford and Robert Kershaw. Baltimore: Murphy & Co., 1859.

Balthasar, Hans Urs von, "Theology and Sanctity," in *Essays in Theology: Word and Redemption, Bk 2.* Translated by A.V. Littledale, 49-86 (Montreal: Palm Publications, 1965).

————. *The Theology of Henri de Lubac.* Translated by Susan Clements. San Francisco: 1991.

————. *The Theology of Karl Barth.* Translated by Edward Oakes, S.J. San Francisco: Ignatius Press, 1992.

Baxter, Michael. "Review Essay: The Non-Catholic Character of the "Public Church." *Modern Theology* 11.2 (April 1995): 243-258.

————. "Notes on Catholic Americanism and Catholic Radicalism: Toward a Counter-Tradition of Catholic Social Ethics." In *American Catholic Traditions: Resources for Renewal,* edited by Sandra Yocum Mize and William Portier, 53-71. Maryknoll, NY: Orbis Press, 1997.

————. "Blowing the Dynamite of the Church:' Catholic Radicalism from a Catholic Radicalist Perspective." In *The Church as Counterculture,* edited by Michael Budde, 195-212. Albany, NY: SUNY Press, 2000.

————. "The Unsettling of Americanism: A Response to William Portier." *Communio* 27 (Spring 2000): 161-170.

————. "The Long Correspondence." *America* (November 8, 2010): online edition.

Bauerschmidt, Frederick. "Confessions of an Evangelical Catholic: Five Theses Related to Theological Anthropology." *Communio* 31 (Spring 2004): 67-84.

————. Holy Teaching: *Introducing the Summa Theologiae of St. Thomas Aquinas.* Grand Rapids, MI: Brazos Press, 2005.

Bellah, Robert, et al, eds. *The Good Society.* New York: Alfred Knopf, 1991.

Bellecio, S.J., Aloysius. *Spiritual Exercises, According to the Method of St. Ignatius Loyola.* Translated by Wm. Hutch. London: Burns Oates, 1883.

Bernardi, S.J., Peter. "Maurice Blondel and the Renewal of the Nature-Grace Relationship." *Communio* 26 (Winter 1999): 806-845.

————. *Maurice Blondel, Social Catholicism & Action Française.* Washington, DC: CUA Press, 2009.

Billot, S.J., Louis. *De ecclesia Christi.* Rome, 1903.

Blanchette, Oliva. *Maurice Blondel: A Philosophical Life.* Grand Rapids, MI: Eerdmans Publishing Co., 2010.

Blondel, Maurice. *The Letter on Apologetics and History and Dogma.* Translated by Alexander Dru and Illtyd Trethowan. New York: Holt, Rinehart and Winston, 1964.

————. *Action (1893).* Translated by Oliva Blanchette. Notre Dame, IN: University of Notre Dame Press, 1984.

————. "The Third 'Testis' Article." Translated by Peter J. Bernardi, S.J. *Communio* 26 (Winter 1999): 846-874.

Boersma, Hans. *Nouvelle Théologie and Sacramental Ontology: A Return to Mystery.* New York: Oxford University Press, 2009

Bonino, O.P., Serge-Thomas, ed. *Surnaturel: A Controversy At the Heart of Twentieth-Century Thomistic Thought.* Translated by Robert Williams and revised by Matthew Levering. Ave Maria, FL: Sapientia Press, 2009.

Bouillard, Henri. *Blondel and Christianity.* Translated by James Somerville. Washington, DC: Corpus Books, 1970.

Boulaye, S.J., H. Pinard de la. *Exercises spirituels selon la method de saint Ignace.* Paris, 1944.

Bouvier, S.J., Pierre. *L'interpretation authentique de la Meditation fondamentale dans les Exercices spirituels de saint Ignace.* Bourges, 1922.

Bremond, Henri, *A Literary History of Religious Thought in France, vol. III.* (translation unknown) New York: The Macmillan Company, 1936.

Buckley, S.J., Michael. "Seventeenth-Century French Spirituality: Three Figures." In *Christian Spirituality III,* edited by Louis Dupre and Don E. Saliers, 28-68. New York: Crossroad, 1989.

Carey, Patrick, ed., *American Catholic Religious Thought: The Shaping of a Theological and Social Tradition.* Mahwah, NJ: Paulist Press,1987.

————. *Catholics in America.* Westport, CT: Praeger Publishers, 2004.

Catherin, S.J., Victor. "De naturali hominis beatitudine." *Gregorianum* 11 (1930).

Certeau, Michel de. *The Mystic Fable, volume 1, The Sixteenth and Seventeenth Centuries.* Translated by Michael B. Smith. Chicago: University of Chicago Press, 1992.

Chautard, Dom Jean-Baptiste. *Soul of the Apostolate.* Translated by J.A. Moran. Gethsemani, KY: Mission Press, 1941.

Chinnici, Joseph. *Living Stones: The History and Structure of Catholic Spiritual Life in the U.S.* Maryknoll, NY: Orbis Books, 1996.

Cogley, John. "Harsh and Dreadful Love." *America* 127 (November 11, 1972).

Cognet, Louis. *Post-Reformation Spirituality.* Translated by P. Hepburne Scott. New York: Hawthorne Books, 1959.

Connell, Francis. Review of *Applied Christianity,* by John J. Hugo, *American Ecclesiastical Review* (July 1945): 69-72.

Connor, S.J., John. "The Catholic Conscientious Objector." *The Ecclesiastical Review* 58 (February 1943): 125-138.

Courel, Francois. "Introduction." *La vie et la doctrine spirituelle de Pere Louis Lallemant.* Paris: Desclee de Brouwer, 1979.

Curran, Charles E., *American Catholic Social Ethics: Twentieth-Century Approaches.* Notre Dame: University of Notre Dame Press, 1982.

Daly, Gabriel. *Transcendence and Immanence: A Study in Catholic Modernism and Integralism.* New York: Oxford University Press, 1980.

Day, Dorothy. "Catholic Worker Retreat." *CW* (September, 1939).

————. "Catholic Worker Holds '40 Retreat at Easton." *CW* (September 1940).

————. "Day after Day." *CW* (July/August 1941).

————. "On Retreat." *CW* (July-August, 1943).

————. "What Dream Did They Dream? Utopia or Suffering?" *CW* (July-August 1947).

————. "Death of Father Onesimus Lacouture, S.J." *CW* (December, 1951).

————. *The Long Loneliness.* New York: Harper & Row Publishers, 1952.

————. *Therese.* Springfield, IL: Templegate Publishing, 1960.

————. "On Pilgrimage." *CW* (September 1976): 2.

————. *Loaves and Fishes*. Maryknoll, NY: Orbis Books, 1997.

————. *Selected Writings*. Edited by Robert Ellsberg. Maryknoll, NY: Orbis Books, 1998.

————. *The Duty of Delight: The Diaries of Dorothy Day*. Edited by Robert Ellsberg. Milwaukee: Marquette University Press, 2008.

————. *All the Way to Heaven: The Selected Letters of Dorothy Day*. Edited by Robert Ellsberg. Milwaukee: Marquette University Press, 2010.

Deville, Raymond. *The French School of Spirituality*. Translated by Agnes Cunningham. Pittsburgh: Duquesne University Press, 1994.

Donovan, C.M., Joseph. "A Bit of Puritanical Catholicity." *Homiletic and Pastoral Review* 48 (August 1948): 807-814.

Downey, Jack Lee. *The Bread of the Strong: Lacouturisme and the Folly of the Cross, 1910-1985*. New York: Fordham University Press, 2015.

Drolet, Jean-Claude. "Un Mouvement de spiritualité sacredotale au Québec as XXe siècle (1931-1965): Le Lacouturisme." *Canadian Catholic Historical Association: Study Sessions, 1973*. (1974): 55-87.

Dulles, Avery. "Jesuits and Theology: Yesterday and Today." *Theological Studies* 52 (September 1991): 524-538.

Evennett, Outram. *The Spirit of the Counter Reformation*. Cambridge: Cambridge University Press, 1968. Faber, Frederick. *Growth in Holiness*. Baltimore: John Murphy, 1854.

Feingold, Lawerence. *The Natural Desire to See God According to St. Thomas Aquinas and His Interpreters*. Ave Maria, FL: Sapientia Press, 2010.

Fenton, Joseph Clifford. *The Concept of Sacred Theology*. Milwaukee: The Bruce Publishing Co., 1941.

————. "Nature and the Supernatural Life." *American Ecclesiastical Review* (January 1946): 54-68.

Fielding, Rosemary. "Anti-Assimilationist Retreat: Becoming Spiritually Inoculated Against Americanism." *Culture Wars* (October 2004): 22-39.

Finney, Torin R.T. *Unsung Hero of the Great War: The Life and Witness of Ben Salmon*. Mahwah, NJ: Paulist Press, 1989.

Fisher, James, T. *The Catholic Counterculture in America, 1933-1962*. Chapel Hill, NC: University of North Carolina Press, 1989.

Forest, Jim. *Love is the Measure*. Mahwah, NJ: Paulist Press, 1986.

Furfey, Paul Hanly. *Fire on the Earth*. New York: Macmillian, 1936.

————. *Three Theories of Society*, New York: Macmillian, 1937.

————. "Unemployment on the Land." *The Catholic Worker* (October 1939): 8.

————. "There are Two Kind of Agrarians." *The Catholic Worker* (December 1939): 7-8.

————. *The Mystery of Iniquity*. Milwaukee: Bruce Publishing, 1944.

Gaillardetz, Richard. "Ecclesiological Foundations of Modern Catholic Social Teaching." In *Modern Catholic Social Teaching*, edited by Kenneth Himes, O.F.M., 72-98. Washington, DC: Georgetown University Press, 2004.

Garrigou-Lagrange, Reginald. *Christian Perfection and Contemplation: according to St. Thomas Aquinas and St. John of the Cross*. Translated by Sr. M. Timothea Doyle. St. Louis: Herder Book Co., 1946.

Gilby, Thomas, O.P., trans. *St. Thomas Aquinas Summa Theologiae vol. 1*. New York: Blackfriars/McGraw-Hill Book Co., 1963.

Gilkey, Langdon. "Symbol, Meaning, and Divine Presence." *Theological Studies* 35 (1974): 249-267.

————. *Reaping the Whirlwind: A Christian Interpretation of History*. New York: Seabury Press, 1976.

————. *Gilkey on Tillich*. New York: Crossroad Publishing Company, 1981.

Gleason, Philip. *Keeping the Faith: American Catholicism Past and Present*. Notre Dame, IN: University of Notre Dame Press, 1987.

————. *Contending With Modernity: Catholic Higher Education in the Twentieth Century*. New York: Oxford University Press, 1995.

Grimm, Eugene, trans. *True Spouse of Christ* by St. Alphonsus de Ligouri. Brooklyn: Redemptorist Fathers, 1929.

Grumett, David. *De Lubac: A Guide for the Perplexed*. New York: T&T Clark, 2007.

Guibert, Joseph de. *The Jesuits: Their Spiritual Doctrine and Practice*. St. Louis: Institute of Jesuit Sources, 1964.

Gustafson, James M. "The Sectarian Temptation: Reflections on Theology, The Church and the University." In *The Catholic Theological Society of America Proceedings of the Fortieth Annual Convention 40*, edited by George Kilcourse. (1985): 83-94.

Halsey, William V. *The Survival of American Innocence: Catholicism in an Era of Disillusionment 1920-1940*. Notre Dame IN: University of Notre Dame Press, 1980.

Healy, Nicholas. "Henri de Lubac on Nature and Grace: A Note of Some Recent Contributions to the Debate." *Communio* 35 (Winter 2008): 535-564.

Heineman, Kenneth. *A Catholic New Deal: Religion and Reform in Depression Pittsburgh.* University Park, PA: Penn State University Press, 1999.

Helms, Chad, ed. and trans. *Fénelon: Selected Writings.* Mahwah, NJ: Paulist Press, 2006.

Henrici, S.J. Peter. "The One Who Went Unnamed: Maurice Blondel in the Encyclical Fides et Ratio." Translated by David L. Schindler *Communio* 26 (Fall 1999): 609-621.

Henry, Paul. "The Christian Philosophy of History." *Theological Studies* 13 (September 1952): 418-432.

Heyer, Kristen. *Prophetic & Public: The Social Witness of U.S. Catholicism.* Washington, DC: Georgetown University Press, 2006.

Himes, Kenneth and Michael Himes. *Fullness of Faith.* Mahwah, NJ: Paulist Press, 1993.

Hooper, S.J., J. Leon. "Dorothy Day's Transposition of Therese's 'Little Way.'" *Theological Studies* 63 (2002): 68-86.

————. "Murray and Day: A Common Enemy, A Common Cause?" *U.S. Catholic Historian* 24 (Winter 2006): 45-61.

Hubbert, C.M., Joseph. "American Ecclesiastical Review." In *The Encyclopedia of American Catholic History,* edited by Michael Glazier and Thomas Shelly, . Collegeville, MN: The Liturgical Press, 1997.

Huff, Peter. *Allen Tate and the Catholic Revival.* Mahwah, NJ: Paulist Press, 1996.

Hugo, John J. "The Realism of Values." *Thought* 9 (December 1935).

————. "Capitalism Impractical." *The Catholic Worker* (CW). (November 1939): 8.

————. "In Defense of the Romantic Agrarians." *CW.* (January 1940): 8.

————. "In the Vineyard," (a ten part series), *CW.* (September 1941-July/August, 1942).

————. "The Weapons of the Spirit," (a six-part series) *CW.* (November 1942-April 1943).

————. "Catholics Can Be Conscientious Objectors." *CW.* (May 1943).

————. "The Superficial Realist." *CW.* (July/August 1943).

————. *Weapons of the Spirit.* New York: Catholic Worker Press, 1943.

————."Going My Way." *CW*. (July/August 1944).

————."The Immorality of Conscription." *CW*. (November 1944).

————. *Applied Christianity*. New York: Catholic Worker Press, 1944.

————. *The Gospel of Peace*. New York: Catholic Worker Press, 1944.

————."Conscience Vindicated." *CW*. (April 1945).

————."Peace without Victory." *CW*. (September 1945).

————."Fathers of the Modern Desert." (four-part series) *CW*. (October 1945-March 1946).

————. *A Sign of Contradiction*. (published by author) 1947.

————. *Nature and the Supernatural: Defense of the Evangelical Ideal*. (published by author) 1949.

————. *St. Augustine on Nature, Sex, and Marriage*. Pittsburgh: Diocese of Pittsburgh, 1968.

————."Love Strong as Death," (eight-part series) *CW*. (October 1968-June 1969).

————. *Love Strong as Death*. Pittsburgh: Diocese of Pittsburgh, 1969.

————."Dorothy Day: Apostle of the Industrial Age." *Pittsburgh Catholic* December12,1980.

————."A Christian Manifesto on War" (published by author) (1981).

————."Dorothy Day: Driven by Love." Memorial Mass for Dorothy Day. Marquette University, Milwaukee, November 2, 1981.

————. *Your Ways Are Not My Ways: The Radical Christianity of the Gospel*, *vol. 2*. Pittsburgh: Encounter With Silence, 1984.

————. *Your Ways Are Not My Ways: The Radical Christianity of the Gospel*, *vol. 1*. Pittsburgh: Encounter With Silence, 1986.

Hunter, S.J., Hugo. *Sketches for the Exercises of an Eight Days' Retreat*. Translated by John B. Kokenge, S.J. St. Louis: Herder, 1919.

Hütter, Reinhard and Matthew Levering. *Ressourcement Thomism: Sacred Doctrine, the Sacraments, and the Moral Life: Essays in Honor of Romanus Cessario, O.P.* Washington DC: Catholic Univeristy Press, 2010.

Hütter, Reinhard. "Theological Faith Enlightening Sacred Theology: Renewing Theology by Recovering its Unity as *sacra doctrina*," *The Thomist* 74 (July 2010).

————. "The Ruins of Discontinuity." *First Things* (January 2011): online edition.

Huxley, Aldous. *The Devils of Loudun*. New York: Harper & Brothers, 1953.

Gleason, Phillip. *Keeping the Faith: American Catholicism Past and Present.* Notre Dame, IN: University of Notre Dame Press, 1987.

————. *Contending with Modernity: Catholic Higher Education in the Twentieth Century.* New York: Oxford University Press, 1995.

James, William. *Varieties of Religious Experience.* New York: New York American Library, 1958.

Kavanaugh, Kieren and Otilio Rodriguez, trans. *The Collected Works of John of the Cross.* Washington DC: ICS Publications, 1979.

Kavanaugh, Kieren. "Spanish Sixteenth Century: Carmel and Surrounding Movements." In *Christian Spirituality III,* edited by Louis Dupre and Don E. Saliers, 69-92. New York: Crossroad, 1989.

Kerlin, Michael. "Maurice Blondel, Philosophy, Prayer, and the Mystical." In *Modernists & Mystics,* edited by C.J.T. Talar, 62-81. Washington, DC: CUA Press, 2009.

Klejment, Anne and Nancy Roberts. *American Catholic Pacifism: The Influence of Dorothy Day and the Catholic Worker Movement.* Westport, CT: Praeger Publishing, Co., 1996.

Kleutgen, S.J., Joseph. *Die Philosophie der Vorzeit, vols. 1-2.* Münster, 1860-3.

Kerr, Fergus. *After Aquinas: Versions of Thomism.* Malden, MA: Blackwell Publishing Co., 2002.

————. *Twentieth-Century Catholic Theologians.* Malden, MA: Blackwell Publishing Co., 2007.

Komonchak, Joseph. "The Enlightenment and the Construction of Roman Catholicism." *Catholic Commission on Intellectual and Cultural Affairs Annual Volume.* 1985: 31-59.

————. "Theology and Culture at Mid-Century: The Example of Henri De Lubac." *Theological Studies* 51 (December 1990): 579-602.

————. "John Courtney Murray and the Redemption of History: Natural Law and Theology." In *John Courtney Murray & The Growth of Tradition,* edited by J. Leon Hooper and Todd David Whitmore, 60-81. Kansas City: Sheed & Ward.

————. "Fenton, Joseph (1906-1969)." "American Ecclesiastical Review." In *The Encyclopedia of American Catholic History,* edited by Michael Glazier and Thomas Shelly, 505-506. Collegeville, MN: The Liturgical Press, 1997.

Longpré, Anselme. *Un Mouvement spiritual au Québec (1931-1962): au retour à l'Evangile.* Montreal: Fides, 1976.

Lubac, Henri de. *Catholicism: Christ and the Common Destiny of Man.* Translated by Elizabeth Englund and Lancelot Sheppard. San Francisco: Ignatius Press, 1988.

———. *At the Service of the Church.* Translated by Anne Elizabeth Englund. San Francisco: Ignatius Press, 1992.

———. "The Internal Causes of the Attenuation and Disappearance of the Sense of the Sacred." In *Theology in History,* translated by Anne Englund Nash, 223-240. San Francisco: Ignatius Press, 1996.

———. "Mystery of the Supernatural." In *Theology in History,* translated by Anne Englund Nash, 281-316. San Francisco: Ignatius Press, 1996.

———. *Mystery of the Supernatural.* Translated by Rosemary Sheedy. New York: Crossroad Publishing Co., 1998.

———. *Augustinianism and Modern Theology.* Translated by Lancelot Sheppard. New York: Crossroad Publishing Co., 2000.

———. *A Brief Catechesis on Nature and Grace.* Translated by Richard Arnandez. San Francisco: Ignatius Press, 1984.

———. "Duplex Hominis Beatitudo (Saint Thomas, Ia 2ae, q62.a1)." Translated by Aaron Riches and Peter Candler. *Communio* 35 (Winter 2008): 599-612.

Mansini, O.S.B., Guy. "The Abiding Theological Significance of Henri de Lubac's *Surnaturel.*" *The Thomist* 73 (October 2009): 1-17.

Massa, Mark. *Catholics in American Culture.* New York: Crossroad Publishing Co., 1999.

Marmion, Columba. *Christ in His Mysteries.* St. Louis: B. Herder Book Co., 1939.

Maturin, B.W. *Self-Knowledge and Self-Discipline.* Paterson, NJ: St. Anthony's Guild Press, 1939.

McCarraher, Eugene, B. "The Church Irrelevant: Paul Hanly Furfey and the Fortunes of American Catholic Radicalism." *Religion and American Culture* 7 (Summer 1997): 163-194.

McCool, Gerald. *Catholic Theology in the Nineteenth Century: The Quest for a Unitary Method.* New York: The Seabury Press, 1977.

———. *The Neo-Thomists.* Milwaukee: Marquette University Press, 1994.

———. "Kleutgen, Joseph." In *Biographical Dictionary of Christian Theologians,* edited by Patrick Carey and Joseph Lienhard, 303-305. Peabody, MA: Hendrickson Publishers, 2002.

McDougall, Alan G., ed. *The Spiritual Doctrine of Father Louis Lallemant.* Westminster, MD: The Newman Book Shop, 1946.

McGreevy, John. *Catholicism and American Freedom.* New York: Norton & Co., 2003.

McInerny, Ralph. *Praeambula fidei: Thomism and the God of the Philosophers.* Washington DC: Catholic University of America Press, 2006.

McKeon, Robert, trans. Jean Pierre Caussade, S.J., *A Treatise of Prayer from the Heart.* St. Louis: Institute of Jesuit Sources, 1998.

McNeal, Patricia. "Catholic Conscientious Objection During World War II." *The Catholic Historical Review* 61 (April 1975): 222-242.

———. *Harder Than War: Catholic Peacemaking in Twentieth-Century America.* New Brunswick, NJ: Rutgers University Press, 1992.

Merriman, O.S.F., Brigid O'Shea. *Searching for Christ: The Spirituality of Dorothy Day.* Notre Dame, IN: University of Notre Dame Press, 1994.

Merton, Thomas. *Ascent to Truth.* New York: Harcourt, Brace and Co., 1951.

Mettepennigen, Jürgen. *Nouvelle Theologie—New Theology: Inheritor of Modernism, Precursor of Vatican II.* New York: T&T Clark, 2010.

Milbank, John. *Theology and Social Theory.* Malden, MA: Blackwell Publishing, 1993.

———. *The Suspended Middle.* Grand Rapids, MI: Eerdmans, 2005.

Miller, William. *A Harsh and Dreadful Love.* Milwaukee: Marquette University Press, 1973. [first edition published by Liveright]

———. *Dorothy Day: A Biography.* San Francisco: Harper & Row, 1982.

———. *All is Grace: The Spirituality of Dorothy Day.* Garden City, NY: Doubleday & Co., 1987.

Mize, Sandra Yocum. "We're Still Pacifists: Dorothy Day's Pacifism During World War II." In *Dorothy Day and the Catholic Worker Movement: Centenary Essays,* edited by Susan Moutin, et al, 465-473. Milwaukee, WI: Marquette University Press, 2001.

Moran, Terrence. "Connell, Francis (1888-1967)." In *The Encyclopedia of American Catholic History,* edited by Michael Glazier and Thomas Shelly, 371-372. Collegeville, MN: The Liturgical Press, 1997.

Muggeridge, Kitty, trans. Pierre Caussade. *The Sacrament of the Present Moment.* San Francisco: Harper Collins, 1989.

Mullan, Elder, trans. *The Spiritual Exercises of St. Ignatius.* St. Louis: The Institute of Jesuit Sources, 1978.

Murray, John Courtney. *We Hold These Truths*. Kansas City: Sheed and Ward, 1960.

Nedoncelle, Maurice, *Is There a Christian Philosophy?* Translated by Illtyd Trethowan. New York: Hawthorn Books, 1960.

Nichols, O.P., Aidan, *Reason with Piety, Garrigou-Lagrange in the Service of Catholic Thought*. Ave Maria, FL: Sapientia Press, 2008.

Niebuhr, H. Richard. *Christ and Culture*. New York: Harper & Row, 1951.

O'Brien, David. *American Catholics and Social Reform: The New Deal Years*. New York: Oxford University Press, 1968.

————. *The Renewal of American Catholicism*. New York: Oxford University Press, 1972.

————. *Public Catholicism*. New York: MacMillan Publishing Co., 1989.

O'Brien, O.P., T.C. trans. *St. Thomas Aquinas Summa Theologiae, vol.26, Original Sin (Ia2ae. 81-85)* New York: Blackfriars-McGraw-Hill Book Company, 1965.

O'Malley, S.J., John. "Early Jesuit Spirituality: Spain and Italy." In *Christian Spirituality III*, edited by Louis Dupre and Don E. Saliers, 3-27. New York: Crossroad, 1989.

Parente, Pascal. "Nature and Grace in Ascetical Theology." *American Ecclesiastical Review* (June 1943): 430-437.

————. *The Ascetical Life*. St. Louis: B. Herder Book Co., 1944.

Peddicord, O.P., Richard. *The Sacred Monster of Thomism, An Introduction to the Life and Legacy of Reginald Garrigou-LaGrange, O.P.* South Bend, IN: St. Augustine's Press, 2005.

Piehl, Mel. *Breaking Bread*. Philadelphia: Temple University Press, 1982.

Pope Leo XII. *Aeterni Patris*. Promulgated on August 4, 1879. Translation from Vatican website.

Pope Pius XII. *Humani Generis*. Promulgated on August 12, 1950. Translation from Vatican website.

Poulain, Auguste. *The Graces of Interior Prayer*. English translation. Trubner & Co., 1928.

Pourrat, S.S., Pierre. *Christian Spirituality volume III: From the Renaissance to Jansenism*. Translated by W.H. Mitchell. London: Burns, Oates and Washbourne, Ltd., 1926.

Portier, William L., "Dorothy Day and Her First Spiritual Director, Fr. Joseph McSorley, C.S.P." *Houston Catholic Worker* 22 (September/October 2002): online edition.

———. "Here Come the Evangelical Catholics." *Communio* 31 (Spring 2004): 35-66

———. "Paul Hanly Furfey: Catholic Extremist and Supernatural Sociologist, 1935-1941." *Josephinum Journal of Theology* 16.1 (Winter/Spring 2009): 25-37.

———. "'Good Friday in December,' World War II in the Editorials of *Preservation of the Faith* Magazine, 1939-1945." *U.S. Catholic Historian* 27.2 (Spring 2009): 25-44.

———. "Twentieth-Century Catholic Theology and the Triumph of Maurice Blondel." *Communio* 38.1 (Spring, 2011).

Portier, William L. and C.J.T. Talar. "Mystical Element of Modernist Crisis." In *Modernists & Mystics*, edited by C.J.T. Talar, 1-22. Washington, DC: CUA Press, 2009.

Puente, S.J., Luis de la. *Vida de la Padre Baltasar Alvarez*. Linkgua ediciones, 2009.

Rahner, S.J., Karl. *Nature and Grace*. Translated by Dinah Wharton. New York: Sheed and Ward, 1964.

Ramiere, S.J., Henri, ed. Pierre de Caussade, *Abandonment to Divine Providence*. Translated by E.J. Strickland. St. Louis: B. Herder Book Co., 1921.

Reardon, Bernard. *Liberalism and Tradition: Aspects of Catholic Thought in Nineteenth-Century France*. New York: Cambridge University Press, 1975.

Reno, Russell. *The Ordinary Transformed: Karl Rahner and the Christian Vision of Transcendence*. Grand Rapids, MI: Eerdmans Publishing Co., 1995.

Richey, Lance. "Stages along Life's Way: House of Hospitality and the Development of Dorothy Day's Spirituality." *American Catholic Studies* 126/1 (Spring 2015).

Rickaby, S.J., Joseph. *The Spiritual Exercises of St. Ignatius of Loyola: Spanish and English, with a continuous commentary*. London: Burns Oates, 1915.

Riegle, Rosalie. *Dorothy Day: Portraits by Those Who Knew Her*. Maryknoll, NY: Orbis Books, 2003.

Schloesser, Stephen. *Jazz Age Catholicism: Mystic Modernism in Postwar Paris, 1919-1933*. Buffalo, NY: University of Toronto Press, 2005.

Schultenover, David. "Billot, Louis." In *Biographical Dictionary of Christian Theologians*, edited by Patrick Carey and Joseph Lienhard, 74-75. Peabody, MA: Hendrickson Publishers, 2002.

Sherley-Price, Leo, trans. Thomas Á Kempis, *Imitation of Christ.* New York: Penguin Books, 1952.

Smith, Anthony. *The Look of Catholics.* Lawrence, KS: University of Kansas Press, 2010.

Simon, Yves. *The Road to Vichy, 1918-1938.* Translated by James Corbett and George McMorrow. Lanham, MD: University Press of America, 1988.

St. Thomas Aquinas. *Summa Theologica.* Translated by Fathers of the English Dominican Province. New York: Benziger Brothers, 1948.

Surin, S.J. Jean-Joseph. *Catéchisme Spirituel De La Perfection Chrétienne.* Paris: Nabu Press, 2010.

Talar, C.J.T. "Prayer at Twilight: Henri Bremond's *Apologie pour Fénelon.*" In *Modernists & Mystics,* edited by C.J.T. Talar, 39-61. Washington, DC: CUA Press, 2009.

———. "Swearing against Modernism: *Sacrorum antistitum* (September 1, 1910)" *Theological Studies* 71 (September 2010): 545-566.

Tentler, Leslie Woodcock. "On the Margins: The State of American Catholic History." *American Quarterly* 45 (March 1993): 104-127.

Thibert, V.H.M., Peronne Marie, ed. and trans. *Francis de Sales, Jane de Chantal: Letters of Spiritual Direction.* Mahwah, NJ: Paulist Press, 1988.

Thompson, William, ed. *Berulle and the French School: Selected Writings.* Translated by Lowell Glendon, S.S. Mahwah, NJ: Paulist Press, 1989.

Thorold, Algor, trans. Pierre Caussade. *On Prayer: Spiritual Instruction on the Various States of Prayer According to the Doctrine of Bossuet, Bishop of Meaux.* Springfield, IL: Templegate Publishers, 1955.

Troester, Rosalie Riegle, ed. *Voices from the Catholic Worker.* Philadelphia: Temple University Press, 1993.

Vann O.P., Gerald. "Nature and Grace." *Orate Fratres* (January 26, 1947): 97-105.

Vidler, Alec. Prophecy and Papacy: *A Study of Lamennais, the Church & Revolution.* New York: Charles Scribner's Sons, 1954.

Vincelette, Alan. *Recent Catholic Philosophers: The Nineteenth Century.* Milwaukee: Marquette University Press, 2009.

Vishnewski, Stanley. *Wings of the Dawn.* New York: The Catholic Worker Press, 1984.

Voderholzer, Rudolf. *Meet Henri de Lubac.* Translated by Michael Miller. San Francisco: Ignatius Press, 2008.

Wangler, Thomas. "John Ireland's Emergence as a Liberal Catholic and Americanist: 1875-1887." *Records of the American Catholic Historical Society of Philadelphia* 81 (June 1970): 67-82.

Weigel, George. *Tranquilitatis Ordinis.* New York: Oxford University Press, 1987.

Wood, Susan. "Lubac, Henri de." In *Biographical Dictionary of Christian Theologians,* edited by Patrick Carey and Joseph Lienhard, 330-333. Peabody, MA: Hendrickson Publishers, 2002.

Zahn, Gordon, *Another Part of the War: The Camp Simon Story.* Amherst, MA: University of Massachusetts Press, 1979.

Zwick, Mark and Louise Zwick. *The Catholic Worker Movement.* Mahwah, NJ: Paulist Press, 2005.

DOROTHY DAY'S
RETREAT NOTEBOOKS

Oakmount, Pa,
ST. Anthony's Village,
Retreat 1942
Fr. John J. Hugo
                    Pittsburgh.
Aug 2 —

Sunday night
Monday
Tuesday,
Friday, Sat,
Also Conferences on Prayer.
          by Fr. Farina.

Oakmont, Pa.
St. Anthony's Village
Retreat 1942
Fr. John J. Hugo
Pittsburgh
Aug 2—
Sunday night
Monday
Tuesday,
Friday, Sat.
Also Conference on Prayer
by Fr. Farina

He who says he has done
enough has already perished
ST? Augustine,

Mass.   8.30.
          9.00   Breakfast
          9.45   Conference.
          11.45   "
          1.00   Dinner
                 private visit
          3.30   Conference.
          5.00   "
            .   Benediction
          7.00   Supper.
          8.30   Conference.
          10.30 lights out

Oh God who didist instruct the hearts
of thy faithful by the light of the Holy
Spirit: grand that by the gift of the
same spirit, we may always to truly
wise, relish what is right, and ever
rejoice in this holy consolation."

He who says he has done
enough has already perished.
St. Augustine

Mass. 8:30
      9:00 Breakfast
      9:45 Conference
      11:45 "
      1:00 Dinner
         private visit
      3:30 Conference
      5:00   "
      Benediction
      7:00 Supper
      8:30 Conference
      10:30 Lights out.

Oh God who didst instruct the hearts
of thy faithful by the light of the Holy
Spirit: grant that by the gift of the
same spirit, we may always be truly
wise, relish what is right, and
ever rejoice in his holy consolation."

Sunday night. Aug. 2. Feast of
St. Alphonsus.
From New York. Peggy Stern.,
Betty Cuda Tina Tamas + I.
Fr. Roy is here. Nancy geneste,
Belle Butos. Loretta Corbin The Sisters are
Zelatrices of the Sacred Heart.

Conditions for good retreat.
1. Silence. Retreat Master The
Holy ghost, "I will lead you
into the desert and there
I will speak to you."
Make promise now to God.
2. Solitude. In the desert.
physical. Ten acres here.
Interior. Put aside sec-
ular activities. even from
thoughts.
3 Prayer. — Lifting of mind
and hearts to God.
Wall with him.

Sunday night, Aug. 2, Feast of
St. Alphonsus.
From New York. Peggy Stern,
Betty Cuda, Tina, Tamar & I.
Fr. Roy is here, Nancy Geneste,
Belle Butes. Loretta ... The Sisters are
Zelatrices of the Sacred Heart.

Conditions for good retreat.
1. Silence. Retreat Master, The
   Holy Ghost " I will lead you
   into the desert and there
   I will speak to you."
   Make promise now to God.
2. Solitude. In the desert
   physical. Ten acres here.
   Interior. Put aside secular
   activities even from
   thoughts
3. Prayer— Lifting of mind
   and hearts to God.
   Walk with him.

Taste and see

1st Problem. To under-
stand supernatural.

Story of Nicodemus John 3.

"How shall we enter, live in
the Kingdom of god
We must be born again.
Born again of water &
Spirit
Physical - human birth.
Rebirth - baptism. new
creature. Share in divine
life. Regeneration. Now
we have natural life. &
supernatural Unless you
live s. life. we cannot
enter Kingdom of God
Grace is share of divine life.

Taste and see

1st Problem. To understand
supernatural.

Story of Nicodemus John 3.

How shall we enter, live in
the Kingdom of God.
We must be born again.
Born again of water &
Spirit
Physical— human birth.
Rebirth—baptism. new
creature. Share in divine
life. Regeneration. Now
we have natural life &
supernatural Unless you
live s. life, we cannot
enter Kingdom of God
Grace is share of divine life.

cornesstone of retreat.
Baptism is like blood transfusion
I possess blood of my parents,
their life. — So also children
of God, heirs of Heaven.
Last Gospel.   John 1.
Sons of God. Raised up
to supernatural plane.
natural, conforming to
   human powers.
Supern. what we can-
not do by ourselves.
We are given power to
become sons of God.

         Ways
Two destinies. Distinguished
in 3 ways.
~~this composition~~

cornerstone of retreat.
Baptism is the blood transfusion.
I possess blood of my parents,
then life. So also children
of God, heirs of Heaven.
Last Gospel. John 1.
Sons of God. Raised up
to supernatural plane.
Natural, conforming to
human powers.
Supern. what we cannot
do by ourselves.
We are given <u>power</u> to
Become <u>sons</u> of God.

Two Ways destinies. Distinguished
in 3 ways.

Two Ways

Two Ways. I

Supernatural.
(Love
charity.
like air)

Natural.
(natural
activity.
eating &
drinking. etc

Sinful

Difference between two actions
is love. Love of God is
make up of Supernatural
world. We have grace,
but we are free.
Meditate on these things

Aristotle wished us to live
according to reason, intellect.
The just (holy) man lives
by faith. Conform our lives
to faith, according to teaching
of Jesus.

Two Ways [of Life]
I
Supernatural. Make up.
Love
charity
like air

Natural.   natural
activity.
Eating &
drinking .etc

Sinful

Difference between two actions
is love. Love of God is
make up of supernatural
world. We have grace,
but we are free.
Meditate on these things

Aristotle wished us to live
according to reason, intellect.
The just (holy) man lives
by faith. Conform our live
to faith, according to teaching
of Jesus.

of Life.

II. ~~grinde (map)~~   III. Term. End.
~~(heartlight)~~
~~faith~~   ↗ (Purg.) Happiness ~~Heaven~~.

reason.   (deTours)   Limbo.

       ↘

appeTites.   Hell.

Faith that works thru hope
love is mark of superior life.
You pick your road by
its destination.
Charity is most important law.
First commandment; That
is law to consider. What makes
us Christian.
    Luke. 18. Jesus + rich youngman

Love is commandment
  " " a virtue.
    choice
    preference.   election.

[Two Ways] of Life

II	III
<u>guide</u> (map)	Term. <u>End.</u>
<u>headlight</u>	
faith	(Purg.) Happiness
	Heaven
reason (Detour)	Limbo.

_____

appetites. <u>Hell.</u>

_____

Faith that works then
love is mark of supern life.
You pick your road by
its destination.
Charity is most important law.
First commandment: That
is law to consider. What makes
us Christians.
Luke 18. Jesus & rich young man

Love is commandment
"   "   a virtue.
         choice
         preference.   election.

If we love God with whole
heart how much *breast* have
we left? Mind, soul, strength.

St. Paul: Col. 3.
If you have risen with
Christ seek things which
are above ... For you are
dead.

We must live this life now.
Nothing will change us
Death changes nothing.

Work now, for night cometh
when no man can work.
Christ said.
As the Tree falls it shall lie.
We must be saints
Only the holy shall see God.
Love & sanctity same. are
    the same.

If we love God with whole
Heart how much heart have
we left? Mind, soul, strength.

St. Paul: Col. 3.
If you have risen with
Christ see things which
are alive... For you are
dead.

We must live this life <u>now.</u>
Nothing will change us
Death changes nothing.

Work now, for night cometh
when no man can work.
Christ said.
As the tree falls it shall lie.
We must be saints
Only the holy shall see God.
Love & sanctity are
the same.

Monday. Aug. 3.
Feast of St. Stephen.
①.
Avoidance ^at mortal sin not mark
of super. life. Gal. 5. 6.
"For in Christ Jesus, neither
circumcision, nor uncir.
but faith which worketh
thru' charity."

Faith — head light
Love — motor.

Meditate on difference between
nat. + sup. happiness.

God is not on the natural road.
to heaven, but supernatural,
another plane. Graces raise
us above natural to divine.

Monday Aug. 3.
Feast of St. Stephen.
     I.
Avoidance of mortal sin not mark
of supern. life Gal. 5-6
"For in Christ Jesus, neither
circumsions , nor uncir.
but faith which worketh
thru charity."

Faith— headlight
Love— motor

Meditate on difference between
<u>nat</u>. & <u>sup</u>. happiness

God is not on the natural road
to heaven, but supernatural,
another plane. Graces raise
us above natural to divine.

Rule: Action and pleasure
are on the same plane.
(pleasure - reward.)
Can't get peaches from apple tree.
Sow wheat, get wheat.
"He who sows in flesh shall
reap corruption."
"He who sows in spirit
shall reap life everlasting."
These truths must go
from mind to heart.

Grace is a share in the
Divine Life. <u>Keystone</u>
of retreat. Raised above
ourselves. Law of S. life
is love. Most important
commandment.
Love demands renunciation
Official meditation during

Rule: Actions and pleasure
are on the same plane.
(pleasure— reward)
Can't get peaches from apple tree.
Sow wheat, get wheat.
"He who sows in flesh shall
reap corruption."
"He who sows in spirit
shall reap life everlasting."
These truths must go
from mind to heart.

Grace is a share in the
Divine Life. <u>Keystone</u>
of retreat. Raised above
ourselves. Law of s. life
is love. Most important
commandment.
Love demands renunciation
Official meditation during

paschal season : Seek things
that are above. Col. 3.
For you are dead and
your life is hid with
Christ in god.

All this is starting point
of Christianity.

(2)nd Conference.

2.⌉ Relationships between natural
point⌋ and supernatural.
What there is that is good?
Before, we have taken
apart; now put together.
Mortify natural to lead
supernatural life. **Kill**
natural.
                   There
But in natural is good.
Certain things evil.
We are like doctors in
destroying natural.

paschal season: Seek things
that are above. Col.3.
For you are dead and
your life is hid with
Christ in God.

All this is starting point
of Christianity.

2nd Conference
2. point
Relationship between natural
and supernatural.
What there is that is good?
Before, we have taken
apart; now put together.
Mortify natural to lead
supernatural life. <u>Kill</u>
natural.
But in natural there is good.
Certain things evil.
We are like doctors in
destroying natural.

There is that which is good
and in harmony with our
supernatural destiny.
A double relationships.
　　　Harmony.
3 ways in which there is
harmony " " in. life is good.

1. Human nature.
2. Natural activity.
3. Natural truth.

1. Body & soul constitute.
human nature. Body
good but less perfect
than soul.
In mortifying natural
we must not injure body
or soul. Not to destroy
but Transform it. as iron
is in fire.

There is that which is good
and in harmony with our
supernatural destiny.
A double relationship.
       Harmony.
3 ways in which there is
harmony " "   n. life is good.

1. Human nature.
2. Natural activity.
3. Natural truth.

1. Body & Soul constitute
human nature. Body
good but less perfect
than soul.
In mortifying natural
we must not injure body
or soul. Not to destroy
But transform it.as iron
is in fire.

Most of our lives unimportant
filled with trivial things.
When transformed by love,
of interest even to angels.
Altho human nature essentially
good it is infected by
orig. sin. Forgiven at baptism
but effects still remain in
soul. Proneness to evil.
Bias toward evil.
"I know that there is not
in my flesh anything that
is good." St. Paul.
There is nothing, either
in body and soul that
is not Tainted by orig.
sin. We must know
how deeply it goes.
Essentially good in
essence. Body + Soul.
Blemish of sin infects all

Most of our lives unimportant
filled with trivial things.
When transformed by love,
of interest even to angels.
Altho human nature essentially
good it is infected by
orig. sin. Forgiven at baptism
but effects still remain in
soul. Proneness to evil.
Bias toward evil.
"I know that there is not
in my flesh anything that
is good." St. Paul.
There is nothing, either
in body and soul that
is not tainted by orig.
sin. We must know
how deeply it goes.
Essentially good in
essence. Body & soul.
Blemish of sin infects all

our actions.
    Example of doctor and
patient.
2nd. Harmony.
    In regard to natural
activity. Eating, drinking
walking, writing, thinking,
Talking, all are good.
We must mortify taste.
hearing, sight — not
activity.   Must keep all
nat. activity and raise
it to supnat. level
The only thing we have
to work with is our
natural activity.
If we wish supernatural
fruit, graft onto natural,
God does not change
our natural activity.
Our reason is same.

our actions.
Example of doctor and
patient.
2nd Harmony
In regard to natural
activity. Eating, drinking
walking, writing, thinking,
talking, all are good.
We must mortify taste,
hearing, sight— not
activity. Must keep all
nat. activity and raise it
to supntl level
The only thing we have
to work with is our
natural activity.
If we wish supernatural
fruit, graft onto natural,
God does not change
our natural activity.
Our reason is same.

grace does not change
our natural activity.
Baptism gives us power
by voluntarily cooperating
with God to supernaturalize
our activity.

Only things are of value
in Christ Jesus. In union
with god, in love of God.

3rd Harmony.   Nat. Truth.
two and two are still four.
I do learn things apparently
conflicting. 2 natures in one
person of Jesus Christ.
Three times one are three.
But 3 persons in 1 God.
Truths of faith are
above and beyond truth
or reason.

Grace does not change
our natural activity.
Baptism gives us <u>power</u>
by voluntarily cooperating
with God to supernaturalize
our activity.
Only things are of value
in Christ Jesus. In union
with God, in love of God.

3rd Harmony.   Nat. Truth.
two and two are still four.
I do learn things apparently
conflicting. 2 natures in one
person of Jesus Christ.
Three times one are three.
But 3 persons in 1 God.
Truths of faith are
above and beyond truth
or reason.

dog has knowledge.
man " " but
higher. No conflict.
Our grasp of truth is
very inadequate compared
with God. We give up
no truths of science, or
history.

We wish to elevate our
human nature. We are
crazy enough in order
of nature without
being crazy in sup. order.
Ostentation – unnoticed
by others.

Practical rule. 1.

Transform nature?
God is love. Life is ruled
by love of God.

dog has knowledge.
Man   "   "   but
higher. No conflict.
Our grasp of truth is
very inadequate compared
with God. We give up
no truths of science or
history.
We wish to elevate our
human nature.

Practical rule. 1.

Transform natural?
God is love. Life is ruled
by love of God.

Where there is no love put
love and you will find love —
St. John of Cross

If I wash dishes for love of
God —. supernaturalized
If I pray for nat. motive —
no good.

How can I know? When
love is active principle,
~~motive~~. A supernatural
motive. Every activity can
be made supernatural.
Except sin.

"Let these things be not
so much as mentioned
amongst you."

1. First rule is to bring love in.
               human
There is animal, pagan, god in us.
     should
" be 3 elements in our action.
Put divine element in." You are
gods." First two elements take
care of themselves. "Whether you
eat or drink do all for glory of God.

Where there is no love put
love and you will find love—

St. John of Cross

If I wash dishes for love of
God— supernaturalized
If I pray for nat. motive
no good.
How can I know? When
love is active principle
A supernatural
motive. Every activity can
be made supernatural.
Except sin.

"Let these things be not
so much as mentioned
amongst you."
1. First rule is to bring love in.
There is animal, human pagan, God in us.
" should be 3 elements in our actions.
Put divine elements in" You are
gods" First two elements take
care of themselves. "Whether you
eat or drink do all for glory of God.

Third Conference.

We can do this by putting
motive in it. Any action
incomplete, not pleasing to
God unless we have divine
element. Poor widow Mark 12.
41. Kings. Samuel sent to
anoint King. Most unsig.,
David chosen by God.
Get habit of judging as Jesus
does.

3.C. Conflict.

Where is seat of infection
in Human Nature.
1. Where conflict is = Motive.
2. Reasons.
3. Why God hates natural
motives.

Third Conference
We can do this by putting
<u>motive</u> in it. Any actions
incomplete, not pleasing to
God unless we have divine
element. Poor widow Mark 12:
41. Kings. Samuel sent to
anoint King. Most insis.,
David chosen by God.
Get habit of judging as Jesus
does.

<u>3.C. Conflict</u>
Where is seat of infection
in Human Nature.

> 1. Where conflict is— in Motive
> 2. Reasons.
> 3. Why God hates natural
> motives.

Order of grace presupposes.
order by nature and does
not destroy it. But there
is a conflict. H. nature
is good but there is conflict
Bias towards creatures.
Imitation Book 3—54. Divers motions of
Nature and grace.
Conflict? motive.
Accumulation of actions
not done for love of god
not pleasing to God.
ST. Paul. 1 Cos. 10. 31.
Whether you eat or drink. 3. Col.

If we do our unpleasant as
well as pleasant duties for
love of God. Eat what is put
in front of us for love of God
Motive is kernel. Gives
vitality. Instrument board.

Order of grace presupposes
order of nature and does
not destroy it. But there
is a conflict. 4. Nature
is good but here is conflict
Bias towards creatures.
Imitation Book 3-54. Divers motions of
Nature and grace.
Conflict? motive.
Accumulation of actions
not done for love of God
not pleasing to God.
St. Paul 1 Cor. 10-31.
Whether you eat or drink.
                3.Col.
If we do our unpleasant as
well as pleasant duties for
love of God. Eat what is put
in front of us for love of God
Motive is kernel. Gives
vitality. Instrument board.

Motives are area of our freedom.
We have free will but
surprising how little freedom
we have.

Of greatest importance.
99 o/o of our action not free.
1 o/o God watches. We
must be like God and watch.

Catholics live like pagans
recreation, way of living.
Defend ourselves by saying
we are in a state of grace.
~~Beginning. We have power.~~

                    one
One [rule] should be.
      [state of grace
      [supernatural motive.

         ing
Bring my soul into state
of grace by baptism or confession

Motives are area of our freedom.
We have free will but
surprising how little freedom
we have.
Of greatest importance.
99% of our action not free.
1% God watches. We
must be like God and watch.

Catholics live like pagans
recreation, way of living.
Defend ourselves by saying
we are in a state of grace.

Our one rule should be.
        state of grace
        supernatural motive.

Bringing my soul into state
of grace by baptism or confession

is like bringing child into
world. Work is only started
If we are in state of grace, we
infants. Maturity is
sanctity.

As long as I'm in a state of
grace I am pleasing to God?
No. Feeble minded
child. Has mind, reason,
potentially, just can't use
it. It is human but
acts like animal.
We act like pagan but in
a state of grace. We throw
away graces.

We are raised to supernatural
but we are free to use
grace or not.

is like bringing child into
world. Work is only started.
If we are only in state of grace, we are
infants. Maturity is
sanctity.

As long as I'm in a state of
grace I am pleasing to God?
No.   Feeble minded
child. Has mind, reason,
potentially, just can't use
it. It is human but
acts like animal.
We act like pagan but in
a state of grace. We throw
away graces.

We are raised to supernatural
but we are free to use
grace or not.

2. Why conflict?
  1. Spiritual life is better.
God invites us. We are
called to be saints.
We are raised to higher
kingdom, not of this world.
We must be holy. We are
sons of God. When we
defend natural we are
in conflict with god's
plan. It is good, yes.
  2. It is a matter of love.
Love of God demands it.
    a.) relationship of love.
    b.) demands supntrl motive.
  a.) children of god. Father
    deep and tender tie.
St. John describes us as
children of god. Also St. Paul
Love of man for woman

2. Why conflict?
1. Spiritual life is better,
God invites us. We are
called to be saints.
We are raised to higher
kingdom, not of this world.
We must be holy. We are
sons of God. When we
defend natural we are
in conflict with God's
plan. It is good, yes.
2. It is a matter of love.
Love of God demands it.
   a.) relationship of love.
   b.) demands supernatural motive.
   c.) children of God. Father
deep and tender tie.
St. John describes us as
children of God. Also, St. Paul.
Love of man for women.

Jesus speaks of himself
as bridegroom. Christian
soul is bride. We should
regard him as bridegroom.
In love with him.
Love creates rivalry,
" is exclusive.
Rivalry between god & world.
Nothing evil in world.
Hatred of world means
indifference.
b.). demands sup. motive.
Principle: We get our
motives from what we
love. James buys flowers,
jewelry because he loves
Martha. If we love world
we get our motives from
world. Motives reveal where
our heart is. Motives

Jesus speaks of himself
as bridegroom. Christian
soul is <u>bride</u>. We should
regard him as bridegroom.
In love with him.
Love creates rivalry,
    "   is exclusive.
Rivalry between God and world.
Nothing evil in world.
Hatred of world means
indifference.
b.) demands sup. motive.
Principle; We get our
motives from what we
love. James buys flower,
jewelry because he loves
Martha. If we love world
we get our motives from
world. Motives reveal where
our heart is. Motives

habitually show where love
is, where heart is.
We may honor god with
our lips not with our
heart.

Question prompted by love
is why? Motive.
We sho can act from motive
of utility or love.
We must use creatures for
motive of utility.
We are not to have any
love for creatures.
We must treat world as
tho it were evil.

How can we know we
have a love of creatures.?
When we use things
habitually without necessity.
or utility.

habitually show were love
is, where heart is
We may honor God with
our lips not with our
heart.
Question prompted by love
is <u>why?</u> Motive.
We can act from motive
of utility or love.
We must use creatures for
motive of utility.
We are not to have any
love for creatures.
We must treat world as
tho it were evil.
<u>How can we know
we have love of creatures?</u>
When we use things
habitually with out necessity
or utility.

3. Why god hates natural
motives. He hates them
so much he will destroy
them himself if we don't.
1 Peter. 1. 6.
Over this rejoice, if you
for a little while, if need
be, be tried.
That is only reason for
suffering.
We are wedded to the
world. All natural
attachments like roots.

Natural motives an insult
to god.
Morning offering is a promise
made to god.
Natural motives lead to sin
Some natural motive lead
directly to sin, practically
all natural motives lead

3.Why God hates natural
motives. He hates them
so much he will destroy
them himself if we don't.
1 Peter 1. 6.
Over this rejoice, if you
for a little while, if need
be, be tried.
That's only reason for
suffering.
We are rooted to the
world. All natural
attachments like roots.

Natural motives an insult
to God.
Morning offering is a promise
made to God.
Natural motives lead to sin.
Some natural motives lead
directly to sin, practically
all natural motive lead

indirectly to sin., Weakens
soul, predisposes to sin
A man dies after
long fast - missing 180
meals. First meal is as
responsible as last.

Sin is never a do sudden
thing - it is a collapse.

Cause of sin is love of creatures
St. Thomas definition:
Sin is a turning away
from God and a turning
to creatures.
St. Augustine's definition
in catechism: "any thought
word or deed against
law of gods."
To Get rid of sin, get rid
of natural motives.

indirectly to sin. Weakens
soul, predisposes to sin
A man dies after
long fast— missing 180
meals. First meal is as
responsible as last.

Sin is never a sudden
thing— it is a collapse.

Cause of sin is love of creatures.
St. Thomas definition:
Sin is a turning away
from God and turning
to creatures.
St. Augustine's definition
in catechism. "Any thought
word or deed against
law of God."
To get rid of sin, get rid
of natural motives.

natural motives are roots.
To enjoy things of this world
and try to avoid mortal
sin as impossible as to
jump from Empire State
and expect to stop before
we get hurt.

Pagan Mentality.

A. Mentality is way of thinking
which is permanent,
characteristic.
Pagan is a natural man.
Christian is a Christ   "
We must change our mentality.
St. Paul. Ephesian. 4 - 22
Put off old man which
is corrupted.   Be you
renewed in spirit of
your mind. Put on new

Natural motives are roots.
To enjoy things of this world
and try to avoid mortal
sin as impossible as to
jump from Empire State
and expect to stop before
we get hurt.

Pagan Mentality

A. Mentality is a way of thinking
which is permanent,
characteristic.
Pagan is a natural man.
Christian is a Christ "
We must change our mentality.
St. Paul, Ephesian 4-22
Put off old man which
is corrupted. Be you
renewed in spirit of
your mind. Put on new

man which is created

Be not conformed to
this world. but reformed
in spirit of your mind.

Have in you that mind
that was in christ Jesus.

We must have helet —
"I always do the things
we please my father."
Mind thinks — forms
rules of action.

Rules of. Pagan ~~soltes~~ Catholics.
  1. The things of the world
  are good, therefore we
  should enjoy them.
      Eat drink and be merry.
  "To enjoy things in this world
  & be happy in the next.

man which is created.

Be not conformed to
this world, but reformed
in spirit of your mind.

Have in you that mind
that was in Christ Jesus.

We must have habit —
"I always do the things
we please my father."
Mind thinks— forms
rules of action.
Rules of Pagan Catholics.
1. The things of the world
are good, therefore we
should enjoy them.
Eat, drink and be merry.
"To enjoy things in this world
& be happy in the next.

2. I'll enjoy the things of
world but avoid mortal
sin.

3. Stay in state of grace, but
enjoy things of world.

If we wish to be renewed
reformed —
If any be in Christ a
new creature, behold
all things are made
new.
Hard to change mentality.
Major problem, big
struggle to get rid of
pagan mentality.
We must blast loose
natural principles,

2. I'll enjoy the things of
world but avoid mortal
sin.

3.Stay in state of grace, but
enjoy things of world.

If we wish to be renewed
reformed—
If any be in Christ a
new creature, behold
all things are made
new.
Have to change mentality.
Major problem, big
struggle to get rid of
pagan mentality.
We must blast loose
natural principles,

Will forms habits —
natural intention. Once
formed it tends to persist.
Mind has series of
ideas . like movies.

Supplementary maxims to
escape responsibility of
being Christian.
1.   It is impossible to be
always thinking about
God . Place burden on
shoulders too heavy.
For pagan it is. We
think of things we love.
It is contrary to our
nature to think of God.
Is it difficult for
people in love to think
of each other ?

Will forms habits—
natural intention. Once
formed it tends to persist.
Mind has series of
ideas, like movies.

Supplementary maxims to
escape responsibility of
being Christian.
1. It is impossible to be
always thinking about
God. Place burden on
shoulder too heavy.
For pagan it is. We
  think of things we love.
It is contrary to our
nature to think of God.
Is it difficult for
people in love to think
of each other?

Jesus said Pray always
Refer all actions to god.
2. Also I have to watch
all my motives. Is god
going to damn us
because of natural
motive — one hears one
candy. Artificial
question.
Not one Termite but
millions.
Our whole life organized
for pleasure.
Chesterton and Belloc
point out neo-paganism
is much worse.
Pius XI condemned black
paganism. Message to
Cleveland Eucharistic Congress.

Jesus said Pray always
Refer all actions to God.

2. Do I have to watch
all my motives. Is God
going to damn us
because of natural
motive— one beer, one
candy. Artificial
question.
Not one termite but
millions.
Our whole life organized
for pleasure.
Chesterton and Belloc
point out neo-paganism
is much worse.
Pius XI condemned black
paganism. Message to
Cleveland Eucharistic Congress.

Evening. 7.30. very loud
cicadas
There are some good nat-
ural motives. Some
untainted? In practice
too hard to distinguish.
Like good and bad germs
For tainted man impossible
Only saint can perform
untainted ᴀ actions.
      natural
Self love ~~noth~~ evil.
root evil.
Even if one could to
act on good natural
motive. Rob ourselves
of grace.
Grace comes from charity,

Maxims of the world.
Saints warn us against
Talking to worldly people

Evening, 7-30 very loud
cicadas
There are some good natural
motives. Some
untainted?
In practice
too hard to distinguish.
Like good and bad germs.
for tainted man impossible.
Only saint can perform
untainted natural actions.
Self love root evil.
Even if we could
act on good natural
motive. Rob ourselves
of grace.
Grace comes from charity.

Maxims of the world
Saints warn us against
Talking to worldly people

we drink in from radio,
newspapers, magazines.
We are all worldly to some
extent.
   Conference. 5.
Jesus speaks of supntrl life.
  Sermon on mount.
Matt... Mark,. Luke..
longest — Math. 5 - 6 - 7
Does not institute Sacra.
ments — does not talk
about Mass.
Christian manifesto.
elementary statement
basic principles
like Com. Manifesto,
    Constitution. sentence.
Summed up in one phrase,
You must cease to be human
begin to be divine.

19. Do not lay up treasures on
earth, but in heaven.

we drink in from radio,
newspapers, magazines.
We are all worldly to some
extent.

Conference 5

Jesus speaks of supernatural life.
Sermon on Mount.
Matt. Mark. Luke..
Longest— Matt. 5-6-7
Does not institute sacraments
--does not talk
about Mass.
Christian manifesto
elementary statement
basic principles
Like Com. Manifesto,
Constitution,
Summed up in one phrase, sentence.
You must cease to be human
begin to be divine.
19. Do not lay up treasures on
earth, but in heaven.

Do not seek things men
seek after. Two divisions
· Condemns pagan, defines
Christian.

       End Means Result
in every action. Condemns
natural end, Means, Result
We always seek after some
good. (end)

       Philosophers say 3 kinds
1. external. 2. bodily good.
3. interior. (joy, peace, gayety,
    knowledge..) Jesus con-
demns them in Beatitudes.
8 Beatitudes - fundamental
principles
      Luke contains condem-
nations.

      Meek persons accepts
trials uncomplainingly,

Do not seek things men
seek after. Two divisions
Condemns pagan, defines
Christian.
    End Means Result
in every action. Condemns
natural end, Means, Result
We always seek after some
good. (end)
    Philosophers say 3 kinds
1.external, 2.bodily good,
3.interior. (joy, peace, gayety
knowledge.) Jesus condemns
them in Beatitudes,
8 Beatitudes —fundamental
principles
Luke contains condemnations.

Meek person accepts
trials uncomplainingly,

Chesterton's picture of Jesus.
what book?

H. Maturin – perfect
combination of gentleness
and strength.
We like to air troubles
complain of others.

Learn of me because I
am meek and humble
of heart.
Meek lack bodily goods,
indifferent to them –

Blessed are they who mourn.
His tenderness is for those
who mourn.
An impoverished idea of
peace. Lake house dog.

10 just men – Sodom & Gomorrah
1 "   "   John.
Nineveh – sackcloth + ashes.

Chesterton's picture of Jesus.
what book?

Fr. Maturin— perfect
combination of gentleness
and strength.
We like to air troubles
Complain of others.

Learn of me because I
am meek and humble
of heart.
Meek lack bodily goods,
indifferent to them.

Blessed are they who mourn.
His tenderness is for those
who mourn.
An impoverished idea of
peace. Like house dog.

10 just men—Sodom & Gomorrah
1 " "   Job
Nineveh— sack cloth— ashes.

Chesterton : Christianity
has been tried but found
too difficult.

Jesus condemns natural
motive Mat. 6. — ~~1. 2. 3.~~
Natural result condemned.
Pharisees good natural men, not
sinners.

v. 20 Unless your justice exceed that of scribes and
pharisees

Jesus define Christian mentality.
                    divine.
Supntrl.   End

      ''   means

      ''   result.

Chesterton: Christianity
has been tried but found
too difficult.

Jesus condemns natural
motive Mat.6.
Natural result condemned
Pharisees good, natural men, not
sinners.

v.20 Unless your justice exceed
that of scribes and
pharisees

Jesus defines Christian mentality.

Divine/ Supernatural   end
      "   means
    "   result

4th Beatitudes gives true
ends. Justice, sanctity.
hunger and thirst after
justice.

Rest of Beatitudes commen-
tary on 4th. When we
become holy, like God.
Mercy, a divine attribute
Pure.
Peacemakers, quality of Trinity
Let your eye be single.

Means: supernatural
motives. Alms, prayer,
fasting for love of God.
Right motive-

Result: Holiness like God's
Be ye therefore perfect.
M. 5-48

4th Beatitude gives true
ends. Justice, sanctity,
hunger and thirst after
justice.

Rest of Beatitude commentary
on 4th. When we
become holy, like God.
Mercy, a divine attribute
Pure
Peacemakers, quality of Trinity
Let you eye be single.

Means: supernatural
motives: Alms, prayer,
fasting for love of God.
Right motive.

Result: Holiness like God's
Be you therefore perfect.
M. 5.48

That you may be children
of your Father.

Seek *first* god.

Conference 6. Tuesday. 9.45.

The law of sin - flesh
Romans - 7-8.
Impossible to lead a good
natural life. So a person
who leads a natural life
is going to hell. He who
lives according to flesh
will die.
Whole civilization built on
sin - depriving labour of wage.

Chesterton Says one doctrine
of original sin can be
proved : Also Plato.
Revelation - own experience.

That you may be children
of your Father

Seek <u>first</u> God.

Conference 6 Tuesday 9:45

The law of sin— flesh
Romans-7-8
Impossible to lead a good
natural life. So a person
who leads a natural life
is going to hell. He who
lives according to flesh
will die.
While civilization built on
sin— depriving laborer of wage.

Chesterton says one doctrine
of original sin can be
proved : Also Plato.
Revelation— own experience.

Natural life.
St. James. 1. 13.
Let terror no man say when
he is tempted

Every man is tempted by
his own desires.
Concupiscence — desires of
fallen man. Prone to
desire earthly creatures.
"Being drawn away and
allured. Passion brings
forth sin.
Monstrous offspring
of our natural desires.
When sin has matured
it begets death.
By baptism
Malice of original sin
Taken away — but
effects remain.

St. James 1. 13
Let no man say when
he is tempted

Everyman is tempted by
his own desires.
Concupiscence— desires o f
fallen man. Prone to
desire earthly creatures.
"Being drawn away and
allured. Passion brings
forth sin.
Monstrous offspring
of our natural desires.
When sin matured
it begets death.
By baptism
Malice of original sin
Taken away— but
effects remain.

Effects:

1 Darkens understanding,
  great pagans prone according to reason that man's
  true happiness consists
  in knowledge and love
  of God. These teachings
  of Aristotle & Plato laid
  down 6 centuries before
  christ. This taught in
  universities even now
  But where are people
  seeking happiness now.
  They have fine minds,
  better than ours.
  Yet this is an elementary
  truth of human reason.
  Pure reason, right reason
  Teaches this.
  But man's reason has
  been darkened by the
  fall.

Effects
1. Darkens understanding
Great pagans prove according
to reason that man's
true happiness consists
in knowledge and love
of God. These teachings
of Aristotle— Plato laid
down 6 centuries before
Christ. This taught in
universities even now.
But where are people
seeking happiness now.
They have fine minds,
better than ours.
Yet this is an elementary
truth of human reason.
Pure reason, right reason
teaches this.
But man's reason has
been darkened by the
fall.

2. Weakens will. We make
resolutions. We make
promises to God.
The evil that I will not,
that I do, and the good
which I love that I do
not.   St. Paul.

We work with broken instruments.

3.) Proneness to evil,
even in little children.
We become sophisticated
hide our vices. Those who
seek God are always,
treated with contempt.

Only God's grace is
strong enough to break
up this law, substituting
another tendency.

2. Weakens will. We make
resolutions. We make
promises to God.
The evil that I will not
that I do, and the good
which I love that I do
not.   St. Paul

We work with broken
instruments.
3. Proneness to evil,
even in little children,
We become sophisticated
hide our vices. Those who
seek God are aliens,
treated with contempt.

Only God's grace is
strong enough to break
up this law, substituting
another tendency.

Newman:
Were it not for the
grace of God what a
dismal event would be
the birth of an infant.

Another starting point
is recognition of fallen
nature. Taken for
granted in Scripture.
Romans. 8. 1. What
mankind looks like
when Christ came.
Nothing good in us but
God's grace.
Romans 8. 5.
The inclination of flesh
is death.
A law works ruthlessly, of
necessity, unsleeping.
Law in our flesh drives us
towards sin

Newman:
Were it not for the
 grace of God what a
dismal event would be
the birth of an infant.

Another starting point
is recognition of fallen
nature. Taken for
granted in Scripture.
Romans 8.1. What
mankind looks like
when Christ came.
Nothing good in us but
God's grace.
Romans 8.5.
The inclination of flesh
is death.
A law works ruthlessly, of
necessity, unsleeping.
Law in our flesh drives us
towards sin.

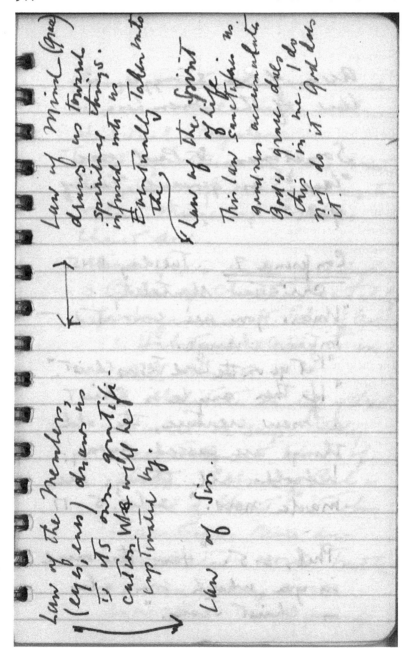

Law of mind (grace)
draws us toward
spiritual things.
infused into us
Eventually taken into
the

Law of the Spirit
of life.
This law sanctifies us
good us accumulate
God's grace does
this in me I do
not do it. God does
it.

Law of the Meadow?
(eyes, ears) draws us
to its own gratifi-
cation. We will be
captivated by.

Law of Sin.

Law of the Members ----------------Law of Mind (grace)
(eyes, ears) draws us   draws us toward
to its owns gratification   spiritual things.
We will be   infused into us
captivated by.   Eventually taken into the

Law of Sin.   Law of the Spirit
    of Life.
    This law sanctifies us
    goodness accumulates
    God's grace does
    this in me. I do
    not do it. God does it.

Area of our struggle is
law of the members.

Sometimes St. Paul uses
"law" as general "law of
God."

Conference 7.   Tuesday 11:45.
Christian Mentality.
"Unless you are converted —
Interior change.
"Put ye on the Lord Jesus Christ."
"If then any be in Christ
a new creature, the old
things are passed away:
behold all things are
made new." 2. Cos. 5. 17.

Phil. 2. 5. "Have this mind
in you which was also
in Christ Jesus."

Area of our struggle is
law of the members.

Sometimes St. Paul uses
"law" as general "law of
God."

Conference 7 Tuesday 11:45
Christian Mentality
"unless you are converted-
interior change.
"Put ye on the Lord Jesus Christ."
"If then any be in Christ
a new creature, the old
things are passed away:
behold all things are
made new." 2 Cor. 5-17.

Phil. 2.5 "Have this mind
in you which was also
in Christ Jesus."

change must be in our mind
because mind guide will.
Habitual, regular.
To act spontaneously, like Christ.
Complexion of mind, so as to
value things of world as
Christ did.

Mind fixes rule principles
3 Rules of Christian mentality
for beginners: St. John of Cross.
1. Habitual desire to im-
state Christ.
2. Meditate on life of Christ
on what he says. Study
New Testament. Words of
christ: "Mind of Paul is
mind of Christ." St John
Chrysostom. Never an
accidental word. Truths.
Treasure every word.
Know them. mainsprings

change must be in our mind
because mind guides will.
Habitual, regular.
To act spontaneously, like Christ,
Complexion of mind, so as to
value things of world as
Christ did.
Mind fixes rule, principles
3 Rules of Christian mentality
for beginners: St. John of Cross
1.Habitual Desire to imitate
Christ.
Meditate on life of Christ.
on what he says. Study
New Testament. Words of
Christ: "Mind of Paul is
mind of Christ." St. John
Chrysostom. Never an
accidental word. Truths,
Treasure every word.
Know them. Mainsprings

of action. Use Bible every
day. St. Francis, St. Dominic
carried a Bible. Like love
letters. Invitation to love.
Read Bible on Sunday,
"come apart and rest
a little."
Capharnaum. Tiberias.
city of pleasure. Let our.
rest be in Christ Jesus.
We do not love Bible because
we do not love God...

Bible speaks to the heart.
from the heart.
1. Cor. 2. 14. The sensual
man does not perceive
the things of God; for it
is foolishness to him, and
he cannot understand
because it is spiritually
examined.

of actions. Use Bible every
day. St Francis, St. Dominic
carried a Bible. Like love
letters. Invitation to love
Read Bible on Sunday.
"Come apart and rest
a little."
Capernaum, Tiberius
city of pleasure. Let our
rest be in Christ Jesus.
We do not love Bible because
we do not love God...

Bible speaks to the heart,
from the heart.
1.Cor. 2.14. The sensual
man does not perceive
the things of God, for it
is foolishness to him, and
he cannot understand
because it is spiritually
examined.

" I live, yet not I, but Christ
liveth in me." St. Paul.

2. If any pleasure presents
itself to your senses and
it be not purely for the glory
of God, you must renounce
it or completely reject it.
Not for our own vanity.
Voluntary and involuntary
pleasure. different.
But we must renounce
desire for pleasure.

3. Agere contra.   St. Ignatius.
                    St. John of Cross.
Prayer of.   St. Francis

" To die without honor, alone
after much suffering." St John
If we ask for what leads to
greater love, we will get those
things.

"I live, not I, but Christ
with in me." St. Paul

2.If any pleasure presents
itself to your senses and
it be not purely for the glory
of God, you must renounce
it or completely reject it.
Not for our own vanity.
Voluntary and involuntary
pleasure. different.
But we must renounce
desire for pleasure.

3. Agere contra. St. Ignatius
St. John of Cross
Prayer of St. Francis

"To die without honor alone
after much suffering." St. John.
If we ask for what leads to
greater love, we will get those
things.

Mind forms principles.
as result of meditation
+ prayer. Then will comes
in. Will loves.

St. John. 6 - 38. Not to do
my own will but the will
of Him who sent me.
Find this many times.
Must renew our intention
many impurities creep in
all day long. How often
do we renew our inten-
tion. Apostleship of Prayer.
we should join. Devotion
to the sacred Heart.
1st degree - Offer all our
our thoughts, works, deeds.
then keep that promise.
More than half of world have
not heard word Jesus.

Mind forms principles.
as result of meditation
& prayer. Then will comes
in. Will loves.

St. John 6-38. Not to do
my own will bet the will
of Him who sent me.
Find this many times.
Must renew our intention
Many impurities creep in
all day long. How often
do we renew our intention.
Apostleship of Prayer.
we should join. Devotion
to the Sacred Heart.
1ˢᵗ degree— offer all our
our thoughts, works, deeds.
then keep that promise.
More than half of world have
not heard word Jesus.

There is no other word by which we may be saved. Don't let morning offering be externalism. Like Phisisees. Not spread by preaching, but by prayer. St. Alphonsus: Renew our intention before every important action. Before Mass, communion before conferences meals. Should not be a matter of strain. We are vigilant on our daily job. Precise attention given to worldly occupation. God gives us a mind to know him, a will to love him. It should be normal, unstrained.

There is no other word by
which we may be saved.
Don't let morning offering
be externalism, like Pharisees.
Not spread by
preaching, but by prayer.
St. Alphonsus: Renew our
intention before every important
action. Before Mass, communion,
before conferences meals.
Should not be a matter of
strain. We are vigilant
on our daily job. Precise
attention given to worldly
occupation. God give us
a mind to know him,
a will to love him.
It should be normal, unstrained.

Supernatural Destiny.

Glory of god.
Folly of Cross.
Supreme Dominion.

Conferences on Prayer.

II

Supernatural Destiny
glory of God
Folly of Cross
Supreme Dominion

Conference on Prayer

II

1. Tuesday.

We must know how to ask.
We may have a good natural
grasp of rules of spiritual
life. Then prayer you
can get all knowledge.
First essential to learn
how to pray, to pray well.
I   Necessity.
II   For what
III Qualities
IV Kinds.
V   Mental Prayer.
VI Prayer of Desire

I. John 15. Without me you
can do nothing.
Natural work — natural
result — more perfect
human beings. I have
right to think, will, talk
act. God will cooperate

1.Tuesday.

We must know how to ask.
We may have a good natural
grasp of rules of spiritual
life. Thru prayer you
can get all knowledge.
First essential to learn
how to pray, to pray well.

I	Necessity
II	For what
III	Qualities
IV	Kinds
V	Mental Prayer
VI	Prayer of Desire.

I. John 15. Without me you
can do nothing.
Natural work— natural
result— more perfect
human beings. I have
right to think, will, talk,
act. God will cooperate

with us. But by baptism
we are given supnatrl
life. Purely a gift at
baptism. Every increase
purely a gift. We must
understand our helplessness,
so we may become true
beggars.
Prayer is an asking. Since
we are commanded to
pray unceasingly;

With God, we get what
we ask. We are praying
all the time. Either for
something selfish, or something
supernatural. If you are
faithful in praying, it is
impossible not to become
a saint.

with us. But by baptism
we are given supernatural
life. Purely a gift at
baptism. Every increase
purely a gift. We must
understand our helplessness,
so we may become true
beggars.
Prayer is an asking. Since
we are commanded to
pray unceasingly.

With God, we get what
we ask. We are praying
all the time. Either for
something selfish or something
supernatural. If you are
faithful in praying it is
impossible not to become
a saint.

Prayer is asking.
Ask and you shall receive.
Sanctity is there for the asking.
I can do nothing of myself.
We depend so much on ourselves.
We must keep quiet and still.
ST. Bonaventure: If you
would endure life patiently,
if you would mortify your
self will; if you would
walk sweetly, like a man
of prayer. Exercise
yourself in prayer.
If you cannot drive from
your soul the flies of vain
anxieties, look to your prayer.
God did not create us
to go to hell but to Heaven.
He has given us this
omnipotent means. ST John
Chrysostom. I can do all things

Prayer is asking.
Ask and you shall receive.
Sanctity is there for the asking.
I can do nothing of myself.
We depend so much on ourselves.
We must keep quiet and still.
St. Bonaventure: If you
would endure life patiently,
if you would mortify your
self will, if you would
walk sweetly, be a man
of prayer. Exercise
yourself in prayer.
If you cannot drive from
your soul the flies of rain
anxieties. look to your prayers.
God did not create us
to go to hell but to Heaven.
He has given us this
omnipotent means. St. John
Chrysostom. I can do all things

thro' him who strengtheneth
me.
     ST. Teresa says:
Sinners should permit
Thee to remain with them
two at least two hours daily,
in return for this violence
they do themselves —

He who goes not to prayer
goes to Temptation; ST John
                 Vianni.

No. amount of knowledge
of spiritual life will
help you.
People refuse to go on
to a higher grade — to
move up. Anyone who
gives himself over to the
spiritual life will cer-
tainly advance.

thru him who strengtheneth
me.
St. Teresa says: Sinners should permit
Thee to remain with them
at least two hours daily.
In return for this violence
they do themselves.—

He who goes not to prayer
goes to temptation: St. John Rossi.

No amount of knowledge
or spiritual life will
help you.

People refuse to go on
to a higher grade— to
move up. Anyone who
gives himself over to the
spiritual life will certainly
advance.

Prayer life energizes spiritual
life. Prayer life is your
love life with god.

Whatever happens never give up.
Burn your ships. Conquer or perish.
Pray to learn how to pray.
Prayer is the heart's desire.

Wednesday. II.
Simplify our intention.
Trick of devil to scatter our
energies.

Intention   Essential.   never refused
of   (necessary.   god's glory
Prayer.   = Our Sanctification

                 accidental. (all
                 not purely necessary.) other.

Prayer life energizes spiritual
life. Prayer life is your
love life with God.

Whatever happens never give up.
Burn you ships. Conquer or perish.
Pray to learn how to pray.
Prayer is the heart's desire.

Wednesday II
Simplify our intention
Trick of devil to scatter our
energies.

Intentions of Prayer

<u>never refused</u>
God's glory

Essential
(necessary)   =   Our sanctification

Accidental
not purely necessary   =   all other

We must trust god entirely
We must learn to be unconcern-
ed. The future is god's.
What ever you want, god.
Love life is scattered. We
must use whatever happens.
Joy and ~~vehicles both~~
suffering both vehicles.

Ask only for god's glory.
God can only love. No
matter what is happening
to me, god is loving me.

Don't ask for any particular
thing — that's presuming
      qualities.
Humility. Humus dirt.

Confidence

Perseverance.

We must trust God entirely
We must learn to be unconcerned.
The future is God's.
Whatever you want, God.
Love life is scattered. We
must use whatever happens.
Joy and suffering both vehicles.

Ask only for God's glory.
God can only love. No
matter what is happening
to me, God is loving me.

Don't ask for any particular
thing— that's presuming
qualities.
Humility— Humus dist.

Confidence

Perseverance

We are high class dirt. Everything we see around us is
dirt. We are going to be
glorified. It is given us to
be glorified. My body is
Temple of Holy Ghost; infused
divine life at baptism.
We must pray as beggars.
3 degrees of humility.
To remember our own
nothingness. Remember
man thou art but
dust.
To want others to treat think us
as nothing. To want.
others to treat us as nothing.

Keep on asking, ex. St Monica
and St. Augustine.
I don't know — excessive faith.
I don't feel. — feeling sense.

We are high class dirt. Everything
we see around us is
dirt. We are going to be
glorified. It is <u>given</u> us to
be glorified. My body is
Temple of Holy Ghost, infused
divine life at baptism.
We must pray as beggars.
3 degrees of humility
To remember our own
nothingness. Remember
man thou art but
dust.
To want others to think us
as nothing. To want
others to treat us as nothing.

Keep on asking. ex. St. Monica
and St. Augustine.
I don't know —exercise faith.
I don't feel —feeling is sense.

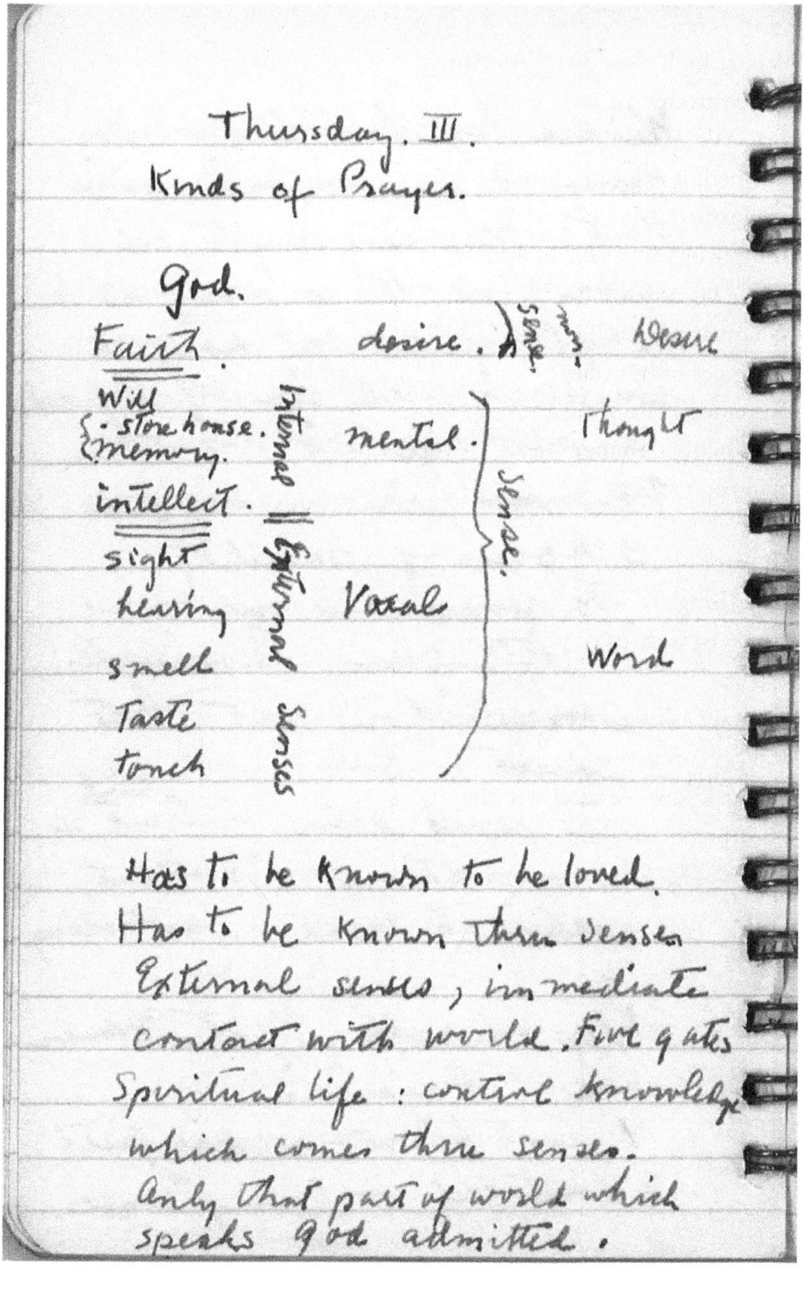

Thursday. III.
Kinds of Prayer.

God.

Faith. | desire. | Desire
Will
· storehouse.
memory.
intellect. | mental. | thought
Internal || External Senses
sight
hearing
smell
Taste
touch | Vocal | Word
sense.

Has to be known to be loved.
Has to be known thru senses
External senses, immediate
contact with world. Five gates
Spiritual life: control knowledge
which comes thru senses.
Only that part of world which
speaks God admitted.

Thursday III
Kinds of Prayer

God.

Faith	desire (nonsense)	Desire
internal		
will		
storehouse	mental (sense)	Thought
intellect		
external senses		
sight	vocal (sense)	
hearing		
smell		Word
taste		
touch		

Has to be known to be loved.
Has to be known thru senses
External senses, immediate
contact with world. Five gates
Spiritual life: control knowledge
which comes thru senses.
Only that part of world which
speaks God admitted.

Quiet them in their eagerness
for world. Senses all help
us to pray. Vocal prayer.
Prayer of external senses.
Hearing:
Prayer by use; prayer by
mortification. Prayer does
not remain in senses but
goes into internal senses;
mental prayer.
Vocal prayer baby prayer.
Mental; controlled by love.
You can meditate on things
and people we love.
It is not intended by God we
remain in mental prayer
but pass on to prayer of
desire. Mental and vocal
called sense prayers.
"Our" effort. We do it as
human beings

Quiet them in their eagerness
for world. Senses all help
us to pray. Vocal prayer.
Prayer of external senses.
Hearing:
Prayer by use: prayer by
mortification. Prayer does
not remain in senses but
goes into internal senses:
mental prayer.
Vocal prayer baby prayer.
Mental, controlled by love.
You can meditate on things
and people we love.
It is not intended by God we
remain in mental prayer
but pass on to prayer of
desire. Mental and vocal
called sense prayers.
"Our" effort. We do it as
human beings

We can learn as much as we
can — we detach world from
us. — Desire, God does it.

Desire.   No rules: We go back,
               and forth. Stay until
               you have exhausted
               these faculties.
thought   Thoughts and word, we
               are acting.
               Prayer not known to
               us.
Word.

God does not have to wait
for your thoughts or word.
He who love us knows our
desire. He who wishes to love
has this desire. God is aware.
We may not be aware of ways.
Loving god, not his consolations.

We can learn as much as we
can —we detach world from
us. —Desire, God does it.

Desire.   No rules. We go back
                   and forth. Stay until
                   you have exhausted
                   their faculties.
Thought.   Thought and word, we
                   are acting.
                   Prayer not known to
                   us.
Word.

God does not have to visit
for you thought or word.
He who love us knows our
desire. He who wishes to love
has this desire. God is aware.
We may not be aware of ways.
Loving God, not his consolations.

God is still giving us grace
but in faith, not sense.
People love consolations, That's
why there are so few saints.
Stay there that period. There are
no end to this. The more
you pray, the worse things
get. Friday. 3. p.m.
Method of Prayer.
To love, serve and honor God,
Ignatian, Sulpician, Salesian methods
"Village" method. Methods are
spiritual book keeping. Must grow out

Know {
1 Presence of God...
2. Fault or virtue...
3 Picture.
4. His life and Our life. read. gospel.
most important 5. Acts of Love. Gaze of love.
serve. { 6. Resolution.
7. Thanksgiving - nosegay.

God is still giving us grace
but in faith, not sense.
People love consolation. That's
why there are so few saints.
Stay there that period. There are
no ends to tests. The more
you pray, the worse things
get.

Friday 3 p.m.
Method of Prayer
To love, serve and honor God.
Ignatius, Sulpician, Salesian method.
"Village" method. Methods are
spiritual book keeping. Must grow
Know
1. Presense of God...
2. Fault of virtue...
3. Picture.
4. His life and our life. read Gospel.
Love most important
5. Acts of love. Gaze of love.
Serve
6. Restoration.
7. Thanksgiving.— Nosegay.

Examine yourself daily, what
makes you happy or sad.
Work on one fault. In your
reading look for that virtue.
Without reading it is almost
impossible to go forward.
Take one text for day.
"In patience you will possess
your souls."
A book worth reading, is worth
reading five times.

How much time in prayer.
1 hour. If you don't pray
you are taking natural satisfaction in work.

For beginners. Read 5 min.
meditate 15. 3 Times.
Use your faculties as long
as you can.

Examine yourself daily, what
makes you happy or sad.
Work on one fault. In your
reading, look for that virtue.
Without reading it is almost
impossible to go forward.
Take one text for day.
"In patience you will possess
your souls."
A book worth reading, is worth
reading five times.

How much time in prayer.
1 hour. If you don't pray
you are taking natural satisfaction
in work.

For beginners. Read 5 min.
meditate 15. 3 times.
 Use your faculties as long
as you can.

"...These accursed occupations".
"Heresy of good works"
St. Bernard, quoted in "The Soul
of the Apostolate."

33 Conference. 5 p.m. Friday.
II Cor. 4-16 Therefore we do not
lose heart: on the contrary
tho' the outer man is decaying,
the inner man is being renewed
from day to day. .. 12:9. Therefore
I glory in mine infirmities that
the power of Christ may dwell in
me.
How God uses creatures as
instruments. The worst
suffering comes thru others.
They are used as blind instruments. God's assistants
are those around you.
They know what they are
doing but are blind to God's plan.

..."These accursed occupations."
"Heresy of good works"
St. Bernard, quoted in "The Soul
of the Apostolate."

23 Conference. 5p.m. Friday,
II Cor. 4-16 Therefore we do not
Lose heart; on the contrary
tho the outer man is decaying,
the inner man is being renewed
from day to day....12:9. Therefore
I glory in mine infirmities that
the power of Christ may dwell in
me.
How God uses creatures as
instruments. The worst
suffering comes thru others.
They are used as blind instruments.
God's assistants
are those around you.
They know what they are
doing but are blind to God's plan.

Jews are being used in Divine
plan. St. Paul. Maritain
Neighbor is conductor. How
can He use them when men
are free. He can use their
activity. We must see God
by faith. "You use an in-
strument according to its nature," St. Thomas.
Our reason and intelligence
are perfection of our nature.
He is nearer to us than we are
to ourselves. Reaching down to
marrow. Hebrews. 1. He controls our heredity, environment,
Teachers, friends etc. Any her-
editary traits controled by law,
that law governed by God. No chance
in our lives. All controlled by
God — watched with Fatherly
interest.

Jews are being made in Divine
Plan. St. Paul. Maritain
neighbor is conductor. How
can He use them when men
are free. He can use their
activity. We must see God
by faith. "You use as an
instrument according to its nature,"
St. Thomas.
Our reason and intelligence
are perfection of our nature.
He is nearer to us than we are
to ourselves. Reaching down to
marrow. Hebrews 1. He controls
our heredity, environment,
teachers, friends etc. Our heredity
traits controlled by law,
that law governed by God. No chance
in our lives. All controlled by
God—watched with Fatherly
interest.

St. Paul Rom 8. For those who love God all things work together unto good, for such as are called to be saints.
God is a surgeon. Thank him, thank instrument.
David stoned. God permitted.
Tobias blinded. Not accidents.
Job accepted. "Even tho thou slay me, still will I trust in Thee."
"One reason why many souls do not become saints, no patience, generosity." St. John of Cross.
We struggle and complain too much.
Council of Trent to reform church St. Chas. Barromeo., Archbishop of Milan started to reform church.
God like a chess player has every situation well in hand, all over world. He puts people together.

St. Paul Rom 8. For those who
love God all things work together
into good, for such as
are called to be saints.
God is a surgeon. Thank him,
thank instrument.
David stoned. God permitted.
Tobias blinded. Not accident.
Job accepted. "Even tho thou
slay me, still will I trust in Thee."
"One reason why many souls do
not become saints, no patience,
generosity." St. John of Cross.
We struggle and complain too
much.
Council of Trent to reform church
St. Chars. Borromeo, Archbishop of
Milan started to reform church
God like a chess player has
every situation well in hand all
over world . He puts people together.

God sanctifies us then fully, stupidity and malice of others.
Divine Providence has forseen
and permitted so in some way
God will change it into his
glory. Sow judgment. We are
opinionated, so bear contradictions patiently. Die to my
reason...
Supreme test of faith. When we
are victims of my notice and
malice, God does not want
malice. He does not want
one man to strike another
but he will use it. God
can use even evil and
sin to further his own ends.
Joseph sold in slavery.
yet then this crime, Jos.
saved them from famine
and preserved Jewish nations.
"God sent me here."

God sanctifies us thru folly, stupidity
and malice of others.
Divine Providence has foreseen
and permitted so in some way
God will change it into his
Glory. Sow judgement. We are
opinionated, so bear contradictions
patiently. Die to my
reason.
Supreme test of faith. When we
are victims of injustice and
malice. God does not want
malice. He does not want
one man to strike another
but he will use it. God
can use even evil and
sin to further his own will.
Joseph sold in slavery
yet thru this crime, Jos.
saved them from famine
and preserved Jewish nations.
"God sent me here."

Devil like dog on leash. (Jat.)
Even he, the prince of this world,
is circumscribed in action.
Jesus used malice of Jews
to save the human race.
"Let Thy will be done." He
did not see The malice of
the Jews. "Shall I not drink the
chalice which my Father hath
prepared." 1 Pet. 2. 18. Servants,
slaves, be subject to your masters,
not only to good, to froward.
Unto this indeed you have
been called to suffer unjustly.
We continue the life of
Christ in our day — stupidity,
folly and malice

25th Conference, Fri. 8·30,
Causade: Garrigou Lagrange.
wrote on Divine Providence. See God
in actions of our Superiors.
Surest way — obedience.

(margin, vertical): Sudden rain storm.

Devil like dog on leash. (Job)
Even he, the prince of this word,
is circumscribed in action.
Jesus used malice of Jews
to save the human race.
"Let Thy will be done." He
did not see the malice of
the Jews. "Shall I not drink the
chalice which <u>my Father</u> hath
prepared." 1 Pet.2.18 Servants,
slaves, be subject to your masters
not only to good, to forward.
Into this indeed you have
been called to suffer unjustly.
We continue the life of
Christ in our day— stupidity,
folly and malice.

sudden rain storm

25ᵗʰ Conference, Friday. 8:30
Caussade: Garrigou Lagrange.
wrote on Divine Providence. See God
in actions of my superiors.
Surest way obedience.

Obedience is that virtue which makes
us acknowledge the will of God

Superior is God's favourite instrument.
Our self will is seat of corruption.
Motive is not seat of imperfection.

Underbrush in wilderness is our
attachment to samples. Pride in our
judgment and our will,

Desire to regulate others sign
of self will. I came not to do my
own will but will of him who
sent me. St Paul. He did not
please himself. We sow our
will by being patient under
contradiction. Interference even
in exercise of duty. Best way of
giving up self will by obedience.
Vows: Poverty — bodily goods.
chastity — affections
obedience — ourselves.

St. Thomas. Obedience + humility
are basic virtues. Foundation Stones.
Christian virtue. for all.
St. Paul. All sin came into world
thru one act of disobedience. All
suffering, misery, wretchedness stems
from that one sin. How God punished
such sin. Saul rejected for 2
small acts of disobedience.
All grace came into the world
because of Jesus' obedience.

Obedience is that virtue which makes
us acknowledge the will of God.
Superior is God's favorite instrument.
Our self will is seat of corruption.
Motive is not seat of infection.
Underbrush in wilderness is our
attachment to samples. Pride in our
judgement and our will.
Desire to regulate others sign
of self will. I came not to do my
own will but will of him who
sent me. St. Paul. He did not
please himself. We sow our
will by being patient under
contradiction. Interference even
in exercise of duty. Best way of
giving of self will by obedience.
Vows, Poverty— worldly goods
          chastity— affections
          obedience— one selves.
St. Thomas, Obedience & humility
are unseen virtues. Foundation stones.
Christian virtues for all.
St. Paul. All sin came into world
thru one act of disobedience. All
suffering, misery, wretchedness stem
form that one sin. How God punished
such sin. Saul rejected for 2
small acts of disobedience.
All grace came into the world
because of Jesus' obedience.

Romans 5. Obedience,
Great sin in world today rebellion
against authority.
Spirit and letter of obedience.
All societies must have a head.
All authority (legitimate) comes
from god. When command is unjust
and sinful not to be obeyed.
"Interfere with vocation" for in-
stance.

" Mediocrity sits in high places."
old saying. It is inconceivable that
the Holy See should give an
unjust command. The
church.
We should scrutinize laws of
the state.
Pastoral letters, encyclical
letters, obey.
Expiation in Present Crisis.
?   1937. Pius XII, like voice
of Samuel. Catholic press
ignored. Peace does not
come from statesmen, If we
had been obedient, there would
be no war Today.
Two terms of obedience,
Visible – superior. Invis. God.
Rebellion always against superior.
whether good or bad.

Romans 5: Obedience.
Great sin in world today rebellion
against authority.
Spirit and letter of obedience.
All societies mush have a head.
All authority (legitimate) comes
from God. When command is unjust
and sinful not to be obeyed.
"interfere with vocation" for instance.

"Mediocrity sits in high places."
old saying. It is inconceivable that
The Holy See should give an
unjust command. The
Church.
We should scrutinize Laws of
the state.
Pastoral letters, encyclical
letters, obey.
Expiration in Present Crisis.
? 1937. Pius XII. Like voice
of Samuel. Catholic press
ignored. Peace does not
come from statesmen. If we
had been obedient, there would
be no war today.
Two terms of obedience.
Visible— superior. Invis. God.
Rebellion always against superior.
whether good or bad.

Jesus was obedient even unto
death.

Obedience of judgment no good,
from supernaturally standpoint.
St. John Baptist de la Salle suspended
on his death bed.
Cure of Ars likes story of St
Vincent because it illustrates
how God will take care of
everything. Obedience is
better than Sacrifice, said
Samuel. It is Supreme.
Sacrifice.

True Devotion to Blessed Mother.

We neglect various devotions
For the Humanity of Jesus.
To the Blessed Mother, necessary
to salvation.
" The flesh of Jesus is the flesh
of Mary." St. Augustine.
Primary instrument is Body of Christ
He satisfied, he redeemed. Blessed
Mother supplied body. Secondary
instrument. We owe personal
debt. Man cannot dispense
with what god fixes as necessary.
All received thru Mary. Ours and
Holy Trinity, thru humanity of Jesus,
thru Mary.

Jesus was obedient even unto death.
Obedience of judgment no good,
from supernatural standpoint.
St. John Baptist de la Salle suspended
on his death bed.
Curé of Ars likes story of St
Vincent because it illustrates
how God will take care of
everything. Obedience is
better than sacrifice, said
Samuel. It is supreme
sacrifice.
<u>True Devotion to Blessed Mother</u>.
We neglect various devotions
for the Humanity of Jesus.
To the blessed Mother necessary
to salvation.
"The flesh of Jesus is the flesh
of Mary." St. Augustine
Primary instrument is Body of Christ
He satisfied, he redeemed, Blessed
Mother supplied body. Secondary
instrument. We owe personal
debt. Man cannot dispense
with what God finds as necessary.
All received thru Mary. Our end
Holy Trinity. Thru humanity of Jesus,
thru Mary.

Saturday. 9.45. 26th Conference

Doctrine of the folly of the cross
is doctrine of the sowing. Unless
the grain of wheat fall into the
ground and die. —
Sow external by almsgiving
       bodily   ,, mortification
       interior   ,, patience.
Natural man knows nothing about
charity. Great pagan writers dealt
with friendship, not charity.
What distinguishes is motive.

By this shall all men know you
that ye love one another.
Christian reform should make rich
men poor. Chesterton: writers
dealing with that text have tried
to decrease size of camel and
increase size of the needle.
"The rich man can't be bribed.
They are bribed already."

Glorify God by imitating Him
in His generosity.
Supreme Dominion. Teaches us
we are stewards. Advocating
poverty of workmen. Jos + Mary.
Cry of modern world. Am I my
brothers keeper?
Folly of Cross.
Poor are porters of the rich.
give them your possessions.
They will carry them into heaven
for you. St John Chrysostom in
breviary. Don't make poor seek
you — seek them.

<u>Saturday 9:45 26th Conference</u>

Doctrine of the folly of the Cross
Is doctrine of the sowing. Unless
the grain of wheat fall into the
ground and die.
Sow external by almsgiving
      bodily   " mortification
      interior " patience.
Natural man knows nothing about
charity. Great pagan writers dealt
with friendship not charity.
What distinguishes is motive!
By this shall all men know you
That ye love one another.
Christian reform should make rich
men poor. Chesterton: writers
dealing with that test have tried
to decrease size of camel
and increase size of the needle.
"The rich man can't be bribed.
They are bribed already."
Glorify God by imitating Him
in His generosity.
Supreme Dominion. Teaches us
We are stewards. Advocates
poverty of workmen. Jos. & Mary.
Cry of the modern world. Am I my
brother's keeper?
Folly of the Cross.
Poor are porters of the rich,
gave them your possessions.
They will carry them into heaven
for you. St. John Chrysostom
for breviary. Don't make poor seek
you—seek them.

How much? Catholic theology
over and beyond our necessities
Not good now because no one
admits he has superfluities.
2nd rule. Tithes. ½o.
Rom. 8.9. He that soweth sparingly, reapeth sparingly.
Sat. 11.45. 27 The Conference.

Sow goods of body by mortification.
1. Need. 2. Doctrine. 3. Practice.
1. According to God's plan. Dying
of natural, cease to be children
of this world, become children of
God. God the Father's plan.
Brothers of Christ live his life.
Christ lives in me. We must
decrease, Christ must increase.
Plan Holy Ghost as his spouse,
give ourselfs. Give our love.
And sin — original. check
proneness toward sin. "
natural habits. Make satisfaction, compensation. '
Jesus is our model. God sees
Jesus in us. loves Jesus in
us.
Doctrine. Mortification is necessary. Unless you do penance,
you shall therefore perish.
Law of fast and abstinence.
Minimum amount is that which

How much? Catholic theology
over and beyond our necessities.
Not good now because no one
admits he has superfluities.
2nd rule. Tithes. 1/10.
Rom. 8-9 He that soweth sparingly,
reapeth sparingly.

Sat. 11:45 27th Conference

Sow goods of body by mortification.
1. Need. 2. Doctrine 3. Practice.
1. According to God's plan. Dying
of natural. Cease to be children
of this world, become children of
God. God the Father's plan.
Brothers of Christ live his life.
Christ lives in me. We must
decrease, Christ must increase.
Plan Holy Ghost as his spouse,
give ourself, give our love.
And sin—original check
proneness toward sin."
Natural habits Make satisfaction,
compensation.
Jesus is our model. God sees
Jesus in us. Loves Jesus in
us.
Doctrine. Mortification is necessary.
Unless you do penance,
you shall therefore perish.
Law of fast and abstinence.
Minimum amount is that which

is fixed by the church.
Pius X: Lost secret of fasting; that
is why there are so many calamities.
More abstinence if one cannot
fast. Keep hour of silence.
Eternal truths remain same.
church is always make adjustments but will never change truth.
External and interior. Sensible
and corporal mortification
Solemn judgments will, attachments interior mortifications
Both kinds necessary.
St. Vincent de Paul. when I hear
anyone praising interior at expense
of the — and not interior, he
does neither. Fr. Faber, also.
get rid of natural motive.
Morti. means. Faber. Penance is
mark of church. (Holiness)
Holiness means being purified
of earthly attachments.
God excuse. Let Providence send
them.
Leo XIII. Pray that his people that
they may have spirit of penance
Prayers without penance are without
love. Pius XI + XII. Increase of
supernatural life would undermine
mine way.
St Paul: I crucify my flesh with
its vices and concupiscences.

is fixed by the Church.
Pius X: Lost secret of fasting: that
is why these are so many callamities.
More abstinence if one cannot
fast. Keep hour of silence.
Eternal truths remain same.
Church is always making adjustments
but will never change Truth.
External and interior. Sensible
and corporal mortification.
Sowing judgments, will, attachments,
interior mortifications
Both kinds necessary.
St. Vincent de Paul when I hear
anyone praising interior
and not interior, he
does neither. Fr. Faber, also
get rid of natural motive,
most means. Faber. Penance
is mark of church. (Holiness)
Holiness means being purified
of earthly attachments,
and excess. Let Providence send
them.
Leo XIII. Pray that his people that
they may have spirit of penance.
Prayers without penance are without
love. Pius XI & XII. Increase of
supernatural life would undermine
war.
St. Paul: I crucify my flesh with
Its vices and concupiscences.

Vision: use only for glory of god.
movies, magazines, papers,
Most "sins enter thru eye.
Eye should be inward. We have
a divine guest.

Ears. not to listen to gossip.
Practice interior solitude. Do not
gossip about priests and nuns or
about fellow catholics. World
gossip. Give up radio alto-
gether. More you sow, more
you reap. Newspapers.
gospel. good news.

Tongue Mortify tongue. Let your
speech be yea, yea, nay, nay.
James. c. 3. Only a perfect
man masters the tongue.
Practice periods of silence and
solitude.

Smell. Put up with offensive odors. Do
not be fastidious. Sour perfume.

Touch. Carriage ^{no} sprawling. Kneeling.
clothes (?)

Taste. Eat what is set before you.
Jesus' rule. Give up eating between
^{meals.}

Imagination thru sight, hearing,
Seat of hope. —

Mortify flesh. Dry up life of sense

<u>Vision</u>: use only for glory of God,
    movies, magazines, papers.
    Most sins enter thru eye.
    Eye should be inward. We have
    a divine guest.
<u>Ear</u>. not to listen to gossip.
    Practice interior solitude. Don't
    gossip about priests and nuns or
    about fellow Catholics. World
    gossip. Give up ration altogether.
    More you sow, more
    you reap. Newspapers.
    Gospel, good news.
<u>Tongue</u> Mortify <u>tongue</u>. Let your
    speech be yea, yea, nay, nay.
    James 8:3. Only a perfect
    man masters the tongue.
    Practice periods of silence and
    solitude.
<u>Smell</u>. Put up with offensive odors. Do
    not be fastidious. Sow perfume.
<u>Touch</u>. ... no sprawling. Kneeling
    clothes (?)
<u>Taste</u>. Eat what is set before you.
    Jesus' rule. Give up eating between
    meals.
<u>Imagination</u> thru sight hearing,
    seat of hope.
Mortify flesh. Dry up life of sense.

Sat. 2. p.m.   28th Conference.

Sowing of Everything.
        <u>Death</u>.

Natural; Sup. ntrl.   Double set.
Consider everything from 2 standpoints.
1. Death is contrary to our soul.
Resolution of our body into its
component parts. Death is
natural for body but not from
soul because it is immortal.
Soul does not like to think of
death from natural point of
view. 2. Death is a punishment
so we do not like to think
of a punishment. 3. Because
of our love for creatures. Means
the end of creature enjoyments.
When we are forced to think
of death. Requiem Mass Wake

Supntrl. Death is beginning.
"I am the resurrection and
the life." "For me to live is
Christ and to die is gain."
Death and suffering are our
two big problems. We must
learn to look it in the face.
"I wish to be dissolved and
to be with christ, a thing

Sat. 2p.m.   28th Conference

Sowing of Everything

Death.

Natural: Supntrl. Double set.

Consider everything from 2 standpoints

1. Death is contrary to our soul.
Resolution of our body into its
component parts. Death is
natural for body but not for
soul because it is immortal.
Soul does not like to think of
death from natural point of
view. 2. Death is a punishment
so we do not like to think
of a punishment. 3. Because
of our love for creatures. Means
the end of creature enjoyments.
When we are forced to think
of death. Requiem Mass Wake.

Supntrl. Death is beginning.
"I am the resurrection and
the life." "For me to live is
Christ and to die is gain."
Death and suffering are our
two big problems. We must
learn to look it in the face.
"I wish to be ... and
to be with Christ, a thing

by far the better; or to be with
you." Always to keep the
thought of death with you.
Perform all your actions as
tho you were going to die
while doing it.
Every day a balancing, monthly
day of recollection, yearly retreat.
St Luke's sermon on death.
C. 12 : V. 16. And He spoke a
certain similitude to them.
A certain rich man had
great fruits   Preoccupied
with earthly things.
King Abimalec and the woman
with the stone. Preoccupied
with how he was to die.
Let your loins be girt and
lamps burning in your hands.
ready for the journey. like
servants waiting for lord
and master.

by far the better: or to be with
you." Always to keep the
thought of death with you.
Perform all your actions as
tho you were going to die
while doing it.
Everyday a balancing, monthly
day of recollection, yearly
retreat.
St. Luke's sermon on death.
L 12:1.16 And He spoke a
certain similitude to them.
A certain rich man had
great fruits. Preoccupied
with earthly things.
King Abimelec and the woman
with the stone. Preoccupied
with how he was to die.
Let your loins be girt and
lamps burning in your hands.
ready for the journey. Like
the servants waiting for Lord
and Master.

Blessed be those servants,
At what hour you think not
It is ordained man once to die
and after death the judgment.
Meditation death once a month.
Prepare. Practice.
Man's home is in San. Fran.
works in Pittsburgh. His picture.
If family. We have samples
here. Reality in heaven.
Be willing to face death.

Rehearse for death by dying
now.
Seek the things that are above
For you are dead, and
your life is hid with God.
Baptism is funeral ceremony
immersed in water.
We are buried with Christ
we have risen with Christ.

Rom.
6. Know ye that all ye
who are baptized in Lord
Jesus are buried with him

Blessed be those servants.
At what hour you think not
it is ordained man once to die
and after death the judgement.
Meditate on death once a month
Prepare. Practice.
Man's home is in San Fran.
works in Pittsburgh. Has picture
of family. We have samples
here. Reality in Heaven.
Be willing to face death.
Rehearse for death by dying
now.
Seek the things that are above.
For you are dead, and
your life is hid with God.
Baptism is funeral ceremony
immersed in water.
We are buried with Christ
we have risen with Christ.
Rom. 6 Know ye that all ye
who are baptized in Lord
Jesus are buried with him

..... Our old man is crucified
with him.
React to world, its joys
its sorrows, as dead even
do. Indifferent.
Mystical Death ∴∴∵∴

Sympathy — to suffer with:
The charity of Christ, compells
us to accept this conclusion.
That if one died for all
then all are dead.
He died for all, now we
live not to ourselves but
to him who died for us &
rose again.

½ on Stone crosses. Indians
begin to weep.
Alhambra — Washington
Irving.

….Our old man is crucified
with him.
React to world, its joys
to sorrows, as dead men
do. Indifferent
Mystical Death.………

Sympathy—to suffer with:
The charity of Christ, impels
us to accept this conclusion.
That if one died for all
then all are dead.
He died for all, now we
live not to ourselves but
to him who died for us &
rose again.

Stone crosses. Indians
began to weep.
　…Alhambra—Washington
Irving

With christ I am nailed
to the Cross, Paul. He knew
only one thing, christ, Far
be it for me to glory save
in one lord Jesus christ.
I am crucified to world and
world is crucified to me.
. At baptism,
Renounce the World.
Renounce the devil & all
his works.

I have a baptism —
and I am straightened
till it be accomplished.
His face was set towards
Jerusalem.
Then let us go and
die with him.

With Christ I am nailed
to the Cross. Paul. He knew
only one thing, Christ. Far
be it for me to glory save
our one Lord Jesus Christ.
I am crucified to world and
world is crucified to me.
At baptism,
Renounce the World.
Renounce the devil & all
his works.

I have a baptism
and I am strengthened
till it be accomplished.
His face was set towards
Jerusalem.
Then let us go and
die with him.

Salve Regina, Mater misericordiae
Vita, dulcedo, et spes nostra salve.
Ad te clamamus, exsules filii Hevae
Ad te suspiramus, gementes et
   flentes in hac lacrimarum valle
Eia ergo, advocata nostra,
Illos tuos misericordes oculos
Ad nos converte
Et Jesum, benedictum fructum
    ventris tui
Nobis post hoc exilium ostende.
O clemens, O pia, O dulcis
   Virgo Maria.

Wynne? When did he go. Jan.? Kay?

Write Fr Hugo - Butlers Saints.
Peter - novel. - food -
sicknesses - obedience conferences
Book - leaflets

Salve Regina, Mater misericordiae
vita, dulcedo, et spes nostra salve.
Ad te clamamus, exsules filii Hevae
Ad te suspiramus, gementes et
flentes in hac lacrimarum valle.
Eia ergo, advocata nostra,
Illos tuos misericordes oculos
Ad nos converte
Et Jesum benedictum fructum
Ventris tui
Nobis post hoc exilium ostende.
O clemens, O pia, O dulcis
Virgo Maria.

Wynn? Where di he go. Jon? Kay?

Write Fr. Hugo—Butlers Saints
Peter—Novel—food
Sicknesses—obedience conference
Book—leaflets

1942 Retreat.   Fr. Hugo.
Pa., Oakmont, St. Anthony's.

Book Two.
   Tuesday 5.pm.
   Wed.
   Thurs
   Fri.

"Take up your Cross daily."
"Lend thine ears to our supplications, O
Lord, and guide, prosper and protect
the journeyings of thy servants, so that
amidst all changes, their paths and
their lives may at all times be
safeguarded by thy helping hand."

Book II
1

1942 Retreat.   Fr. Hugo
Pa., Oakmont, St. Anthony's

Book Two
Tuesday 5 p.m.
Wed.
Thurs.
Fri.

"Take up your Cross daily."
"Lend thine ear to our supplication. O
Lord, and guide, prosper and protect
the journeyings of thy servants, so that
amidst all changes, their paths and
their lives may at all times be
safeguarded by thy helping hand."

Four principles of spiritual life.

1. Supernatural Destiny
2. Glory of God.
3. Glorifying God thru Samples
4. Folly of the Cross.
5. Glorifying God thru his
   Suprema Dominion (Providence)

Four principles of spiritual life.
1. Supernatural Destiny
2. Glory of God.
3. Glorifying God through Samples
4. Folly of the Cross.
5. Glorifying God thru his
   Supreme Dominion (Providence)

8th. Conference   5 p m.
Obligation to be saints

If we did not think of Jesus as
sovor of god is mad. Mark 3.
Jesus spoke in scene of pastoral
quietness, peacefully, he
dismisses all our efforts to
excuse ourselves. "This is not
for me." Who was Jesus talking to. No Carmelites, no
Carthusians, Ordinary people,
fishermen, farmers, shepherds
housewives. People from little
villages. This legislation
was for all, lay people
or religious.
We are not to be like
Saints or angels. But be
ye perfect as your Heavenly
Father is perfect.

8th Conference   5 pm
Obligation to be saints

If we did not think of Jesus as
Son of God is mad. Mark. 5
Jesus spoke in scene of pastoral
quietness, peacefully; he
dismisses all our efforts to
excuse ourselves. "This is not
for me." Who was Jesus talking
to. No Carmelites, no
Carthusians. Ordinary people,
fishermen, farmers, shepherds,
housewives. People from little
villages. This legislation
was for all, lay people
or religious.
We are not to be like
saints or angels. But be
ye perfect as your Heavenly
Father is perfect.

Be ye imitators of me as
I also of Christ Jesus.
Jesus Christ calls all
men to holiness. No
distinction between monk
and man in world.
St. John Chrysostom:
God will be more severe
on lay people. They
have natural supports
Only difference between
monk and lay person,
man in world is married
This holds for 1942
Truth is eternal and
unchangeable.
Human distinction
6th century. Benedict
Scholastica. Desert Fathers.
Christians lived in the
world intensely.

Be ye imitators of me as
I also of Christ Jesus.
Jesus Christ calls all
men to holiness. No
distinction between monk
and man in world.
St. John Chrysostom:
God will be more severe
on lay people. They
have natural supports.
Only difference between
monk and lay person,
man in world is married.
This holds for 1942.
Truth is eternal and
unchangeable.
Human distinction
6th century. Benedict
Scholastica. Desert Fathers.
Christians lived in the
world. Intensely.

Was Christ Divided?
Ridiculous these distinctions
to be baptized in name
of Benedict Francis.
Were they crucified for us.
To unite all men, that
they may be one. One
God, one Faith, one
baptism. All frustrate
Christianity.
All sponsors of Jesus.
All children of God.
Who has passed from
death to life? You are
a royal priesthood, a
chosen nation, a
A religious has a
double obligation. He has
taken an oath. To
reinforce my obligation
That is only difference.

5T
Peters

Was Christ divided?
Ridiculous these distinctions.
Is he baptized in name
of Benedict Francis.
Were thy crucified for us.
To unite all men, that
they may be one. One
God, one Faith , one
baptism. All first rate
Christianity.
All spouses of Jesus.
All children of God.
Who has passed from
death to life? You are
a royal priesthood, a
chosen nation
St. Peter..
A religious has a
double obligation. He has
taken an oath to
reinforce my obligation.
That is only difference.

They Take 3 vows —.
Primary obligation from
baptism which makes us
seek after perfection.

Pius XI   3 centenary St. Francis
de Sales. He took holiness
out of cloister and put it
into the world.
Pius XI made him
patron of modern layman.
Lived in 16 Century, in
modern times. He wrote
2 books. Which made him
Teacher of church.
" Christ has constituted
church holy and all
who take her for guide
and Teacher must
tend to holiness. ✶
This is will of God,

They take 3 vows—
Primary obligation from
baptism which makes us
seek after perfection.

Pius XI 3 Century St. Francis
de Sales. He took holiness
out of cloisters and put it
into the world.
Pius XI made him
patron of modern laymen.
Lived in 16 Century, in
modern times. He wrote
2 books. Which made him
Teacher of church.
"Christ has constituted
church holy and all
who take her for guide
and teacher must
tend to holiness—
This is will of God,

your sanctification.
Let know one think
this is addressed to a
select few and that
others are permitted to
remain in an inferior
degree of perfection."

What is perfection?

Divine + human.
Human is perfection of
an artist - perfect piece
of human work.
Impossible. Even Homer nods,
Christ talks of divine
perfection. - so we must
understand it in super-
natural sense. Divine
perfection is possible.

your sanctification.
Let know one think
this is addressed to a
select few and that
others are permitted to
remain in an inferior
degree of perfection."

What is perfection?

Divine & human
Human is perfection of
an artist—perfect piece
of human work.
Impossible. Even Homer nods.
Christ talks of Divine
perfection.—so we must
understand it in supernatural
sense. Divine
perfection is possible.

Perfection does not require culture, good manners,

What is it, in divine sense.

Perfection is love. God is love. 1 John. 4. 16. Love of God + love of neighbor..

Sacrament is sign which gives grace: Perfection means love of God, love of neighbor. Holiness, Sanctity, righteousness, justice. Love is all embracing. St. Thomas asks this same question. A thing is perfect when it achieves the

Perfection does not require
culture, good manners,

What is it, in divine sense.

Perfection is love. God
is love 1 John 4.16
Love of God & love of
neighbor...

Sacrament is sign which
gives grace: Perfection
means love of God, love
of neighbor.
Holiness, sanctity,
righteousness, justice.
Love is all embracing.
St. Thomas asks this
same question.
A thing is perfect
when it achieves the

end for which it is made.
Man is made perfect
by that which unites
us to god. Charity unites
us to God. God is our
last end. Perfection
is love. As I advance
in love of god & neighbor
the more I am holy.

God perfects us.
Perfection in us is work
of god's grace. We cannot
even take name of God
but by his grace.

Procedure - recipe
How do we go about it.
The way we work to
become perfect is to

end for which it is made.
Man is made perfect
by that which unites
us to God. Charity unites
us to God. God is our
last end. Perfection
is love. As I advance
in love of God—neighbor
the more I am holy.

God perfects us.
Perfection in us is work
of God's grace. We cannot
even take name of God
but by his grace.

Procedure—recipe
How do we go about it.
The way we work to
become perfect is to

St Thomas. Aquinas.
Remove from our souls
whatever is opposed to
our movement toward God.
1. Mortal sin. 2. venial sin.
Venial sin is greater evil
than war, famine.
We can get rid of all
deliberate venial sin.
A just man falls seven
times a day. indeliberate
3. attachment to creatures
of world.

In obedience to first commandment we must be
perfect. A commandment.
      Way of Perfection.
One perfection. Two ways
to achieve it. One goal.
1. Christian religious
2   "   laity.

St. Thomas Aquinas

remove from our souls
whatever is opposed to
our movement toward God
1.Mortal sin 2. venial sin.
Venial sin is greater evil
than war, famine.
We can get rid of all
deliberate venial sin. A just man falls seven
times a day. indeliberate.
3. Attachment to creatures
of world.

In obedience to first commandment
we must be
perfect. A commandment.
          Way of Perfection
One perfection. Two ways
to achieve it. One goal.
          1.Christian religions
          2.   "   laity.

1. Following counsels.
cannot own, borrow property,
cannot marry, live in
family life Obedience,
give up our will.

Counsel is recommendation
not binding on all.
Counsels point out way,
best way. Means

Perfection is a precept, not
a counsel.
Religious life is not a
sacrament. Marriage is.
a means of perfection,
a vocation...
Encyclical on Marriage. Pius XI
" First purpose.
" in forming themselves and
perfecting themselves in interior
life. For all men without

1. Following counsels.
cannot own, borrow property,
cannot marry, live in
family life. Obedience,
give up our will.

Counsel is recommendation
not binding on all.
Counsels point out way,
Best way. Means

Perfection is a precept, not
a counsel.
Religious life is not a
sacrament. Marriage is
a means of perfection,
a vocation.
Encyclical on Marriage Pius XI
"First purpose in forming themselves and
perfecting themselves in interior
life. For all men without

partnership in virtue
especially virtue of love
" All men of every condition
in whatever honorable
walk of life they may be,
can and ought to imitate
Jesus Christ and by
God's help assure at
summit of perfection "

St. Francis Borgia

St. Paul: Women can be
sanctified by bearing of
children.

Laymen not bound by
letter of counsels but
they are bound by
spirit.

partnership in virtue
especially virtue of love.
"All men of every condition
in whatever honorable
walk of life they may be,
can and ought to imitate
Jesus Christ and by
God's help arrive at
summit of perfection"

St. Francis Borgia

St. Paul: Women can be
sanctified by bearing of
children.

Laymen not bound by
letter of counsels but
they are bound by
spirit.

The function of church is
to teach and to sanctify.
Home also.

9th Conference.
Tues. 8·30

"Grant us to relish what is
right and even more to
rejoice in His consolation."
So far we have talked only
of relation of natural and
supernatural.
There are 4 principles
of spiritual life.
1. Supernatural Destiny
2. Glory of God.
                    of living divine life
Difficulties: we are human,
we live in midst of creatures
nowhere do we get vision of
Creator.

The function of church is
to teach and to sanctity
Home also.

9th Conference
Tues. 8:30

"Grant us to relish what is
right and even more to
rejoice in His consolation."
So far we have talked only
of relation of natural and
supernatural.
There are 4 principles
of spiritual life.
 1. Supernatural Destiny
   2. Glory of God.
   of living divine life
Difficulties: we are human,
we live in midst of creatures.
No where do we get vision of
Creator.

What is God's plan for
creatures - what principle
will govern this activity.
End or goal of plan.
Means to attain.
Study of glory of God reveals
God's plan for creatures.

St. Augustine. Glory is
"luminous knowledge
joined to praise."
Two ways in which creatures
glorify God. Flowers, planets
trees glorify God. Of necessity
unconsciously. Man consciously. He can refuse. He is free.
Man's is more perfect.
  Only men have knowledge.
So only a really can glorify.
A. What God's glory means to God
                                    to man.

What is God's plan for
creatures—what principle
will govern His activity.
End or goal of plan.
Means to attain.
Study of glory of God reveals
God's plan for creatures.

St. Augustine. Glory is
"luminous knowledge
joined to praise."
Two ways in which creatures
glorify God. Flowers, plants,
trees glorify God. Of necessity
unconsciously. Man consciously.
He can refuse. He is free.
Man's is more perfect.
    Only men have knowledge.
So only " really can glorify.
A. What God's glory means to God

                            to man.

Praise of glory — Watkin

1. primary purpose of Creation.
2. dominating idea
3. principle preoccupation

"Heavens declare the glory of
God + the firmament show
the work of His hands."

All intelligent actions have
a motive.
God's purpose is infinite.
God creates all things for
Himself. God is His own end.
Beings act to get some goods
All action is inspired by good.
Vast manifestation of goodness
Man acts to get good
God " to give good
Man has such needs he must
give good to get good.
God is all good, overflowing

Praise of glory—Watkin

1. primary purpose of Creation.
2. dominating idea
3. principle preoccupation.

"Heaven's declare the glory
of God & the firmament show
the work of His hands."

All intelligent actions have
a motive.
God's purpose is infinite.
God creates all things for
Himself. God is His own end.
Beings act to get some good.
All action is inspired by good.
Vast manifestation of goodness.
Man acts to get good
God "   to give good.
Man has such needs he must
give good to get good.
God is all good, overflowing

Gospel means good news. to.
Teach us His love.
What are purpose of creatures
What did God intend for
creatures. They are good
but not here to enjoy.
but to manifest God's
goodness. All talents are
to glorify God. All actions.
Whether we eat or drink do
all for glory.   St Ignatius
For greater glory of God.
Use our senses

2./ Dominating idea...
Everything capable. God is
perfect workman. So we
cannot judge others, our-
selves.

Gospel means good news. To
teach us His love.
What are purpose of creatures
What did God intend for
creatures. They are good
but not here to enjoy
but to manifest God's
goodness. All talents are
to glorify God. All actions.
Whether we eat or drink do
all for glory.   St. Ignatius
For greater glory of God.
Use our senses.

2. Dominating idea...
Everything capable. God is
perfect workman. So we
cannot judge others, ourselves.

3. God shows His concern
for His glory by picking
unfit instruments.
Judith; Gideon;
Gideon was one of
the Judges. Ordinarily
Jews ruled by prophets
patriarchs. God always
punished following
falling away from Him
by war.
Idolatry — love of creatures.

Samuel called for penance
Armies, peace conferences;
statesmen cannot
bring peace. Only prayer
and penance.
Possibilities of a permanent
peace become more and
more remote. Not by armies

3. God shows his concern
for His glory by picking
unfit instruments.
Judith : Gideon:
Gideon was one of
the Judges. Ordinarily
Jews ruled by prophets
patriarchs. God always
punished
falling away from Him
by war.
Idolatry—love of creatures.

Samuel called for penance
Armies, peace conferences,
statesmen cannot
bring peace. Only prayer
and penance.
Possibilities of a permanent
peace become more and
more remote. Not by armies.

glory of god is man's happiness.

Gideon: I, a nobody, to save
my nation. No parade
for Gideon. Glory to God.
St Joan, St. Catherine,
St. Margaret Mary.
God uses men of talent too.
St. Augustine, St. Thomas.

What God's glory means for man.
1. Man's happiness.
Fundamental urge of man.
Very consoling doctrine.
Happiness is only reward
for working for God. He is
source of all joy, wisdom,
love.   He has made our
nature in such a way
as only to achieve happiness
in Him.

Glory of God is man's happiness.

Gideon: I, a nobody, to save
    my nation. No parade
    for Gideon. Glory to God.
    St. Joan, St. Catherine,
    St. Margaret Mary.
    God uses men of talent too
    St. Augustine, St. Thomas.

What God's glory means for man.
1.<u>Man's happiness.</u>
Fundamental urge of man.
 Very consoling doctrine.
 Happiness is reward
for working for God. He is
source of all joy, wisdom,
love. He has made our
nature in such a way
as only to achieve happiness
in Him.

Men end in despair, mad-
ness. Hound of Heaven,
of Francis Thompson.
Our hearts were made for
Thee O God and never
rest until they rest in Thee.
　　　　St. Augustine.
The more closely united, more
happy.
　　2 Man's way of thanking
Him. Praise Him and glorify
Him.
　　3. Man's continual preoccupation. If we are to be
divine beings we must spend
our lives in giving glory.
Offer all work. Eliminate
self seeking, self gratification.
Much self seeking in apostolate.
St. Paul. "They seek the things
which are their own and not

Men end in despair, madness.
Hound of Heaven,
of Francis Thompson.
Our hearts were made for
Thee O God and never
rest until they rest in Thee.
        St. Augustine.
The more closely united, more
happy.
        2. <u>Man's way of thanking</u>
<u>Him</u> Praise Him and glorify
Him.
        3.Man's continual preoccupation.
If we are to be
divine beings we must spend
our lives in giving glory.
Offer all work. Eliminate
self seeking, self gratification.
Much self seeking in apostolate.
St. Paul "They seek the things
which are their own and not

the things of Jesus Christ.
Only when we are
purified God uses us. When
we are selfless.
St Alphonsus says vanity is
like a robber among trav-
ellers, insinuating himself
as a friend.
Paul. 1 Cor. 1. 27.
But God has chosen the
foolish things of the world
that He may confound the
wise: and the weak things
of the world hath God
chosen, that he may con-
found the strong. And
the base things of the
world, and the things
that are contemptible,
hath god chosen, that
he might bring to nought

the things of Jesus Christ.
Only when we are
purified God uses us. When
we are selfless.
St. Alphonsus says vanity is
like a robber among travelers,
insinuating himself
as a friend.
Paul 1 Cor. 1.27
But God has chosen the
foolish things of the world
that He may confound the
wise: and the weak things
of the world hath God
chosen, that he may confound
the strong. And
the base things of the
world, and the things
that are contemptible,
hath God chosen, that
he might bring to nought

things that are: that
no flesh should glory in
his sight.
St. Isaac Joques. 1 convert
St. John Brebeuf. 20 converts
We must not expect results.

Apostle is like a wire.
Power house supplies light

Vain man is a non conductor.
People with whom you are
working turn on lights.
We have nothing to say
as to whether God provides
or they turn on.
We can be most sure
when there is no results

things that are: that
no flesh should glory in
his sight.
St. Isaac Jogues. 1 convert
St. John Brebeuf. 20 converts
We must not expect results.

Apostle is like a wire—
Power house supplies light.

Vain man is a non conductor.
People with whom you are
working turn on the lights.
We have nothing to say
as to whether God provides
or they turn on.
We can be most sure
when there is no results.

Wednesday.   10th Conference. 9.45
                        very chilly.

Means to glorify God.
        The Samples.
As the Artist leaves mark of his
genius in his work, Bears mark
of his divine perfections.
Every creature reflects God.
ST. Bonaventure, de Sales, says
all creatures sample of divine
perfections, Why God made
creatures so good. So thru
them we may rise to knowledge
of God. The only way we
can know God is glory,
"He that has made the
eye, shall he not see?"
We are not to worship samples.
Wisdom 13. Samples.
Rom. 1. 18.... God is made
manifest to them. For from

Wednesday. 10th Conference 9:45
very chilly

Means to glorify God.
The Samples.
As the artist leaves mark of his
genius in his work, Bears mark
of his divine perfections.
Every creature reflects God.
St. Bonaventure, de Sales, says
all creatures sample of divine
perfections. Why God made
creatures so good. So thru
them we may rise to knowledge
of God. The only way we
can know God is glory,
"He that has made the
eye, shall he not see?"
We are not to worship samples.
Wisdom 13. Samples.
Romans 1.18... God is made
manifest to them. For from

the creature of the world
his invisible attributes are
clearly seen. His everlasting
power, his divinity because
they are understood in the
things that are made.

Use the samples — to compare
them to God. — to know God.
Duration, quality, intensity

Happiness primarily spiritual
this of different order.
Things of material order are
truly samples.
Things are contemptible
compared to God.
More intense happiness from
possessing God. We must renounce samples here and now
yet. we will have happiness here just the same
spiritual

the creatures of the world
his invisible attributes are
clearly seen. His everlasting
power, his divinity because
they are understood in the
things that are made.

Use the samples—to compare
them to God—to know God.
Duration, quality, intensity.

Happiness primarily spiritual
tho of different order.
Things of material order are
Truly samples.
Things are contemptible
compared to God.
More intense happiness from
possessing God. We must renounce
samples here and now
yet we will have spiritual happiness here just the same.

life of grace is beginning
of life of glory. This life
differs from life eternal
like acorn from oak.
Faber.
Grace is glory in exile,
as glory is grace at home

St Paul. Kingdom of
Heaven is not eating and
drinking but joy in the
Holy Ghost.
Saints possess God in this
world, but must renounce
samples.
1. Cor.
Sensual man does not per-
ceive the things of the
spirit. It is foolishness
to him because it must
be examined spiritually.

Life of grace is beginning
of life of glory. This life
differs from life eternal
like acorn from oak.
Faber.
    Grace is glory in exile,
    as glory is grace at home.

St. Paul. Kingdom of
    Heaven is not eating and
    drinking but joy in the
    Holy Ghost.
    Saints possess God in this
    world, but must renounce
    samples.
    1 Cor.
    Sensual man does not perceive
    the things of the
    spirit. It is foolishness
    to him because it must
    be examined spiritually.

like St. Anthony in the desert
"The dawn comes too soon."

To achieve holiness we do
not need to do extraordinary
things[x], but they are a
lesson to us.   We are
spiritually attrophied.
No joy in anticipation of
spiritual life.
More you get of material pleasure less you want; more
of spiritual you get, more
you want.   No satiety.
No revulsion.
"Eating always spoils my
appetite." says small boy.
How Jesus used samples
To teach. We all have to
learn thru senses.
Everything is sample to
Jesus. Goodier's life of
Jesus. Vine, hen, sheep.
in the gospel.

Like St. Anthony in the desert
"the dawn comes too soon."

To achieve holiness we do
not need to do extra ordinary
things, but they are a
lesson to us. We are
spiritually atrophied.
No joy in anticipation of
spiritual life.
More you get of natural pleasures
less you want; more
of spiritual you get, more
you want. No satiety.
No revulsions.
"Eating always sparks my
appetite." Says small boy.
How Jesus used sample
To teach. We all have to
learn thru senses.
Everything is sample to
Jesus. Goodness life of
Jesus. Vine, hen, sheep
in Gospel.

What water does for parched
body, Christ does for soul

What meat does for body,
god's will does for the soul
"My meat is to do the will
of him that sent me."

First use of water is to
glorify god. Second use
is to sustain us.

Loaves and fishes: parables
in action. Spiritual implications. Labor not for food
which perisheth. I am
bread of life. What bread
does for body, Jesus does for
soul. The bread that
I will give is my flesh.
Heaven is a banquet.

What water does for parched
body, Christ does for soul.

What meat does for body,
God's will does for the soul.
"My meat is to do the will
of him that sent me."

First use of water is to
glorify God. Second use
is to sustain us.

Loaves and fishes: parables
in action. Spiritual implications.
Labor not for food
which perisheth. I am
bread of life. What bread
does for the body, Jesus does for
soul. The bread that
I will give is my flesh.
Heaven is a banquet.

11th Conference. 11.45.

1. Doctrine will help to dry
up life of the senses.
Gal. 5. 16. For the flesh
lusts against the spirit
and the spirit against
the flesh For these two
are opposed.

Whenever you love anything
you become like unto it.
— or its slave. St John of Cross
Tyrannized over by our
senses.
Great difficulty is we live
in world of sense. Hence
difficulty! We are smothered
by world of senses, but
doctrine of sample shows
us escape. We are as
though trapped in a world.

11th Conference. 11:45

1. Doctrine will help to dry
up life of the senses.
Gal. 5.16. For the flesh
lusts against the spirit
and the spirit against
the flesh. For these two
are opposed.

Whenever you love anything
you become like unto it.
-or its slave: St. John of Cross
Tyrannized over by our
senses.
Great difficulty is we live
for world of sense. Hence
difficulty. We are smothered
by world of senses, but
doctrine of samples shows
us escape. We are as
though trapped in a ~~world~~

submarine

~~of those~~ Samples are
like a submarine valve
Where there is attachment
there is union. Shows
us these things are not
to be used for our en-
joyment but as a means
of getting to God.

2. Develops life of spirit

Shows us how to meditate
"Eye has not seen nor
ear heard, nor has it
entered into the heart
of man what god has
prepared for them that
love him."
Atrophy hearing.
qualities in human
beings, virtues, beauties.

submarine. Samples are
like a submarine valve.
Where there is attachment
there is union. Shows
us these things are not
to be used for our enjoyment
but as a means
of getting to God.

2. Develops life of spirit

Shows us how to mediate
"Eye has not seen nor
ear heard, nor has it
entered into the heart
of man what God has
prepared for them that
love him.
Atrophy hearing.
Qualities in human
beings, virtues, beauties.

Distractions: food, work,
" helps us to meditate.

Do we have to give up
music etc. No god not
put creatures here to
give them up, no to teach
us about god.
"Best thing to do with
the best of things is to
give them up."

St. John Cross: If anything,
leads you immediately
to contemplation of
God, go ahead.
But if y. it causes you
to become attached, give
up.

Distractions: food, work.
   "   helps us to meditate.

Do we have to give up
music etc. No God not
put creatures here to
give them up. No, to teach
us about God.
"Best thing to do with
the best of things is to
give them up."

St. John Cross: If anything,
leads you immediately
to contemplation of
God, go ahead.
But if it causes you to
become attached, give
up.

Difference between spiritual
and supernatural.

Music, art, architecture was
used for glory of god as
before renaissance.

3. Doctrine of samples explains nature of temptation.

Minimum degree of love:
we must prefer him
above every creature.
Love of preference.

Temptation is an opportunity
to make an act of living
love.
Faith: do I prefer my
reason or god's. My
intelligence sample of divine.

Difference between spiritual
and supernatural.

Music, art architecture was
used for glory of God as
before renaissance.

3.Doctrine of samples explains
nature of temptation.

Minimum degree of love:
we must prefer him
above every creature.
Love of preference.

Temptation is an opportunity
to make an act of living
love.
Faith: do I prefer my
reason or God's. My
intelligence sample of divine,

Human love sample of divine. Strongest temptation is desire to love, give love.

We are in this world to be tried. Devil is like a general trying to take a city, St. Ignatius said. Watch and pray.

4. Teach us reason for failure of our spiritual effort.

5. God has commissioned us to save all men. Holy Father has called all Christians to help.
Despite outlay of energy and wealth — failure.
Purpose to extend Kingdom of Christ on earth.

Human love sample of
divine. Strongest temptation
is desire to love, give love.

We are in this world to be tried.
Devil is like a general trying
to take a city, St. Ignatius
said. Watch and pray.

4.Teach us reason for failure
of our spiritual effort.

God has commissioned us to
save all men Holy Father
has called all Christian to
help.
Despite…of energy and
wealth— failure.
Purpose to extend Kingdom
of Christ on earth.

Karl Adam. speaking of
Western civilization.
"Cause of failure, worldli-
ness of the West."

Keymark-recreation. Early
christians died rather than
participate in pleasures of
pagans

Will - heart. Synonymous
Will has great urgency
to love. Will is blind.
It will love that which
mind presents to it as
loveable. I love what my
mind is filled with.
The only way to correct is
to fill my mind with
God. Then my will
reaching out, loves that

Karl Adam speaking of
Western civilization.
"Cause of failure, worldliness
of the West."

Keymark—recreation. Early
Christians died rather than
participate in pleasures of
pagans.

Will—heart. synonymous.
Will has great urging
to love. Will is blind.
It will love that which
mind presents to it as
loveable. I love what my
mind is filled with.
The only way to correct is
to fill my mind with
God. Then my will
reaching out, loves that

which it finds.
To teach children. Every
sense brings to us the
knowledge of God.
Sear this into the mind.
Creatures are not to be
enjoyed, but used as
samples.
This is problem of Christian
education, parents in
the home.

'

which it finds.
To teach children. Every
sense brings to us the
knowledge of God.
Sear this into the mind,
Creatures are not to be
enjoyed, but used as
samples.
This is problem of Christian
education, parents in
the home.

5. p m Conference.
Folly of the Cross.

Leo XIII speaks of it as the law.
Not so much symbolism
as in middle ages. Of all
symbols. Cross is characteristic symbol of Christianity.
More than a symbol. Contains
a doctrine a way of life.
Curious, extraordinary symbol
of pain.

Why did St Paul stand on his
dignity as Roman citizen.

St Luke 9.23. If any one
wishes to come after me
let him deny himself daily,
and take up his cross
and follow me. Best short

5 pm. Conference
Folly of the Cross

Leo XIII speaks of it as the law.
Not so much symbolism
as in middle ages. Of all
symbols. Cross is characteristic
symbol of Christianity
More than a symbol. Contains
a doctrine, a way of life.
Curious, extraordinary symbol
of pain.

Why did St. Paul stand on his
dignity as Roman citizen.

St. Luke 9.23. If anyone
wishes to come after me
let him deny himself daily,
and take up his cross
and follow me. Best short

Summary. Jesus gave of
Christianity. Summary.

Conditions for following.
1. Let him deny myself.
repudiate ego. selflove.
Contrast with philosophy of
world. Express yourself.
Sign of contradiction.
2. Take up his cross daily.

We must die to the natural
and out of this death comes
life. Phoenix was symbol
of supernatural. Out of
ashes a new life. St Paul
speaks of it as death.
death to what is natural
this death must take place
independently of sin.
Not because of original

summary Jesus gave of
Christianity. Summary.

Conditions for following:
1. Let him deny myself
   repudiate ego. self love.
Contrast with philosophy of
world. Express yourself,
Sign of contradiction.
2.Take up his cross daily.

We must die to the natural
and out of this death comes
life. Phoenix was symbol
of supernatural. Out of
ashes a new life. St. Paul
speaks of it as death,
death to what is natural.
This death must take place
independently of sin.
Not because of original

Sin or actual sin.
Even Blessed Mother subject
to law of cross. Jesus was
sinless yet he submitted
to it. Renewed human
body and soul.

Consequence of doctrine
that we are children of god.

In reference to standard
of the world, folly,
foolishness to the world.

1 Cor. 3 chapters, Folly of
the Cross.
Isaiah 29.14
To bring world shattering news
1st official act to reject money.
to be born in a stable.
We have nearly passed be-

sin or actual sin.
Even Blessed Mother subject
to law of cross. Jesus was
sinless yet he submitted
to it. Remained human
body and soul.

Consequences of doctrine
that we are children of God.

In reference to standard
of the world, folly,
foolishness to the world.

1 Cor. 3 chapters, Folly of
the Cross
Isaiah 29.14
To bring world shattering news
1st official act to reject money,
to be born in a stable.
We have never passed beyond

yond Graeco Roman culture.
No universities for Jesus.
He did not study under Gamaliel. He worked first
as a carpenter, then he
went out as a tramp.
Chose 12 men, illiterate,
workers.
In Nazareth they thought
him mad.
If any man think himself
wise, let him become a
fool that he may be wise.
Foolishness of God is wiser
than mens

Our vocation to live the
cross — not only as far as
Cannan but to Calvary.

Greco Roman culture.
No universities for Jesus.
He did not study under Gamaliel.
He worked first
as a carpenter, then he
went out as a tramp.
Chose 12 men, illiterate,
workers.
In Nazareth they thought
him mad.
If any man think himself
wise, let him become a
fool that he may be wise.
Foolishness of God is wiser
than men.

Our vocation to live the
cross— not only as far as
Canaan but to Calvary.

<u>Not sin</u>

Reasons. Why must we
die to the natural,
It is a law (like law of gravity)
Law of the Cross. If you
reject Cross.
Governs nature too, life
comes from death.
"Corruption of one thing
is generation of another."
ancient axiom.
Dead plants are fuel.
Unless grain of wheat
falls into the ground and
dies.
Luke 9. He who will save
his life will lose it. He
that loveth his life shall
lose it

2. Sanctity of God requires it
   1 " divine attribute
   2. " is love for god.
   3. " is freedom from imperfection

Reasons. <u>Not sin</u> Why must we
die to the natural.
It is a law (like law of gravity).
Law of the Cross. If you
reject Cross.
Governs nature too. Life
comes from death.
"Corruption of one thing
is generation of another."
ancient axiom.
Dead plants are food.
Unless grain of wheat
fall onto the ground and
dies.
Luke 9. He who will save
his life will lose it. He
that loveth his life shall
lose it.
2.Sancitiy of God requires it
  1. "   divine attribute
  2. " is love for God.
  3. " is freedom from imperfection.

Saint is a man who brings
something divine into the world.
We don't need books to prove
saints are human.

v. 16.
1 St. Peter summarizes in one
sentence all we have said
quoting Leviticus. "You
shall be holy because I
am holy."

1. St. John. 3. 1-3 We are
now the children of God and
it doth not yet appear
what we shall be. We know
that when he shall appear
we shall be like him, because
we shall see him as he is.
And everything one that
hath this hope in him

Saint is a man who brings
something divine into the world.
We don't need books to prove
saints are human.

1 St. Peter 1.16 summarizes in one
sentence all we have said
quoting Leviticus. "You
shall be holy because I
am holy."

1.St. John. 3.23 We are
now the children of God and
it doth not yet appear
what we shall be. We know
that when he shall appear
we shall be like him, because
we shall see him as he is.
And everyone that
hath this hope in him

sanctifieth himself, as he also
is holy.

Everylove not centered in Him
is imperfection in His sight.

Without holiness no man can
see God. All imperfection
must be removed.

Flesh and blood cannot see God.
Every natural attachment,
every n. motive.

Newman:

Dream of Gerontius.

A worldly person would be
unhappy in heaven.

"Heaven would be hell for
an unholy soul."

ex. reason of folly of the Cross.

angels, supernatural destiny,
before sin entered, in he asked
them to accept Cross. Fathers

sanctifieth himself, as he also
is holy.
Every love not centered in Him is
imperfection in His sight.
Without holiness no man can
see God. All imperfection
must be removed.
Flesh and blood cannot see God.
Every natural attachment,
every n. motive.
Newman:
Dream of Gerontius
A worldly person would be
unhappy in heaven.
"Heaven would be hell for
an unholy soul."
ex. reason of folly of the Cross.
Angels. supernatural destiny,
before sin entered in he asked
them to accept Cross. Fathers

of the church -. They were asked
to do homage to the human
Jesus. Renounce reason and
will, two highest attributes.
Lucifer & his followers refused,
damned for living according
to their will.
Before sin existed required
to deny themselves.
ex. Adam and Eve.
Test of holiness, to give
up their will
Their crime was to act
like pagans, not to act
like devils.

of the church—They were asked
to do homage to the human
Jesus. Renounce reason and
will, two highest attributes.
Lucifer & his followers refused,
damned for living according
to their will.
Before sin existed required
to deny themselves.
ex. Adam and Eve.
Test of foolishness, to give
up their will
Their crime was to act
like pagans, not to act
like devils.

It is getting dark now at 8·30
Damp and chilly. Warm day.

Wed.   8·30· p m Conference.

Christ's humanity was crushed.
He did not have to give up sin
Mortified. Our mother too.
Our lady had to die to natural.
Physically she was put to one
side. Naturally he would
have stayed at home and
taken care of her. "Who are
my brethren? my mother,
my sister and my brother
are those who do my will

Cosmic law of Folly of Cross.
Just as much a law as law
of gravity. Life comes from
death. John 15; I am true
vine and my Father is
husbandmen. Every branch
that beareth not fruit he

It is getting dark now at 8:30
Damp and chilly. Warm day.

Wed. 8:30 p.m. Conference

Christ's humanity was crushed.
He did not have to give up sin.
Mortified. Our mother too.
Our Lady had to die to natural.
Physically she was put to one
side. Naturally he would
have stayed at home and
taken care of her. "Who are
my brethren? My mother,
my sister and my brother
are those who do my will.

Cosmic law of Folly of Cross.
Just as much a law as law
of gravity. Life comes from
death. John 15. I am true
vine and my Father is
husbandmen. Every branch
that bearith not fruit he

will cut off.   Pruning that
they may bear more fruit.
Kills it to get more life.
Take this for granted but it
is not logical. Cuts it
shorter to grow taller, thins
ant in order to grow more
thickly.
Strengthens life of plant to
cut off blooms. Same law
applies to us.
God still uses suffering
as punishment for wicked
but also to purify the good.
Secret of fruitfulness is
suffering, pruning.
Life of sacrifice, prayer,
suffering. We have to do
God's work, God's way.

will cut off. Pruning that
they may bear more fruit.
Kills it to get more life.
Take this for granted but it
is not logical. Cuts it
shorter to grow taller, thins
out in order to grow more
thickly.
Strengthens life of plant to
cut off blooms. Same law
applies to us.
God still uses suffering
as punishment for wicked,
but also to purify the good.
Secret of fruitfulness is
suffering, pruning.
Life of sacrifice, prayer,
suffering. We have to do
God's work, God's way.

Negative Christianity (pruning)
Fasting and mortification
are positive. Farmer does
not use pruning knife to
destroy but to make fruitful.

No other secret of fruitfulness.
Sufferings are roots of flower.

John 12.^{24} He was Master of
his Father's secrets.

The hour is come for the Son
of man to be glorified.
Unless the grain of wheat
fall into the ground and
die, itself remains alone,
but if it die it brings
forth much fruit.

Negative Christianity (pruning)
Fasting and mortification
are positive. Farmer does not use
pruning knife to
destroy but to make fruitful.

No other secret of fruitfulness.
Sufferings are roots of flower.

John 12.24 He was Master of
his Father's secrets.

The hour is come for the Son
of Man to be glorified.
Unless the grain of wheat fall
into the ground and
die, itself remains alone,
but if it dies it brings
forth much fruit.

Contrary to etro logic. Comes
from that strange law
"Life comes from death."

Sow creature, possess Creator.
Sow pleasures, reap happiness.
Sow our life, reap life eternal.

What to do with samples? sow them.
Farmer is picture of christian
life. Hard life, inclement
weather, sowing.   ST. Paul —
Singing and making melody
in your hearts to the Lord.
Rejoice in the crop.
Keep your mind on the crop.
Sow with abandon.
Sow sparingly, reap sparingly.
What shall we sow. Jesus
says everything. Our life.

Contrary to logic. Comes
from that strange law
"Life come from death."

Sow creature, possess Creator.
Sow pleasures, reap happiness,
Sow our life, reap life eternal.

What to do with samples? Sow them.
Farmer is picture of Christian
life. Hard life, inclement
weather, sowing.   St. Paul—
Singing and making melody
in your hearts to the Lord.
Rejoice in the crop.
Keep your mind on the crop.
Sow with abandon.
Sow sparingly, reap sparingly.
What shall we sow. Jesus
says everything. Our life.

Sow creatures, Money,
give to poor, to Church.
Money is not to be hoarded
in banks. It is to be wasted.
Too human in prudence.
Make act of faith.

Sow time. Time is money
Sow by wasting it for God,
  going to church, prayers,
   serving poor.
Sow time. Reap eternity.
Time is sample of eternity.
Prayer is only road to God.
One hour a day.
Hundred fold in this life and
in the life to come, life ever-
lasting.
Cannot live divine life without
prayer.

Sow creatures. Money,
give to poor, to Church.
Money is not to be hoarded
in banks. It is to be wasted.
Too human in prudence.
Make act of faith.

Sow time. Time is money.
Sow by wasting it for God,
going to church, prayer,
serving poor.
Sow time. Reap eternity.
Time is sample of eternity.
Prayer is only road to God.
One hour a day.
Hundred fold in this life and
in the life to come, life everlasting.

Cannot live divine life without
prayer.

Can you not spend one hour with me?

St. Frances de Sales. 1 hr.
St. Teresa, minimum 1 hr.
not including Mass. No Bible,
no rosary, no stations, no prayer
book.
St. Ignatius says don't let
devil cheat you out of one
minute.
Without prayer, soldiers without
weapons.

St. Teresa

Can you not spend one hour with
me?

St. Frances de Sales. 1 hr.
St. Teresa, minimum 1 hr.
Not including Mass. No bible,
no rosary, no stations, no prayer
book.
St. Ignatius says don't let
devil cheat you of one
minute.
Without prayer, soldiers without
weapons.

St. Teresa

Love of God.

Thursday. 9.45. 16th Conference.

Finished preliminary survey
of principles. Today doctrine
of samples, basic. How to increase our love of God.
We acquire it thru faculties
Know him, esteem him + love.
Our mind must be filled
with knowledge of God —
thru samples. Above all
the sample — our neighbor.
In practice the way to love God
is to love our neighbor.
This is the law and the
prophets. He reduces it
still further. Do to others
as you would have others do
unto you. This is law
Teaching of prophets. That is
reason 2 commandments are

Love of God

Thursday 9:45 16ᵗʰ Conference.

Finished preliminary survey
of principles. Today doctrine
of samples, basic. How to increase
our love of God.
We acquire if thru faculties
know him, esteem him & love.
Our mind must be filled
with knowledge of God—
thru samples. Above all
the sample—our neighbor.
In practice the way to love God
is to lover our neighbor.
This is the law and the
prophets. He reduced it
still further. Do to others
as you would have others do
unto you. This is the law
and the teaching of the prophets. This is
reason 2 commandments are

so closely connected. We cannot
see our neighbor but we can
not
see god.

Owe no man anything
but to love one another,
If there is any commandment
it is summed up. Love is
fulfilment of the law.
Love of god & neighbor one
commandment. Cannot
separate.

Worst sin is coldhearted lack of
charity. Lazarus & Dives.
St. James & do honor poor
by making distinctions. There
should be no respect of persons,
Treat each alike. Live by
Faith not by eyesight.
See Christ in each one.

so closely connected. We can
see our neighbor but we can
not see God.
Owe no man anything
but to love one another,
if there is any commandment
it is summed up. Love is
fulfillment of the law.
Love of God & neighbor one
commandment. Cannot
separate.

Worst sin is cold hearted lack of
charity. Lazarus & Dives
St. James: dishonor poor
by making distinctions. There
should be no respect of persons,
treat each alike. Live by
Faith, not by eyesight.
See Christ in each one.

St. James chap.
2. and 5.

Come now ye rich, weep and
howl over your miseries.
Your riches will be a witness
against you.
Blood Tie; but we are related
by blood of Jesus Christ.
Grace tie is stronger.
Includes all mankind, not
just Catholics.
Christ came to unite all
men.
Who is our neighbor. All
men are our neighbors.
The more difficult, the more
wonderful an act of faith.

1. St. John. Love of neighbor.
A new commandment I
give you - that you love

St. James   chap 2. and 5

Come now ye rich, weep and
howl over your miseries.
Your riches will be a witness
against you.
Blood tie; but we are related
by blood of Jesus Christ.
Grace tie is stronger.
Includes all mankind, not
just Catholics.
Christ came to unite all
men.
Who is our neighbor. All
men are our neighbors.
The more different, the more
wonderful an act of faith.

1. St. John. Love of neighbor.
A new commandment I
give you—that you love.

By this shall all men know
you — that you love one
another.

2:9. He who says he is in
the light, and hates his
brother, 'he is, you are in darkness.

"For him there is no stumbling"

3:16. In this we have come
to know His love for us;
we ought likewise to lay
down his life for the
brethren.
He who has the goods of
this world and see his
brother in need, how does
he have the love of God
with him.

By this shall all men know
you— that you love one
another.
2.9. He who says he is in
the light, and hates his
brother, he is in darkness.

"For him there is no stumbling".

3.16. In this we have come
to know His love for us:
we ought likewise to lay
down his life for the
brethren.
He who has the goods of
this world and sees his
brother in need, how does
he have the love of God
with him.

We know that we have
passed from death to
life because we have
loved.
Everyone who hates is a
murderer.
4. 7. My beloved, let us
love one another for love
is of god.

He has first loved us.
He who abides in love abides
in god.
Anyone who says he loves
god and hates his brother
is a liar.

Esteem god, prefer Him
give up attachments.

We know that we have
passed from death to
life because we have
lived.
Everyone who hates is a
murderer.
4.7. My beloved let us
love one another for love
is of God.

He has first loved us.
He who abides in love abides
in God.
Anyone who says he loves
God and hates his brother
is a liar.

Esteem God, prefer Him
give up attachments.

Cardinal Newman.
Sermon on love of god,
Comforts of life are chief
cause of lack of love of god.
It seems trivial.
Full meals, soft raiment
Secure life, ease and comfort
all these things close up
in your souls the avenues
by which God can come
to you.

Love is union with a certain
Communi-
cation. St John of the Cross
One way is active life of Service; direct union in
prayer. Both necessary.

Cardinal Newman.
Sermon on Love of God.
Comforts of life are chief
cause of lack of love of God.
It seems trivial.
Full meals, soft garment,
secure life, ease and comfort,
all these things close up
in your soul the avenue
by which God can come
to you.

Love is union with a certain communication.
St. John of the Cross
One way is active life of service:
direct union in
prayer. Both necessary.

Characteristics:
Reciprical
To give our life as victim
It means reparation,
penance suffering.
Three Hearts - Yeo.
Pius XI. Encyc. on Sacred Heart.
St. Paul. I die daily.
Love is surrender.
A giving of oneself.

Exclusive.
Human love is sample. It
is indeed a hard saying.
Whole heart whole soul
whole mind, whole strength.
You cannot serve God and
mammon. He that
gathereth not with me
scattereth. How exclusive?
a virtue by which we love

Characteristics:
Reciprocal
To give our life as victim
It means reparation,
penance, suffering.
Three Hearts.—Yes.
Pius XI. Encyc. on Sacred Heart.
St. Paul. I die daily.
Love is surrender.
A giving of oneself.

Exclusive.
Human love is sample. It
is indeed a hard saying.
Whole heart, whole soul,
whole mind, whole strength.
You cannot serve God and
mammon. He that
gathereth not with me
sattereth. How exclusive?
A virtue by which we love

gods on account of his
goodness, and our neighbor
in god.   Husband + wife,
brother and sister, children
towards parents.
Image of god, redeemed by
Jesus, set over them by god
Love; friendship raised
to supernatural.

"Men descend to meet." Imit.
We should support one
another in charity.
You cannot live this life
alone. Need friends.

God on account of his
goodness, and our neighbor
in God. Husband & wife,
brother and sister, children
towards parents.
Image of God, redeemed by
Jesus, set over them by God.
Love: friendship raised
to supernatural.

"Men descend to meet." Imit.
We should support one
another in charity.
You cannot live this life
alone. Need friends.

Thurs. - 10.45.   17.Th Conference.

Love is Absolute. No lessening
Total love and end toward
which we work. We must aim
at daily increase in love.
Substantial even unto death.
Not a matter of fervor and
feeling. Love is in the will.
Feelings belong to body, not
to soul. Show love by perseverance

St. Thomas says. Even highest
degrees of love is put upon us
as commandment.

Urgent. Charity of Christ
Constrains us, forces itself
upon us. Vow.
Like marriages. Suppose
James left to travel after marriage
"I'll come home when I'm old."

Thurs.—11:45 17th Conference

Love is Absolute. No lessening
Total love and end toward
which we work. We must aim
at daily increase in love.
Substantial even unto death.
Not a matter of fervor and
feeling. Love is in the will.
Feelings belong to body, not
to soul. Show love by perseverance.

St. Thomas says. Even highest
degrees of love is put upon us
as commandment.

Urgent. Charity of Christ
constrains us, forces itself
upon us. Now.
Like marriage. Suppose
James left to travel after marriage
"I'll come home when I'm old."

This retreat is a call.
The pagan in us like a roly-poly
doll. Jesus never condoned
mediocrity. If he calls at
third hour, we must listen.
God may withdraw his grace.
1. Rom. God's withdraws grace.
Without me you can do nothing.
We may be left helpless. like
newborn baby.
Rom. 11.   God has given
them a spirit of stupor.
Grace illuminates minds
        inspires wills.
God always accepts sinner
on condition sinner repents.

Love is the measure by which
we shall be judged.

This retreat is a call.
The pagan in us like a roly-poly
doll. Jesus never condoned
mediocrity. If he calls at
third hour, we must listen.
God may withdraw his grace.
1. Rom. God's withdraws grace
Without me you can do nothing.
We may be left helpless like
newborn baby.
Rom.11. God has given
them a spirit of stupor.
Grace illuminates minds
        inspires wills.
God always accepts sinners
on condition sinner repents.

Love is the measure by which
we shall be judged.

Contempt of the world
    Opposite to love of god.
Like convex and concave
go together. Cannot be separated.
Must have right idea of
this harsh word.
Holy indifference.
When we compare creatures
to god, they are contemptible

Man is midway between heaven
and world. Inverse relationships
Pittsburgh and N.Y. Nearer
we are to one, the farther
from other.

God's part is to infuse
grace into our soul.
Charity is infused virtue.
We can dispose ourselves
to receive. To empty our hearts.

Contempt of the world
Opposite to love of God.
like convex and concave
go together. Cannot be separated.
Must have right idea of
this harsh word.
Holy indifference.
<u>When we compare creatures</u>
<u>to God, they are contemptible.</u>

Man is midway between Heaven
and world. Inverse relationship.
Pittsburgh and N.Y. Nearer
we are to one, the farther
from other.

God's part is to infuse
grace into our soul.
Charity is infused virtue.
We can dispose ourselves
to receive. To empty our hearts.

In practice we must keep
our eyes on the unpleasant
part. With joy.
St. Frances de Sales.
Man's heart is finite.
We must empty oneselves,
like wine barrell.
Practical principle of first
importance.

Hatred of world Jansenism,
Manicheists?
God's world: man's world.

The world
{
God's.   love it as sample
          not for itself.
          reflected love.
          must to be loved
          as an end.

Man's.   in itself   society
          abstract.   art
                      literature
          not to be loved.
          in
          concrete.
          as it
          is.
}

In practice we must keep
our eyes on the unpleasant
part. With joy.
St. Frances de Sales
Man's heart is finite.
We must empty ourselves,
like wine barrel.
Practical principle of first
importance.

Hatred of world Jansenism,
Manicheists?
God's world: Man's world

The World $\Big\{$

God's: Love it a sample
not for itself
reflected love
not to be lived
as an end

Man's: in itself
abstract.
Not to be loved in concrete
as it
is.
society
art
literature

the only ones who love
creatures are those who renounce them.

One literature may be better
than others but even best ~~is old~~.
World is Christ's enemy
Devil is prince of this world.
The world and me hath no part.
Paraclete, whom the world
cannot receive.
John 13, 14, 15, 16, 17.
Fear not.
I have overcome the world
14 : 17. The world cannot
see or know spirit of truth
17 : 9. I do not pray for
the world.
Our enemy is not sin
it is the world. The
world will oppose you.

the only ones who love
creatures are those who renounce
them.

One literature may be better
than other but even best
World is Christ's enemy.
Devil is prince of this world.
The world and me hath no part.
Paraclete, whom the world
cannot receive.
John 13, 14, 15, 16, 17
Fear not.
I have overcome the world.
14.17 The world cannot
see or know spirit of truth
17.9 I do not pray for
the world.
Our enemy is not sin
It is the world. The
world will oppose you.

Those who live godly lives will
suffer persecution.

Fr. Faber: at first ridicule.

The disciple is not above his
master.

John 15. If the world hate you,
know that it has hated me
before you.

I have chosen you out of the
world and the world will
hate you.

Newman.

When world no longer persecutes the church, the church
is no longer preaching the
truth.

Mariner does not watch waves
but the polestar.

1. Cor. 7. 29.   First example
marriage.

Those who live godly lives will
suffer persecution.
Fr. Faber: at first ridicule.
The disciple is not above his
master.
John 15. If the world hate you,
know that it has hated me
before you.
I have chosen you out of the
world and the world will
hate you.
Newman.
When world no longer persecutes
the church, the church
is no longer preaching the
truth.
Mariner does not watch waves
but the polestar.
1. Cor. 7.29 First example
marriage.

As tho not weeping; not rejoicing. They that buy as
tho they possessed not.
And they that use this
world as if they used it not.
For the rank and file.

Thursday. 5.p.m.

St. Anthony's Village is in Ox.
mount — an hour's ride by bus
north east of Pittsburgh. You get
off the bus and walk a mile or
so up hill — a long climb on a
hot day.
The Village is one of children,
and nuns, and in the summer
a few visiting priests and
forty or so retreatants. It is
here members of the CW groups
also had their retreat this summer.

As tho not weeping: not rejoicing.
They that long as
tho they possessed not.
And they that use this
world as if they used it not.
For the rank and file.

Thursday 5 p.m.

St. Anthony's Village is in Oakmont
—an hour's ride by bus
Northeast of Pittsburgh. You get
off the bus and walk a mile or
so up hill—a long climb on a
hot day.
The Village is one of children
and nuns, and in the summer
a few visiting priests and
forty or so retreatants. It is
here members of the CW groups
also had their retreat this summer.

There are 10 acres of grounds,
a salad and herb garden
a little orchard — and many
weeping willow trees. They are
the kind of trees neither goats
nor children can hurt.
Down one side of the grounds
there is even a hedge of these
trees.

Surrounding a statue of St
Anthony in the center of the
front lawn are flowers,
at his feet in boxes and jars,
at the foot of the pedestal
in a circular bed — a border
of some fragrant herb, petunias,
geraniums + phlox. There is
nicotine a and, in other beds
around the grounds and
at night the fragrance comes
into the chapel during night
prayers.

There are 10 acres of grounds,
a salad and herb garden
a little orchard—and many
weeping willow trees. They are
the kind of trees neither goats
nor children can hurt.
Down one side of the grounds
there is even a hedge of these
trees.
Surrounding a statue of St.
Anthony in the center of the
front lawn are flowers,
at his feet in boxes and, also
at the foot of the pedestal
in a circular bed—a border
of some fragrant herb, petunias,
geraniums. There is
nicotiana & phlox in the other beds
around the grounds and
at night the fragrance comes
into the chapel during night
prayers.

Small boys were cutting grass
with er and there were
additional smells of cut
grass and the exhaust
from the gasoline motor.
There was also the smell
of Italian working which
reminded us of Mott St.

18the Conference. thus. 5.ᵃ.

Hatred of the world.
1 John 2 - 15. love not
the world nor the things we
are in the world. Any one
loves the world, love of
God is not in him.
James 4. 4
Adulterers. Do you not
know that friendship of
this world is enmity with
God.

Small boys were cutting grass
and there were
additional smells of cut
grass and the exhaust
from the gasoline motor.
There was also the smell
of Italian cooking which
reminded us of Mott St.

18th conference Thurs. 5:00

Hatred of the world.
1 John 2-15. have not
the world nor the things we
are in the world. Anyone
loves the world, love of
God is not in him.
James4.4
Adulteress. Do you not
know that friendship of
this world is enmity with
God.

We are adulterers when we
love the world. Fornicators,
idolators.
Phil. 3. 18. For many walk. who
are enemies of the cross of
Christ, whose god is their belly.
Those who mind earthly
things, who glory in things
they should be ashamed of.
3. 5. a Hebrew of the Hebrews
things that were gain to me,
now I count them as loss.
I count everything loss for
the excellent knowledge
of Jesus Christ my Lord,
for whom I suffered the loss
of all things and count
them all as dung.

Jesus used even more
vehement language:

We are adulterers when we
love the world. Fornications,
idolaters.
Phil.3.18. For many walk who
are enemies of the cross of
Christ, whose God is their belly.
Those who mind earthly
things, who glory in things
they should be ashamed of.
3.5. a Hebrew of the Hebrews
things that were gain to me,
now I count them as loss.
I count everything loss for
the excellent knowledge
of Jesus Christ our Lord,
for whom I suffered the loss
of all things and count
them all as dung.

Jesus used even more
vehement language:

Unless a man hate his
father, mother, sister, brother,
children.

Practice of Contempt of World.

War destroys great cities
Real contempt of the
world. More extreme.
We must distinguish
different kinds of samples

1. Necessary Samples.
   Captivating "   .
   Indifferent "
   Forbidden "

1. Food, drink, rest, recreation.
   Rules to guide us. Farmer
   is model. Enough keps
   to sustain life, sow rest.
   Not stingy with self and family.

Unless a man hate his
father, mother, sister, brother,
children.

Practice of Contempt of World.

War destroys great cities.
Real contempt of the
world more extreme.
We must distinguish
different kinds of samples.

1.Necessary Samples.
  Captivating   "
  Indifferent   "
  Forbidden   "

1. Food, drink, rest, recreation.
Rules to guide us. Farmer
is a model. Enough kept
to sustain life, sow rest.
Not stingy with self and family.

To take our recreation to
serve God better. 2 hrs daily.
St. John - bow. and arrow.
Set not your hearts on them.
St Francis de Sales. Chapters
on recreation.
Don't let it become an occupation — that takes too
long, or is exhausted.
What we are always thinking
about.
St. John Chrysostom: Christians
seem more His enemies than
his friends.

19th Conference. 8.30. Thursday.

God uses those creatures which
most captivate us to test us.
What is our most c. sample.
Love of ease when a person.

To take our recreation to
serve God better. 2 hrs daily.
St. John—bow and arrow.
Set not your heart on them.
St. Frances de Sales. Chapter
on recreation.
Don't let it become an occupation—
that takes too
long , or is exhausted.
What we are always s thinking
about.
St. John Chrysostom: Christians
seem more His enemies than
his friends.

19th Conference. 8:30. Thursday.

God uses those creatures which
most captivate us to test us.
What is our most c. sample.
Love of ease when a person

has a position of responsibility.
Sloth one of deadly sins. Leads
to sensuality, impurity.
Vanity. faults grow. Saul good
while young man. strong, modest,
handsome. Deterioration. Jealousy
Life became passion to kill David.
A minor fault can grow up to
destroy. Vanity in a man leads
to injustice. In woman, impurity.
Sensuality, gluttony, intemperance. Devil starts with innocent things. Use something
for pleasure.
Fr. Scupoli - favorite Trick of
devil is to quit Tempting.
Then it comes back with seven
other devils. We will never be
relieved as long as we are
here in this world. Prepare
for violent temptations every day

has a position of responsibility.
Sloth one of deadly sins. Leads
to sensuality, impurity
Vanity. faults grow. Saul good
while young man. Strong, modest,
handsome. Deterioration. Jealousy.
Life became passion to kill David.
A minor fault can grow up to
destroy. Vanity in a man leads
to injustice. In woman, impurity.
Sensuality, gluttony, intemperance.
Devil starts with innocent things. Use something
for pleasure.
Fr. Scupoli—favorite trick of
devil is to quit tempting.
Then it comes back with seven
other devils. We will never be
relieved as long as we are
here in this world. Prepare
for violent temptations every day

by mortifying himself every day.
Refrain ourselves from all things
to gain incorruptible crown.
We fall by little and little.
No satisfaction in work, in prayer
no sensible support. Revolt
against cross.
    Indifferent samples.
Philosophers say 2 kinds of
action. Intrinsically bad. steal.
giving alms.   "   good.
indifferent   walking. swimming
                drinking, smoking, dance
The attitude we have of treating
things as indifferent, is false.
Error in such a way of speaking
in considering an action in the
abstract, in itself.
Classifying actions in abstract
is for philosophers, convenience.
In concrete, actions are good or bad

by mortifying himself every day.
Refrain ourselves from all things
to gain incorruptible crown.
We fall by little and little.
No satisfaction in work, in prayer
no sensible support. Revolt
against cross.
Indifferent samples.
Philosophers say 2 kinds of
action.   Intrinsically bad. steal,
giving alms   "   good.
indifferent   walking, swimming
                        drinking, smoking, dance
The attitude we have of treating
things as indifferent, is false.
Error is such a way of speaking
in considering an action in the
abstract, in itself.
Classifying actions in abstract
is for philosophers, convenience.
In concrete, actions are good or bad

There is no such thing as an
indifferent action in concrete
reality.   St. Thomas.
Either leads us nearer to or
further from God. Every
action has its effect on our
soul.   Intention gives character
to action. Circumstance of
place, time, manner.

In order to be good every
circumstance must be good.
Principle of Christian ethics +.
Motive of utility, necessity.
20th Conference. Friday. 9.45.
St. John of Cross deliberate
Any habitual, attachment is sufficient to prevent all progress
in the spiritual life. No
matter how small. We are
on a Treadmill.

There is no such thing as an
indifferent action in concrete
reality.   St. Thomas.
Either leads us nearer to or
further from God. Every
action has its effect on our
soul. Intention gives character
to action. Circumstance of place, time, manner.

In order to be good every
circumstance must be good.
Principle of Christian ethics &
motive of utility, necessary.
20ᵗʰ Conference. Friday 9:45
St. John of Cross
Any habitual deliberate attachment is sufficient
to prevent all progress
in the spiritual life. No
matter how small. We are
on a treadmill.

Doctor of nothing. Nada.

impossible to go on. Ex. '
Habit of much speaking.
Habit of news.
attachment for object - books.
Room - place - house + dress
Hearing or seeing. music, art.
curiosity. Smoking, drinking.
Ex. It makes no difference if
bird is tied by heavy or
slender cord. Smaller is
easier to break but until it
be broken, it cannot fly.
Ex. Sucking fish. If it became attached to a ship
the ship cannot sail.
Some souls like rich ships
laden down with riches,
but they cannot sail on
In the doldrums.
    Unless you renounce all that
you possess. – Christ.

Doctor of Nothing. Nada

impossible to go on. Ex.
Habit of much speaking
Habit of news.
Attachment for object—books.
Room—place—house—dress,
Hearing or seeing , music, art.
curiosity. Smoking drinking.
Ex. It makes no difference if
bird is tied by heavy or
slender wire. Smaller is
easier to break but until it
be broken, it cannot fly.
Ex. sucking fish. If it became
attached to a ship
the ship cannot sail.
Some souls like rich ships
laden down with riches,
but they cannot sail on
in the doldrums.
Unless you renounce all that
you possess.—Christ.

Forbidden Samples. (under
pain of sin.). Why? Every
sample has a purpose – for
the glory of God – and for particular purpose. Misuse of samples.
Final end of marriage is to
glorify God ; for children;
mutual happiness. If used
only for gratification for
private end, forbidden.
It means nothing to God if
we break commandments – no
diminution of His glory.
Harm to man and society.
Falling away of population.
Unhappy marriage. family,
children.
Love is union of wills. Love
of God constrains us to keep
His commandments.
Love God and do as you will.
                St. Augustine.

Forbidden Samples. (under
pain of sin.) Why? Every
sample has a purpose—for
the glory of God—and for particular
purpose. Misuse of samples.
Final end of marriage is to
glorify God; for children;
mutual happiness. If had
only for gratification, for
private end, forbidden.
It means nothing to God if
we break commandments—no
diminution of His glory.
Harm to man and society.
Falling away of population.
Unhappy marriage, family,
children.
Love is union of wills. Love
of God constrains us to keep
His commandments.
Love God and do as you will.
St. Augustine.

Even imperfections seperate us
from the love of God.
St. Teresa: I would die for a rubric.
St. Ignatius: We should be willing
to die rather than com. a vbnial sin.
Avoid mortal sin is no good as
a rule. no love in it, only paganism,
impossible in world, condemned
by Jesus. Mortal sin is deicide,
murder of divine life in us. If
we love god we will do his
will.
(If you do not desire perfection,
try to content yourself with just being
in a "state of grace". it is impossible
Need air: prayer: food: grace.
mortification, meditation.
To live is to act. Life is activity.
Either under law of the members,
or law of grace. Pagan
and Christian. Law of sin, law
of spirit

Even imperfections separate us
from the love of God.
St. Teresa: I would die for a rubric.
St. Ignatius: We should be willing
to die rather than com. a venial sin.
Avoid mortal, sin is no good as
a rule. No love in it, only paganism,
impossible in world, condemned
by Jesus. Mortal sin is deicide,
murder of divine life in us. If
we love God we will do his
will.
If you do not desire perfection,
try to content yourself with just being
in a "state of grace." It is impossible.
Need aim: prayer: food: grace.
mortification, meditation.
To live is to act. Life is activity.
Either under law of the members,
or law of grace. Pagan
and Christian. Law of sin, law
of spirit.

1 John 5:19 We know that we are of God but the whole world is seated in wickedness: The whole world is in the power of the evil one. ST. Alphonsus says a soul in deliberate venial sin in a worse state than a man who occasionally commits a mortal sin.

Apoc 3; 16. To a Bishop, lukewarm, I know thy works that thou art neither cold, nor hot. But because I would that thou wert cold or hot. But because thou art lukewarm, and neither hot nor cold, I will begin to vomit thee out of my mouth. Because thou sayest: I am rich, and made wealthy, and have need of nothing, and knowest not, that thou art wretched, and miserable, and

1 John 5:19 We know that we are
of God but the whole world is
seated in wickedness : the whole
world is in the power of the evil
one. St. Alphonsus says a
soul in deliberate venial sin in
a worse state than a man who
occasionally commits a mortal sin.

Apoc 3;16 To a Bishop, lukewarm
I know thy works that thou
art neither cold, nor hot.
I would that thou were
cold or hot. But because thou
are lukewarm, and neither hot
nor cold, I will begin to vomit
thee out of my mouth. Because
thou sayest: I am rich, and made
wealthy, and have need of nothing
and knowest not, that thou art
wretched, and miserable, and

poor, and blind, and naked.
Such as I love, I rebuke and
chastise. Be zealous therefore
and do penance. Behold I
stand at the door and knock.
If any man shall hear my
voice, and open to me the door,
I will come in to him, and
will sup with him, and he
with me.

Jesus always asked maximum
not minimum. He does not
want us to take a single
step in the wrong direction.
Maximum. Purity of heart
21 ST Conference. Supreme Dominion
We glorify God in what he
does. In Samples "   "   . io.
Power, omnipotence.
S. D. governs all things in world
that they may accomplish its purpose.

poor, and blind, and naked.
Such as I love, I rebuke and
chastise. Be zealous therefore
and do penance. Behold I
stand at the door and knock.
If any man shall hear my
voice, and open to me the door,
I will come in to him, and
will sup with him, and he
with me.
Jesus always asked maximum
not minimum. He does not
want us to take a single
step in the wrong direction.
Maximum. Purity of heart
21ˢᵗ Conference. Supreme Dominion
We glorify God in what he
does. In Sample " " " is.
Power, omnipotence.
S. D. governs all things in world
that they may accomplish its purpose.

God's Providence <u>universal</u>: birds
of the air, grass of field,
hairs of your head. Nothing
too small. Every action in
human life. All we need
to know that it is universal.
Very beautiful and consoling.
It is efficacious, powerful.
It is <u>sweet</u>. Does not force
anyone. Does not destroy our
freedom intelligence.

Nothing happens except thru
providence of God.

Very great importance. Final
importance.

Basic : Supernatural Life.
Central: Cross,
Final: Providence.

We decrease our attachments
to increase our love of God

God's Providence <u>universal</u>: birds
of the air, grass of field,
hairs of your head. Nothing
too small. Every action in
human life. All we need
to know that it is universal.
Very beautiful and consoling.
It is <u>efficacious</u>, powerful.
It is <u>sweet</u>. Does not force
anyone. Does not destroy our
freedom, intelligence.
Nothing happens except thru
providence of God.
Very great importance. Final
importance.
Basic: Supernatural Life.
Central: Cross,
Final: Providence.

We decrease our attachments
to increase our love of God.

To have more love we must have
more faith. Faith, Hope, Charity
all grow together like fingers
on a hand. God increases our
faith by trials, sufferings, so
as to see God in every event.
Job is example of faith.
Look beyond natural and human
and see divine.
Faith is spotlight. Faith pre-
cedes love..
Theologians say God spends more care
on each soul than on whole
universe. Tries souls in different ways, according to needs.
Why does God sanctify us thru
trials? Christ is way.
Doctrine: St. Thomas calls it doctrine
of assimilation. Steps of creation:
minerals, plants, animals, human,
God. God creates all. All tend

To have more love we must have
more faith. Faith, Hope, Charity.
All grow together like fingers
on hand. God increases our
faith by trials, sufferings, so
as to see God in every event.
Job is example of faith.
Look beyond natural and human
and see divine.
Faith is spotlight. Faith proceeds
Love.
Theologians say God spends more care
on each soul than on whole
universe. Tries souls in different
ways, according to needs.
Why does God sanctify us thru
trials? Christ is way.
Doctrine: St. Thomas calls it doctrine
of assimilation. Steps of creation:
minerals, plants, animals, human,
God. God creates all. All tend

back toward God. He is last end.
We gather within ourselves all orders
of creation. Every level is picked
up and brought one step higher.
Assimilation, becoming similar to
1. John. 3. 2
        Dearly beloved, we are now
the sons of God: and it hath
not yet appeared what we
shall be. We know that
when he shall appear, we shall
be like him; because we
shall see him as he is.
        minerals destroyed, plants
destroyed, animals destroyed.
Man also must cease to be
human. God must remove
our corruptions.
        Why do we have to become
divine. St John. Because we
shall see him as he is. It is

back toward God. He is last end.
We gather within ourselves all order
of creation. Every level is picked
up and brought one step higher.
Assimilation, becoming similar to
1.John. 3.2
Dearly beloved, we are now
the sons of God: and it hath
not yet appeared what we
shall be. We know that
when he shall appear, we shall
be like him; because we
shall see him as he is.
Minerals destroyed, plants
destroyed, animals destroyed.
Man also must cease to be
human. God must remove
our corruptions.
Why, do we have to become
divine. St. John. Because we
shall see him as he is. It is

our destiny.

Now we look at God as a dog
looks at his master.

Knowledge demands equality
Love demands equality.
Love creates equality

The scriptures are given us
for our consolation.
St. Paul: I delight in my suffering.
St. Peter: Rejoice in tribulation.
Hebrews. 12. 1.

Having so many witnesses,
laying aside every weight
and sin which surrounds
us, let us run by faith
patience to the fight proposed
to us, looking on Jesus, the
author and finisher of faith,
who having joy set before him,
endured the cross.

our destiny.
Now we look at God as a dog
looks at his master.
Knowledge demands equality
Love demands equality.
Love creates equality.

The scriptures are given us
for our consolation.
St. Paul: I delight in my suffering.
St. Peter: Rejoice in tribulation.
Hebrews. 12:1.
 Having so many witnesses,
laying aside every weight
and sin which surrounds
us, let us run by.
patience to the fight proposed
to us, looking on Jesus, the
author and finisher of faith,
who having joy set before him,
endured the cross.

You have not resisted unto
blood, striving against sin.

"Wherefore lift up the hands
which hang down, and
the feeble knees, and
make straight steps.
Follow peace with all men,

You have not resisted unto
blood, striving against sin.

"Wherefore lift up the hands
which hang down, and
the feeble knees, and
make straight steps.
Follow peace with all men.

How many children
what ages.
How many nuns.
Get names for monthly day of *recollection*
Fr. Farina + Mrs Fahey
Get extra book of St John of the Cross
for John monastery.
Telegraph Peter + Dave.

Con, ✝

sloth a venial sin?
Expiation in Present Crisis. 1937
Pius XI or XII ?
What book - Chesterton's picture of Jesus

How many children
What ages
How many nuns
Get names for monthly day of recollection.
Fr. Farina & Mrs. Fahey
Get extra book of St. John of Cross
from John Monahan.

sloth a venial sin?
Expiation in Present Crisis. 1937
Pius XI or XII ?
What book—Chesterton's picture of Jesus

INDEX

A

Action française 156–158, 165–166
agere contra 48, 110, 353
Alumbrados 104, 119
American Ecclesiastical Review 17,
36, 171, 174, 189, 193, 201, 204,
248, 250, 252
American neo-Thomists 174,
180, 184–186, 195, 201–202,
205–206, 223, 226, 235, 243
apocalyptic sectarianism 15, 223
Applied Christianity 14, 17, 42,
54–56, 60, 64, 66, 68–70, 72,
74–76, 78–81, 83–84, 86–87,
90, 143, 171, 186–187, 189–191,
194–195, 197, 204, 212–215,
236, 247, 251

B

Balthasar, Hans Urs von 245
Bauerschmidt, Frederick C. 207,
231, 234, 237, 239, 245
Baxter, Michael 229, 245
Bernardi, Peter 149, 154, 156,
161–167, 246
Billot, Louis 158, 256
Blanchette, Oliva 160–165, 246
Blondelian Jesuits 161
Blondel, Maurice 246
Bremond, Henri 246
Buckley, Michael 7, 119–126, 246

C

Cajetanian Thomists 150
"Catholics Can Be Conscientious
Objectors" 165, 181, 250
Catholic "public" theology 229–230
Catholic radicals 12, 15, 38, 165,
208, 226, 231, 233, 237

Certeau, Michel de 132, 247
Chinnici, Joseph 38–39, 247
Christian mentality 70, 72, 108
concupiscence 209
Connell, Francis 17, 143, 186,
189–197, 202, 204, 205, 226,
247, 254
Curran, Charles 227–237, 247

D

Daly, Gabriel 247
datum optimum 153
Day, Dorothy 247
donum perfectum 153, 155, 222, 232
Downey, Jack Lee 8, 96, 98, 194,
197, 248
Dulles, Avery 248
duplex hominis beatitudo 148
Duty of the Present Moment 87

E

eschatological humanism 225–226,
233
Ellsberg, Robert 15, 44, 188, 222,
248
exaggerated supernaturalism 176,
191–192, 209, 213, 224, 227,
233, 237
extrinsicist monophorism 161

F

Fahey, Peter Claver 27, 241, 581
Farina, Louis 11, 16–17, 42, 54–55,
78, 261, 581
Fénelon, François 129–133,
136–137, 250, 257
Fenton, Joseph Clifford 248
Fielding, Rosemary 248
Fisher, James 248

Folly of the Cross 78–80, 84, 89–90, 99, 210, 221
Furfey, Paul Hanly 248

G

Gaillardetz, Richard 249
Gilkey, Langdon 249
Gleason, Philip 252
grace builds on nature 228, 234
gratia elevans 65, 116, 155, 219–221, 232
gratia non tollat naturam sed perficiat 234
Grumett, David 249

H

Henrici, Peter 161, 166, 250
Heyer, Kristen 228–237, 250
Himes 161, 166, 250
Humani Generis 12, 45, 138, 141, 143, 154, 159–160, 167, 255

I

Imitation of Christ, The 44–45, 97, 100
Incarnational humanism 226

J

Jansenism 13, 15, 30, 36–37, 75, 91, 118, 128, 131–133, 139, 147, 161, 176, 196, 215, 237, 255

K

Kerlin, Michael 252
Kerr, Fergus 252
Komonchak, Joseph 252

L

Lacouture, Onesimus 6, 12, 14, 16–18, 22, 25–26, 37, 40–44, 54–55, 60, 93–101, 107–114,
117, 119, 121, 125–127, 135, 138–139, 160, 164, 168, 187, 194, 247
Lallemant, Louis 95, 104, 119–127, 132–135, 137–139, 144, 155, 158, 168, 212, 219, 243, 247, 254, 585
Long Loneliness, The 13, 16, 27, 40–41, 45, 48–49, 51, 53, 85, 91, 141, 143, 188, 194, 222–223, 247
Longpre, Anselm 94, 194, 252
Lubac, Henri de 159, 253, 258

M

Marquette University 19, 21, 40–42, 45–46, 53, 222, 248, 253–254, 257
Maryfarm 16, 25, 30, 32, 40–41, 193
Maurin, Peter 21, 23, 28, 37, 50, 93, 164, 227
McCool, Gerald 12, 13, 141, 253
McNeal, Patricia 24, 181, 182, 186, 254
merely natural 48, 57, 61, 63, 67–68, 78, 111, 116–117, 166, 210–211, 215, 221, 236, 241
McSorley, Joseph 38, 88, 122, 135–136, 139, 255
Merriman, Brigit O'Shea 7, 9, 25–28, 40,–41, 51, 54, 94, 254
Milbank, John 254
Miller, William 254
Murray, John Courtney 255

N

natural happiness 43, 47–48, 58–60, 63, 70, 223
natural life 56–61, 65, 68, 73, 78, 211
natural motive 22, 57, 65–69, 71, 73, 78, 190, 195, 210–211, 215

Nature and the Supernatural: A Defense of the Evangelic Ideal 190
neo-Thomism 12–13, 52, 67, 136, 138, 149, 151, 167–168, 175–176, 205, 208
New Social Catholics 192

O

Oath against Modernism 138, 166
O'Brien, 16, 182, 216–218, 223–224, 227,–228, 233, 255
O'Malley, John 99–104, 106–107, 118, 119, 125, 127, 152
original justice 147, 214–218, 221

P

pagan mentality 66, 68, 70, 108
Parente, Pascal 191–195, 255
Pascendi Dominici Gregis 158
perfectionists 228, 233
perfect nature 147, 216, 218–219, 221, 236
Piehl, Mel 255
pious naturalism 197, 199, 213, 236
Pope Francis 117
Portier, William 255–256
practical mysticism 105, 115, 125–126, 155, 584
Principle and Foundation 100, 109–112, 114–115
prune 211
pure nature 112, 147–148, 150–151, 218–219

Q

Quietism 89, 126–129, 132, 136, 147, 197

R

Realist Agrarians 172

ressourcement 13–14, 92, 95–96, 127, 138–139, 144, 152, 168, 240, 243
Ressourcement Thomists 149
Riegle, Rosalie 256
Romantic Agrarians 172, 250

S

sacramental approach 230–233
sacrament of the present moment 88, 135, 212
samples 20, 75–78, 80, 83–84, 190, 211, 214
Semaines sociales 156, 164–166
separated theology 39, 141, 148, 151
Sign of Contradiction, A 42, 94–96, 98, 171
sin mentality 198–199, 213, 237
Social Catholicism 149, 156, 162, 167, 192, 246
sowing 44, 50–51, 80, 89–90, 211
Spiritual Doctrine of Father Louis Lallemant, The 121–122, 254
Spiritual Exercises of Ignatius of Loyola 14, 99, 101
St. Alphonsus de Liguori 66, 71, 87
St. Ignatius of Loyola 38, 54, 93–94, 99, 256
St. John of the Cross 50, 63, 71, 76, 85, 126, 138, 201, 249
strict observance Thomism 12, 158, 175
St. Thomas Aquinas 138, 148, 216, 222, 234, 246, 248–249, 255, 257
supernatural life 27, 35–36, 41, 50, 56–58, 61, 64, 66, 68, 70–73, 78, 80, 84, 89–90, 99, 101, 134, 186, 202, 213–214, 220, 223, 238, 240–241
supernatural motive 29, 42, 57, 64–65, 67–68, 71, 73, 89, 168, 195

Surin, Jean Joseph 95, 120,–121, 123, 125, 128, 134, 137–138, 243, 257
Surnaturel 143, 145, 149, 151, 246, 253

T

Talar, C.J.T. 128–138, 257
Tanq corps 188
Testis 164–166, 246
thematize 230
Thomism in action 215
Thomist Resurgence 148

V

Vishnewski, Stanley 29–32, 51, 257

W

Weigel, George 224–225, 258

Y

Yocum, Sandra 9, 35, 41, 49, 159, 223, 245, 254
Your Ways Are Not My Ways 18–19, 55, 94, 251

Z

Zahn, Gordon 180, 258